IFIP Advances in Information and Communication Technology 661

Editor-in-Chief

Kai Rannenberg, Goethe University Frankfurt, Germany

Editorial Board Members

IFIP – The International Federation for Information Processing

IFIP was founded in 1960 under the auspices of UNESCO, following the first World Computer Congress held in Paris the previous year. A federation for societies working in information processing, IFIP's aim is two-fold: to support information processing in the countries of its members and to encourage technology transfer to developing nations. As its mission statement clearly states:

> *IFIP is the global non-profit federation of societies of ICT professionals that aims at achieving a worldwide professional and socially responsible development and application of information and communication technologies.*

IFIP is a non-profit-making organization, run almost solely by 2500 volunteers. It operates through a number of technical committees and working groups, which organize events and publications. IFIP's events range from large international open conferences to working conferences and local seminars.

The flagship event is the IFIP World Computer Congress, at which both invited and contributed papers are presented. Contributed papers are rigorously refereed and the rejection rate is high.

As with the Congress, participation in the open conferences is open to all and papers may be invited or submitted. Again, submitted papers are stringently refereed.

The working conferences are structured differently. They are usually run by a working group and attendance is generally smaller and occasionally by invitation only. Their purpose is to create an atmosphere conducive to innovation and development. Refereeing is also rigorous and papers are subjected to extensive group discussion.

Publications arising from IFIP events vary. The papers presented at the IFIP World Computer Congress and at open conferences are published as conference proceedings, while the results of the working conferences are often published as collections of selected and edited papers.

IFIP distinguishes three types of institutional membership: Country Representative Members, Members at Large, and Associate Members. The type of organization that can apply for membership is a wide variety and includes national or international societies of individual computer scientists/ICT professionals, associations or federations of such societies, government institutions/government related organizations, national or international research institutes or consortia, universities, academies of sciences, companies, national or international associations or federations of companies.

More information about this series at https://link.springer.com/bookseries/6102

Victor Grimblatt · Chip Hong Chang ·
Ricardo Reis · Anupam Chattopadhyay ·
Andrea Calimera (Eds.)

VLSI-SoC: Technology Advancement on SoC Design

29th IFIP WG 10.5/IEEE International Conference
on Very Large Scale Integration, VLSI-SoC 2021
Singapore, October 4–8, 2021
Revised and Extended Selected Papers

 Springer

Editors
Victor Grimblatt ⓘD
Synopsys Chile R&D Center
Vitacura, Chile

Chip Hong Chang ⓘD
Nanyang Technological University
Singapore, Singapore

Ricardo Reis ⓘD
Universidade Federal do Rio Grande do Sul
Porto Alegre, Brazil

Anupam Chattopadhyay ⓘD
Nanyang Technological University
Singapore, Singapore

Andrea Calimera ⓘD
Politecnico di Torino
Turin, Italy

ISSN 1868-4238   ISSN 1868-422X (electronic)
IFIP Advances in Information and Communication Technology
ISBN 978-3-031-16820-8   ISBN 978-3-031-16818-5 (eBook)
https://doi.org/10.1007/978-3-031-16818-5

This Springer imprint is published by the registered company Springer Nature Switzerland AG
The registered company address is: Gewerbestrasse 11, 6330 Cham, Switzerland

Preface

This book contains extended and revised versions of the highest quality papers, presented during the 29th edition of the IFIP/IEEE WG 10.5 International Conference on Very Large Scale Integration (VLSI-SoC 2021), a global system-on-chip design and computer-aided design conference. The 29th edition of the conference was held during October 4–8, 2021, virtually from Singapore. Previous conferences have taken place in Edinburgh, Scotland (1981); Trondheim, Norway (1983); Tokyo, Japan (1985); Vancouver, Canada (1987); Munich, Germany (1989); Edinburgh, Scotland (1991); Grenoble, France (1993); Chiba, Japan (1995); Gramado, Brazil (1997); Lisbon, Portugal (1999); Montpellier, France (2001); Darmstadt, Germany (2003); Perth, Australia (2005); Nice, France (2006); Atlanta, GA, USA (2007); Rhodes, Greece (2008); Florianopolis, Brazil (2009); Madrid, Spain (2010); Kowloon, Hong Kong (2011); Santa Cruz, CA, USA (2012); Istanbul, Turkey (2013); Playa del Carmen, Mexico (2014); Daejeon, South Korea (2015); Tallin, Estonia (2016); Abu Dhabi, United Arab Emirates (2017); Verona, Italy (2018); Cuzco, Peru (2019); and Salt Lake City (2020, virtual edition).

The purpose of this conference, sponsored by IFIP TC 10 Working Group 10.5, the IEEE Council on Electronic Design Automation (CEDA), and the IEEE Circuits and Systems Society, with the In-Cooperation of ACM SIGDA, is to provide a forum for the presentation and discussion of the latest academic and industrial results and developments as well as the future trends in the field of system-on-chip (SoC) design, considering the challenges of nano-scale, state-of-the-art, and emerging manufacturing technologies. In particular, VLSI-SoC 2021 addressed cutting-edge research fields like emerging technologies, analog and mixed-signal circuits, VLSI and embedded system design, testing and verification, computer-aided design, design for security, reliable in-memory computing, secure hardware architectures, and cyber-physical systems on heterogeneous system-on-chips. The chapters of this new book in the VLSI-SoC series continue its tradition of providing an internationally acknowledged platform for scientific contributions and industrial progress in this field.

For VLSI-SoC 2021, 44 papers out of 75 submissions were selected for oral and poster presentations. There was an average of 3.45 reviews of each paper in the conference selection process and out of the 44 full papers presented at the conference, 12 papers were chosen by a special selection committee to have an extended and revised version included in this book. The selection process of these papers considered the evaluation scores during the conference review process as well as the review forms provided by members of the Technical Program Committee and the session chairs as a result of the presentations. After the authors sent their extended versions, the book co-editors reviewed the final papers.

The chapters of this book have authors from Canada, France, Italy, Germany, Singapore, and the USA. The Technical Program Committee for the regular tracks comprised 125 members from more than 25 countries.

VLSI-SoC 2021 was the culmination of the work of many dedicated volunteers: paper authors, reviewers, session chairs, invited speakers, and various committee chairs. We thank them all for their contributions.

This book is intended for the VLSI community at large, and in particular the many colleagues who did not have the chance to attend the conference. We hope you will enjoy reading this book and that you will find it useful in your professional life and for the development of the VLSI community as a whole.

August 2022

Victor Grimblatt
Chip Hong Chang
Ricardo Reis
Anupam Chattopadhyay
Andrea Calimera

Organization

The IFIP/IEEE International Conference on Very Large Scale Integration System-on-Chip (VLSI-SoC) 2021 took place during October 4–8, 2021, virtually from Singapore. VLSI-SoC 2021 was the 29th in a series of international conferences, sponsored by IFIP TC 10 Working Group 10.5 (VLSI), IEEE CEDA, and ACM SIGDA. The Organization Committee of the conference consisted of the following colleagues:

General Chairs

Anupam Chattopadhyay	NTU, Singapore
Andrea Calimera	Politecnico di Torino, Italy

Technical Program Chairs

Chip Hong Chang	NTU, Singapore
Victor Grimblatt	Synopsys, Chile

Special Sessions Chairs

Francesco Regazzoni	University of Amsterdam, The Netherlands, and Università della Svizzera italiana, Switzerland
Mohammed Sabry	NTU, Singapore

PhD Forum Chairs

Shivam Bhasin	NTU, Singapore
Trevor Carlson	NUS, Singapore

Local Chairs

Manimuthu Arunmozhi	NTU, Singapore
Nandeesh Veeranna	ST Microelectronics, Singapore

Industrial Chair

Annamalai Muthu	CME Labs, Singapore

Publicity Chairs

Swaroop Ghosh	Pennsylvania State University, USA
Shahar Kvatinsky	Technion, Israel

| Farhad Merchant | RWTH Aachen University, Germany |
| Ian O'Connor | ECL, France |

Publication Chair

| Nicola Bombieri | University of Verona, Italy |

Finance Chair

| Debjyoti Bhattacharjee | IMEC, Belgium |

Web Chairs

| Valentino Peluso | Politecnico di Torino, Italy |
| Roberto G. Rizzo | Politecnico di Torino, Italy |

VLSI-SoC Steering Committee

Graziano Pravadelli	University of Verona, Italy
Ibrahim Elfadel	Khalifa University, UAE
Manfred Glesner	TU Darmstadt, Germany
Matthew Guthaus	University of California, Santa Cruz, USA
Luis Miguel Silveira	INESC-ID, Portugal
Fatih Ugurdag	Ozyegin University, Turkey
Salvador Mir	TIMA, Université Grenoble Alpes, France
Ricardo Reis	Universidade Federal do Rio Grande do Sul, Brazil
Chi-Ying Tsui	Hong Kong University of Science and Technology, Hong Kong, China
Ian O'Connor	ECL, France
Masahiro Fujita	University of Tokyo, Japan

As for the technical program committee, it was composed as follows

Technical Program Committee

Analog, Mixed Signal, Sensors and RF

Track Chairs

| Salvador Mir | TIMA, Université Grenoble Alpes, France |
| Ross Walker | University of Utah, USA |

Track Members

Armin Tajalli	University of Utah, USA
Piero Malcovati	University of Pavia, Italy
Jacob Rosenstein	Brown University, USA

Marie-Minerve Louerat   Sorbonne University, France
Matthew Johnston   Sorbonne University, France
Krishna Vamshi   Renesas, India
Helmut Graeb   Technical University of Munich, Germany
Sylvain Bourdel   RFIC-Lab, Université Grenoble Alpes, France
Tetsuya Iizuka   University of Tokyo, Japan
Manuel Barragán   Université Grenoble Alpes, France
Sai Manoj   George Mason University, USA
Hossein Kassiri   York University, Canada
Zhangming Zhu   Xidian University, China

VLSI Circuits and SoC Design

Track Chairs

Ibrahim Elfadel   Khalifa University, UAE
Chun-Jen Tsai   National Chiao Tung University, Taiwan

Track Members

Kenji Kise   Tokyo Institute of Technology, Japan
Yu-Hsin Chen   Facebook, USA
Christoph Studer   Cornell University, USA
Lirong Zheng   Fudan University, China
Mario R. Casu   Politecnico di Torino, Italy
Joo-Young Kim   Korea Advanced Institute of Science and Technology,
                                 South Korea
Hayden K. H. So   University of Hong Kong, Hong Kong, China
Maurizio Palesi   University of Catania, Italy
H. Fatih Ugurdag   Ozyegin University, Turkey
Adam Teman   Bar-Ilan University, Israel
Ozgur Tasdizen   ARM, UK
Sezer Gören   Yeditepe University, Turkey
Ali Akoglu   University of Arizona, USA
Peng Liu   Zhejiang University, China
Carlos Silva-Cárdenas   Pontificia Universidad Catolica del Peru, Peru
Vojin G. Oklobdzija   University of California, USA
Per Larsson-Edefors   Chalmers University of Technology, Sweden
Tolga Yalcin   Northern Arizona University, USA

Embedded Systems Design and Software

Track Chairs

Wei Zhang   Hong Kong University of Science and Technology,
                                 Hong Kong, China
Mohamed Sabry   Nanyang Technological University, Singapore

Track Members

Ibrahim Elfadel	Khalifa University, UAE
Luc Claesen	Hasselt University, Belgium
Maciej Ogorzalek	Jagiellonian University, Poland
Giovanni Ansaloni	Swiss Federal Institute of Technology Lausanne, Switzerland
Donatella Sciuto	Politecnico di Milano, Italy
Dimitrios Soudris	National Technical University of Athens, Greece
Gianvito Urgese	Politecnico di Torino, Italy
Philippe Coussy	Université de Bretagne Sud, France
Lars Bauer	Karlsruhe Institute of Technology, Germany
Eugenio Villar	University of Cantabria, Spain
Wenjing Rao	University of Illinois at Chicago, USA
Domenico Balsamo	University of Newcastle, Australia
Sharad Sinha	Indian Institute of Technology Goa, India

CAD Tools and Methodologies for Digital IC Design and Optimization

Track Chairs

Ricardo Reis	Universidade Federal do Rio Grande do Sul, Brazil
Aida Todri-Sanial	LIRMM, University of Montpellier, CNRS, France

Track Members

L. Miguel Silveira	Universidade de Lisboa, Portugal
Srinivas Katkoori	University of South Florida, USA
Shao-Yun Fang	National Taiwan University of Science and Technology, Taiwan
Azemard Nadine	University of Montpellier, France
Rongmei Chen	Interuniversity Microelectronics Centre, Belgium
Yuanqing Cheng	Beihang University, China
Vasilis Pavlidis	University of Manchester, UK
Tsung-Yi Ho	National Tsing Hua University, Taiwan
Xing Huang	Technical University of Munich, Germany
Daniele Pagliari	Politecnico di Torino, Italy
Stefania Carapezzi	University of Montpellier, France
Gracieli Posser	Cadence, USA
Laleh Behjat	University of Calgary, Canada

Verification, Modeling and Prototyping

Track Chairs

Graziano Pravadelli	Università di Verona, Italy
Yakir Vizel	Technion, Israel

Track Members

Katell Morin-Allory	Université Grenoble Alpes, France
Tiziana Margaria	Lero, Ireland
Robert Wille	Johannes Kepler Universitat Linz, Austria
Tara Ghasempouri	Tallinn University of Technology, Estonia
Daniel Grosse	Johannes Kepler Universitat Linz, Austria
Doowon Lee	IBM, USA
Pierluigi Nuzzo	University of Southern California, USA
Vladimir Herdt	University of Bremen, Germany
Alexander Iivri	IBM, Israel
Alessandro Cimatti	Fondazione Bruno Kessler, Italy

Design for Testability, Reliability and Fault Tolerance

Track Chairs

Matteo Sonza Reorda	Politecnico di Torino, Italy
Xinmiao Zhang	Ohio State University, USA

Track Members

Alberto Bosio	Ecole Centrale de Lyon, France
Arnaud Virazel	University of Montpellier, France
Michele Portolan	Université Grenoble Alpes, France
Mottaqiallah Taouil	Delft University of Technology, The Netherlands
Tiago Balen	Universidade Federal do Rio Grande do Sul, Brazil
Maksim Jenihhin	Tallinn University of Technology, Estonia
Gurgen Harutyunyan	Synopsys, Armenia
Nicola Nicolici	McMaster University, Canada
Leticia Bolzani Poehls	RWTH Aachen University, Germany
Chia Yee Ooi	Universiti Teknologi Malaysia, Malaysia
Xiaoqing Wen	Kyushu Institute of Technology, Japan
Sachin Sapatnekar	University of Minnesota, USA
Huawei Li	Institute of Computing Technology, Chinese Academy of Science, China

Hardware Security

Track Chairs

Yue Zheng	Nanyang Technological University, Singapore
Domenic Forte	University of Florida, USA

Track Members

Rajat Chakraborty	IIT Kharagpur, India
Adib Nahiyan	Intel, USA
Xiaolin Xu	Northeastern University, USA

Gang Qu	University of Maryland, USA
Chester Rebeiro	IIT Madras, India
Sheng Wei	Rutgers University, USA
Tamzidul Hoque	University of Kansas, USA
Stjepan Picek	Delft University of Technology, The Netherlands
Xiaolu Hou	Nanyang Technological University, Singapore
Fan Zhang	Zhejiang University, China
Itamar Levi	Bar-Ilan University, Israel
Song Bian	Kyoto University, Japan
Ayesha Khalid	Queen's University Belfast, UK
Sujoy Sinha Roy	TU Graz, Austria
Youssef Souissi	Secure-IC, France

Emerging Technologies and New Computing Paradigms

Track Chairs

| Leonel Sousa | Universidade de Lisboa, Portugal |
| Yang (Cindy) Yi | Virginia Tech, USA |

Track Members

Joseph Friedman	University of Texas at Dallas, USA
Sébastien Le Beux	Concordia University, USA
Alexandre Levisse	École Polytechnique Fédérale de Lausanne, Switzerland
Elena Ioana Vatajelu	TIMA, Université Grenoble Alpes, France
Walter Weber	TU Wien, Austria
Shigeru Yamashita	Ritsumeikan University, Japan
Zhaohao Wang	Beihang University, China
Jie Han	University of Alberta, Canada
Sorin Cotofana	Delft University of Technology, The Netherlands
Mohammad Mansour	American University of Beirut, Lebanon
Hongyu An	Michigan Technological University, USA
Cheng Zhuo	Zhejiang University, China
Xiang Chen	George Mason University, USA

Contents

On the Efficiency of AdapTTA: An Adaptive Test-Time Augmentation Strategy for Reliable Embedded ConvNets

Luca Mocerino[1]([✉]), Roberto G. Rizzo[1], Valentino Peluso[2], Andrea Calimera[1], and Enrico Macii[2]

[1] Department of Control and Computer Engineering, Politecnico di Torino, 10129 Turin, Italy
{luca.mocerino,robertogiorgio.rizzo,andrea.calimera}@polito.it
[2] Interuniversity Department of Regional and Urban Studies and Planning, Politecnico di Torino, 10129 Turin, Italy
{valentino.peluso,enrico.macii}@polito.it

Abstract. Test-Time Augmentation (TTA) is a popular technique that aims to improve the accuracy of Convolutional Neural Networks (ConvNets) at inference-time. TTA addresses a limitation inherent to any deep learning pipeline, that is, training datasets cover only a tiny portion of the possible inputs. For this reason, when ported to real-life scenarios, ConvNets may suffer from substantial accuracy loss due to unseen input patterns received under unpredictable external conditions that can mislead the model. TTA tackles this problem directly on the field, first running multiple inferences on a set of altered versions of the same input sample and then computing the final outcome through a consensus of the aggregated predictions. TTA has been conceived to run on cloud systems powered with high-performance GPUs, where the altered inputs get processed in parallel with no (or negligible) performance overhead. Unfortunately, when shifted on embedded CPUs, TTA introduces latency penalties that limit its adoption for edge applications. For a more efficient resource usage, we can rely on an adaptive implementation of TTA, *AdapTTA*, that adjusts the number of inferences dynamically, depending on the input complexity. In this work, we assess the figures of merit of the AdapTTA framework, exploring different configurations of its basic blocks, i.e., the augmentation policy, the predictions aggregation function, and the model confidence score estimator, suitable for the integration with the proposed adaptive system. We conducted an extensive experimental evaluation, considering state-of-the-art ConvNets for image classification, MobileNets and EfficientNets, deployed onto a commercial embedded device, the ARM Cortex-A CPU. The collected results reveal that thanks to optimal design choices, AdapTTA ensures substantial acceleration compared to a static TTA, with up to 2.21× faster processing preserving the same accuracy level. This comprehensive analysis helps designers identify the most efficient AdapTTA configuration for custom inference engines running on the edge.

© IFIP International Federation for Information Processing 2022
Published by Springer Nature Switzerland AG 2022
V. Grimblatt et al. (Eds.): VLSI-SoC 2021, IFIP AICT 661, pp. 1–23, 2022.
https://doi.org/10.1007/978-3-031-16818-5_1

Keywords: Test-time augmentation · Deep learning · Embedded systems

1   Introduction

1.1   Context

Convolutional Neural Networks (ConvNets) are the backbone of many computer vision applications, thanks to their ability to recognize complex data structures with good generalization capability. However, state-of-the-art ConvNets are far from the robustness of the human vision systems, which can deal with abstract changes in structure and style and are rarely misled by spatial changes in images or forms of corruption such as blur, snow, noise, and a combination of them. Achieving this level of generalization is an essential target for intelligent systems, especially in safety-critical applications. Still, current ConvNets suffer from accuracy drop when ported to real-life scenarios and operated on input patterns that differ substantially from those used at training time, which often represents only a limited subset of all the possible patterns. This issue gets critical in high-dimensional problems like image classification, for which covering the large variability across different data samples is unfeasible. For example, the most common sources of misprediction are the discrepancy in size and orientation of the objects caught in the image [1], as well as different light conditions or contrast.

The first actions to address this problem can be taken at training time. Among the possible options, data augmentation is one of the most common techniques, thanks to its straightforward integration in standard training pipelines. It consists of applying random transformations on the input data to increase the diversity of the training samples, with the final goal of improving the generalization capability. The most simple implementations used in computer vision problems rely on a set of geometric and graphical transformations, often hand-tuned by domain experts to match the conditions of real-life scenarios [2,3]. More advanced strategies aim to automate the design of the augmentation policy, for instance, through a grid search [4], reinforcement learning [5], or gradient-based optimization [6]. Some of these strategies have been successfully integrated with the training of state-of-the-art ConvNets [7].

Despite these efforts, ConvNets may still fail to handle unpredictable changes in the data distribution [8,9] in real-life scenarios. For a more robust generalization, recent works proposed complementary strategies operating at inference time [10,11]. Among them, Test-Time Augmentation (TTA) is a valuable option for ConvNets hosted in the cloud and operated for visual tasks like image classification [2,12,13]. It is a simple yet efficient strategy that leverages multiple predictions to increase the model's confidence. Specifically, it involves the aggregation of partial predictions over a set of transformed versions of the same input image. In practice, the transformations applied are inspired by the data augmentation techniques typically adopted during training.

Different implementations of TTA exist, yet all of them have been validated only on high-performance platforms for cloud applications. In this work, we focus

Table 1. Inference latency (ms) of state-of-the-art ConvNets measured at different batch sizes (1, 5, and 10) on a cloud GPU (NVIDIA Titan Xp with 3840 CUDA cores) and an embedded CPU (ARM Cortex-A53 with 4 cores).

ConvNet	NVIDIA Titan Xp			ARM Cortex-A53		
	1	5	10	1	5	10
MobileNetV1	18.2	18.6	18.7	53.1	290.6	569.9
MobileNetV2	12.1	12.4	12.9	44.2	261.8	513.5
MobileNetV3	19.0	20.1	21.3	46.2	221.3	470.6
EfficientNet-B0	21.3	22.4	22.6	68.5	358.9	682.3
EfficientNet-B1	31.9	33.4	33.9	103.4	536.4	1290.2
EfficientNet-B2	33.2	35.7	38.4	122.6	591.9	1360.4

instead on the portability of TTA to inference engines running on embedded systems integrating low-power CPUs. This shift raises several challenges due to the limited computational resources of embedded systems, as detailed in the following sub-section.

1.2 Motivations

Conventional TTA policies have been conceived for high-performance architectures like GPUs, which offer thousands of parallel processing cores. For example, a commercial device like the NVIDIA Titan XP hosts 3840 CUDA cores. These architectures enable to process multiple inputs in parallel with a single feed-forward pass, a procedure commonly called *batch inference*. When implemented on cloud GPUs, TTA relies on batch inference to process the augmented images with negligible performance overhead (see Table 1). The same does not hold on the edge, where ConvNets are made run on mobile devices powered by low-power CPUs with limited resources [14–16] (e.g., 4 cores in the ARM Cortex-A53). On low-power CPUs, a single image is enough to saturate all the available computing units. Table 1 demonstrates this observation with a quantitative comparison, showing that batch inference raises a prohibitive latency overhead on embedded CPUs, which in turn prevents the portability of TTA. Specifically, batch inference gets 5.5× (batch size = 5) and 11.2× (batch size = 10) slower than a single inference (batch size = 1), therefore it is even less efficient than sequential processing.

In our recent work [17], we introduced *AdapTTA*, an adaptive implementation of TTA suited for embedded systems. Unlike static TTA strategies, where the number of modified samples fed to the ConvNet is fixed, AdapTTA self-regulates the number of transformations and feed-forward passes dynamically. The transformed images are generated and processed sequentially till the model achieves good confidence in the main outcome. In other words, it only runs those inferences that make the model confident enough about the prediction. Specifically, AdapTTA relies on the fact that different inputs have different intrinsic complexity and the minimum number of transformations needed to reach an accurate classification changes on a sample basis. This suggests that the number of feed-forward passes can be adjusted at run-time depending on the confidence level accumulated. The processing gets faster for "easy" images and slower for the most "complex" ones. Leveraging the statistics of the input patterns, AdapTTA allows a substantial average speed-up compared to the original static approach.

1.3   Contributions

Starting from the findings of AdapTTA, we further investigate the design of a TTA framework for embedded ConvNets, exploring different implementations of its basic components and quantifying their impact on accuracy gain and performance. Specifically, the design and the optimization of AdapTTA involve three main choices: (i) the augmentation policy, i.e., the set of transformations to apply to the input image; (ii) the aggregation function, i.e., the method to combine the partial predictions; (iii) the confidence score estimator, i.e., a proxy to control the number of transformations needed for each input. For all three blocks, we consider different options borrowed from the literature, focusing on those configurations that fit the target of our adaptive strategy, i.e., systems with limited computing resources.

The remainder of this paper is organized as follows. After a brief description of data augmentation and TTA, we report the most recent advancements in cloud-based TTA policies (Sect. 2). We then introduce the architecture of AdapTTA, discussing the viable options for the implementation of augmentation policy, aggregation function, and confidence score (Sect. 3). To assess the figures of merit of AdapTTA, we considered two families of ConvNets for image classification, MobileNets and EfficientNets, running on a commercial off-the-shelf embedded platform powered by an ARM Cortex-A53 CPU (Sect. 4). The results collected from the comprehensive analysis of different AdapTTA configurations guide designers towards the understanding of the best practices for an efficient porting of AdapTTA to embedded platforms (Sect. 5). Finally, a summary of the main achievements concludes the work (Sect. 6).

2   Background and Related Work

2.1   Data Augmentation for Training

The main bottleneck for training reliable ConvNets lies in imperfections in the data. The most critical aspects to consider include (i) domain mismatch when the data used for training differs from that processed on the field, (ii) data bias when the data is imbalanced towards specific classes or categories, (iii) data noise when the data is cluttered or corrupted.

Data augmentation is one of the simplest solutions to deal with these problems. It consists of adding additional training data through the application of random transformations on the available training samples. In computer vision tasks,

Geometric transformations

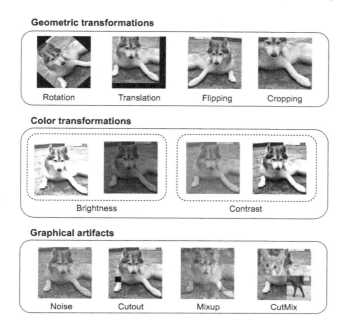

Fig. 1. Example of data augmentations for an image classification task.

the most popular augmentation procedures involve a set of geometric transformations (e.g., translation, rotation, flipping) and color transformations (e.g., brightness, contrast, saturation) that try to reproduce the conditions of the application domain [2,3] (Fig. 1). More sophisticated techniques introduce graphical artifacts injecting random noise, masking random regions on the input (*Cutout* [18]), or mixing multiple samples in a single image (*Mixup* [19] and *CutMix* [20]). The generated samples help the model learn features that make the classification more robust to changes in objects' position, lighting conditions, and scales.

Common training pipelines combine multiple transformations to further increase the diversity of data. The set of the transformations selected defines the augmentation policy. At each training iteration, a random subset of these transformations are applied sequentially to the original data. Augmentation policies can be hand-crafted or built with automatic techniques. For example, the optimal selection can be driven by a random search engine to adapt the augmentation policy to different contexts [4]. In general, automatic solutions outperform manual designs, motivating their integration in the training flow of state-of-the-art ConvNets [7,21].

Rather than transforming the original input, alternative solutions are proposed to extend the training dataset with synthetic images that preserve the features of the original data. These solutions rely on generative models, like Variational Autoencoders [22] or Generative Adversarial Networks [23], that are trained on the available samples together with the classification model. Despite the potential benefits, the additional training operations generate a substantial computational overhead, which hinders the adoption of these methods.

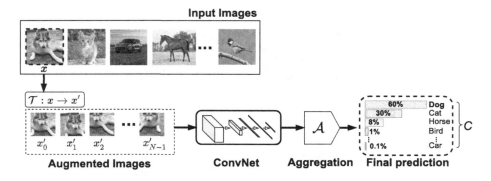

Fig. 2. Flow diagram of static TTA policy for an image classification task.

2.2 Test-Time Augmentation

Even if trained with complex augmentation policies, ConvNets still remain susceptible to unpredictable changes in the data distribution due to the shift from laboratory conditions to real-life scenarios [9]. TTA has emerged as a common strategy integrated with prediction services hosted in the cloud to increase the model robustness. In practice, TTA employs the same transformations for data augmentation to generate altered versions of an input sample. The generated instances are fed to the ConvNet, and the partial predictions are aggregated to compute the outcome. The rationale behind this process is that an altered version of the same input data increases the information contents provided to the model, improving the decision-making process.

Like data augmentation, most research efforts to optimize TTA focused on the search for the transformations that maximize the accuracy gains. Early works in the literature adopted hand-crafted policies based on basic spatial transformations such as image cropping & flipping and input resolution re-scaling [2,12,13,24]. More recent studies investigated algorithms for the automatic design of the TTA policy. For example, the selection of the transformations can be driven by a greedy exploration [8] or even tailored to each input sample [25]. However, automatic methods share an import shortcoming, that is, they require the training of additional modules or the re-training of the entire ConvNets.

Regardless of the transformations adopted, the major limitation of all the TTA implementations lies in their *static* behavior: they apply a predefined number of transformations to each input data without discriminating their features and complexity. Figure 2 shows a more detailed view of the execution flow of a generic TTA strategy. It depicts an image classification problem involving C classes. First, a set of N augmented versions x' of the input image x is generated through the application of a set of transformations included in the augmentation policy $\mathcal{T} : x \rightarrow x'$. Second, the generated images are fed to the ConvNet in parallel or sequentially (more details in Sect. 5). Third, the N outputs are processed by a softmax layer to score the available labels. Finally, the resulting partial predictions are aggregated through a function $\mathcal{A}$ that returns the final outcome. The parameter N is fixed at design time by the TTA policy, therefore each prediction encompasses the same number of inferences for each input image.

Existing TTA policies address a single optimization goal that is the accuracy gain. They have been conceived and integrated with ConvNets running on cloud systems, which can process a high number of transformations still without saturating the available processing units thanks to the extensive parallelism of GPUs. On the contrary, embedded systems cannot offer comparable levels of parallelism, and even the inference of a single image requires the full utilization of resources. Besides accuracy, latency is an important variable to consider for the efficiency of TTA on low-power devices. This is a less explored problem, which motivated the design of AdapTTA.

3   Adaptive Test-Time Augmentation

Static TTA policies might be too conservative for most input samples, especially for specific inputs with well-exposed features that ConvNets can spot with a single or few feed-forward passes. Therefore, we conceived AdapTTA with a specific goal: provide a more flexible TTA mechanism that monitors intermediate predictions to minimize the number of transformations needed to return a reliable classification.

The schematic flow of Fig. 3 illustrates the working principle of AdapTTA. The flow is iterative, and the number of iterations changes on a sample basis depending on the level of *confidence* of the classification. In each iteration, the ConvNet takes as input an altered version of the original data x_i', which is generated with a transformation defined in the augmentation policy $\mathcal{T}$. Then, the ConvNet returns a partial prediction p_i, which contains the probabilities over the C classes. The partial predictions are aggregated class-wise after each inference using the aggregation function $\mathcal{A}(p_i)$. The resulting probability distribution P_A is evaluated with the confidence score CS to decide whether to process to the next transformation or return P_A to infer the final output. Specifically, if the confidence score satisfies a user-defined threshold τ, i.e., $CS > \tau$, the prediction is deemed reliable, and the TTA loop ends. The class with the largest probability in P_A is then selected as the label of the input image. In other words, AdapTTA implements an adaptive mechanism to control the augmentation passes at runtime based on the confidence level accumulated across repeated inferences. In the worst-case scenario, namely, if CS falls below the threshold τ for each iteration, the entire set of augmented samples extracted from the policy $\mathcal{T}$ is evaluated. In this case, AdapTTA delivers the same predictions as the static TTA, with the same computing effort and accuracy gain.

The flow depicted in Fig. 3 is kept general to underline that, in principle, AdapTTA is compatible with different augmentation policies, aggregation functions, and confidence scores. However, the design and optimization of these components are paramount to build an efficient adaptive scheme that maximizes the accuracy gain with minimum computational effort. Regarding the augmentation

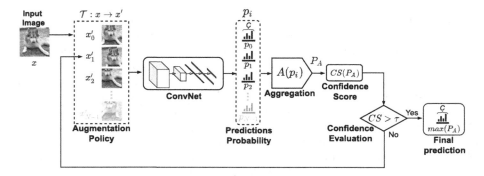

Fig. 3. AdapTTA schematic flow. Augmented images are generated and fed sequentially to the ConvNet. After each iteration, the predictions are aggregated, and the confidence score is computed. Depending on its value, the following transformation is applied and evaluated, or the loop is interrupted. In the example, only x'_0, x'_1, and x'_2 get processed by the ConvNet to compute the final prediction. The label with the largest probability in P_A is assigned to the input.

policies and aggregation functions, we considered solutions already adopted in static TTA strategies. The confidence score, on the contrary, is the fundamental component that distinguishes AdapTTA from the static approach, as it regulates the dynamic behavior of the proposed flow. For such reason, it is critical to identify a good proxy to evaluate the confidence of a model prediction. For such purpose, we considered different metrics that investigated the level of correctness of a classification taken from the recent literature [26–30]. Compared to these works, the novelty of our contribution lies in the application of the confidence score for the optimization of TTA.

Among the possible design choices for the above mentioned blocks, only a subset of them is compliant with the systems having limited computing resources. Therefore, we conducted our analysis considering the portability ops such blocks to embedded systems as a primary constraint (more details in the following subsections).

3.1 Augmentation Policy

The augmentation policy $\mathcal{T}$ defines the set of transformations that generate N different versions of the input image. In resource-constrained environments, the design of the augmentation policies should follow two important considerations. First, the augmentation policy should keep N as small as possible, as larger values of N imply more network feed-forward passes, which can affect both latency and power dissipation [31]. Second, the execution time needed to process a transformation should be negligible compared to that needed for inference.

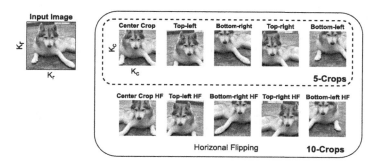

Fig. 4. Example of 5-Crops and 10-Crops TTA policies. HF denotes the application of horizontal flipping.

Following these observations, we considered only simple spatial manipulations, i.e., cropping & flipping. We integrated them into two TTA policies, *5-Crops* and *10-Crops*, inspired by the early implementations of TTA [2,12,13,24]. These two policies fit our design target. On the ARM Cortex-A53 CPU, cropping requires only 0.8 ms and horizontal flipping 0.9 ms, which is negligible compared to the tens of ms needed for network inference. Specifically, the two policies can be described as follows:

5-Crops (5C) - This policy takes as input a $K_r \times K_r$ image (the leftmost in Fig. 4) and extracts consecutively a set of five crops of size $K_c \times K_c$, with $K_c < K_r$, from different areas of the input image. Specifically, it returns the center crop and the four corner crops (top-left, top-right, bottom-left and bottom-right).

10-Crops (10C) - This policy is an extension of the 5C policy; it applies the left-to-right horizontal flipping to the five crops of 5C for a total of 10 images (Fig. 4). Doubling the number of transformations (from 5C to 10C) should increase the accuracy gain at the cost of a higher overall inference latency.

3.2   Aggregation Function

The aggregation function $\mathcal{A}(p_i)$ defines how to combine the partial predictions p_i generated at the different iterations of the flow in Fig. 3. The study in [26] reported the most common implementations adopted in cloud-based TTA, *Max* and *Mean* aggregation. Although introduced for the cloud, we imported these two functions to our design target. Their execution, consisting of simple arithmetic operations, is negligible compared to the intensive workloads of ConvNets, and makes these functions a good fit for systems with limited computing resources. We summarize them as follows:

Max Aggregation - The *Max* function selects the distribution p_i that contains the class with the largest score among all the partial predictions. Therefore, the outcome of this function rewards only a single prediction and discards the contribution of the other ones.

Mean Aggregation - The *Mean* function performs the class-wise average of the partial predictions p_i. Different from *Max*, this aggregation function gives the same importance to all the partial predictions. For higher accuracy, it is possible to apply a weighted average, where the weights are trained with a dedicated procedure [26]. However, this procedure requires additional calibration data, which might be unavailable in the deployment phase. Therefore, our analysis considers only the arithmetic average.

In static TTA, the aggregation is performed after processing all the transformations defined in the augmentation policy. In AdapTTA, the aggregated probability P_A is instead updated after every inference to evaluate the classification confidence at the end of each iteration.

3.3   Confidence Score Estimator

The confidence score estimates the correctness of the classification and regulates the dynamic behavior of AdapTTA. A proper definition of the confidence score should guarantee two essential properties: (i) an high confidence value should correspond to a correct prediction, avoiding early stops of AdapTTA; (ii) low confidence should be assigned only to those inputs that need more transformations for committing the correct prediction, avoiding waste of computing resources.

Estimating the classification confidence of a ConvNet is not a new research problem; still, it remains an open issue. Among the viable options, we considered the following approaches:

MaxP - This function selects as confidence score the largest probability in P_A [26], over the C classes. This function considers only the top-1 probability, thus it may be misleading if all class probabilities have similar values.

Score Margin (SM) - It denotes the difference between the first and second largest probabilities over the C classes contained in P_A [27,28].

$$SM = P_{Atop1} - P_{Atop2} \tag{1}$$

Intuitively, low values of SM denote that the model is uncertain between the two most likely classes.

Entropy - In information theory and statistics, entropy represents the informative content of a random variable [32]. For this reason, it has been adopted as an uncertainty metric in many deep learning problems like active learning [29] and unsupervised learning [33]. For the AdapTTA design, we computed the normalized entropy H_n [34] of P_A (over the C classes).

$$H = - \sum_{c=0}^{C-1} P_{Ac} \cdot log(P_{Ac}) \tag{2}$$

$$H_n = 1 - \frac{H}{log(C)} \tag{3}$$

In this way, the *Entropy* score ranges in $[0, 1]$ like the above mentioned confidence metrics, where lower values imply higher uncertainty and larger values indicate stronger confidence.

Similar to the aggregation functions, these confidence scores are suitable for low-power systems as they only require simple arithmetic operations with negligible computational overhead compared to the execution of a ConvNet.

4   Experimental Setup

This section describes the hardware platforms and the software environment for AdapTTA deployment. In addition, we discuss the ConvNets families used as benchmarks for the experiments.

4.1   Hardware Platform and Software Setup

The Odroid-C2 platform, powered by the Amlogic S905 SoC, serves as the hardware testbench. The CPU is a quad-core ARM Cortex-A53 with a nominal frequency of 1.5 GHz. The board runs Ubuntu Mate 18.04 with Hardkernel's version 3.16.72-46. TensorFlow Lite 1.14 is the inference engine, and it includes a collection of neural-network procedures tailored for the ARM Cortex-A architecture. TensorFlow Lite is cross-compiled in our environment using the GNU ARM Embedded Toolchain (version 6.5) [35].

4.2   ConvNet Benchmarks

The adopted benchmarks are pre-trained models from TensorFlow Hub [36] and TensorFlow Hosted Models [37] repository. Specifically, they belong to two families of ConvNets that represent the state-of-the-art for image classification tasks for the mobile segment: *MobileNets* [38–40] and *EfficientNets* [7]. All the models were trained on the ImageNet [41] dataset and quantized to 8 bits, which is a standard solution for edge inference as it provides a smaller memory footprint and faster processing with negligible accuracy loss when compared to floating-point.

Table 2 reports structural properties (memory footprint and latency) and functional (the classification accuracy) of the ConvNets under test. Specifically, the column **Storage** collects the size (in MB) of the ConvNet in .tflite format,

Table 2. Storage requirements, input resolution (K_c), top-1 accuracy without TTA (Top-1), and inference latency (L_{nom}) of the selected benchmarks.

ConvNet	Storage [MB]	K_c	Top-1 [%]	L_{nom} [ms]
MobileNetV1	4.3	224	70.0	53.1
MobileNetV2	3.4	224	70.8	44.2
MobileNetV3	4.2	224	72.2	46.2
EfficientNet-B0	5.4	224	74.4	68.5
EfficientNet-B1	6.4	240	75.9	103.4
EfficientNet-B2	6.9	260	77.0	122.6

which includes the model weights and additional metadata (i.e., the topology description) to deploy the model on the target device. The metric **Top-1** refers to the top-1 classification accuracy measured on the ImageNet validation set, which consists of 50k images split into 1k different classes. The accuracy is evaluated without TTA, i.e., with a standard pre-processing pipeline consisting of resizing the images to a fixed resolution of $K_r \times K_r$ pixels and extracting the central crop of shape $K_c \times K_c$ ($K_r = K_c + 32$). Finally, the column L_{nom} reports the nominal latency of a single inference running at the maximum available resources (4 threads @1.5 GHz).

5 Results

5.1 Design and Optimization of AdapTTA

The primary goal of any TTA strategy, static or adaptive, is to improve classification accuracy. For this reason, our first analysis aims to identify the most accurate static configurations that will serve as baselines to assess the quality of AdapTTA. In the static TTA, the design choices that impact the accuracy are the augmentation policy and the aggregation function. Therefore, we conducted an exhaustive exploration that considers all the possible combinations of the augmentation policies and aggregation functions under investigation.

Specifically, the results in Table 3 report the accuracy gain achieved by *Max* and *Mean* aggregation functions with the 5C and 10C policies for the entire benchmark suite. Regardless of the design choices, TTA improves the classification quality, yet with different benefits depending on the configuration. The accuracy gain ranges from 0.5% (MobileNetV3) to 2.70% (MobileNetV1) for 5C policy and from 0.9% (EfficientNet-B2) to 3.1% (MobileNetV1) for 10C policy. In general, a larger number of transformations brings higher accuracy. Moreover, the *Mean* aggregation function always outperforms *Max*, with relative improvements up to 1.2% (MobileNetV2 with 5C policy). The two functions only reach the same accuracy level for MobileNetV3 with the 5C policy. For two ConvNets (MobileNetV2 and EfficientNet-B0), *Mean* with 5C shows even a larger gain than

Table 3. Accuracy gain (in %) of 5-Crops (**5C**) and 10-Crops (**10C**) TTA policies with **Max** and **Mean** aggregation functions.

ConvNet	5C		10C	
	Max	Mean	Max	Mean
MobileNetV1	2.4%	**2.7%**	2.8%	**3.1%**
MobileNetV2	1.0%	**2.2%**	1.8%	**2.9%**
MobileNetV3	**0.5%**	**0.5%**	1.0%	**1.2%**
EfficientNet-B0	0.7%	**1.1%**	0.9%	**1.3%**
EfficientNet-B1	1.9%	**2.2%**	2.2%	**2.5%**
EfficientNet-B2	0.7%	**0.8%**	0.9%	**1.1%**

Max with 10C, suggesting that the proper selection of the aggregation function enables a smaller number of transformations, retaining the same accuracy.

Our findings confirm the analyses conducted in previous studies like [26], which reported similar trends on a different set of networks and datasets. We believe that the *Max* function is susceptible to wrong classifications due to a partial prediction that erroneously overestimates a class probability. In these cases, the other predictions would be simply discarded. On the contrary, the *Mean* function mitigate this effect, as averaging over all the predictions can distribute the influence of outliers over the final decision. Motivated by these observations, we selected *Mean* as the aggregation function for both the static TTA used as a reference and the implementation of AdapTTA (more details about their comparison in Sect. 5.2).

As described in Sect. 3, the dynamic behavior of AdapTTA is controlled by the confidence score and the corresponding value of the confidence threshold τ (set as a hyper-parameter). We then focus on understanding which confidence estimator provides the most reliable evaluation of the classification correctness. For this purpose, we validated the three candidate functions (*MaxP*, *Entropy*, *SM*) in AdapTTA and we measured the accuracy gain for different values of $\tau \in [0.1, 0.9]$, with a step of 0.1. Notice that $\tau = 0$ is equivalent to classification without TTA, and $\tau = 1$ corresponds to the static TTA (all the transformations get processed).

The results are reported in Figs. 5 and 6 for the MobileNet and EfficientNet families, respectively. *SM* is the only metric that, with appropriate values of τ, ensures the same accuracy as the static TTA (dashed grey line in the plots). In general, *SM* always outperforms the other metrics, even at lower values of τ. The same trend holds for all the ConvNets and augmentation policies (5C and 10C). The most representative example is MobileNetV2 with the 5C policy (Fig. 5-b left). In this case, *SM* keeps almost the maximum level of accuracy even with $\tau = 0.4$, while *MaxP* and *Entropy* reduce accuracy by 1.48%. In summary, with *SM* the accuracy shows a lower sensitivity to the variations of τ. This is a desirable property, as lowering the value of τ could enable higher acceleration. Intuitively, if the classification is deemed correct even at "low" confidence lev-

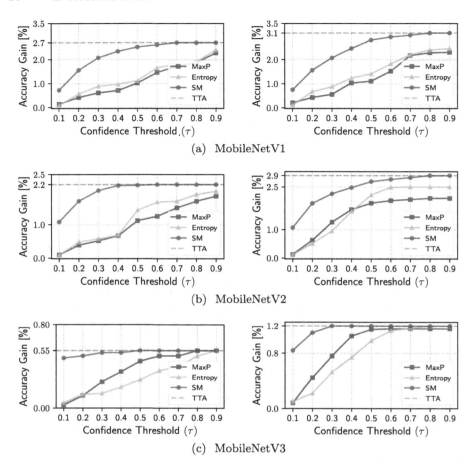

Fig. 5. Accuracy gain of AdapTTA for different confidence scores (MaxP, Entropy, SM) using 5C policy (left) and 10C policy (right). Results on the MobileNets family.

els, fewer transformations must be processed to return the final prediction (see Sect. 5.3 for more details). In MobileNetV3 with 10C policy (Fig. 5-c right) and EfficientNet-B2 with 5C policy (Fig. 6-c left), *SM* shows the lowest sensitivity to τ: the accuracy gain quickly saturates to the maximum level of accuracy starting from $\tau \geq 0.3$.

5.2   Comparing Static TTA and AdapTTA

We compared the computational efficiency of a standard static TTA and AdapTTA, measuring the average prediction rate (in FPS) across the ImageNet validation set (50k images). For the static TTA, we benchmarked two different implementations:

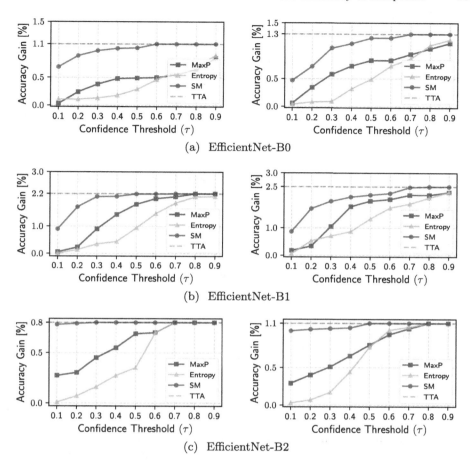

Fig. 6. Accuracy gain of AdapTTA for different confidence scores (MaxP, Entropy, SM) using 5C policy (left) and 10C policy (right). Results on the EfficientNets family.

Batch-TTA - the augmented images get processed in parallel through batching (the batch size is equal to the number of transformations);
Seq-TTA - the augmented images get processed sequentially.
The overall inference time includes the data augmentations latency measured on the target device (0.8 ms for cropping and 0.9 ms for horizontal flipping).

In all cases, we considered the *Mean* aggregation, and we studied both the 5C and 10C policies. For AdapTTA, we fixed $\tau = 0.8$ to ensure the same accuracy gain of the static TTA, although this high value could limit the potential acceleration of AdapTTA. However, we opted for this conservative choice to assess the feasibility of AdapTTA decoupling our analysis from the optimization of τ.

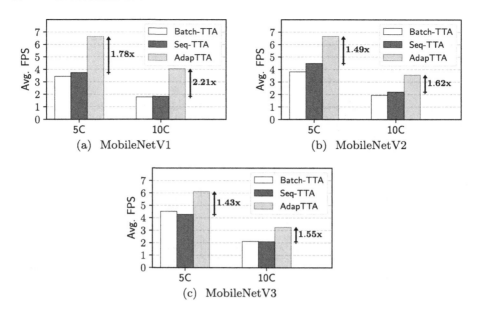

Fig. 7. Average prediction rate (Avg. FPS - the higher, the better) for 5C and 10C policies of the static implementations (Batch-TTA and Seq-TTA) and AdapTTA. The arrows indicate the relative speed-up of AdapTTA compared to Seq-TTA. Results on the MobileNets family.

Figures 7 and 8 summarize the collected results for the two families of benchmarks. As mentioned in Sect. 1, batching turns out to be inefficient on embedded CPUs due to the low number of parallel cores (4 in the Cortex-A53); hence, Seq-TTA is slightly faster than Batch-TTA. Also, AdapTTA enables substantial acceleration, with much faster prediction rates ranging from 1.16× to 1.78× in 5C and from 1.19× to 2.21× in 10C. In MobileNetV1, AdapTTA on 10C outperforms Seq-TTA on 5C in both accuracy (+3.1% vs. +2.7%) and speed (4.05 FPS vs. 3.73 FPS). The reason can be inferred from Table 4, which reports the average number of inferences needed to run a prediction with AdapTTA. AdapTTA needs less than 5 (4.57) inferences on average (row MobileNetV1, column 10C), achieving superior performance than a static 5C implementation. A comprehensive analysis on all the benchmarks shows that the average number of images ranges from 2.81 to 4.32 for 5C and from 4.57 to 8.41 for 10C at the same accuracy level, demonstrating that static TTA is too conservative in most cases and unreliable for less frequent complex inputs.

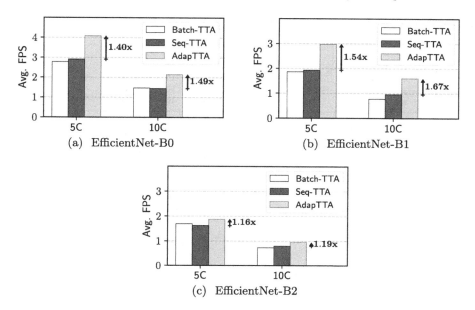

Fig. 8. Average prediction rate (Avg. FPS - the higher, the better) for 5C and 10C policies of the static implementations (Batch-TTA and Seq-TTA) and AdapTTA. The arrows indicate the relative speed-up of AdapTTA compared to Seq-TTA. Results on the EfficientNets family.

Table 4. Average number of inferences in AdapTTA for the 5-Crops (5C) and 10-Crops (10C) policies.

ConvNet	5C	10C
MobileNetV1	2.81	4.57
MobileNetV2	3.37	6.26
MobileNetV3	3.48	6.54
EfficientNet-B0	3.57	6.75
EfficientNet-B1	3.24	6.02
EfficientNet-B2	4.32	8.41

5.3   Accuracy vs. Performance Trade-Offs

This section aims to assess the sensitivity of AdapTTA efficiency on the hyper-parameter τ. Even though we selected the same value ($\tau = 0.8$) for all the networks in the preliminary analysis of Sect. 5.2, more precise control of τ could enable additional margins of optimization. Indeed, a too low value of τ can limit the accuracy gains of AdapTTA, while a too high value can lower the prediction rate as unneeded transformations get processed. Here, we aim to quantify the maximum speed-ups that can be achieved while retaining the maximum accu-

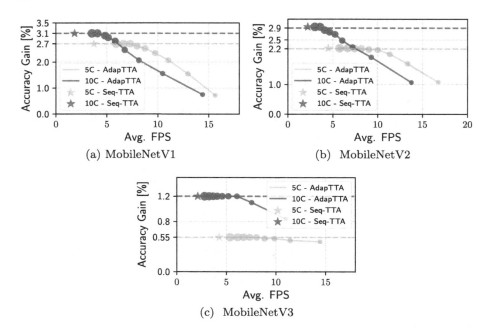

Fig. 9. Accuracy gain (in %) vs. average prediction rate (Avg. FPS) at different values of τ for 5C and 10C policy. The size of the circles is proportional to τ (a larger size indicates a higher τ). Results on the MobileNets family.

racy. For this purpose, we evaluated a discrete set of values of τ, ranging from 0.1 to 0.9, with a step of 0.1. The experiments were conducted on the ImageNet validation set.

The main outcome of the analysis is that the minimum value of τ ensuring the highest accuracy gain differs across the selected benchmarks: from 0.7 for MobileNetV1 in 5C policy to 0.3 for MobileNetV3 in 10C policy (Fig. 9). This translates to additional acceleration: in MobileNetV1 5C policy, the prediction rate increases from 6.64 FPS ($\tau = 0.8$) to 7.28 FPS ($\tau = 0.7$) on average; in MobileNetV3 10C policy, from 3.26 FPS ($\tau = 0.8$) to 6.07 FPS ($\tau = 0.3$). Similar trends do hold for the EfficientNet family (Fig. 10). Besides a different topology, these networks followed a different training protocol, e.g., integrating different data augmentation pipelines [7,38]. This observation suggests that training hyper-parameters can affect the efficiency of AdapTTA, and potentially corrective actions applied at training time could reduce the number of transformations needed at test time.

Moreover, the circles in the plots represent different operating points that can be selected at run-time to enable a fine-grain trade-off between accuracy and speed. This can be helpful when the application has to rescale its energy footprint (e.g., together with DVFS [42], if the mobile system is running out of battery) or when the classification task is not a critical application (some accuracy loss is tolerable). For example, with $\tau = 0.5$, MobileNetV1 reaches 8.7 FPS, yet with a

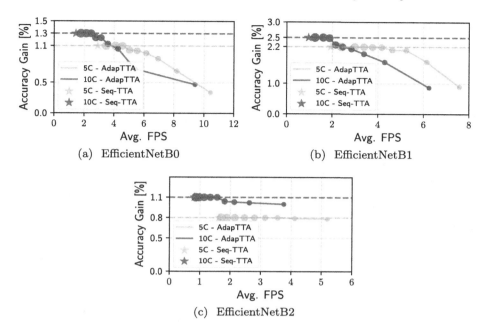

Fig. 10. Accuracy gain (in %) vs. average prediction rate (Avg. FPS) at different values of τ for 5C and 10C policy. The size of the circles is proportional to τ (a larger size indicates a higher τ). Results on the EfficientNets family. (Color figure online)

marginal accuracy loss with respect to Seq-TTA ($< 0.5\%$). Also, a more in-depth analysis of the collected results reveals an interesting relationship between the value of τ and the policy selection. In all the networks except MobileNetV3 and EfficientNet-B2, the 10C (blue) and 5C (yellow) curves show a point of intersection. This point qualitatively delimits the boundary of two working conditions, *high-accuracy* on the left and *high-performance* on the right. For high-accuracy, 10C always outperforms 5C, while, for high-performance, the opposite consideration holds. This is due to the rapid drop in the accuracy observed in the 10C policy at lower values of τ. In summary, the maximum efficiency can be reached only with the joint optimization of τ and the augmentation policy. However, MobileNetV3 (Fig. 9-c) and EfficientNet-B2 (Fig. 10-c) show different trends. As mentioned, the accuracy of these networks is less sensitive to the variations of τ, resulting in almost flat curves in the accuracy vs. performance space. Specifically, the 10C curve never intersects the 5C curve, indicating that the 10C policy is the most practical choice for these networks. The 5C policy could be taken into account only for smaller values of τ (the two rightmost points in this case), which can still guarantee high-performance operating conditions with limited accuracy loss ($<0.4\%$ for MobileNetV3 and $<0.7\%$ for EfficientNet-B2).

6 Conclusions

AdapTTA introduced a dynamic implementation of TTA targeting low-power applications deployed on embedded systems. Specifically, AdapTTA minimizes the number of augmented samples to process, with the final goal of reducing the computational effort while preserving the same accuracy benefits. To validate the efficiency of AdapTTA, we conducted a comprehensive analysis of different components and configurations of the proposed framework. We explored different TTA policies, aggregation functions, and confidence scores, assessing their impact on accuracy and performance. Our analyses serve as practical guidelines for designers and end-users to identify the most efficient configuration. Moreover, extensive experiments on a large variety of benchmarks reveal that AdapTTA reaches substantial acceleration, from $1.16\times$ to $2.21\times$ compared to static TTA policies, with no loss of prediction accuracy.

References

1. Hendrycks, D., Dietterich, T.G.: Benchmarking neural network robustness to common corruptions and perturbations. In: 7th International Conference on Learning Representations, ICLR 2019, New Orleans, LA, USA, 6–9 May 2019 (2019)
2. Krizhevsky, A., Sutskever, I., Hinton, G.E.: ImageNet classification with deep convolutional neural networks. In: Advances in Neural Information Processing Systems 25: 26th Annual Conference on Neural Information Processing Systems 2012. Proceedings of a Meeting Held, Lake Tahoe, Nevada, USA, 3–6 December 2012, pp. 1106–1114 (2012)
3. Simard, P.Y., Steinkraus, D., Platt, J.C.: Best practices for convolutional neural networks applied to visual document analysis. In: 7th International Conference on Document Analysis and Recognition (ICDAR 2003), Edinburgh, Scotland, UK, 3–6 August 2003, vol. 2, pp. 958–962. IEEE Computer Society (2003)
4. Cubuk, E.D., Zoph, B., Shlens, J., Le, Q.V.: RandAugment: practical automated data augmentation with a reduced search space. In: 2020 IEEE/CVF Conference on Computer Vision and Pattern Recognition, CVPR Workshops 2020, Seattle, WA, USA, 14–19 June 2020, pp. 3008–3017. Computer Vision Foundation/IEEE (2020)
5. Cubuk, E.D., Zoph, B., Mané, D., Vasudevan, V., Le, Q.V.: AutoAugment: learning augmentation strategies from data. In: IEEE Conference on Computer Vision and Pattern Recognition, CVPR 2019, Long Beach, CA, USA, 16–20 June 2019, pp. 113–123. Computer Vision Foundation/IEEE (2019)
6. Hataya, R., Zdenek, J., Yoshizoe, K., Nakayama, H.: Faster AutoAugment: learning augmentation strategies using backpropagation. In: Vedaldi, A., Bischof, H., Brox, T., Frahm, J.-M. (eds.) ECCV 2020. LNCS, vol. 12370, pp. 1–16. Springer, Cham (2020). https://doi.org/10.1007/978-3-030-58595-2_1
7. Tan, M., Le, Q.V.: EfficientNet: rethinking model scaling for convolutional neural networks. In: Proceedings of the 36th International Conference on Machine Learning, ICML 2019, Long Beach, California, USA, 9–15 June 2019. Proceedings of Machine Learning Research, vol. 97, pp. 6105–6114. PMLR (2019)

8. Lyzhov, A., Molchanova, Y., Ashukha, A., Molchanov, D., Vetrov, D.P.: Greedy policy search: a simple baseline for learnable test-time augmentation. In: Proceedings of the Thirty-Sixth Conference on Uncertainty in Artificial Intelligence, UAI 2020, Virtual, 3–6 August 2020. Proceedings of Machine Learning Research, vol. 124, pp. 1308–1317. AUAI Press (2020)

9. Recht, B., Roelofs, R., Schmidt, L., Shankar, V.: Do imagenet classifiers generalize to imagenet? In: Proceedings of the 36th International Conference on Machine Learning, ICML 2019, Long Beach, California, USA, 9–15 June 2019. Proceedings of Machine Learning Research, vol. 97, pp. 5389–5400. PMLR (2019)

10. Sun, Y., et al.: Test-time training with self-supervision for generalization under distribution shifts. In: Proceedings of the 37th International Conference on Machine Learning, ICML 2020, Virtual, 13–18 July 2020. Proceedings of Machine Learning Research, vol. 119, pp. 9229–9248. PMLR (2020)

11. Kim, J., Kim, H., Kim, G.: Model-agnostic boundary-adversarial sampling for test-time generalization in few-shot learning. In: Vedaldi, A., Bischof, H., Brox, T., Frahm, J.-M. (eds.) ECCV 2020. LNCS, vol. 12346, pp. 599–617. Springer, Cham (2020). https://doi.org/10.1007/978-3-030-58452-8_35

12. Howard, A.G.: Some improvements on deep convolutional neural network based image classification. In: 2nd International Conference on Learning Representations, ICLR 2014, Banff, AB, Canada, 14–16 April 2014. Conference Track Proceedings (2014)

13. Szegedy, C., et al.: Going deeper with convolutions. In: IEEE Conference on Computer Vision and Pattern Recognition, CVPR 2015, Boston, MA, USA, 7–12 June 2015, pp. 1–9. IEEE Computer Society (2015)

14. Peluso, V., Rizzo, R.G., Cipolletta, A., Calimera, A.: Inference on the edge: performance analysis of an image classification task using off-the-shelf CPUs and open-source convnets. In: Sixth International Conference on Social Networks Analysis, Management and Security, SNAMS 2019, Granada, Spain, 22–25 October 2019, pp. 454–459. IEEE (2019)

15. Peluso, V., Rizzo, R.G., Calimera, A.: Performance profiling of embedded convnets under thermal-aware DVFs. Electronics 8(12), 1423 (2019)

16. Grimaldi, M., Peluso, V., Calimera, A.: Optimality assessment of memory-bounded convnets deployed on resource-constrained RISC cores. IEEE Access 7, 152 599–152 611 (2019)

17. Mocerino, L., Rizzo, R.G., Peluso, V., Calimera, A., Macii, E.: AdapTTA: adaptive test-time augmentation for reliable embedded convnets. In: 29th IFIP/IEEE International Conference on Very Large Scale Integration, VLSI-SoC 2021, Singapore, Singapore, 4–7 October 2021, pp. 1–6. IEEE (2021)

18. Devries, T., Taylor, G.W.: Improved regularization of convolutional neural networks with cutout. CoRR, vol. abs/1708.04552 (2017)

19. Zhang, H., Cissé, M., Dauphin, Y.N., Lopez-Paz, D.: Mixup: beyond empirical risk minimization. In: 6th International Conference on Learning Representations, ICLR 2018, Vancouver, BC, Canada, 30 April–3 May 2018. Conference Track Proceedings (2018)

20. Yun, S., et al.: CutMix: regularization strategy to train strong classifiers with localizable features. In: 2019 IEEE/CVF International Conference on Computer Vision, ICCV 2019, Seoul, Korea (South), 27 October–2 November 2019, pp. 6022–6031. IEEE (2019)

21. Tan, M., Le, Q.V.: EfficientNetV2: smaller models and faster training. In: Proceedings of the 38th International Conference on Machine Learning, ICML 2021, Virtual, 18–24 July 2021. Proceedings of Machine Learning Research, vol. 139, pp. 10 096–10 106. PMLR (2021)
22. Jorge, J., Vieco, J., Paredes, R., Sánchez, J., Benedí, J.: Empirical evaluation of variational autoencoders for data augmentation. In: Proceedings of the 13th International Joint Conference on Computer Vision, Imaging and Computer Graphics Theory and Applications (VISIGRAPP 2018), Volume 5: VISAPP, Funchal, Madeira, Portugal, 27–29 January 2018, pp. 96–104. SciTePress (2018)
23. Antoniou, A., Storkey, A., Edwards, H.: Augmenting image classifiers using data augmentation generative adversarial networks. In: Kůrková, V., Manolopoulos, Y., Hammer, B., Iliadis, L., Maglogiannis, I. (eds.) ICANN 2018. LNCS, vol. 11141, pp. 594–603. Springer, Cham (2018). https://doi.org/10.1007/978-3-030-01424-7_58
24. Simonyan, K., Zisserman, A.: Very deep convolutional networks for large-scale image recognition. In: 3rd International Conference on Learning Representations, ICLR 2015, San Diego, CA, USA, 7–9 May 2015. Conference Track Proceedings (2015)
25. Kim, I., Kim, Y., Kim, S.: Learning loss for test-time augmentation. In: Advances in Neural Information Processing Systems 33: Annual Conference on Neural Information Processing Systems 2020, NeurIPS 2020, Virtual, 6–12 December 2020 (2020)
26. Shanmugam, D., Blalock, D.W., Balakrishnan, G., Guttag, J.V.: Better aggregation in test-time augmentation. In: 2021 IEEE/CVF International Conference on Computer Vision, ICCV 2021, Montreal, QC, Canada, 10–17 October 2021, pp. 1194–1203. IEEE (2021)
27. Park, E., et al.: Big/little deep neural network for ultra low power inference. In: 2015 International Conference on Hardware/Software Codesign and System Synthesis, CODES+ISSS 2015, Amsterdam, Netherlands, 4–9 October 2015, pp. 124–132. IEEE (2015)
28. Mocerino, L., Calimera, A.: Fast and accurate inference on microcontrollers with boosted cooperative convolutional neural networks (BC-Net). IEEE Trans. Circuits Syst. I Regul. Pap. **68**(1), 77–88 (2020)
29. Joshi, A.J., Porikli, F., Papanikolopoulos, N.: Multi-class active learning for image classification. In: 2009 IEEE Computer Society Conference on Computer Vision and Pattern Recognition (CVPR 2009), Miami, Florida, USA, 20–25 June 2009, pp. 2372–2379. IEEE Computer Society (2009)
30. Wang, K., Yan, X., Zhang, D., Zhang, L., Lin, L.: Towards human-machine cooperation: Self-supervised sample mining for object detection. In: 2018 IEEE Conference on Computer Vision and Pattern Recognition, CVPR 2018, Salt Lake City, UT, USA, 18–22 June 2018, pp. 1605–1613. Computer Vision Foundation/IEEE Computer Society (2018)
31. Rizzo, R.G., Peluso, V., Calimera, A.: TVFS: topology voltage frequency scaling for reliable embedded convnets. IEEE Trans. Circuits Syst. II Express Briefs **68**(2), 672–676 (2020)
32. Shannon, C.E.: A mathematical theory of communication. ACM SIGMOBILE Mob. Comput. Commun. Rev. **5**(1), 3–55 (2001)
33. Melacci, S., Gori, M.: Unsupervised learning by minimal entropy encoding. IEEE Trans. Neural Netw. Learn. Syst. **23**(12), 1849–1861 (2012)

34. Hassibi, B., Shadbakht, S.: Normalized entropy vectors, network information theory and convex optimization. In: Proceedings of the IEEE Information Theory Workshop on Information Theory for Wireless Networks, Solstrand, Norway, 1–6 July 2007, pp. 1–5. IEEE (2007)
35. Linaro toolchain. https://www.linaro.org/downloads/
36. Tensorflow Hub. https://tfhub.dev
37. Tensorflow lite hosted models. https://www.tensorflow.org/lite/guide/hosted_models
38. Howard, A.G., et al.: MobileNets: efficient convolutional neural networks for mobile vision applications. CoRR, vol. abs/1704.04861 (2017)
39. Sandler, M., Howard, A.G., Zhu, M., Zhmoginov, A., Chen, L.: MobileNetV2: inverted residuals and linear bottlenecks. In: 2018 IEEE Conference on Computer Vision and Pattern Recognition, CVPR 2018, Salt Lake City, UT, USA, 18–22 June 2018, pp. 4510–4520. Computer Vision Foundation/IEEE Computer Society (2018)
40. Howard, A., et al.: Searching for MobileNetV3. In: 2019 IEEE/CVF International Conference on Computer Vision, ICCV 2019, Seoul, Korea (South), 27 October–2 November 2019, pp. 1314–1324. IEEE (2019)
41. Deng, J., et al.: ImageNet: a large-scale hierarchical image database. In: 2009 IEEE Computer Society Conference on Computer Vision and Pattern Recognition (CVPR 2009), Miami, Florida, USA, 20–25 June 2009, pp. 248–255. IEEE Computer Society (2009)
42. Peluso, V., Rizzo, R.G., Calimera, A., Macii, E., Alioto, M.: Beyond ideal DVFS through ultra-fine grain Vdd-hopping. In: Hollstein, T., Raik, J., Kostin, S., Tšertov, A., O'Connor, I., Reis, R. (eds.) VLSI-SoC 2016. IAICT, vol. 508, pp. 152–172. Springer, Cham (2017). https://doi.org/10.1007/978-3-319-67104-8_8

Low-Overhead Early-Stopping Policies for Efficient Random Forests Inference on Microcontrollers

Francesco Daghero[1]([✉]), Alessio Burrello[2], Chen Xie[1], Luca Benini[2,3],
Andrea Calimera[1], Enrico Macii[1], Massimo Poncino[1],
and Daniele Jahier Pagliari[1]

[1] Politecnico di Torino, Turin, Italy
{francesco.daghero,chen.xie,andrea.calimera,enrico.macii,
massimo.poncino,daniele.jahier}@polito.it
[2] University of Bologna, Bologna, Italy
{alessio.burrello,luca.benini}@unibo.it
[3] ETH, Zurich, Switzerland
benini@iis.ee.ethz.ch

Abstract. Random Forests (RFs) are popular Machine Learning models for edge computing, due to their lightweight nature and high accuracy on several common tasks. Large RFs however, still have significant energy costs, a serious concern for battery-operated ultra-low-power devices. Following the adaptive (or dynamic) inference paradigm, we introduce a hardware-friendly early stopping policy for RF-based classifiers, halting the execution as soon as a sufficient prediction confidence is achieved. We benchmark our approach on three state-of-the-art datasets relative to different embedded classification tasks, and deploy our models on a single core RISC-V microcontroller. We achieve an energy reduction ranging from 18% to more than 91%, with an accuracy drop lower than 0.5%. Additionally, we compare our approach with other early-stopping policies, showing that we outperform them.

Keywords: Machine learning · TinyML · Adaptive inference · Dynamic inference · Energy-efficiency · Random forests · Microcontrollers

1 Introduction

Machine Learning (ML) inference is one of the core components of an increasing number of Internet of Things (IoT) applications, from time-series processing to computer vision [12,31]. The cloud-based paradigm is the most popular deployment approach for this kind of application, relying on a powerful high-end server performing the inference with a computationally expensive and accurate model. IoT devices are instead only responsible for the data collection and transmission, offloading almost all the computations to the cloud and receiving back the final output of the inference.

© IFIP International Federation for Information Processing 2022
Published by Springer Nature Switzerland AG 2022
V. Grimblatt et al. (Eds.): VLSI-SoC 2021, IFIP AICT 661, pp. 25–47, 2022.
https://doi.org/10.1007/978-3-031-16818-5_2

This approach however presents several limitations, mostly stemming from the need to continuously send data to remote hardware [33, 36]. A stable and reliable internet connection is in fact permanently necessary, an assumption that may not always hold (e.g. for a wearable system used in a remote area). Even when present, wireless connectivity may be unstable or slow, increasing the inference latency in an unpredictable way, and posing a serious challenge for real-time applications. Additionally, transmitting possibly sensitive data over an untrusted network poses a challenge to security, leading to privacy-related concerns. Last but not least, sending large amounts of data to the cloud is an energy-hungry operation [40], reducing the lifetime of battery-operated devices.

For all the above reasons, *edge computing* is becoming an increasingly popular approach for ML-based IoT applications [33, 36], consisting of an on-device deployment of the ML model, which completely eliminates (or limits to particularly complex tasks) the interaction with remote servers. Performing all computations locally eliminates latency and privacy concerns at the source, while also possibly obtaining higher energy efficiency.

However, directly deploying ML models at the edge is not easy due to their memory and computational requirements, which clash with the tight constraints of IoT nodes, mostly based on Microcontrollers (MCUs). Deep Learning (DL) approaches, in particular, while reaching state-of-the-art accuracy on many domains, maintain high complexity even after applying multiple optimizations [10, 18], and are often too expensive, in terms of energy consumption and memory occupation, for MCU-based edge devices.

There are however lightweight alternatives to DL, particularly suited for easy recognition tasks such as the ones involved in IoT applications. Among them, tree-based ensemble models, and in particular Random Forests (RFs) [5], are increasingly popular. Their success stems from their inexpensive inference, requiring often a small number of compare and branch operations, while also having a compact memory footprint. At the same time, Random Forests (RFs) [5] often reach an accuracy close to DL models and good resistance to overfitting for simple IoT tasks, such as human activity recognition, ECG analysis, and seizure detection [14, 15, 30, 35]. For instance, the DL-based classifiers proposed by the authors of [30] for an Electrocardiogram (ECG) anomaly detection requires around 200k arithmetic operations and the storage of a similar amount of parameters, while in Sect. 6, we show that an RF can achieve comparable accuracy with ≈2k parameters and less than 1k operations.

Although less expensive than DL, the inference time and energy consumption of RFs can nonetheless have a relevant impact on the battery lifetime of MCU-based systems. Hence, inference optimization techniques are fundamental even for these simple models.

In this work, which extends [11], we propose one such optimization originating from the observation that, for single-core MCUs, RF inference time and energy costs are *linearly dependent on the number of trees* (the forest "width"). In fact, the MCU will evaluate all the Decision Trees (DTs) that constitute the ensemble in a sequential fashion, one after the other. However, evaluating the whole forest may be necessary only for a subset of complex input samples, while being wasteful in terms of energy for easy inputs. Intuitively, if the initial bunch of trees executed during an inference predicts that the output belongs to a specific class with *very high confidence*, it becomes unlikely (or even impossible) that the remaining DTs will overturn that prediction. Thus, the execution of the latter can be *skipped completely*, reducing the total time and energy, while not affecting the final accuracy negatively.

Leveraging this idea, we propose an *early stopping* mechanism for RF inference, which stops the evaluation of DTs as soon as a user-defined confidence level has been reached. While *adaptive (or dynamic) inference* approaches such as this are widely adopted for DL [6,19,20,22,28,37], to the best of our knowledge, we are the first to consider them for RFs, with a focus on embedded/IoT deployment. In fact, the few existing techniques for tree-based models [16,39] have been studied only theoretically, without evaluating a practical implementation on a low-power device, hence largely ignoring some important overheads derivating from their deployment. In contrast, our proposed method is designed specifically for embedded RFs, being based on low-overhead early stopping policies, easy to execute efficiently at runtime, with minimal latency/energy overheads.

We benchmark our approach on three different embedded tasks, i.e., human activity recognition, heart failure detection, and gesture recognition. Deploying our models on a popular single-core RISC-V MCU, we obtain an energy reduction ranging from 18% to 91% with less than 0.5% accuracy drop, with respect to a standard (i.e., static) RF inference.

2   Background

2.1   Decision Trees and Random Forests

When used in a supervised learning setting, Decision Trees (DTs) learn a set of decision rules extracted at training time from the data features, in order to perform either a classification or regression task. Several training algorithms for DTs have been proposed in the literature [23], differing in the criteria used for selecting the features and decision thresholds considered at each internal node. The details of the training phase are out of the scope of this work, and interested readers may refer to [23]. Since this work proposes an *inference* optimization, herein we detail only the operations of the inference phase.

Figure 1 shows a high-level overview of a "grown" (i.e., trained) DT used for a 2-class classification task, in which leaf nodes are depicted as rectangles and other nodes as circles. Leaf nodes contain the probabilities of the input belonging to a specific class, while each non-terminal node stores the index of the input data feature considered for branching in that node, and the threshold that determines the left or right branch.

The DT inference pseudo-code is shown in Algorithm 1, where Root(T) denotes the root node and Leaves(T) the set of leaves. Feature(n) and Threshold(n) are the input feature and comparison threshold considered in the n-th node, and Left(n) and Right(n) are the left and right children of the node. Finally, Prediction(n) is only defined for leaves and contains the corresponding

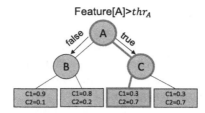

Fig. 1. High-level overview of a DT structure for a 2-class classification problem. The leaves are represented as rectangles, each storing the class probabilities of an input belonging to that path. Other nodes are represented as circles

---

Algorithm 1: Decision Tree inference.

1   $n = \text{Root}(T)$
2   **while** $n \notin \text{Leaves}(T)$ **do**
3   **if** $\text{Feature}(n) > \text{Threshold}(n)$ **then**
4 | $n = \text{Right}(n)$
5   **else**
6 | $n = \text{Left}(n)$
7   **end**
8   **end**
9   $out = \text{Prediction}(n)$

---

output prediction (an array of probabilities for a classification, and a continuous scalar value for regression).

The time complexity of Algorithm 1 is $O(D)$, where D denotes the tree depth, i.e., the maximum length of a path from the root to the leaves. For a classification, an additional $O(M)$ scan over the output probabilities is then needed to determine the final class label, where M is the number of classes. The memory complexity, instead, grows with $O(2^D)$, i.e., it is proportional to the total number of nodes, which is at most 2^D in the case of a *balanced and unpruned* DT, with all root-leaf paths having the same length [23].

DTs are prone to over-fitting, suffer from high variance even with small perturbations in the training data, and introduce biases when used with unbalanced datasets. In order to overcome these limitations, Random Forests (RFs) have been proposed [5]. RFs are ensembles of DTs (called "weak learners"), trained with *bagging* (bootstrap aggregating) and, more recently, random features selection [29]. In practice, each DT is trained on a random subset of the training samples, drawn with replacement, and on a limited set of the input features, thus ensuring a low correlation among weak learners, which reduces overfitting.

At inference time, the individual DTs predictions are combined to obtain the final RF output, as shown in Fig. 2. Specifically, in early implementations of RFs for classification, each weak learner outputs a class prediction, then aggregated with a majority voting. In contrast, modern RF libraries [29] store in the leaf nodes of the trees the entire set of class probabilities, thus allowing the final

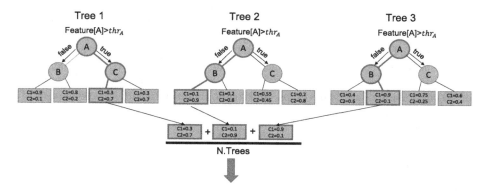

Fig. 2. High-level overview of a RF inference with width 3 and depth 3. The output of each DT is averaged to obtain the final predictions of the ensemble.

predictions to be computed as the average (or sum) of all the weak learners' class probabilities. The final label is then selected as the argmax of the array.

Algorithm 2 reports the pseudo-code of a RF inference pass, for an implementation that loops sequentially over the weak learners (such as the one for a single-core processor). The function DecisionTreeInference corresponds to Algorithm 1. From a complexity point of view, a RF of *width* N, i.e., including N trees, has a time and memory complexity of $O(ND)$ and $O(N2^D)$ respectively, where D is the maximum depth over all weak learners. Lastly, the argmax that extract the predicted label has time complexity $O(M)$, as for a single DT.

Algorithm 2: Random Forest Classification.

---

1 $out = \mathbf{0}_M$ //array of 0s of size M
2 **for** $T \in$ Forest **do**
3 $\quad \mid \quad out = out + \text{DecisionTreeInference}(T)$
4 **end**
5 $class = \arg\max(out)$

2.2   IoT End Nodes

The great majority of IoT end-nodes are based on low-power microcontrollers (MCUs), whose main compute unit is a general-purpose CPU, typically based on a RISC instruction set [17]. This is mainly due to their employment on extremely low-cost devices. In this context, the flexibility and high programmability of MCUs make them preferable to custom Application-Specific Integrated Circuits (ASICs), potentially orders of magnitude more efficient, but whose design and manufacturing costs are only affordable for high-end, high-volume devices.

Specifically, the RISC-V Instruction Set Architecture (ISA) is recently becoming more and more adopted both in the research world and in companies for the realization of IoT devices [13,34]. Following this trend, we benchmark our results on a RISC-V processor from the PULP family [8]. Given the very low-power requirements and tight cost constraints of our target applications, we select one of the smallest architectures in the family, the single-core *PULPissimo*. This device is based on a RI5CY core with a 4-stage, in-order, single-issue pipeline. The core implements the *RV32IMC* ISA, enhanced with domain-specific extensions for DSP, such as Single Instruction Multiple Data (SIMD) operations, hardware-loops, and loads/stores with index increment, and no caches, all design choices aimed at providing significant speedups and energy saving for ML applications.

2.3 Machine Learning at the Edge

In order to bridge the gap between the computational requirements of Machine Learning models and the limited resources of IoT end nodes, several works have introduced optimizations with the goal of making the inference as energy efficient as possible, without affecting significantly its accuracy [1,9,15,19,21,27,28,37]. These optimizations can be divided into two categories: *static* and *adaptive*.

The first category optimizes a model before deployment, usually at training or post-training, with the goal of reducing the inference latency, energy, or the memory required to store the classifier parameters. Pruning and quantization are among the most popular static optimizations for DL [18,26], reducing models' complexity respectively through the removal of redundant parameters or by using low-precision arithmetic. Notably, pruning can also be applied to DTs and RFs during their training (or growth), with the goal of eliminating unimportant nodes from the trees, hence reducing the number of parameters of the model [25].

Static approaches are, by definition, unable to efficiently support multiple runtime operating modes, with different complexity versus accuracy trade-offs. Nonetheless, this would be useful to respond to changes in external conditions, such as the remaining battery life of the device or, more interestingly, to promptly adapt to variations the complexity of the task being executed [9,28].

The naive solution to achieve such runtime flexibility is deploying multiple, independent models, each with a different accuracy and computational complexity, and selecting the most appropriate model at any given time. However, this approach is often unfeasible due to the limited memory of IoT end nodes, which makes it impossible to store a large number of models on a single device.

Adaptive (or *dynamic*) inference techniques try to overcome these limitations, proposing a set of optimizations, mostly orthogonal to static ones, that allow multiple operating points at runtime with limited memory overheads. These optimizations are based on the concept that *not all inputs are equally hard to process* for a ML model, and that easy inputs are often far more common than difficult ones. Adapting the computational effort spent for inference based on the difficulty of the processed input (i.e., reducing the effort for easy inputs and increasing it for difficult ones), could then enable significant energy savings, while keeping the classification accuracy unchanged. Accordingly, one of the focal points of any adaptive inference technique is the design of an automatic mechanism (or *policy*) for discerning between easy and hard inputs. Furthermore, this policy should introduce low computational overheads, which do not overshadow the energy savings obtained thanks to the adaptive effort tuning.

3   Related Works

In the literature, adaptive inference implementations have been proposed by multiple works, with a particular focus on DL. One of the earliest endeavors proposed the so-called Big-Little scheme [28], combining two deep neural networks with different complexity and accuracy. At runtime, the inexpensive yet less accurate network, named "little", performs the first inference on each input. The confidence of this model is then evaluated, stopping the execution in case it surpasses a user-defined threshold. Otherwise, the input is fed to the second model, an accurate yet more complex network named "big", and its output is taken as final prediction. The rationale of this technique is that, as long as the easy inputs, predicted with high confidence by the "little" model, are more common than hard ones, the average energy required for inference will decrease significantly. At the same time, the final accuracy is not affected, since complex inputs are still re-directed to the "big" model. The main flaw of this approach, however, lies in its considerable memory overhead, since it requires the deployment of two completely separate networks on the edge device.

Based on this observation, multiple subsequent works have proposed alternative adaptive inference schemes for DL, that try to address the memory overhead problem. For instance, deriving the "little" network from the "big" model by using only a subset of the layers, channels or a lower bit-width quantization may reduce significantly the number of parameters that need to be stored [19,27,37]. On an orthogonal direction, other works enhanced the Big-Little paradigm by increasing the number of cascaded models to more than two, or improving the stopping mechanism to handle class-specific confidence [9,37].

Applications of the adaptive paradigm to shallow ML models, and in particular to tree-based ones, are far less common compared to DL [16,32,39]. The authors of [32] propose an early stopping criterion for RFs and other tree ensembles, which allows reducing the number of trees invoked for inference on easy inputs, modeling it with a binomial or multinomial distribution (depending on the number of classes). The approach is benchmarked on 7 small public datasets and one private, showing that, for ensembles with a large amount of trees, they reduce the average number of weak learners required for inference by 63%. However, the proposed criterion requires the storage of a large lookup table with a dimension in the order of $O(N^2)$, which introduces a significant memory overhead (10s of kB) for large forests.

In another work, the authors of [16] propose an approach to determine the best order of execution for weak learners depending on the most likely class indicated by the DTs that have been already executed. This selection happens at runtime, and takes into account the different computational costs associated to weak learners due to their reliance on different features, finding the optimal trade-off between complexity and accuracy to select the next DT. The authors leverage a mixture of Gaussian distributions to design a probabilistic model of the classifier, exploiting it to trigger an adaptive early stopping based on the posterior probabilities. Furthermore, they also introduce a dimensionality reduction technique to prune the number of computations required to perform the selection of the following DT. However, on an ultra-low-power MCU-based device, the introduced overhead would overshadow the energy savings obtained by performing the inference on a subset of the weak learners. Hence, as stated by the authors in the original paper, this approach becomes effective only if the target task involves *very complex feature extractions*, which is rarely the case for simple IoT applications.

The work closest to ours is named Quit When You Can (QWYC) [39]. In this case, the authors focus on binary classification tasks and propose a simple early stopping based on two probabilities thresholds (ϵ_- and ϵ_+) derived statically post-training. Additionally, the authors propose a static sorting of the weak learners, so that the DTs most likely to trigger an early stop are executed first. At inference time, as soon as one of the probabilities of the last executed DT is either lower than ϵ_- or higher than ϵ_+, the early stop mechanism is triggered, selecting the negative or positive class as the final prediction, respectively.

While QWYC requires a small overhead at runtime (only two comparisons), the extension to a multi-class problem is not straightforward. The authors propose a possible implementation of the multi-class version, but do not show any results for it, leaving its effectiveness yet to be tested. Moreover, their approach is still not tested on a real low-power IoT node.

In summary, all the works mentioned above are purely theoretical, and their effectiveness is evaluated only from a complexity reduction point of view, i.e., computing the average number of DTs executed for inference, with no deployment on a real embedded device. Additionally, many of these works introduce considerable overheads either in terms of memory or time/energy, both of which are very precious resources on IoT devices. In our work, we compare the proposed approach with QWYC [39], showing that we obtain similar or better performance, despite the higher simplicity and generality of our method.

4   Motivation and Goal

RFs generally use a large number of trees N (e.g., between 10 and 100) to improve the accuracy over single DTs. Indeed, using many weak learners instead of a single powerful one is demonstrated to reduce the overfitting and the bias of the model, leading to a better generalization on new unseen data and higher accuracy overall. On the other hand, easy inputs would be correctly classified also by means of fewer trees than the ones present in the complete forest. In this case, employing the full set of trees of the RF is sub-optimal, leading to a possible increment of energy consumption and higher latency, which could be critical for IoT devices. Nonetheless, deploying a smaller RF with N' trees, where $N' < N$ may result in errors when classifying more complex samples, and therefore in a reduction of the overall accuracy.

Our work is based on these observations: our aim is to design an adaptive early stopping policy for tree-based ensembles, minimizing the DTs executed to correctly classify easy inputs, while exploiting more DTs (up to the entire RFs) to classify the most complex ones. The key to achieve high energy saving through this method lies in the light but accurate mechanism to distinguish easy from hard inputs. Therefore, the main goal of this work is the search for a way to allow an early stopping of the inference, before the execution of the whole RF, without affecting the final accuracy. At the same time, we also look for a *lightweight early-stopping policy*, to avoid overshadowing the savings obtained thanks to the lower number of weak learners executed.

5   Methodology

5.1   Aggregated Score Thresholds for Early Stopping

Among the various confidence metrics introduced in the literature for adaptive early-stopping in classification problems, the most common ones are based on the output probabilities (P^t) produced by the last model t executed. A first approach considers the highest probability (i.e. the one associated with the most likely class) to compute the confidence of the model. A large maximum probability denotes a classifier confident in its prediction, while a small value is associated with an uncertain classification. We name this approach *Max Score* (or simply *Max*). This metric is fast to compute at runtime, requiring $O(M)$ pairwise comparisons. The second approach, named *Score Margin* (SM), extends the Max policy by considering the two largest probabilities of the model. For a target model t, we can compute its SM as:

$$SM = \max(P^t) - \max_{2nd}(P^t) \qquad (1)$$

where $\max_{2nd}(P^t)$ denotes the second largest value in vector P^t. Even though the SM requires more operations compared to the simpler Max (around twice), it makes the computation of the confidence more robust. For instance, the max value for a 11-class prediction problem will be 0.5 in case of a distribution of $P^0 = 0.5$, $P^1 = 0.5$, and $P^{2-10} = 0$, which corresponds to a very uncertain prediction, but also in the case of $P^0 = 0.5$, $P^{1-10} = 0.05$, which is instead a quite reliable output. On the other hand, the SM would be 0 in the first case and 0.45 in the second, correctly capturing the different confidence of the model in the two cases. From this example, the reader can understand why the SM metric has become so popular in recent literature.

To determine when early-stopping should be performed, a threshold α is compared with the selected confidence metric (Max or SM): when the metric is higher than α, the inference is stopped and the output prediction is produced based on (some of) the outputs of the classifiers that have been already executed. Therefore, the value of α directly controls the energy vs accuracy trade-off, since it determines how many classifiers are executed on average.

The advantage of this early-stopping criterion lies in its inexpensive derivation (requiring a single comparison after the computation of the corresponding metric), while being accurate as long as the classifiers' output probabilities are *calibrated* (i.e., proportional to the likelihood of the class to be the correct one). Furthermore, the threshold α can be changed at run-time, e.g., based on the system condition (level of battery charge, period of the day, etc.), to produce more accurate or more energy-efficient classifications.

Normally, the confidence metric (Max or SM) is computed using the output probabilities of the *last executed classifier* t, neglecting the outputs of the models executed before it, i.e., the "history" of the ensemble. This approach is ideal for cascades of increasingly accurate classifiers, since taking into account the $t - 1$-th classifier output may actually worsen the prediction of the (much more accurate) t-th model [19, 28]. However, it is not appropriate for an ensemble of *equally predictive* weak learners, such as a RF.

Starting from this observation, we extend the policies described above so that the early stopping is triggered using the aggregated predictions of *all the already executed classifiers* ($P^{[1,t]}$). Noteworthy, easy inputs will in fact have partial aggregated probabilities already skewed towards one class even after the execution of just a few DTs. Therefore, it is unlikely or even mathematically impossible that when the aggregated probabilities are sufficiently skewed toward one specific class, the remaining DTs will overturn the prediction, which makes their execution not necessary to improve the accuracy of the prediction.

We define the partial output of a RF after executing t trees as:

$$P^{[1:t]} = \sum_{i=1}^{t} P^i \tag{2}$$

where P^i denotes the vector of output probabilities of the i-th weak learner. We then define the *Aggregated Max Score* (S) early-stopping policy after the execution of the t-th classifier as the rule:

$$S^t = \max(P^{[1:t]}) > \alpha \tag{3}$$

while the *Aggregated Score Margin* SM policy is defined as:

$$SM^t = \max(P^{[1:t]}) - \max_{2nd}(P^{[1:t]}) > \alpha \tag{4}$$

In our experiments, we consider both of these policies, with a tunable threshold α, to determine when to perform early-stopping in a RF ensemble. To the best of our knowledge, we are the first to propose an early-stopping approach that considers the aggregated probabilities of the weak learners, while being based on a lightweight comparison with a threshold. Our results show that we outperform other state-of-the-art approaches that leverage only the last weak learner of the ensemble, achieving higher energy efficiency during the inference while also avoiding large accuracy drop.

Figure 3 shows a high-level overview of the adaptive inference mechanism proposed in this work, for the case of the SM policy and with a batch $B = 1$ (see Sect. 5.3 below). The RF represented has $N = 3$, $M = 2$, and $D = 3$. Orange nodes are those "selected" by the series of compare-and-branch operations for a hypothetical input. In a nutshell, after executing each DT, the partial predictions are accumulated and used to determine whether the confidence of the inference up to tree t is enough to trigger an early stop, based on α.

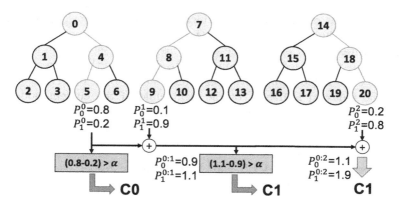

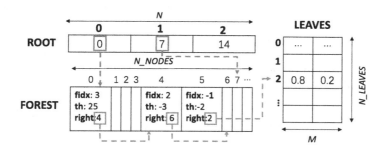

Fig. 3. High-level overview of the proposed adaptive inference method for RFs, for $B = 1$. At each step, the SM is computed on the partially aggregated scores.

5.2 Deployment on MCUs

Due to the lack of open-source RF libraries tailored for the target MCU (described in Sect. 6), we design and deploy an optimized implementation in C language of both the traditional RF and of our adaptive version, i.e., a RF augmented with the early-stop mechanism described above.

We take inspiration from the open-source implementation available in OpenCV [4], optimizing it for our target ultra-low-power platform. The main difference resides in the way RF nodes, leaves, and thresholds are stored: OpenCV lists are replaced with C arrays in our version, both to save precious memory space and to improve the memory locality of the data. Figure 4 shows the three main arrays that compose our RF representation, i.e., FOREST, ROOT, and LEAVES.

Fig. 4. C data structures of our RF implementation.

The array **FOREST** stores in each element a "struct" with the information relative to a node belonging to one of the RF trees. The struct has three member variables:

- *fidx* is the index of the feature on which the split has been performed. It is used to select the correct value from the input feature array to be compared with the threshold *th* at inference time. This value is set to -1 in leaf nodes.
- *th*: the value to be used as a comparison to determine the following node to visit; left child if the input feature is lower than *th*, right otherwise.
- *right*: the index in FOREST of the right child of the current node. Note that to reduce the memory occupation, the left child is always stored as the following element of the array. For leaf nodes, the right child index stores the index of the corresponding leaf probabilities in the LEAVES array.

The other two arrays, **LEAVES**, and **ROOT**, store respectively the output probabilities of each leaf and the indexes of the root node of each DT in FOREST.

Figure 4 reports some data structure values corresponding to the RF shown in Fig. 3. In particular, it shows the elements of FOREST which correspond to the nodes in the decision path of the leftmost DT in Fig. 3.

To further compress the memory required to store our RFs, we quantize to 16-bit integers all the fields of the FOREST and LEAVES arrays, simplifying also the deployment on MCUs not equipped with a Floating Point Unit. We verified that quantizing the inputs, comparison thresholds, and output probabilities to 16-bit integers yields close to 0 accuracy drop, compared to the original floating-point model. We also reduce to 16-bit the precision of the ROOT elements, which guarantees the possibility of deploying large RFs (up to 2^{16} nodes), while significantly reducing the memory overhead of this vector.

5.3   Tree Batching

One of the main advantages of the aggregated Score Margin and Max early-stop policies lies in their lightweight nature. Specifically, their time complexity at inference time is $O(M)$ to find either the highest or the two highest probabilities and $O(1)$ to compare with the threshold α. In the case of dynamic inference systems for deep learning [28,37], this computational overhead is negligible w.r.t the execution of the individual neural networks. On the other hand, when working on lightweight classifiers such as RFs, the computation of either the aggregated Max or the SM can affect negatively the energy gains obtained by avoiding the execution of the full forest. In fact, as introduced in Sect. 2, the time complexity for a single DT inference is $O(D)$, plus $O(M)$ for the argmax over classes. Large yet shallow adaptive RFs may then have a significant overhead for the early-stopping decision (when D is comparable or lower than M), becoming significantly less efficient than a static forest with fewer trees.

In order to tackle this problem, we propose a simple but effective approach to reduce the impact of the early stopping policy, named *tree batching*. Rather than evaluating the aggregated confidence metric after every DT inference, we instead perform its computation after a *batch* of B trees. This additional hyperparameter has a contrasting effect on the energy consumption of the system. In fact, larger batch sizes can reduce the overhead introduced by the computation of the confidence metric by a factor of B, thus saving additional energy. On the other hand, evaluating the stopping criterion every B trees may cause the classifier to perform up to $B-1$ additional inferences that could be avoided with $B = 1$. Empirically we show that depending on the dataset, the results obtained setting $B > 1$ can outperform the ones of $B = 1$ in terms of accuracy vs energy.

Algorithm 3 reports the pseudo-code of the adaptive inference with batch size B, where $Batch(b)$ denotes the subset of weak learners belonging to the b-th batch. $Metric(out)$ represents instead the computation of the confidence metric at tree t, e.g., $SM^{1:t}$ in case of the aggregated Score Margin.

Algorithm 3: Adaptive Random Forest Classification.

1 **for** $b \in [0, N/B]$ **do**
2   **for** $T \in Batch(b)$ **do**
3          $out = out + \mathrm{DecisionTreeInference}(T)$
4   **end**
5   **if** $Metric(out) > \alpha$ **then**
6   break
7   **end**
8 **end**
9 $class = \arg\max(out)$

5.4 Tree Ordering

The introduction of an early stopping mechanism that depends on the output probabilities of each DT makes the inference results become dependent on the order of the weak learners. As opposed to the classic approach, which sums or averages the contributions of all DTs, the adaptive inference will, for most of the inputs, leverage only the probabilities of a subset of them. As a consequence, invoking first the most informative and confident DTs increases the probability that the early-stopping mechanism will be triggered sooner, and therefore the energy savings. Intuitively, one could then think of finding an optimal ordering of the DTs on a subset of the training data (e.g. the validation set), by means of a search algorithm such as greedy, random, exhaustive search, or others. As mentioned in Sect. 3, multiple previous works including QWYC [39] have proposed mechanisms to determine such a "hardcoded" ordering of the classifiers.

However, in our experiments, we demonstrate that such an optimized ordering does not actually provide statistical advantages over executing the DTs in a random order. In fact, we compare multiple permutations of the DTs composing the ensembles, showing that those orderings that reduce the average number of weak learners per inference on the validation dataset, do not obtain comparable results on the test set. In other words, there is no correlation between the "goodness" of a given ordering on the two data subsets.

Therefore, we conclude that an optimized hard-coded ordering of weak learners do not provide advantages, at least in our considered scenario, i.e., for a RF classifier and considering the simple early-stopping policies described above. In contrast, input-dependent DTs reordering could be effective, but is extremely difficult to implement at low overhead [16], hence we leave it to future work.

6   Results

6.1   Benchmarks, Deployment Setup, and Comparisons

We evaluate the proposed technique on three different datasets for popular tiny-ML tasks: ECG5000 [7], Ninapro DB1 [2], and UniMiB-SHAR [24].

ECG5000 [7] features annotated electrocardiogram (ECG) data, provided already preprocessed in windows of $0.8\,$s, each containing a single heartbeat. We perform the same task as the authors of [30], which consists in detecting whether congestive heart failure happens. For this dataset, we take as a baseline for comparison a static RF with $N = 40$ and $D = 3$. Our adaptive model uses an identical RF structure, but dynamically reduces the number of trees executed at runtime as described in Sect. 5.

The second set of experiments is performed on the popular **Ninapro** DB1 [3], featuring Electromyography (EMG) signals of 27 healthy subjects performing different hand movements. We follow the experimental setup proposed in [3], performing the classification of 14 hand movements using a 10-channel EMG signal. In order to do so, we employ the same preprocessing used by the authors of [3]. Our starting RF for this task has $N = 24$ and $D = 12$.

Finally, **UniMiB-SHAR** [24] is a Human Activity Recognition (HAR) dataset featuring a tri-axial accelerometer signal collected from a sensor mounted on a smartphone. The recorded motions belong either to one out of 9 daily-life activities (e.g. walking, sitting, etc.) or one out of 8 kinds of falls. The signals are collected $50\,$Hz, and already provided in fixed-size windows of 151 samples, centered around peaks. We keep the same preprocessing as proposed in [24], benchmarking our results on the AF-17 task, which is the one considering all the target classes in the dataset. We derive the adaptive RFs from a baseline with $N = 32$ and $D = 9$.

The three datasets refer to tasks with a significant difference in the level of complexity, ranging from a binary classification (ECG5000) to a 17-classes one (UniMiB-SHAR). Accordingly, the time and energy associated with the accumulation of output probabilities during inference vary significantly, which influences our policies' overheads, as explained in Sect. 5.3. As shown in the following section, however, our approach remains effective even in conditions far from ideal ($M \approx D$). Additionally, after benchmarking the RFs both with raw data and simple embedded-friendly features extracted in the time domain, we always achieve higher accuracy with the former. Therefore, we report for all the three datasets results obtained using raw data as input.

Due to the class imbalance of all three datasets, we always report the scoring metric proposed in [24], i.e., the top-1 macro-average accuracy. All results are reported on each dataset's test set.

We deploy all RFs on PULPissimo [8], a 32-bit single-core RISC-V MCU belonging to the PULP family of architectures. Specifically, we refer to a 22 nm realization of PULPissimo running at 205 MHz and equipped with 520 KB of L2 memory [13]. We estimate the inference clock cycles using a virtual platform [38], deriving the energy values from [13]. Concerning the software stack, we train the Random Forests using the open-source package scikit-learn [29] in Python 3.8. The inference phase uses the MCU-oriented C language implementation described in Sect. 5.2 both for the baseline and adaptive classifiers.

We compare the proposed approach with a static RF, the standard Max/SM policies evaluated on the last DT (as proposed in [28,37]), and the QWYC method [39]. Concerning the latter, we limit the comparison to the binary ECG5000 task, since as mentioned in Sect. 3, QWYC is only benchmarked on binary problems. Independently on the early stopping criterion, the baseline models have been derived from the RFs with the N and D reported above for each dataset.

6.2   Hardware-Independent Results

Since all previous works on adaptive inference for RFs have only been evaluated in theoretical terms, without any real deployment at the edge, we perform a first hardware-independent comparison.

To this end, we consider the *average number of trees executed per inference* as a metric to quantify the complexity of the various techniques. This is a reasonable proxy for the time and energy consumption of inference, especially for a single-core platform (such as an MCU) that executes weak learners sequentially. Of course, this evaluation is unable to factor in the additional overhead introduced by the evaluation of the early stopping policy, thus possibly favoring accurate yet complex mechanisms to stop the inference. Thus, these results are meaningful under the assumption that evaluating a single weak learner has a significantly higher complexity than evaluating the early stopping criterion.

Figures 5–9 report the results of this experiment. Specifically, they report Pareto fronts obtained by the various considered techniques in terms of accuracy versus the average number of DTs per inference (N.Trees). In case of adaptive methods, different points of the curve, when present, are obtained by varying the early stopping threshold (α in Eqs. 3 and 4). Furthermore, all graphs also report, as a comparison baseline, the results obtained with a static RF. In this case, different points refer to ensembles with progressively fewer weak learners (i.e., decreasing N), which have been retrained from scratch each time.

State-of-the-Art Comparison. Figure 5 compares one of our proposed policies (the Aggregated SM) with the standard SM applied to the last executed model (as in [9,28,37]), and with a static RF. Additionally, for the binary ECG5000, we also report the results obtained with QWYC, both with and without the static ordering of the DTs. We do not apply tree batching yet.

For all three datasets, the Aggregated Score Margin with $B = 1$ lies on the Pareto front, often outperforming both other adaptive approaches and static

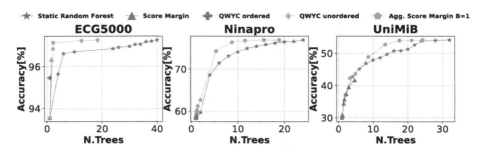

Fig. 5. Accuracy versus average number of trees. Each point represents either a different static RF for the baseline or the same RF with different early-stopping thresholds for adaptive ones.

RFs. On the other hand, the classic SM computed only on the last tree either obtains close results to the baseline or is underperforming. The only notable exception is represented by the ECG5000 dataset, where with few DTs the classic SM is able to achieve results comparable to our method. Nonetheless, that technique is unable to further grow in terms of prediction quality when changing the early stopping threshold.

Both QWYC versions, lie close to the global Pareto front. However, we found that even when testing several values of the hyperparameters that determine ϵ (the parameter used to decide for early stopping in QWYC), the average number of trees executed remains almost unchanged. Most importantly, the maximum accuracy that we were able to obtain with QWYC on ECG500 is significantly lower than with our approach, or with the largest static RF. Additionally, we found that the DT sorting proposed in QWYC actually underperforms on our dataset, leading to lower accuracy than the "unordered" version.

Considering the whole set of trade-off points of our approach, we obtain a reduction in terms of average trees executed per inference of up to 93% on ECG5000, with respect to a static RF achieving the same accuracy (2.26 vs 34 DTs on average, at 97% accuracy. On Ninapro, we achieve up to 47% reduction (10.47 vs 20 average DTs at 76.5% accuracy), and on UniMiB up to 43% (12.5 vs 22 DTs at 52% accuracy).

Batch Size Exploration and Criteria Comparison. Figures 6, 7, 8, 9 report a detailed comparison of the two proposed metrics (Aggregated SM and Aggregated Max.) for different tree batching conditions (i.e., B values).

Intuitively, since these results still do not consider the overheads of the early stopping criterion, increasing B should worsen the results. In fact, $B = 1$ theoretically offers a finer granularity of control on the early stopping, allowing to interrupt an inference just after executing the *first* DT that makes the aggregated SM or Max. overcome the threshold α. This is indeed what happens on average, as shown by the fact that curves relative to larger B values come closer to the static RF ones. However, it is not a hard rule, since the random sampling

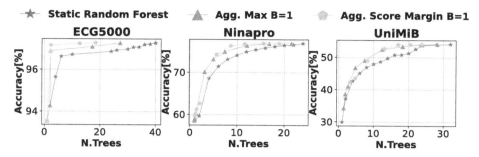

Fig. 6. Hardware-independent comparison of the two proposed metrics for $B = 1$.

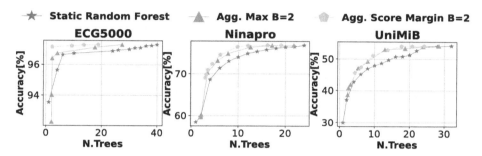

Fig. 7. Hardware-independent comparison of the two proposed metrics for $B = 2$.

and feature selection used to train the DTs can lead to a non-monotonically increase in prediction quality when adding weak learners. For instance, for the UniMiB dataset, the Aggregated Max with $B = 8$ obtains the largest reduction in the average number of DTs without accuracy drop with respect to the complete static RF (20.82 trees on average with $+0.2\%$ accuracy). On the contrary, Ninapro shows the expected results, with the Aggregated SM with $B = 1$ yielding the least average DTs for the same accuracy as the static RF (18.73).

Table 1 reports the detailed results of this comparison. Specifically, we show the average number of trees executed by the different variants of the adaptive inference policy, for two different accuracy conditions, i.e., to reach iso-accuracy with the original RF (Drop 0.0%) or allowing a negligible degradation (Drop 0.5%) The *Red.RF* column reports smallest static RF obtaining the same accuracy. Since the standard Score Margin and QWYC only achieved accuracy values with drops larger than 0.5% with respect to the original RF, they are not reported in the table.

On the ECG dataset we are able to reduce the average number of trees by 57% (17.18 vs 40) with no accuracy loss. Concerning the Ninapro dataset, the proposed approach can reduce the number of weak learners by 22% (18.73 vs 24), while on UniMiB by 35% (20.82 vs 32).

When accepting an accuracy drop of 0.5%, we achieve a reduction in the average DTs executed of 91% with respect to the closest RF (Red. RF column)

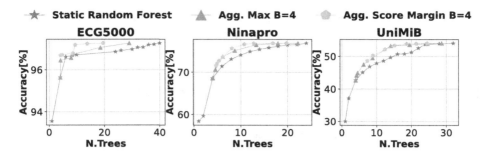

Fig. 8. Hardware-independent comparison of the two proposed metrics for $B = 4$.

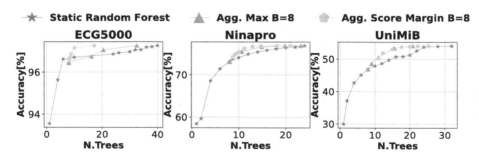

Fig. 9. Hardware-independent comparison of the two proposed metrics for $B = 8$.

on the ECG dataset (2.1 vs 24 DTs). On Ninapro, we avoid the execution of 51% weak learners (9.73 vs 20) while for UniMiB of 29% (17.02 vs 24).

6.3   Tree-Ordering Analysis

As anticipated in Sect. 5.4, our results demonstrate that an optimized hardcoded ordering of DTs to favour early exit does not provide practical advantages. A first indication of this is shown in Fig. 5, where QWYC with optimized tree ordering performs significantly worse than the randomly ordered one in terms of accuracy, for a negligible reduction in the number of invoked trees.

A further confirmation is provided in Fig. 10. To generate it, we shuffled the DTs of the original RF 20 times at random. For each ordering, we then compared the early-stopping results on the validation and on the test set of each dataset. Specifically, we selected an α threshold so that the accuracy drop is 0% with respect to the static RF (as done in Table 1) and we then extracted the average number of DTs executed with that threshold on the two data subsets. We considered the Aggregated SM policy and a batch $B = 1$ for this experiment.

Two interesting results appear from the figure. First, tree ordering could ideally play a significant role in the early stopping effectiveness. In fact, the average number of DTs executed on the full test set varies by up to ± 15 depending on the weak learners' permutation. However, obtaining the optimal ordering on a

Table 1. Average number of trees for different accuracy drops with respect to a full RF.

Data	Full RF	Red. RF	Aggr. Max				Aggr. SM			
			B = 1	B = 2	B = 4	B = 8	B = 1	B = 2	B = 4	B = 8
Drop: 0%										
ECG	40	40	27.22	27.38	28.95	32.55	18.39	18.78	19.58	**17.18**
Ninapro	24	24	21.52	21.72	22.14	23.07	**18.73**	18.95	19.62	20.94
UniMiB	32	32	28.41	28.6	28.94	**20.82**	24.21	24.46	24.97	25.85
Drop: 0.5%										
ECG	40	24	**2.1**	17.63	18.54	20.43	2.19	2.23	8.64	8.86
Ninapro	24	20	12.02	12.56	13.26	14.83	11.55	**9.73**	10.69	12.83
UniMiB	32	24	23.76	24.08	19.34	20.82	**17.02**	17.64	18.41	17.43

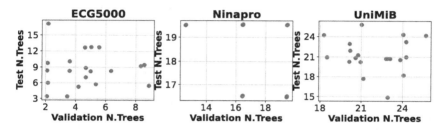

Fig. 10. Average number of DTs executed with the aggregated SM policy to reach the same accuracy as the original static RF on the Validation and Test sets respectively. Each point represent a different ordering of weak learners.

different data subset (in our case, the validation set) does not work, as evident by the lack of correlation in the scatter plots.

The "optimal ordering" must therefore be computed dynamically based on the processed input. How to do so while keeping a low overhead will be subject of our future work.

6.4   Deployment Results

In this section, we report the results obtained with the proposed adaptive inference method when deployed on the target edge device. Figure 11 shows the Pareto fronts in terms of accuracy versus average energy consumption per inference on PULPissimo. For each dataset, we report the results of static RFs with different numbers of weak learners, as well as both our proposed early-stopping policies (Aggregated Max Score and Aggregated SM), with two batch sizes ($B = 1$ and $B = 2$). Differently from Sect. 6.2, here energy results include also the overheads for evaluating the early-stopping policies.

Indeed, as expected, while the curves are similar to the ones reported in Fig. 5, the early stopping overhead becomes visible. This brings the adaptive

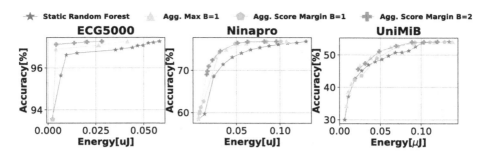

Fig. 11. Accuracy versus average energy per inference.

approach closer to the baseline. Nonetheless, our proposed method still significantly outperforms static RFs. In detail, at iso-accuracy with a static RF, we obtain energy savings up to 26% on the UniMiB dataset, up to 91% on ECG5000 and up to 45% on Ninapro.

Table 2 reports the detailed energy results on each dataset, under the same conditions described in Table 1. While the top-performing approaches are similar to the hardware-independent case, some notable exceptions occur. For instance, on Ninapro, the aggregated Score Margin with $B = 2$, although requiring slightly more trees on average, requires less energy than the one with $B = 1$. This becomes even more evident for $B = 4$, requiring 0.67 additional trees on average than $B = 2$, while "costing" only 0.02 nJ more. Regarding the UniMiB dataset, the aggregated Score Margin with $B = 1$ requires the least amount of trees, however, it has a higher cost in terms of energy than all the other batched versions. Globally, these results show once again that properly accounting for the early stopping policy overheads is fundamental in order to assess the *real* effectiveness of an adaptive inference method.

Table 2. Average energy consumption, in nJ, for different accuracy drops with respect to a full RF.

Data	Full RF	Red. RF	Aggr. Max				Aggr. SM			
			$B=1$	$B=2$	$B=4$	$B=8$	$B=1$	$B=2$	$B=4$	$B=8$
Drop: 0%										
ECG	58.27	58.27	41.46	40.87	44.17	47.68	28.31	28.14	30.15	**25.77**
Ninapro	129.64	129.64	106.85	104.05	104.5	108.24	100.64	**95.5**	95.52	99.42
UniMiB	134.15	134.15	138.32	133.24	130.2	**96.33**	128.5	119.91	115.16	117.76
Drop: 0.5%										
ECG	58.27	35.32	**4.17**	26.68	28.95	31.21	4.3	4.29	13.66	13.59
Ninapro	129.64	108.54	61.32	61.76	64.23	71.27	63.56	**50.56**	53.52	62.29
UniMiB	134.15	101.21	115.92	112.52	89.18	96.33	92.41	88.61	87.69	**82.28**

7 Conclusions

In this work, we have presented an adaptive inference approach for RFs on MCUs, based on executing only a subset of the weak learners in order to save energy. To control this early-stopping mechanism, we have proposed two different lightweight policies which use the class probabilities produced in output by DTs to estimate the partial prediction confidence. In order to validate our approach, we have performed extensive experiments on three state-of-the-art datasets concerning popular embedded tasks. Moreover, we have deployed the proposed method on a single-core RISC-V MCU, showing that even when taking into account the overhead associated with the evaluation of the early stopping policy, we are able to save significant energy with respect to a static model, up to more than 90% for the same accuracy.

References

1. Anguita, D., Ghio, A., Oneto, L., Parra, X., Reyes-Ortiz, J.L.: Human activity recognition on smartphones using a multiclass hardware-friendly support vector machine. In: Bravo, J., Hervás, R., Rodríguez, M. (eds.) IWAAL 2012. LNCS, vol. 7657, pp. 216–223. Springer, Heidelberg (2012). https://doi.org/10.1007/978-3-642-35395-6_30
2. Atzori, M., et al.: Building the Ninapro database: a resource for the biorobotics community. In: 2012 4th IEEE RAS & EMBS International Conference on Biomedical Robotics and Biomechatronics (BioRob). IEEE, pp. 1258–1265 (2012)
3. Atzori, M., et al.: Electromyography data for non-invasive naturally controlled robotic hand prostheses. Sci. Data **1**(1), 1–13 (2014)
4. Bradski, G.: The OpenCV library. In: Dr. Dobb's Journal of Software Tools (2000)
5. Breiman, L.: Random forests. Mach. Learn. **45**(1), 5–32 (2001). https://doi.org/10.1023/a:1010933404324
6. Burrello, A., et al.: Embedding temporal convolutional networks for energy-efficient PPG-based heart rate monitoring. ACM Trans. Comput. Healthcare, **3**(2) (2022). issn: 2691–1957. https://doi.org/10.1145/3487910.
7. Chen, Y., Hao, Y., Rakthanmanon, T., Zakaria, J., Hu, B., Keogh, E.: A general framework for never-ending learning from time series streams. Data Min. Knowl. Disc. **29**(6), 1622–1664 (2014). https://doi.org/10.1007/s10618-014-0388-4
8. Conti, F., Rossi, D., Pullini, A., Loi, I., Benini, L.: PULP: a ultra-low power parallel accelerator for energy-efficient and flexible embedded vision. J. Signal Proc. Syst. **84**(3), 339–354 (2015). https://doi.org/10.1007/s11265-015-1070-9
9. Daghero, F., et al.: Energy-efficient adaptive machine learning on IoT end-nodes with class-dependent confidence. In: 2020 27th IEEE International Conference on Electronics, Circuits and Systems (ICECS), pp. 1–4 (2020). https://doi.org/10.1109/ICECS49266.2020.9294863
10. Daghero, F., et al.: Energy-efficient deep learning inference on edge devices. In: Hardware Accelerator Systems for Artificial Intelligence and Machine Learning. Ed. by Shiho Kim and Ganesh Chandra Deka, vol. 122. Advances in Computers. Elsevier, pp. 247–301 (2021)
11. Daghero, F., et al.: Adaptive random forests for energy-efficient inference on microcontrollers. In: 2021 IFIP/IEEE 29th International Conference on Very Large Scale Integration (VLSI-SoC). IEEE, pp. 1–6 (2021)

12. Daghero, F., et al.: Ultra-compact binary neural networks for human activity recognition on RISC-V processors. In: Proceedings of the 18th ACM International Conference on Computing Frontiers, pp. 3–11 (2021)
13. Di Mauro, A.Q., et al.: Always-on 674μ W@ 4GOP/s error resilient binary neural networks with aggressive SRAM voltage scaling on a 22-nm IoT endnode. In: IEEE Transactions on Circuits and Systems I: Regular Papers, vol. 67, no. 11, pp. 3905–3918 (2020)
14. Donos, C., Dümpelmann, M., Schulze-Bonhage, A.: Early seizure detection algorithm based on intracranial EEG and random forest classification. Int. J. Neural Syst. **25**(05), 1550023 (2015). https://doi.org/10.1142/S0129065715500239
15. Fan, L., Wang, Z., Wang, H.: Human activity recognition model based on decision tree. In: Proceedings of the 2013 International Conference on Advanced Cloud and Big Data. CBD 2013. USA. IEEE Computer Society, pp. 64–68. isbn: 9781479932610 (2013). https://doi.org/10.1109/CBD.2013.19
16. Gao, T., Koller, D.: Active classification based on value of classifier. In: Shawe-Taylor, J., et al., (eds.) Advances in Neural Information Processing Systems 24. Curran Associates Inc, pp. 1062–1070 (2011). http://papers.nips.cc/paper/4340-active-classification-based-onvalue-of-classifier.pdf
17. Garofalo, A., et al.: PULP-NN: accelerating quantized neural networks on parallel ultra-low-power RISC-V processors. Philos. Trans. R. Soc. A Math. Phys. Eng. Sci. **378**(2164), 20190155 (2020). https://doi.org/10.1098/rsta.2019.0155
18. Jacob, B., et al.: Quantization and training of neural networks for efficient integer-arithmetic-only inference. In: Proceedings of the IEEE Conference on Computer Vision and Pattern Recognition (CVPR) (2018)
19. Jahier Pagliari, D., et al.: Dynamic bit-width reconfiguration for energy-efficient deep learning hardware. In: Proceedings of the International Symposium on Low Power Electronics and Design. ISLPED 2018. New York, NY, USA. ACM, vol. 47, no. (1–47), p. 6. isbn: 978-1-4503-5704-3 (2018). https://doi.org/10.1145/3218603.3218611
20. Jahier Pagliari, D., et al.: Sequence-to-sequence neural networks inference on embedded processors using dynamic beam search. Electronics, **9**(2) (2020). issn: 2079–9292
21. Jahier Pagliari, D., et al.: CRIME: input-dependent collaborative inference for recurrent neural networks. IEEE Trans. Comput. 1 (2020). issn: 1557–9956. https://doi.org/10.1109/TC.2020.3021199
22. Jahier Pagliari, D., et al.: Input-dependent edge-cloud mapping of recurrent neural networks inference. In: 2020 57th ACM/IEEE Design Automation Conference (DAC), pp. 1–6 (2020). https://doi.org/10.1109/DAC18072.2020.9218595
23. Maimon, O.Z., Rokach, L.: Data mining with decision trees: theory and applications, vol. 81. World scientific (2014)
24. Micucci, D., et al.: Unimib shar: a dataset for human activity recognition using acceleration data from smartphones. Appl. Sci. **7**(10), 1101 (2017)
25. John Mingers, J.: An empirical comparison of pruning methods for decision tree induction. Mach. Learn. **4**(2), 227–243 (1989). https://doi.org/10.1023/A:1022604100933
26. Molchanov, P., et al.: Pruning convolutional neural networks for resource efficient inference. In: 5th International Conference on Learning Representations, ICLR 2017, Toulon, France, 24–26 April 2017, Conference Track Proceedings. OpenReview.net (2017). https://openreview.net/forum?id=SJGCiw5gl

27. Panda, P., Sengupta, A., Roy, K.: Conditional deep learning for energy-efficient and enhanced pattern recognition. In: Proceedings of the 2016 Conference on Design, Automation & Test in Europe. DATE 2016, San Jose, CA, USA. EDA Consortium, pp. 475–480 (2016). isbn: 9783981537062
28. Park, E., et al.: Big/little deep neural network for ultra low power inference. In: 2015 International Conference on Hardware/Software Code- sign and System Synthesis (CODES+ISSS), pp. 124–132 (2015). isbn: 978-1-4673-8321-9. https://doi.org/10.1109/CODESISSS.2015.7331375
29. Pedregosa, F., et al.: Scikit-learn: machine learning in python. J. Mach. Learn. Res. **12**, 2825–2830 (2011)
30. Pereira, J., Silveira, M.: Learning representations from healthcare time series data for unsupervised anomaly detection. In: 2019 IEEE International Conference on Big Data and Smart Computing (BigComp). IEEE, pp. 1–7 (2019)
31. Samie, F., et al.: From cloud down to things: an overview of machine learning in internet of things. IEEE Internet Things J. **6**(3), 4921–4934 (2019). issn: 2327–4662. https://doi.org/10.1109/JIOT.2019.2893866
32. Schwing, A.G., et al.: Adaptive random forest - how many "experts" to ask before making a decision? In: CVPR 2011, pp. 1377–1384 (2011). https://doi.org/10.1109/CVPR.2011.5995684
33. Shi, W., et al.: Edge computing: vision and challenges. In: IEEE Internet Things J. **3**(5), 637–646 (2016). issn: 2327–4662. https://doi.org/10.1109/JIOT.2016.2579198
34. SiFive. SiFive Core IP. (2021). https://www.sive.com/risc-v-core-ip
35. STMicroelectronics. iNEMO inertial module: always-on 3D accelerometer and 3D gyroscope. Website (2019). www.st.com/resource/en/datasheet/lsm6dsox.pdf
36. Sze, V., et al.: Efficient processing of deep neural networks: a tutorial and survey. Proc. IEEE, **105**(12), 2295–2329 (2017). issn: 00189219. https://doi.org/10.1109/JPROC.2017.2761740, arXiv: 1703.09039
37. Tann, H., et al.: Runtime configurable deep neural networks for energy-accuracy trade-off. In: Proceedings of the Eleventh IEEE/ACM/IFIP International Conference on Hardware/SoftwareCodesign and System Synthesis - CODES 2016, pp. 1–10 (2016). isbn: 9781450344838. https://doi.org/10.1145/2968456.2968458, arXiv: arXiv:1508.06655v1, http://dl.acm.org/citation.cfm?doid=2968456.2968458
38. The PULP Platform. GVSOC: PULP Virtual Platform (2020). https://github.com/pulp-platform/gvsoc
39. Wang, S., et al.: Quit when you can: efficient evaluation of ensembles by optimized ordering. ACM J. Emerg. Technol. Comput. Syst. (JETC) **17**(4), 1–20 (2021)
40. Zhou, Z., et al.: Edge intelligence: paving the last mile of artificial intelligence with edge computing. Proc. IEEE, **107**(8), 1738–1762 (2019). issn: 1558–2256 VO - 107. 2918951. https://doi.org/10.1109/JPROC.2019.2918951

Transformative Hardware Design Following the Model-Driven Architecture Vision

Zhao Han[1,2(✉)], Gabriel Rutsch[1], Deyan Wang[1,2], Bowen Li[1,2],
Sebastian Siegfried Prebeck[1,2], Daniela Sanchez Lopera[1,2],
Keerthikumara Devarajegowda[1], and Wolfgang Ecker[1,2]

[1] Infineon Technologies AG, Am Campeon 1-15, 85579 Neubiberg, Germany
{Zhao.Han,Gabriel.Rutsch,Deyan.Wang,Bowen.Li,Sebastian.Prebeck,
Daniela.Lopera,Keerthikumara.Devarajegowda,Wolfgang.Ecker}@infineon.com
[2] Technical University Munich, Arcisstraße 21, 80333 Munich, Germany

Abstract. Despite the high configurability of IPs and hardware generators, code modifications are still required to introduce aspect-oriented
instrumentation to satisfy emerging aspectual design requirements such
as on-chip debug and functional safety. These code modifications escalate
development, verification efforts, and deteriorate code reuse. This paper
proposes a highly efficient transformative hardware design methodology
that leverages graph-grammar-based model transformations. Following
the proposed methodology, main design functionalities and aspectual
instrumentation are separately developed, automatically integrated, and
verified. To demonstrate the applicability, industrial SoCs were transformed to support on-chip debug. Compared to the manual RTL coding,
the proposed transformative methodology needed less than 32x Lines of
Code (LoC) to develop and integrate the aspectual instrumentation. In
particular, our approach enables high code reusability, as the implementation of the transformation script is a one-time effort, and can be applied
to all evaluated SoCs. This high LoC gain and code reuse promote the
overall productivity of digital design.

Keywords: Electronic design automation · Aspect-oriented
programming · Model-driven architecture

1 Introduction

With growing complexity in System on Chips (SoCs), the hardware development cycle is prolonged and the cost increases. Intellectual Property (IP) reuse
is a major productivity booster in hardware development and helps to promote
code reuse. Following the IP reuse methodology, designers are encouraged to
build configurable IPs that encapsulate verified design implementations. After,
IPs are adapted and integrated to build large and complex designs to accelerate the development cycle. For further code reuse, hardware generators are

© IFIP International Federation for Information Processing 2022
Published by Springer Nature Switzerland AG 2022
V. Grimblatt et al. (Eds.): VLSI-SoC 2021, IFIP AICT 661, pp. 49–70, 2022.
https://doi.org/10.1007/978-3-031-16818-5_3

built to encode design knowledge with hardware generation frameworks [1–5]. Hardware generators enable design customization reuse and are implemented with high-level programming languages such as Scala and Python. Making use of modern programming paradigms such as object orientation, hardware generators can adapt highly complex configurations and generate adequate Hardware Description Language (HDL) code.

However, beyond main functionalities, aspectual design requirements such as On-Chip Debug (OCD) [6] and functional safety [7] have emerged over the years and are essential for product success. On-chip instrumentation satisfying these design requirements is dependent on core functionality realizations and demands system-wide support. Towards this end, code pieces are scattered across different IPs to implement the required on-chip instrumentation. For example, to support OCD, not only debug IPs (e.g. JTAG) but also special features are needed in existing IPs, e.g. hardware breakpoints in the CPU. But due to the absence of aspect orientation [8] in state-of-the-art HDLs (e.g. SystemVerilog [9]) and hardware generation frameworks (e.g. Chisel [2]), the OCD instrumentation is either always implemented [10] or configurable by increasing the IP generality [11]. The former option results in an additional chip area and introduces possible security breaches, whereas escalated development and verification efforts are expected in the latter one [12]. In this paper, we use the term *design aspects* to describe these scattered and tangled aspect-oriented on-chip instrumentation. Design aspects pose new challenges in hardware development, because the scattering and tangling make the hardware implementations hard to understand, maintain, and reuse.

To address these issues, we propose to weave aspect-oriented instrumentation by transforming existing designs leveraging graph grammar [13]. The proposed transformative hardware design methodology is built on top of a model-driven hardware generation framework, which follows the Model-Driven Architecture® (MDA®) vision [14]. The intermediate layer of this framework contains platform-independent design models that capture intended microarchitectures. Design models are graph-based: Hierarchical and logic components are vertices, whereas connections among ports and hierarchizations of components are edges. The proposed methodology transforms existing design models to incorporate desired aspect-oriented instrumentation. Model transformations are formalized and guided by graph grammar. Thus, the main contributions of this paper are: (1) Main functionalities and design aspects are decoupled and addressed separately with the proposed methodology. This separation of design concerns promotes modularity, reduces development efforts, and enables high code reuse. (2) For quality assurance, design constraints are developed to validate introduced design modifications. Besides, formal properties are automated to verify transformed designs. (3) One Domain-Specific Language (DSL) is used to construct and transform designs. This consistent design environment prevents semantic gaps and lowers integration and maintenance burdens.

The rest of the paper is organized as follows: Related work is discussed in the next section. Section 3 depicts the underlying model-driven hardware generation framework. After, the proposed transformative hardware design methodology is elaborated in Sect. 4. To demonstrate the applicability, Sect. 5 presents an industrial case study on RISC-V OCD transformation and discusses the experimental results. The last section concludes the significance of this paper.

2   Related Work

High-level languages such as SystemC are used to describe hardware and compiled to HDL to improve design productivity [15]. To further reuse design customizations, hardware generation frameworks such as Genesis2 [1] are proposed. However, they fail to separate design aspects from main functionalities. Designers must consider aspect-oriented instrumentation during the implementation of the main functionality. Consequently, the scattered and tangled-up aspect-oriented instrumentation leads to increased development and verification efforts [12].

Moreover, the intermediate layer of the hardware generation framework used by Chisel is called Flexible Intermediate Representation for RTL (FIRRTL) [3]. FIRRTL enables instrumentation insertion by rewriting its abstract syntax tree. In doing so, simple circuits such as hardware counters can be inserted into designs. Also, PyRTL [4] and PyMTL [5] follow the same idea to enable instrumentation transformation. Furthermore, FTI [16] provides a graphical user interface to assist hardware engineers to harden a design step by step. Internally, FTI translates designs written in VHDL to tree-based AIRE-CE representations [17].

However, there are three main drawbacks of these approaches. First, the underlying tree-based data structure is inappropriate, as it is not the intrinsic structure of circuits, i.e., graphs. As a result, development efforts escalate, which diminishes the gained design productivity. Second, the employment of different languages for design construction and transformation introduces semantic gaps and complicates hardware development. Most importantly, they do not generate verification artifacts to assure the quality of transformed designs.

3   Model-Driven Hardware Generation Framework

MDA® [18] established itself as an important part of modern development processes over the last decades. Following MDA®, a model-driven hardware generation framework called MetaRTL has been developed to improve hardware design productivity [14]. With this design-centric framework, designers can focus on design intent instead of implementation details such as code formatting.

MetaRTL consists of three layers: *Things*, *Design*, and *View* (Fig. 1). The things layer captures specification items into the *Formal Specification Model*. For satisfying specifications, designs are constructed with the expressive MetaRTL DSL [19] and stored as platform-independent *Design Models*. Subsequently, *Target Code Models* are derived for different HDLs and technologies (e.g. FPGA) in the view layer. State-of-the-art HDLs such as VHDL [20], Verilog [21], and SystemVerilog [9] are supported as the possible generator outputs.

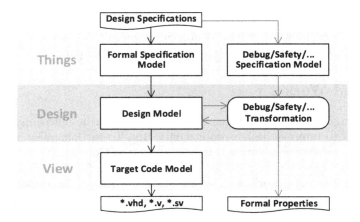

Fig. 1. Model-driven hardware generation framework (MetaRTL). The generation framework is extended with the transformative hardware design methodology as depicted in the right part.

A hardware generation flow starts from a formalized specification, which includes all must-have features and properties. In the main stage, i.e., design layer, the translation from the specification model to a design model is conducted by making use of a design template [22]. Design models are abstract RTL models and include all high-level design details, for instance, port connections among different logic gates. Next, the design model is translated to a target HDL code model by a view template [23], which includes target-specific aspects. Finally, the HDL code is derived from the target code model.

4   Transformative Hardware Design Methodology

The proposed methodology is implemented as part of the MetaRTL in Fig. 1. The left part in the figure shows the hardware generation flow, whereas the right part addresses design aspects with the transformative hardware design methodology. The proposed methodology integrates aspect-oriented instrumentation by transforming design models leveraging graph grammar. For easing hardware transformation development, various transformation utilities and reusable basic transformations are provided by the hardware transformation system. To assure quality, modified design models are validated with design constraints and transformed designs are verified with automated formal properties.

4.1   Graph-Based Design Model

In the main stage of MetaRTL, platform-independent design models capture microarchitectures. For describing microarchitectures, four types of components can be included in a design model [24]:

- *Descriptive* components indicate design hierarchies and description styles in the MetaRTL DSL [25].
- *Behavioural* components describe hardware behavior on a high level, such as finite state machines.
- *Sequential* components such as register store information, as their outputs depend on past and current inputs.
- *Primitive* components describe combinatorial logic, such as bitwise AND.

Hardware designs are usually represented as schematic diagrams, which use graphs to depict the instantiated components and connections among them. The design model is graph-based as well. Let LAB be an arbitrary but fixed set of suitable labels. A design model can be formalized with a hierarchical port graph [24]:

$$H = (V, P, E, (s_i, t_i)_{i \in \{G,T\}}, \mathfrak{p}, \mathfrak{t}, \mathfrak{d}, l)$$

- V is a finite set of vertices (components).
- P is a finite set of ports.
- $E = E_G \cup E_T$ are finite sets of graph and tree edges.
- s_G, s_T are source functions for graph and tree edges respectively.
- t_G, t_T are target functions for graph and tree edges respectively.
- $\mathfrak{p} : P \to V$ is a parent function that returns the parent component of a port.
- $\mathfrak{t} : V \to Descriptive \cup Behavioural \cup Sequential \cup Primitive$ is the type function for vertices (components).
- $\mathfrak{d} : P \to \{In, Out, Inout\}$ is the direction function for ports.
- $l : V \cup P \to LAB$ is a labeling function for vertices and ports.

The hierarchy in design models is a tree spanning over the same set of vertices V. This means, some vertices in design models are subgraphs that contain other vertices. These vertices are descriptive components, since they indicate design hierarchies and contain sub-components in design models. Hence, a vertex $v \in V$ can be denoted as

$$v = (V_v, P_v, E_v, (s_{i.v}, t_{i.v})_{i \in \{G,T\}}, \mathfrak{p}_v, \mathfrak{t}_v, \mathfrak{d}_v, l_v)$$

It is noteworthy that $V_v \subseteq V$, $E_V \subseteq E_G$, and $P_V \subseteq P$. Besides, these functions are restricted by the functions of the graph. This means, the global functions apply to subgraphs as well, i.e.,

$$v = (V_v, P_v, E_v, (s_i, t_i)_{i \in \{G,T\}}, \mathfrak{p}, \mathfrak{t}, \mathfrak{d}, l)$$

When a vertex $v \in V$ is not a descriptive component, then it does not contain any sub-component or edge, i.e., $V_v = v, E_v = \emptyset$. In contrast, when a vertex $v \in V$ is the top-level component, then $V_v = V, P_v = P$, and $E_v = E$. The top-level component is not a target of any tree edge.

For an illustrative example, the hierarchical port graph of a half adder is shown in Fig. 2. Labels of components and ports are illustrated, e.g. $l(v_0) = $ "*halfAdder*". The descriptive component v_0 indicates a hierarchy, i.e.,

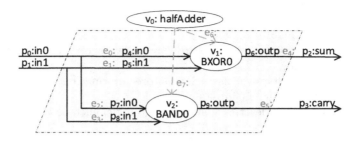

Fig. 2. Hierarchical port graph for a half adder. Solid black edges describe connections among ports and dashed grey edges depict hierarchizations of vertices (components). (Color figure online)

$t(v_0) \in Descriptive$. Where $V_{v_0} = \{v_1, v_2\}$, $P_{v_0} = \{p_0, p_1, ..., p_9\}$ and $E_{v_0} = \{e_0, e_1, ..., e_7\}$. Components v_1, v_2 are bitwise XOR and AND respectively.

Ports belong to components, i.e., $p(p_i)_{i \in \{0,1,2,3\}} = v_0$, $p(p_i)_{i \in \{4,5,6\}} = v_1$, and $p(p_i)_{i \in \{7,8,9\}} = v_2$. Directions of ports are: $\partial(p_i)_{i \in \{0,1,4,5,7,8\}} = In$ and $\partial(p_i)_{i \in \{2,3,6,9\}} = Out$. Connections among ports are identified by their source and target ports in the graph:

$$s_G(e_0) = p_0, t_G(e_0) = p_4$$
$$s_G(e_1) = p_1, t_G(e_1) = p_5$$
$$s_G(e_2) = p_0, t_G(e_2) = p_7$$
$$s_G(e_3) = p_1, t_G(e_3) = p_8$$
$$s_G(e_4) = p_6, t_G(e_4) = p_2$$
$$s_G(e_5) = p_9, t_G(e_5) = p_3$$

In a design model, a port might be connected to multiple ports. But connections across hierarchies are forbidden. Therefore, a port such as p_4 can only be connected to another port that belongs to the current hierarchy (e.g. p_0) or a component in the current hierarchy (e.g. p_9). The port direction must be considered as well. A connection between two ports $p_i, p_j \in P$ is represented as $e_G \in E_G$, e.g. $e_0 = (p_0, p_4)$. Whilst, a tree edge $e_T \in E_T$ describes the hierarchical inclusion between two components $v_i, v_j \in V$, e.g. $e_7 = (v_0, v_2)$.

The uniqueness of labels is only assured inside a design hierarchy and among ports of the same component. Therefore, labels maybe not unique in a design model, e.g. $l(p_4) = l(p_7)$. To locate an exact component, additional hierarchical information is required. To this end, let $\mathfrak{h}$ be a *hierarchical path* from v_i to v_j, where $t(v_i) \in Descriptive$. A hierarchical path $\mathfrak{h}$ is a sequence of vertices $v_i, v_{i+1}, ..., v_j$ such that, for any $x = i, i+1, ..., j$, there exists an edge $e_T \in E_T$, that $s_T(e_T) = v_x$ and $t_T(e_T) = v_{x+1}$. That is, the previous descriptive component contains the next component in a hierarchical path.

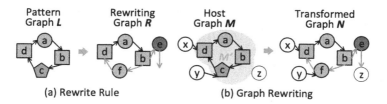

| Pattern Graph L | Rewriting Graph R | Host Graph M | Transformed Graph N |

(a) Rewrite Rule   (b) Graph Rewriting

Fig. 3. Graph grammar. (a) A rewrite rule consists of a pattern graph L and a rewriting graph R. (b) By matching the subgraph M' in host graph M according to the pattern graph L, design modifications indicated by the rewriting graph R are inserted automatically to form the transformed graph N.

4.2 Design Model Transformation

The design model transformation can be referred to as graph rewriting. A graph rewriting is guided with graph grammar, which describes an iterative process of applying a set of rewrite rules on the matched subgraphs in the host graph [26]. For this purpose, the definition of graph morphisms and subgraphs is adapted for hierarchical port graphs.

Let M and N be two hierarchical port graphs. A *hierarchical port graph morphism* $\mathfrak{f}$ from M to N consists of three functions: $\mathfrak{f}_V$, $\mathfrak{f}_P$, and $\mathfrak{f}_E$. The interrelations of edges, hierarchical inclusions between components, labels and types of components, labels and directions of ports are preserved, i.e., for any $v_M \in V_M$, $p_M \in P_M$, $e_{M.G} \in E_{M.G}$, and $e_{M.T} \in E_{M.T}$, the following properties hold:

$$\mathfrak{f}_P(s_{M.G}(e_{M.G})) = s_{N.G}(\mathfrak{f}_E(e_{M.G}))$$
$$\mathfrak{f}_P(t_{M.G}(e_{M.G})) = t_{N.G}(\mathfrak{f}_E(e_{M.G}))$$
$$\mathfrak{f}_V(s_{M.T}(e_{M.T})) = s_{N.T}(\mathfrak{f}_E(e_{M.T}))$$
$$\mathfrak{f}_V(t_{M.T}(e_{M.T})) = t_{N.T}(\mathfrak{f}_E(e_{M.T}))$$
$$l(v_M) = l(\mathfrak{f}_V(v_M)) \wedge \mathfrak{t}(v_M) = \mathfrak{t}(\mathfrak{f}_V(v_M))$$
$$l(p_M) = l(\mathfrak{f}_P(p_M)) \wedge \mathfrak{d}(p_M) = \mathfrak{d}(\mathfrak{f}_P(p_M))$$

Further, let M be a *subgraph* of a hierarchical port graph N, denoted as $M \subseteq N$, where $V_M \subseteq V_N$, $P_M \subseteq P_N$ and $E_M \subseteq E_N$, and the functions of M are restrictions of those in N. For any $v \in V_M$, if $\mathfrak{t}(v) \in Descriptive$, then all subcomponents and edges in this descriptive component in N should be included in M as well, i.e., $V_{N.v} \subseteq V_M$, $P_{N.v} \subseteq P_M$, and $E_{N.v} \subseteq E_M$.

Algorithm 1 describes the graph-grammar-based design model transformation. A graph grammar consists of a set of rewrite rules $\mathfrak{R}$. A rewrite rule $r \in \mathfrak{R}$ consists of two graphs: left-hand-side pattern graph L and right-hand-side rewriting graph R (Fig. 3a).

The application of a rewrite rule consists of three steps:

1. *Match* a subgraph M' in host graph M that has a graph morphism from pattern graph L to M' (Fig. 3b).

Algorithm 1: Design Model Transformation

Input : Host graph $M = (V_M, P_M, E_M, (s_{M.i}, t_{M.i})_{i \in \{G,T\}}, \mathfrak{p}_M, \mathfrak{t}_M, \partial_M, l_M)$,
           Rules $\mathfrak{R} = \{r_0, r_n, ..., r_n\}$
Output: Transformed Graph N
Let N be the duplication of M
for $r = (L, R) \in \mathfrak{R}$ **do**
  $M' = \text{match}(M, L)$
  for $v \in V_L$ **and** $v \notin V_R$ **do**
  | $V_N = V_N \setminus \{v\}$
  end
  for $e \in E_L$ **and** $e \notin E_R$ **do**
  | $E_N = E_N \setminus \{e\}$
  end
  for $v \in V_R$ **and** $v \notin V_L$ **do**
  | $V_N = V_N \cup \{v\}$
  end
  for $e \in E_R$ **and** $e \notin E_L$ **do**
  | $E_N = E_N \cup \{e\}$
  end
end
return $N = (V_N, P_N, E_N, (s_{N.i}, t_{N.i})_{i \in \{G,T\}}, \mathfrak{p}_N, \mathfrak{t}_N, \partial_N, l_N)$

---

2. *Remove* the components, ports and edges that belong to L but not R.
3. *Add* the components, ports and edges that belong to R but not L.

In the algorithm, the function $\text{match}(M, L)$ returns the found subgraph M'. During transformations, graph functions such as labeling function l are updated automatically when the host graph is modified.

To find the subgraph M' in host graph M, components in M are located for every vertex in L with its hierarchical path, name, and type. Since the name and direction of ports are preserved in the matched subgraph, connections are recognized by locating the linked ports. The located components, ports, and edges compose the matched subgraph M'. In doing so, a graph morphism from M' to L is derived. Based on such graph morphism, design modifications described by the rewriting graph R are incorporated automatically to form the transformed graph N.

Design construction is a special case of design transformation, where the pattern graph L is always a subgraph of the rewriting graph R in rewrite rules. That is, the removal of components, ports, and connections is absent in design construction. Inspired by this observation, we use the MetaRTL DSL to not only construct but also transform designs.

4.3 Hardware Transformation System

To ease hardware transformation development, a hardware transformation system is developed (Fig. 4). Essential operations such as *Localization*, *Removal*, and *Addition* of components, ports, and connections are needed during design model transformations. These operations are performed with the *Transformation Utilities*. Making use of transformation utilities, various *Transformations* are developed. Transformations are classified into *Basic*, *Design-Independent*,

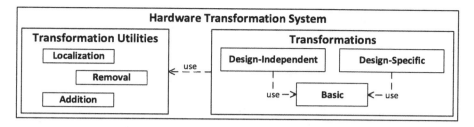

Fig. 4. Hardware transformation system. Transformation utilities consist of localization, removal, and addition utilities for components, ports, and connections. Making use of these utilities, basic transformations introduce elementary design modifications and are reused to construct complex design-independent and design-specific transformations.

and *Design-Specific* transformations. A basic transformation introduces an elementary design modification, which affects only a few components, ports, and connections in design models. In contrast, by reusing basic transformations, complex design-independent and design-specific transformations are developed with reduced efforts for systematic design modifications. These systematic transformations differ due to microarchitectural dependency.

Transformation Utilities. During hardware transformation, specific components, ports, and connections are modified to introduce design modifications. For this purpose, hardware transformations start with the localization of target components, ports, and connections. This step is formalized as the first application step of rewrite rules. To assist this step, the MetaRTL DSL offers localization utilities. For example, a simplified component localization function is shown in Listing 1.1.

```
1  def componentLocalization(hierarchy, name, comp_type, path, designModel)
   :
2    founds = list()
3    for comp in hierarchy.getComponents():
4      currentHierarchicalPath = getHierarchicalPath(comp, designModel)
5      if currentHierarchicalPath in path:
6        if isinstance(comp, Descriptive):
7          foundComps = componentLocalization(comp, name, comp_type, path,
             designModel)
8          founds.extends(foundComps)
9      elif currentHierarchicalPath == path:
10       if comp.getName() == name:
11         if isinstance(comp, comp_type):
12           founds.append(comp)
13     continue
14   return founds
```

Listing 1.1. Component Localization Function. This function localizes a component based on its name, type, and hierarchical path. In doing so, adequate components in the design model are located and returned as a list.

The shown component localization function has five arguments: the current design *hierarchy*, target component *name*, *comp_type*, its absolute hierarchical *path*, and the *designModel*. First, components under the current design hierarchy are iterated in line 3. The absolute hierarchical path of the iterated component (*comp*) is retrieved with the *getHierarchicalPath* function in line 4. By comparing the retrieved hierarchical path (*currentHierarchicalPath*) to the given path, different steps are followed: If the retrieved hierarchical path is part of the given absolute hierarchical path and the iterated component is a descriptive component (lines 5–6), target components are located in the design hierarchy indicated by the iterated component. Then, the localization process conducts further inside the iterated component in line 7. But if the retrieved hierarchical path is identical to the given absolute hierarchical path, component name and type are then compared (lines 9–11). When all these search criteria are satisfied, the current iterated component is marked in line 12. However, if the retrieved hierarchical path does not satisfy the previous conditions, the component localization function continues to iterate the next component in the current design hierarchy.

After the localization step in model transformations, components, ports, and/or connections are removed from and/or added in located subgraphs to introduce design modifications. During this process, three graph-based operations are observed: remove, add, and replace. The remove and add operations are supported inherently by the MetaRTL DSL [19], while the replace operation is the composition of remove and add operations. For example, an exemplary component replacement function is shown in Listing 1.2.

```
1  def componentReplacement ( original , new ) :
2    hierarchy = original . parent
3    for port in original . getPorts () :
4      newPort = new . getPort (Name=port . getName ())
5      connections = getConnections ( port , hierarchy )
6      for connection in connections :
7        connection . delConnector ( port )
8        connection . addConnector ( newPort )
9    hierarchy . delComponent ( original )
10   hierarchy . insComponent ( new )
```

Listing 1.2. Component replacement function. This simplified function considers only components with identical port definitions in terms of name, type, and number.

The shown component replacement function replaces the *original* component with the *new* component. The target design *hierarchy* is located in line 2. Since both components have identical port definitions, connections linking the ports of the original component are rewired in lines 3–8. To do this, the port *newPort* of the new component is retrieved with the *getPort* function by the name of the iterated *port* in line 4. The *connections* linking the iterated *port* under the current design hierarchy are then obtained with the *getConnections* function in line 5. Later, these connections are rewired by replacing the iterated port with the *newPort* (lines 6–8). Afterward, the original component is removed and the new component is placed under the same design hierarchy (lines 9–10).

Moreover, design details such as the related connections and connected ports of the target port are often required in model transformations. For this purpose, transformation utilities for connections such as *getConnections* in Listing 1.2 are provided. Various transformation utilities are served as the intuitive programming interface for hardware transformation and are the fundament of the hardware transformation system.

Basic Transformations. Basic transformations introduce elementary design modifications into design models. Exemplary basic transformations are the naming convention transformation and safety mechanism transformations.

A basic transformation for the naming convention has been developed [25] to adapt component and port names to different design projects. That is, specific prefixes and suffixes are often predefined for different design elements to avoid ambiguity and assist readability. For example, ports are named with the prefix "p_". Also, the name suffix "_i" or "_o" of ports indicates the direction. With this naming convention transformation, component and port names are adapted automatically to meet coding guidelines in the target design project.

Moreover, the transformation system offers basic transformations for various safety mechanisms [27]. Safety mechanisms introduce redundancy into the system to enable error detection (and correction). In doing so, the system is maintained in a safe state and, thus, dangerous consequences caused by malfunctions are reduced. The introduced redundancy has three categories: information redundancy, hardware redundancy, and time redundancy [7]. For introducing information redundancy into the hardware system, basic transformations are provided for parity error detection code, CRC, hamming code, etc. Whilst, basic transformations for hardware redundancy mechanisms such as Dual Modular Redundancy (DMR) and Triple Modular Redundancy (TMR) are also provided. But time redundancy safety mechanisms are software-based [28] and, thus, not offered as basic transformations.

Basic transformations are implemented in a configurable and modular manner. Hereby, basic transformations can serve as building blocks and form the "transformation library". This modularity and reusability assist and ease the complex hardware transformation development.

Design-Specific/-Independent Transformations. To address aspectual design requirements such as on-chip debug [6] and functional safety [7], design-specific and -independent transformations introduce systematic design modifications to design models. As the name indicates, design-specific transformations are dependent on the microarchitecture and, thus, are applicable to only a set of designs. Whereas, design-independent transformations have no such restrictions and are applicable to all designs.

Design-specific transformations are highly dependent on the microarchitecture. For example, the RISC-V OCD transformation introduces on-chip debug support in a CPU subsystem that implements RISC-V ISA [29]. In this ISA specification, the exception handling behavior and related information storage are detailed for RISC-V architecture. If the target architecture does not support the RISC-V ISA, these design details may differ and, thus, the RISC-V OCD transformation is not applicable anymore.

In contrast, design-independent transformations are independent of the microarchitecture. For example, a systematic functional safety transformation has been developed [27]. This functional safety transformation reuses basic transformations for safety mechanisms to harden sequential components such as registers and memories in a design. Moreover, different design projects may have different coding requirements for e.g. linting checks and code review. Thus, different RTL coding styles may be required. For this purpose, design-independent model transformations have been developed to fine-tune design models to vary IP-coding styles [25].

4.4 Quality Assurance

Model Validation. After transformations, modified design models are validated against design constraints. This validation assures the consistency of design models, which ensures that the generated HDL code is synthesizable. Following design constraints must be satisfied by all design models:

– *Multiple Connections*: For any two connections $e_i, e_j \in E_G$, their source and target can not be identical at the same time.

$$s_G(e_i) = s_G(e_j) \wedge t_G(e_i) \neq t_G(e_j) \vee$$
$$s_G(e_i) \neq s_G(e_j) \wedge t_G(e_i) = t_G(e_j) \vee$$
$$s_G(e_i) \neq s_G(e_j) \wedge t_G(e_i) \neq t_G(e_j)$$

– *Cross-Hierarchy Connections*: Connections across hierarchies are not allowed. To simplify the notation, we introduce a helper function $\mathfrak{s} : V \to V$ that returns the parent component of a component. For any connection $e \in E_G$, its source and target port must belong to the same hierarchy, i.e.,
  - if $\mathfrak{t}(\mathfrak{p}(s_G(e))), \mathfrak{t}(\mathfrak{p}(t_G(e))) \notin Descriptive$, then

  $$\mathfrak{s}(\mathfrak{p}(s_G(e))) = \mathfrak{s}(\mathfrak{p}(t_G(e)))$$

  - if $\mathfrak{t}(\mathfrak{p}(s_G(e))) \in Descriptive$ and $\mathfrak{t}(\mathfrak{p}(t_G(e))) \notin Descriptive$, then

  $$\mathfrak{s}(\mathfrak{p}(s_G(e))) = \mathfrak{s}(\mathfrak{p}(t_G(e))) \vee$$
  $$\mathfrak{p}(s_G(e)) = \mathfrak{s}(\mathfrak{p}(t_G(e)))$$

  - if $\mathfrak{t}(\mathfrak{p}(s_G(e))), \mathfrak{t}(\mathfrak{p}(t_G(e))) \in Descriptive$, then

  $$\mathfrak{s}(\mathfrak{p}(s_G(e))) = \mathfrak{s}(\mathfrak{p}(t_G(e))) \vee$$
  $$\mathfrak{p}(s_G(e)) = \mathfrak{s}(\mathfrak{p}(t_G(e))) \vee$$
  $$\mathfrak{s}(\mathfrak{p}(s_G(e))) = \mathfrak{p}(t_G(e))$$

– *Dangling Connections*: For any connection $e \in E_G$, there must exist a source and a target port, i.e.,
$$s_G(e), t_G(e) \in P$$

- *Valid Connections*: For any connection $e \in E_G$, it must be feasible in terms of port directions. As an exception, a connection is always feasible, if any of the connected ports has the direction "Inout". Thus, following constraints apply to a connection $e \in E_G$ that connects ports with direction either "In" or "Out", i.e., $\mathfrak{d}(s_G(e)), \mathfrak{d}(t_G(e)) \in \{In, Out\}$.
  - If two connected ports belong to components under the same hierarchy, i.e., $\mathfrak{s}(\mathfrak{p}(s_G(e))) = \mathfrak{s}(\mathfrak{p}(t_G(e)))$, then connector directions must differ.

$$\mathfrak{d}(s_G(e)) \neq \mathfrak{d}(t_G(e))$$

  - If two connected ports belong to components under different hierarchies, i.e., $\mathfrak{s}(\mathfrak{p}(s_G(e))) \neq \mathfrak{s}(\mathfrak{p}(t_G(e)))$. This means, one of these components is a descriptive component that contains the other connector's parent, then connector directions must be identical.

$$\mathfrak{d}(s_G(e)) = \mathfrak{d}(t_G(e))$$

- *Zero-Driven Connections*: Except input ports of the top component, for any port $p \in P$, there exists $e \in E_G$ such that

$$t_G(e) = p$$

- *Multi-Driven Connections*: For any two connections $e_i, e_j \in E_G$, they must have different targets.

$$t_G(e_i) \neq t_G(e_j)$$

- *Unconnected Component*: For any port $p \in P$, it must be connected, i.e., there exists a connection $e \in E_G$ such that

$$s_G(e) = p \vee t_G(e) = p$$

- *Single Hierarchy*: For any component $v \in V$, it must be located in only one hierarchy. This means, for any two hierarchical inclusions $e_i, e_j \in E_T$, their targets must be different.

$$t_T(e_i) \neq t_T(e_j)$$

Design Verification. To verify the design functionality, two verification suites are employed: existing regressions tests for main functionalities and newly automated formal properties for introduced design modifications.

Existing regression tests consisting of verification artifacts such as testbenches are developed for existing designs. Because the proposed approach targets design aspects, the main functionalities should stay intact. Thus, with adequate additional constraining, transformed designs must behave identically as original designs in regression tests.

Further, a formal property generation framework is used to automate formal properties for introduced design modifications [30]. The meta-information produced by applying a rewrite rule indicates the component and connection modifications. With this information, the property templates developed from design specifications generate suitable formal properties. For example, a rewrite rule is developed to harden a General-Purpose Register (GPR) *sp* under the register file (*RF*) with DMR. The DMR inserts a duplicated register *sp_copy*. A new signal *err_det* indicates an error when the outputs of *sp* and *sp_copy* differ. Afterward, we apply this rule to a design model, where *RF* is in instruction decode stage *ID* in *CPU*. Alongside the rewrite rule application, formal properties are generated in SystemVerilog Assertions to verify the inserted DMR (Listing 1.3).

```
1  property  RegisterFile_sp_DMR_ErrorFree  ;
2       ( CPU.ID.RF.sp.Out == CPU.ID.RF.sp_copy.Out)
3       |->
4       ( CPU.ID.RF.sp.err_det == 0 ) ;
5  endproperty
6  property  RegisterFile_sp_DMR_ErrorDetection  ;
7       ( CPU.ID.RF.sp.Out != CPU.ID.RF.sp_copy.Out)
8       |->
9       ( CPU.ID.RF.sp.err_det == 1 ) ;
10 endproperty
```

Listing 1.3. Generated properties for DMR transformation. The first property verifies the error-free scenario, whereas the second property is for the erroneous scenario.

The proposed methodology complements the hardware generation. By rewriting existing design models following graph-grammar-based transformations, design aspects are addressed separately from main functionalities. This separation of design concerns reduces complexity in hardware generators, which can be developed and verified with decreased efforts. Moreover, the development of hardware transformations is assisted with the transformation utilities and reusable basic transformations provided by the hardware transformation system. After transformation, modified design models are validated by design constraints and formal properties are generated to verify introduced aspect-oriented instrumentation. In particular, because one DSL is used for design construction and transformation, the proposed approach avoids semantic gaps, lowers integration, and maintenance burdens.

5   Case Study

In this section, a case study is conducted on the RISC-V OCD transformation. To demonstrate the applicability, we apply the OCD transformation to different industrial SoCs. Resource utilization and the time to conduct hardware transformations are discussed. Subsequently, the achieved code reusability and required development efforts are analyzed.

5.1   RISC-V On-Chip Debug Automation

With the increasing complexity in chips and stringent time to market requirements, post-silicon firmware debug solutions such as In-Circuit Emulator (ICE) becomes rapidly unfavorable because of the high cost and long development time.

Whereas, with low-cost hardware probes, OCD instrumentation provides dedicated debug circuitry for a reasonable area increase. An OCD system provides advanced functionalities such as hardware breakpoints, single stepping, register, and memory accesses [6]. To support these OCD features, system-wide design modifications are required. For instance, the CPU needs to allow external register accesses and the bus matrix needs to support external memory accesses. It is also important to note that these design modifications are highly microarchitecture-specific. To separate these design concerns, the OCD automation is developed following the proposed transformative hardware design methodology.

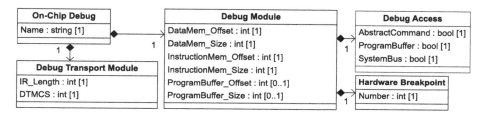

Fig. 5. RISC-V on-chip debug specification metamodel. This metamodel captures the main features of the debug transport module, debug module, and required system-wide support.

For formalizing the OCD requirements, the *On-Chip Debug* metamodel is abstracted from the RISC-V debug specification [6] (Fig. 5). Other than design-specific information such as the *Debug Transport Module* (DTM) instruction register length (*IR_Length*), memory offset and size, and the *Number* of supported *Hardware Breakpoints*, *Debug Accesses* can be configured as well. That is, the *Debug Module* (DM) may support different debug accesses: *AbstractCommand*, *ProgramBuffer*, and *SystemBus*. Since it is mandatory to support GPR accesses with the abstract command, these debug accesses differ in terms of Control and Status Registers (CSRs) and memory access methods. In this case study, abstract-command-based OCD implementation is used as an example.

The OCD transformation consists of basic transformations for enabling external register access, inserting hardware breakpoint CSRs, supporting breakpoint exception in the exception pipeline, etc. These basic transformations target different system parts and insert design modifications depending on the microarchitecture. In this paper, we focus on basic transformations for two essential design modifications: *register access* and *hardware breakpoint (HWBP)*.

The register access transformation adds several multiplexers for accessing the *GPR and CSR Units* (Fig. 6). The GPR unit supports two concurrent register read accesses. These registers are addressed by the *rs1_addr* and *rs2_addr*. Ports *rs1_data* and *rs2_data* indicate respective register data. The write access is supported by the *rd_addr*, *rd_data*, and *wr_en*. They carry the address, data, and write enable signals respectively. In contrast, the CSR unit supports only

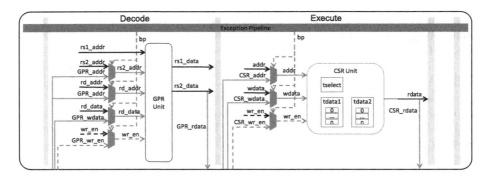

Fig. 6. On-chip debug transformation of RISC-V CPU. The CPU has a superscalar five-pipeline-stage architecture [31]. For simplicity, only transformation-related design details in the Decode and Execute stages are depicted.

one concurrent read or write access. Thus, the CSR unit has a much simpler interface: *addr*, *wdata*, *wr_en*, and *rdata*.

```
1  def transformGPRUnit(designModel, debugModule):
2    EP = componentLocalization(designModel, "ExceptionPipeline")
3    GPRUnit = componentLocalization(designModel, "GPRUnit")
4    bp_sig = EP.getPort(Name="bp")
5    transform_dict = {"rs2_addr" : "GPR_addr",
6    "rd_addr" : "GPR_addr",
7    "rd_data" : "GPR_wdata",
8    "wr_en" : "GPR_wr_en",
9    "rs2_data" : "GPR_rdata"}
10   for orig_sig, debug_sig in transform.iteritems():
11     target_port = GPRUnit.getPort(Name=orig_sig)
12     mux = Mux(Name="{}_mux".format(orig_sig), Sel=bp_sig, parent=GPRUnit
         ._Parent)
13     connection = getConnection(target_port, GPRUnit._Parent)
14     connection.delConnector(target_port)
15     connection.addConnector(mux.addIn())
16     debug_port = debugModule.getPort(Name=debug_sig)
17     mux.addIn().connect(debug_port)
18   rs2_data = GPRUnit.getPort(Name="rs2_data")
19   GPR_rdata = debugModule.getPort(Name="GPR_rdata")
20   rs2_data.connect(GPR_rdata)
```

Listing 1.4. Register accesses transformation of the GPR unit. This transformation locates and rewrites the rs2 and rd of the GPR unit for the read and write access respectively.

The transformation that enables external GPR accesses is shown in Listing 1.4. In the *transformGPRUnit*, the exception pipeline (*EP*) and GPR unit (*GPRUnit*) are first located in lines 2–3. The signal *bp_sig* provided by the exception pipeline indicates whether the CPU enters debug mode or not (line 4). Signals such as *GPR_addr*, *GPR_wdata*, *GPR_wr_en*, and *GPR_rdata* belong to the *debugModule* and indicate the current debug GPR access. For allowing the external GPR accesses in CPU, a mapping of ports of the GPR unit and DM is defined in lines 5–9. Based on this port mapping, target input ports of the GPR unit are located and their connections are reworked (lines 10–17). In doing so, the target inputs of the GPR unit are re-connected to insert several multiplexers (*mux*). These multiplexers are controlled by the *bp_sig*. That is, when the CPU enters debug mode, the GPR unit is accessed by the DM, otherwise, by the CPU. After, the *rs2_data* signal is connected to the *GPR_rdata* (lines 18–19). Following similar steps, external CSR accesses are enabled.

Furthermore, the HWBP transformation transforms specific CSRs [6] in the *CSR unit*: *tselect, tdata1, tdata2* (Fig. 6). The tdata1 stores the configuration of an HWBP, whereas the tdata2 stores the comparison data, e.g. target instruction address. For supporting multiple HWBPs, the tdata1 and tdata2 are designed as virtual CSRs, where multiple CSRs are accessible with the same CSR address. The tselect CSR determines the current accessible HWBP CSRs.

```
1  class TSELECT(Descriptive):
2    def __init__(self, DebugMoT)
3  class TDATA1(Descriptive):
4    def __init__(self, DebugMoT)
5  class TDATA2(Descriptive):
6    def __init__(self, DebugMoT)
7  def transformHWBP(designModel, DebugMoT):
8    CSRUnit = componentLocalization(designModel, "CSRUnit")
9    tselect = componentLocalization(CSRUnit, "tselect")
10   tdata1 = componentLocalization(CSRUnit, "tdata1")
11   tdata2 = componentLocalization(CSRUnit, "tdata2")
12   componentReplacement(tselect, TSELECT(DebugMoT))
13   componentReplacement(tdata1, TDATA1(DebugMoT))
14   componentReplacement(tdata2, TDATA2(DebugMoT))
```

Listing 1.5. Hardware breakpoint transformation of the CSR unit. This transformation is simplified, since it only considers the scenarios, when inadequate hardware breakpoint CSRs are already implemented.

Listing 1.5 illustrates the HWBP transformation in the CSR unit. In this transformation, the target design hierarchy (*CSRUnit*) and *tselect, tdata1*, and *tdata2* CSRs are located in lines 8–11. By replacing these original CSRs with the instantiated HWBP CSRs according to the *DebugMoT*, the HWBP transformation is complete (lines 12–14). The component replacement utility (*componentReplacement*) is part of transformation utilities.

Following the proposed methodology, the OCD transformation serves as the single source for implementing and integrating RISC-V OCD support. Subsequently, the transformed design models are validated against design constraints and the inserted OCD instrumentation is verified exhaustively with the automated formal properties.

5.2   Results

Five industrial 32-bit RISC-V SoCs with different feature sets targeting the powertrain market are evaluated. Besides peripherals such as Serial Peripheral Interface (SPI) and timers, the supported ISA extensions differ as well. Other than the base integer instruction set, SoCs may support standard extensions such as compressed instructions [29]. Additionally, customized multiply-accumulate instructions can be supported to boost the execution of machine learning applications. The more features are supported, the more complex is the design as shown in Fig. 7.

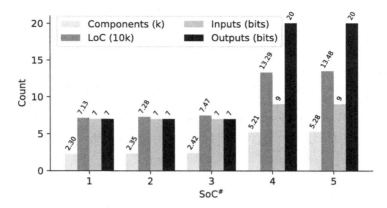

Fig. 7. Design complexity of experimented SoCs. The complexity is indicated by four factors: the number of components, LoC of the code base, bit width of input, and output ports.

Since the GPR and CSR units in evaluated SoCs have the same interface, the register access basic transformation introduces the same design modifications. To diversify the inserted design modifications, different amounts of HWBPs are enabled in SoCs, i.e., 4 HWBPs are enabled in SoC^1, SoC^2 and SoC^3, whereas SoC^4 and SoC^5 are enabled with 8 and 12 HWBPs respectively.

The resource utilization of SoCs is reported by the Vivado® v2018.1 design tool targeting the Arty-7 FPGA board from Xilinx®. All experiments are conducted on an Intel Xeon CPU E5-2690 v4 machine.

Design Area. Figure 8 shows the register and Look-Up-Table (LUT) utilization for the SoCs with and without OCD respectively. Resource utilization indicates the design area. A similar design area increase is observed in SoC^1, SoC^2 and SoC^3. With more HWBPs supported, SoC^4 and SoC^5 require more resources. The area penalty introduced by OCD cannot be neglected, which implies the importance of the RISC-V OCD automation.

Transformation Time. The time consumption of transforming an existing design model into a new design model is defined as the transformation time (Fig. 9). In general, more components and LoC of an SoC indicate a more complex graph representation in terms of vertices, ports, and edges. The increasing graph elements complicate the first step of the rewrite rule application, i.e., subgraph matching. However, around 1.1 s was used to enable external register access for SoCs with different design complexity. The reason is that the proposed approach can match a subgraph efficiently with hierarchical information.

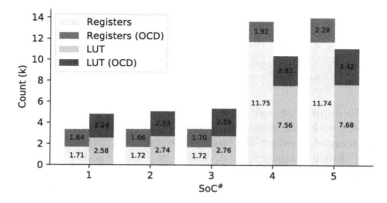

Fig. 8. Resource utilization before and after RISC-V On-Chip Debug (OCD) transformation. Light colors show the resource utilization of experimented SoCs, whereas dark colors depict utilization changes after RISC-V OCD transformation. (Color figure online)

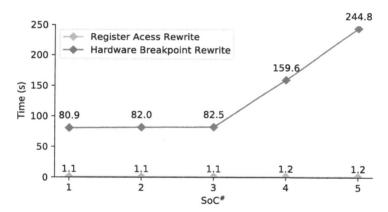

Fig. 9. Transformation time to apply rewrite rules. The hardware breakpoint rewrite rule introduces more design modifications when more hardware breakpoints are enabled. Whereas, the register access rewrite rule introduces the same design modifications in experimented SoCs.

Furthermore, a proportional relationship is observed between the number of enabled HWBPs and the transformation time. This shows, the transformation time for HWBPs increases linearly with introduced design modifications and is independent of the design complexity of target SoCs. This observation confirms the scalability and efficiency of the proposed methodology.

Development Efforts. Table 1 shows the required LoC for hardware transformations in the *MetaRTL* and state-of-the-art manual *VHDL* coding. Following the proposed transformative design methodology, 1.8k LoC is required to implement the RISC-V OCD automation. Whilst, at least 59k LoC needs to

Table 1. On-chip debug development efforts (LoC)

Platform	SoC^1	SoC^2	SoC^3	SoC^4	SoC^5
VHDL		59.0k	60.4k	62.3k	66.5k	73.1k
MetaRTL	1.8k	–	–	–	–

be revisited to implement and integrate the RISC-V OCD instrumentation for evaluated SoCs with the manual approach. As a result, an LoC gain of more than 32x is observed. Further, the error-prone manual approach is replaced with the proposed design transformation, which promotes further modularity and automation in hardware development. Finally, it is important to note that the development efforts with MetaRTL are shown only for SoC^1 in the second row. This means, the transformation script requires only one-time implementation efforts and is applicable for all evaluated SoC models. The actual LoC gain and the code reusability factors are high.

6   Conclusion

In this paper, we propose to satisfy emerging aspectual design requirements such as On-Chip Debug (OCD) and functional safety with the transformative hardware design methodology. The proposed methodology is supported by graph-grammar-based model transformations that are implemented as part of a model-driven hardware generation framework. The model transformations enable aspect orientation in the conventional hardware generation. The aspect orientation separates design concerns and assures high modularity in hardware development. As a result, the complexity of hardware generators is reduced since their focal point is the core functionalities. Whilst, the aspect-oriented instrumentation is separately developed and automatically incorporated with model transformations. For easing transformation development, transformation utilities and reusable basic transformations are provided in the hardware transformation system. To assure quality, introduced design modifications are validated against design constraints and formal properties are generated to verify the transformed designs. Of note, we use one DSL to construct as well as transform designs, which prevents semantic gaps and lowers integration and maintenance burdens in hardware development. To demonstrate the applicability, the RISC-V OCD transformation was implemented and applied to different industry-strength SoCs. Compared to manual VHDL development, the LoC to develop and integrate the OCD instrumentation is reduced more than 32x with the proposed methodology. In particular, the transformation script requires only one-time implementation efforts and is applicable for different SoCs. The achieved high LoC gain and code reuse improve the overall productivity of digital design.

Acknowledgements. The work described herein is partly funded by the German Federal Ministry of Education and Research (BMBF) as part of the research project Scale4Edge (16ME0122K). It has its roots in the BMBF funded projects SAVE4I and COMPACT.

References

1. Shacham, O., et al.: Avoiding game over: bringing design to the next level. In: DAC Design Automation Conference 2012, pp. 623–629. IEEE (2012)
2. Bachrach, J., et al.: Chisel: constructing hardware in a scala embedded language. In: DAC Design Automation Conference 2012, pp. 1212–1221. IEEE (2012)
3. Izraelevitz, A., et al.: Reusability is FIRRTL ground: hardware construction languages, compiler frameworks, and transformations. In: Proceedings of the 36th International Conference on Computer-Aided Design, pp. 209–216. IEEE Press (2017)
4. Clow, J., Tzimpragos, G., Dangwal, D., Guo, S., McMahan, J., Sherwood, T.: A pythonic approach for rapid hardware prototyping and instrumentation. In: 2017 27th International Conference on Field Programmable Logic and Applications (FPL), pp. 1–7. IEEE (2017)
5. Jiang, S., Pan, P., Ou, Y., Batten, C.: PyMTL3: a python framework for open-source hardware modeling, generation, simulation, and verification. IEEE Micro **40**(4), 58–66 (2020)
6. Tim, N., Megan, W.: RISC-V external debug support version 0.13.2. Technical report, SiFive Inc. (2019)
7. ISO, ISO26262: 26262: Road Vehicles-Functional Safety. International Standard ISO/FDIS, vol. 26262 (2011)
8. Kiczales, G., et al.: Aspect-oriented programming. In: Akşit, M., Matsuoka, S. (eds.) ECOOP 1997. LNCS, vol. 1241, pp. 220–242. Springer, Heidelberg (1997). https://doi.org/10.1007/BFb0053381
9. Marconi, S., Conti, E., Placidi, P., Christiansen, J., Hemperek, T.: IEEE standard for SystemVerilog-unified hardware design, specification, and verification language (2013)
10. Traber, A., et al.: PULPino: a small single-core RISC-V SoC. In: 3rd RISCV Workshop (2016)
11. Asanovic, K., et al.: The rocket chip generator. EECS Department, University of California, Berkeley, Technical report UCB/EECS-2016-17 (2016)
12. Gajski, D.D., Wu, A.C.-H., Chaiyakul, V., Mori, S., Nukiyama, T., Bricaud, P.: Embedded tutorial: essential issues for IP reuse. In: Proceedings of the 2000 Asia and South Pacific Design Automation Conference, pp. 37–42 (2000)
13. Ehrig, H., Habel, A., Kreowski, H.-J.: Introduction to graph grammars with applications to semantic networks. Comput. Math. Appl. **23**(6–9), 557–572 (1992)
14. Ecker, W., Devarajegowda, K., Werner, M., Han, Z., Servadei, L.: Embedded systems' automation following OMG's model driven architecture vision. In: 2019 Design, Automation & Test in Europe Conference & Exhibition (DATE), pp. 1301–1306. IEEE (2019)
15. Moiseev, M., Popov, R., Klotchkov, I.: SystemC-to-verilog compiler: a productivity-focused tool for hardware design in cycle-accurate SystemC. In: Design and Verification Conference and Exhibition (DVCon) Europe (2020)
16. López-Ongil, C., Entrena, L., García-Valderas, M., Portela-García, M.: Automatic tools for design hardening. In: Velazco, R., Fouillat, P., Reis, R. (eds.) Radiation Effects on Embedded Systems, pp. 183–200. Springer, Dordrecht (2007). https://doi.org/10.1007/978-1-4020-5646-8_9
17. Reshadi, M.H., Gharehbaghi, A.M., Navabi, Z.: AIRE/CE: a revision towards CAD tool integration. In: ICM 2000. Proceedings of the 12th International Conference on Microelectronics. (IEEE Cat. No. 00EX453), pp. 277–280 (2000)

18. Kleppe, A.G., Warmer, J., Warmer, J.B., Bast, W.: MDA Explained: The Model Driven Architecture: Practice and Promise. Addison-Wesley Professional (2003)
19. Han, Z., Devarajegowda, K., Werner, M., Ecker, W.: Towards a python-based one language ecosystem for embedded systems automation. In: 2019 IEEE Nordic Circuits and Systems Conference (NorCAS): NORCHIP and International Symposium of System-on-Chip (SoC), pp. 1–7. IEEE (2019)
20. I. Societies and the Standards Coordinating Committees of the IEEE Standards Association (IEEE-SA) Standards Board. IEEE Standard VHDL Language Reference Manual. IEEE (2000)
21. Sutherland, S.: The IEEE Verilog 1364–2001 standard what's new, and why you need it. In: 9th International HDL Conference (HDLCon) (2000)
22. Schreiner, J., Findenigy, R., Ecker, W.: Design centric modeling of digital hardware. In: 2016 IEEE International High-Level Design Validation and Test Workshop (HLDVT), pp. 46–52. IEEE (2016)
23. Schreiner, J., Willgerodt, F., Ecker, W.: A new approach for generating view generators. In: Design and Verification Conference and Exhibition (DVCon) (2017)
24. Han, Z., et al.: Aspect-oriented design automation with model transformation. In: 2021 IFIP/IEEE International Conference on Very Large Scale Integration (VLSI-SoC). IEEE (2021)
25. Han, Z., Devarajegowda, K., Neumeier, A., Ecker, W.: IP-coding style variants in a multi-layer generator framework. In: Design and Verification Conference and Exhibition (DVCon) Europe (2020)
26. Drewes, F., Hoffmann, B., Plump, D.: Hierarchical Graph Transformation. J. Comput. Syst. Sci. **64**(2), 249–283 (2002)
27. Bavache, V.B., Han, Z., Hartlieb, H., Kaja, E., Devarajegowda, K., Ecker, W.: Automated SoC hardening with model transformation. In: 2020 17th Biennial Baltic Electronics Conference (BEC), pp. 1–6. IEEE (2020)
28. Dubrova, E.: Fault-Tolerant Design. Springer, Heidelberg (2013). https://doi.org/10.1007/978-1-4614-2113-9
29. Waterman, A., Asanović, K.: The RISC-V instruction set manual. Volume I: Unprivileged v (2020)
30. Devarajegowda, K., Ecker, W., Kunz, W.: How to keep 4-eyes principle in a design and property generation flow. In: MBMV 2019; 22nd Workshop-Methods and Description Languages for Modelling and Verification of Circuits and Systems, pp. 1–6. VDE (2019)
31. Patterson, D.A., Hennessy, J.L.: Computer Organization and Design: The Hardware/Software Interface (2012)

Exploiting Program Slicing and Instruction Clusterization to Identify the Cause of Faulty Temporal Behaviours at System Level

Moreno Bragaglio, Samuele Germiniani$^{(\boxtimes)}$, and Graziano Pravadelli

Department of Computer Science, University of Verona, Verona, Italy
{Moreno.Bragaglio,Samuele.Germiniani,Graziano.Pravadelli}@univr.it

Abstract. Several verification strategies exist to identify unexpected behaviours due to the presence of bugs in system-level HW/SW descriptions. However, when the bug is found, further effort must be spent by the design team to understand its cause and then fix the originating error. This requires a tedious and time-consuming process, generally based on the manual inspection of the execution traces of the design under verification (DUV). This process becomes even more demanding for systems whose behaviours span across wide time windows. Nevertheless, in these cases, usually only a few instructions belonging to long execution traces are relevant for understanding the cause of the unexpected behaviour. Then, we propose a tool that supports the verification engineers in the identification of such a few instructions, to focus their attention on the actual origin of the bug. The tool works by combining dynamic program slicing with a clustering procedure on the execution traces corresponding to unexpected behaviours. Firstly, program slicing is applied to remove instructions not belonging to the cone of influence of the unexpected behaviour. Then, clusters of instructions based on store operations at the LLVM intermediate representation of the DUV are created to guide the heuristic in removing further irrelevant instructions.

Keywords: Bug explanation · Clusterization · Temporal assertions · Program slicing · LLVM · LTL

1 Introduction

Early identification and correction of bugs is a key point in order to save money and speed up the time-to-market of modern embedded systems. In this context, while designers focus on generating a bug-free implementation that meets the specifications, verification engineers work to check that such an implementation indeed satisfies the initial specifications without including unexpected behaviours. Thus, many approaches have been developed both from the point of

© IFIP International Federation for Information Processing 2022
Published by Springer Nature Switzerland AG 2022
V. Grimblatt et al. (Eds.): VLSI-SoC 2021, IFIP AICT 661, pp. 71–92, 2022.
https://doi.org/10.1007/978-3-031-16818-5_4

view of the designers and of the verification engineers to detect bugs and, more generally, unexpected behaviours in system-level descriptions, before they are propagated throughout the lower design levels. However, when such behaviours are found, the verification engineer still has to understand their cause through manual inspection of the execution traces of the design under verification (DUV).

In the context of temporised DUVs, functional requirements involve the concept of time, where behaviours are allowed to span across multiple time units. These behaviours are usually verified using assertions formalised through temporal logic such as linear temporal logic (LTL). Due to its complex nature, understanding and fixing a bug involving temporal logic is way more demanding than finding the cause of an error observable through the failure of a simple propositional assertion. Nonetheless, in both scenarios, understanding the cause of a bug requires a long and tedious manual process of inspection of the execution traces. In most cases, this process is unnecessarily long, since only a few instructions of the execution traces are relevant for understanding and fixing the unwanted behaviours.

To fill in the gap, we present a new methodology and a related tool to automatically remove irrelevant instructions from the execution traces of unexpected temporal behaviours such that verification engineers can focus on the real cause of the problem when debugging their DUV. The tool works on any system-level implementation that can be compiled into a Low-Level Virtual Machine (LLVM) bitcode [1]. Given an unexpected behaviour formalised by means of a propositional assertion, the tool provides the user with a reduced execution trace that still triggers such behaviour, thus highlighting the essential instructions related to it. The underpinning methodology applies a sequence of reductions to the execution trace through a program-slicing-based technique. After each reduction, we verify by simulation if the remaining trace is still an executable program capable of triggering the unexpected behaviour. This procedure works in two phases. Firstly, we remove all the instructions not belonging to the cone of influence of the unexpected behaviour by exploring the dynamic program dependency graph (DPDG). Secondly, we apply a heuristic based on an instruction-clustering procedure to further reduce the remaining trace. In this work, we extend the methodology described in [2] to perform bug explanation of unexpected behaviours modelled as temporal assertions.

The rest of the paper is organised as follows. In Sect. 2, we report the related work. In Sect. 3, we provide a few preliminary definitions necessary to clearly understand the proposed approach. In Sect. 4, we overview the methodology, then we describe in detail each step. In Sect. 5, we describe how to extend the methodology to perform bug explanation with temporal assertions. In Sect. 6, we report the experimental results; finally, in Sect. 7, we draw our conclusions.

2   Related Work

In the last decades, several methodologies, mainly in the software field, have been proposed to tackle the aforementioned problem. A well-known technique to perform fault localisation and bug explanation is, in particular, program slicing.

The original notion of a program slice was proposed by Weiser [3]. Weiser defined a program slice as a reduced program obtained from a program p by removing statements, such that the slice replicates part of the behavior of p. Program slicing techniques fall in two main categories: static and dynamic program slicing. A static slice is computed without making assumptions regarding the input of the program while a dynamic slice relies on some specific test case. Several techniques have been proposed to produce a static slice using reachability algorithms on program dependency graphs (PDG) [4–8]. A PDG is an intermediate program representation to make explicit both data and control dependencies in a program.

Dynamic program slicing was first introduced by Korel and Laski in [9], which allows extracting a (small) executable section of the original program that preserves part of the program's behaviour for a specific input with respect to a subset of selected variables, rather than for all possible computations. One of the most popular applications of dynamic program slicing consists of comparing two or more slices to identify differences or similarities. In [10], the authors present a technique to isolate the region of the bug by computing the difference between a correct slice and the faulty one; likewise, [11] propose an approach to find a correct slice that is the nearest to a related faulty slice. Similar techniques based on intersections and unions between dynamic slices are reported in [12]. In [13], the authors describe a tool to find the cause of a bug by comparing a faulty slice with several correct slices generated through symbolic simulation and converted to sequences of strings. A dynamic program dependency graph is usually employed in conjunction with program slicing as a dynamic variant of a PDG. In a DPDG, dependencies consider a specific occurrence of a certain instruction as there may be several repetitions in a single execution trace. The paper in [14] describes several techniques to exploit a DPDG while performing dynamic program slicing.

Several approaches have been proposed to generate slices by exploiting both static and dynamic information [15–20].

Other approaches rely on statistical methods to perform fault localisation [21,22]. These techniques aim at gathering coverage details of correct and faulty executions over a bugged program, then they rate each programming element in terms of their suspiciousness. In [23] the authors combine dynamic program slicing with statistical methods to build program slicing spectra to rank suspicious elements.

With regard to the use of clustering techniques, Wang et al. [24] proposed a guided technique called "hierarchical program slicing", where the execution trace is divided into phases to simplify the comprehension of data and control dependencies between the instructions in the trace.

The above works provide valid solutions to help the verification engineers in the process of bug localisation and explanation. However, these solutions are usually available only for specific application domains and do not offer a standardised way of defying unexpected behaviors. Furthermore, none of the previous works is capable of providing a reduced execution trace for expected behaviours modelled as temporal assertions.

3   Preliminary Definitions

Definition 1. *An **instruction** is a programming statement following the LLVM bitcode syntax [25].*

Definition 2. *An **execution trace** is a sequence of instructions representing an executable instance of a program.*

Definition 3. *Let i_1 and i_2 be two instructions, i_2 is **data dependent** on i_1 if i_2 accesses a portion of memory allocated or modified by i_1.*

Definition 4. *Let i_1 and i_2 two instructions, where i_1 is a branch with multiple branch targets, if changing the branch target of i_1 may cause i_2 is not executed, then i_2 is **control dependent** on i_1.*

Definition 5. *A **dynamic program dependence graph** is a structure composed of nodes and edges where each node represents an instruction of an execution trace and each edge represents a data or control dependency between instructions. Let n_1, n_2 be two nodes of a DPDG, if n_2 has an incoming edge e_1 connecting n_2 with n_1, then the instruction represented by n_2 is either data dependent or control dependent on the instruction represented by n_1.*

Figure 3 shows an example of a DPDG where red edges are data dependencies and blue edges are control dependencies.

Definition 6. *Linear temporal logic (LTL) is a modal temporal logic used to formalise behaviours spanning multiple instants of time. In LTL, one can encode formulae about the future of paths, e.g., a condition will eventually be true, a condition will be true until another fact becomes true, and so on. We recommend [26] for a full reference of the semantics.*

Definition 7. *An **assertion** is a logic property that must hold during the execution of the design. They are divided into two main categories. I) immediate assertion: a function assert defined inside the source code of the design; it checks if a propositional formula is satisfied when assert is called during execution. A proposition can be any kind of Boolean expression that can be constructed in C by connecting variables using boolean, relational or arithmetic operators. II) temporal assertions: a logic formula formalised using LTL. The truth value of the formula is checked by the simulator independently from the execution of the design. In this work, we allow the formalisation of assertions following the grammar in Fig. 1.*

Definition 8. *Let as be an assertion and $A = \{a_0, a_1, ..., a_n\}$ the set of memory addresses of variables $v_0, v_1, ..., v_n$ on which as predicates, then the memory address a^f is a **fundamental address** of as if $a^f \in A$.*

```
template : G(implication)

implication : tformula -> tformula
        | tformula => tformula
        | {sere} |-> tformula
        | {sere} |=> tformula

tformula: proposition
      | (tformula) | !tformula | tformula && tformula
      | tformula || tformula | tformula xor tformula
      | tformula U tformula | tformula W tformula
      | tformula R tformula | tformula M tformula
      | X [N..(N)?] tformula | X tformula
      | F tformula | {sere}

sere : proposition | (sere) | {sere}
      | sere | sere | sere & sere | sere && sere
      | sere;sere | sere:sere | sere[*N(..N)?]
      | sere[*] | sere[+] | sere[=N(..N)?]
      | sere[->N(..N)?] | ##N sere | ##[N(..N)?] sere
      | sere ##N sere | sere ##[N(..N)?] sere
```

Fig. 1. Temporal assertion grammar

4   Methodology

As shown in Fig. 2, the proposed tool is composed of 3 main steps executed sequentially. The inputs of the tool are the LLVM code of the DUV and a set of propositional assertions capturing the expected behaviours. Additionally, the user can provide the sequences of inputs that eventually falsify the assertions, thus highlighting the presence of a bug. For each failed assertion, the tool produces a sequence of minimal instructions explaining the cause of the failure, i.e., the reason for the bug. Hereafter, we provide an overview of the 3 main steps.

1. **Trace Extraction:** given the failure of an assertion, in the first step of the methodology, we extract the sequences of LLVM instructions that brings the execution to activate the unexpected behaviours. This procedure may occur in two ways, depending on whether the user provided the sequences of inputs or only the assertion. In the first case, the sequence of instructions firing the unexpected behaviour is extracted by executing the implementation with the given inputs until the related assertion fails. In the latter case, we use symbolic simulation to find a sequence of instructions capable of falsifying the assertion.

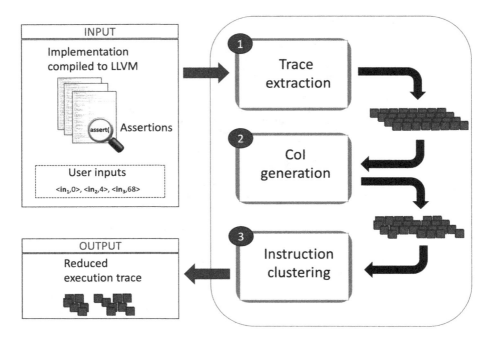

Fig. 2. Methodology execution flow

2. **Cone of Influence Generation:** each trace extracted in the previous step is reduced by applying a dynamic program slicing algorithm to eliminate all instructions not belonging to the cone of influence (CoI) of the assertion. For each trace, we generate a DPDG characterising control and data dependencies between instructions. After that, we apply a reachability algorithm to determine what instructions influence the value of the variables contained in the assertions. The instructions not selected by the above procedure are removed from the trace.

3. **Instruction Clustering:** in the last step of the methodology, we apply a clustering procedure to further reduce the remaining instructions. Our approach consists of dividing the instructions into independent clusters such that applying any reduction procedures to one cluster would not prevent a satisfying minimisation in another. Once such clusters are identified, we apply a combinatorial-based reduction to obtain the minimal sequence in each cluster.

To simplify the exposition, we apply the proposed methodology to the example shown in listing 1.1. It consists of a design written in C implementing a simple arithmetic transformation. The code is decorated with an immediate assertion (line 16) specifying a property that must hold during execution.

```
1  int  in ;
2  int  main ( )  {
3        int  a=0;
4        int  b=5;
5        while  (1)  {
6              in= getNextInput () ;
7              if  ( in == 0)  {
8                    a=4;
9                    a++;
10             } else  if  ( in < 5)  {
11                   a+=10;
12                   a--;
13             } else  if  ( in > 90)  {
14                   a-=2;
15                   b+=3;
16                   assert ( a != 12) ;
17             }
18       }
19 }
```

Listing 1.1. Running example

4.1   Trace Extraction

In the first step of the methodology, we extract the sequences of LLVM instructions that expose the unexpected behaviour, namely, sequences starting with the first instruction of the program and ending with the assertion failure.

In Table 1 we report an execution trace falsifying the assertion contained in the running example. The instructions are labelled with two identifiers: the first uniquely identifies each LLVM instruction, the second links each instruction to its corresponding high-level statement in listing 1.1. To extract such an execution trace, we symbolically simulate the DUV, until we find an execution path that falsifies the target assertion. To accomplish that, we exploit the symbolic simulation engine provided by KLEE [27]. To simulate the DUV with KLEE, the DUV inputs are marked as "symbolic" to declare where symbolic values should be injected. For example, to symbolically simulate the running example, line 6 must be replaced by *klee_make_symbolic(in)*, since variable *in* is the only input. Then the symbolic simulation explores the various paths of the running example, until it finds a path that makes the assertion at line 16 fail. Such a path has the following symbolic constraints: ($in1 == 0$, $in2 < 5$, $in3 > 90$), where the subscript i of ini refers to the value of the variable *in* at the symbolic iteration i.

Symbolic simulation is quite expensive in terms of computational resources. As a matter of fact, it is an exponential-time algorithm; however, if the user already has the required sequence of inputs to activate the bug, it can be run in a linear-time constrained mode, since only one path needs to be explored. In the running example, we assumed the following sequence of inputs: $\{\langle in1, 0\rangle,$

Table 1. LLVM execution trace of the running example

<label>:0:	**<label>:14:**
[0, 1] %1 = alloca i32	[26, 11] %15 = load i32, i32* %2
[1, 3] %2 = alloca i32	[27, 11] %16 = add add nsw i32 %15,10
[2, 5] %3 = alloca i32	[28, 11] store i32 %16, i32* %2
[3, 1] store i32 0, i32* %1	[29, 12] %17 = load i32, i32* %2
[5, 3] store i32 0, i32* %2	[30, 12] %18 = add nsw i32 %17, -1
[7, 4] store i32 5, i32* %3	[31, 12] store i32 %18, i32* %2
[8, 5] br label %4	[32, 18] br label %31
<label>:4: //in=0	**<label>:31:**
[9, 6] store i32 getNextInput(), i32* %1	[33, 5] br label %4
[10, 7] %6 = load i32, i32* %1	**<label>:4:** //in=125
[11, 7] %7 = icmp eq i32 %6, 0	[34, 6] store i32 getNextInput(), i32* %1
[12, 7] br i1 %7, label %8, label %11	[35, 7] %6 = load i32, i32* %1
<label>:8:	[36, 7] %7 = icmp eq i32 %6, 0
[13, 8] store i32 4, i32* %2	[37, 7] br i1 %7, label %8, label %11
[14, 9] %9 = load i32, i32* %2	**<label>:11:**
[15, 9] %10 = add nsw i32 %9, 1	[38, 10] %12 = load i32, i32* %1
[16, 9] store i32 %10, i32* %2	[39, 10] %13 = icmp slt i32 %12, 5
[17, 18] br label %31	[40, 10] br i1 %13, label %14, label %19
<label>:31:	**<label>:19:**
[18, 5] br label %4	[41, 13] %20 = load i32, i32* %1
<label>:4: //in=4	[42, 13] %21 = icmp sgt i32 %20, 90
[19, 6] store i32 getNextInput(), i32* %1	[43, 13] br i1 %21, label %22, label %31
[20, 7] %6 = load i32, i32* %1	**<label>:22:**
[21, 7] %7 = icmp eq i32 %6, 0	[44, 14] = load i32, i32* %2
[22, 7] br i1 %7, label %8, label %11	[45, 14] %24 = sub nsw i32 %23, 2
<label>:11:	[46, 14] store i32 %24, i32* %2
[23, 10] %12 = load i32, i32* %1	[47, 15] %25 = load i32, i32* %3
[24, 10] %13 = icmp slt i32 %12, 5	[48, 15] %26 = add nsw i32 %25, 3
[25, 10] br i1 %13, label %14, label %19	[49, 15] store i32 %26, i32* %3
	[50, 16] %27 = load i32, i32* %2
	[51, 16] %28 = icmp ne i32 %27, 12
	[52, 16] %29 = zext i1 %28 to i32
	[53, 16] %30 = call @assert

$\langle in2, 4 \rangle$, $\langle in3, 125 \rangle$}. Therefore, the symbolic simulation must explore only one path with the following constraints: $in1 == 0$, $in2 == 4$, $in3 == 125$ producing the sequence of instructions reported in Table 1.

4.2   Cone of Influence Generation

In the second step of the methodology, the execution trace extracted in the previous phase is reduced by applying a dynamic program slicing algorithm. The remaining elements of the execution trace correspond to instructions involved directly (or indirectly through association) in data or control dependencies with the variables contained in the failed assertion, that is, the cone of influence of the assertion. The procedure works in three main sub-steps.

In the first step, we generate the DPDG of the execution trace extracted in the first step of the methodology. In the last decades, many algorithms have been proposed to generate DPDGs efficiently, one of which can be found in [28]; therefore, we do not describe such an algorithm in this paper. Figure 3 shows the DPDG for the execution trace listed in Table 1.

In the second step, we identify all *store* instructions in the execution trace accessing fundamental addresses for the target assertion. These are the only instructions that can modify the variables on which the assertion predicates, and therefore, that can change its truth value. We call $fundInst$ the set of instructions collected with the above procedure. Since the algorithm to identify $fundInst$ is trivial, we do not give any further details on it. In the running example, there is only one fundamental address, namely, the memory address of variable a in assertion $a! = 12$. Such an address is allocated by instruction 3 of Table 1 and saved in the LLVM label %2. In this example, $fundInst$ is composed of the store instructions $\{5, 13, 16, 28, 31, 46\}$, which are accessing the address in label %2.

In the last step, we traverse the generated DPDG starting from each store instruction in $fundInst$ and going backward through the incoming edges until a node with no incoming edges is found. By construction, the generated DPDG is an acyclic direct graph, therefore the whole procedure has worst-case time-complexity of $O(V)$, where V is the number of nodes in the DPDG. Each instruction represented by a node in the DPDG that is not visited in the aforementioned procedure will be removed from the execution trace. The whole procedure is formalised in function $extractCoI$ of Algorithm 1.

The inputs of this function are the identifiers corresponding to fundamental instructions $fundInst$, the execution trace $trace$ and the DPDG $dpdg$. First, $visited$ and $reducedTrace$ are declared and initialised (line 2, 3); the first variable contains the visited nodes, while the latter contains the reduced execution trace. After that, we apply the function $backwardDFS$ to all the nodes representing the fundamental instructions in $fundInst$ (line 4–6). Each node is retrieved from the DPDG through the method $getNodeFromeId$ (line 5) which returns a node data structure for a given instruction identifier. The function $backwardDFS$ performs a depth-first search algorithm going backward from the incoming edges of each node. First, the function marks the current node as visited (line 17). After that, it iterates through all the incoming edges of the current node (line 18). Then, it retrieves the source node $sourceNode$ connected to $node$ through $edge$ using the method $getSource$ (line 19). If $sourceNode$ is not already marked (line 20), then we apply $backwardDFS$ recursively using $sourceNode$ as input (line 21).

Algorithm 1. Cone of influence extraction

```
 1: function extractCoI(fundInst, trace, dpdg)
 2:     visited = ∅
 3:     coi_Trace = ∅
 4:     for all fi_id in fundInst do
 5:         node = dpdg.getNodeFromId(fi_id)
 6:         backwardDFS(node, visited)
 7:     end for
 8:     for id = 0, id < trace.size(), id++ do
 9:         if !visited.contains(id) then
10:             reducedTrace.pushBack(trace[id])
11:         end if
12:     end for
13:     return reducedTrace
14: end function
15:
16: function backwardDFS(node, &visited)
17:     visited.insert(node)
18:     for all edge in node.getInEdges() do
19:         sourceNode = edge.getSource()
20:         if !visited.contains(sourceNode.getId()) then
21:             backwardDFS(sourceNode, visited)
22:         end if
23:     end for
24: end function
```

When all the visits are concluded, we iterate on all the instructions in *trace* (line 8) and we add to *coi_Trace* the instructions that do not have a corresponding marked node (line 9–10), that is, that do not have a corresponding node stored in *visited*. Finally, the reduced trace is returned (line 13).

If we apply the above procedure to the running example, the instructions corresponding to nodes 2, 7, 47, 48, 49 are removed from the trace. These nodes are highlighted in red in Fig. 3. Intuitively, these instructions refer to the declaration and utilisation of variable b, which does not have any control or data dependency with variable a in the assertion. From now on, we will use the term *CoI-Trace* to refer to the execution trace reduced with the above procedure.

4.3 Instruction Clustering

In the last step of the methodology, we apply a heuristic procedure to further reduce the remaining instructions in the CoI-Trace. Further reductions are necessary because in most cases, step two of our methodology can not produce a minimal sequence of instructions falsifying an assertion. Consider, for example, the high-level instructions $a++$ and $a--$ contained, respectively, at lines 9 and 12 of the running example. Since the assertion predicates on variable a, which is data-dependent on these instructions, the previous step is not capable

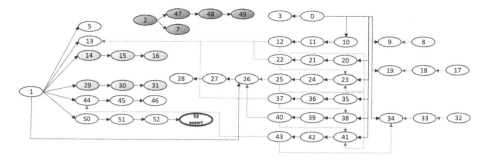

Fig. 3. DPDG of the running example (Color figure online)

of removing them. In theory, any subsequence of instructions of the execution trace could be a minimum sequence of instructions explaining the unexpected behaviour. Therefore, any algorithm seeking to find the minimal sequence would suffer from exponential complexity, and hence, scalability issues. To tackle this problem, our approach splits the instructions of the CoI-Trace into independent clusters such that applying any reduction to one cluster would not prevent a satisfying reduction to another cluster. Since every cluster contains a small number of instructions, it is feasible to quickly find the optimal reduction for each cluster. We generate such clusters by grouping store instructions accessing the same memory address. Note that this is just one method of clustering the instructions, the whole methodology can be still applied with different heuristics. Our clustering heuristic does not produce clusters completely data/control independent from one another; nonetheless, they provide a satisfying amount of independence to apply effective individual reductions. Since each store instruction can only access one memory address, the required clustering procedure is straightforward. In the running example, the clustering procedure produces two clusters for the execution trace of Table 1: $c_1 = \{13, 16, 28, 31, 46\}$ for the stores instructions accessing to the address of variable a, and $c_2 = \{9, 19, 34\}$ for the address of variable in.

Let $a_i, a_2, ..., a_k$ be the addresses accessed in the store instructions of the CoI-Trace, $C = \{c_1, c_2, ..., c_k\}$ is the set of clusters generated with the above procedure, where c_i contains the store instructions for address a_i. We define the **optimal reduction** as the biggest set of instructions $optRed_i = \{i_1, i_2..., i_m\}$ in a cluster c_i such that if the execution trace is stripped of the instructions contained in $optRed_i$, the trace is still an executable program capable of falsifying the assertion. For each cluster, we find its optimal reduction and we remove the respective instructions from the execution trace. In the running example, instructions 16 and 31 correspond to the optimal reduction of cluster c_1. We identify a candidate optimal reduction $optRed_i$ of a cluster c_i by applying a "select and test" procedure. Firstly, we select a subset $s_i \subseteq c_i$, then we remove the selected instructions from the trace. Secondly, we test if the execution trace is still an executable program capable of falsifying the assertion. To perform such

Algorithm 2. Reduction through clustering and slicing

```
 1: function reduce(trace,dpdg)
 2:     finalTrace = trace
 3:     C = generateClusters(trace)
 4:     for all cᵢ in C do
 5:         for s = cᵢ.size(), s > 0, s−− do
 6:             combs = getCombs(cᵢ.size(), s)
 7:             for all combᵢ in combs do
 8:                 c_sel = select(cᵢ, combᵢ)
 9:                 traceˢ = strip(c_sel, finalTrace)
10:                 if test(traceˢ) then
11:                     removeLooseInst(c_sel, dpdg, traceˢ)
12:                     finalTrace = traceˢ
13:                     goto newCluster
14:                 end if
15:             end for
16:         end for
17:         label newCluster
18:     end for
19:     return finalTrace
20: end function
21:
22: function removeLooseInst(c_sel,dpdg,&traceˢ)
23:     for all cⱼ in c_sel do
24:         visited = ∅
25:         node = dpdg.getNodeFromId(cⱼ)
26:         removeLooseNodes(node, visited)
27:         traceˢ.erase(visited)
28:     end for
29: end function
30:
31: function findLooseNodes(node,&visited)
32:     if node.getInEdges().size() > 1 then
33:         return
34:     end if
35:     visited.insert(node)
36:     for all edge in node.getInEdges() do
37:         sourceNode = edge.getSource()
38:         findLooseNodes(sourceNode, visited)
39:     end for
40: end function
```

a test, we exploit the KLEE LLVM interpreter to re-execute the reduced trace. This procedure can produce only three outcomes: (1) the assertion fails during execution; (2) the assertion does not fail; (3) a branch instruction jumps to a different target than the one in the original trace.

In the first scenario, removing the instructions does not affect the truth value of the assertion, hence, the removed instructions are considered a candidate optimal reduction. On the contrary, in the second and third scenario, the removed instructions were necessary to, respectively, falsify or reach the assertion, therefore, they can not be removed from the trace. The biggest candidate optimal reduction identified with the above procedure is the optimal reduction for the given cluster. Step three of our methodology is completely formalised in the function *reduce* of Algorithm 2. First, the function generates the clusters of stores instructions (line 3) through the method *generateClusters*. Then, the selection and test procedure is performed for all clusters. The selection phase works by selecting progressively smaller combinations of cluster instructions (lines 4–8). For example, let $c_p = \{23, 45, 98\}$ be a cluster of instructions, the selection phase starts by selecting combinations of size 3, which is only $\langle 23, 45, 98 \rangle$. After that, it continues with combinations of size two, which are $\langle 23, 45 \rangle$, $\langle 23, 98 \rangle$, $\langle 45, 98 \rangle$ and finishes with combinations of size 1, which are $\langle 23 \rangle$, $\langle 45 \rangle$, $\langle 98 \rangle$. For each combination, a new reduced trace $trace^s$ is generated by removing the corresponding instructions using function *strip* (line 9). $trace^s$ is re-executed through function *test* (line 10). If *test* returns true, then we are in scenario 1 of the aforementioned procedure and c_{sel} is an optimal reduction of c_i. In this case, the newly reduced trace is saved in $finalTrace$ (line 11) and the execution moves to the next cluster (line 13). Finally, when the trace is reduced using all clusters, we return the final trace (line 19). If we apply this procedure to cluster c_1 and c_2 of the running example, we discover that there is no candidate reduction for c_2 as all its store instructions are necessary to explain the unexpected behaviour; on the contrary, cluster c_1 admits an optimal reduction consisting of instructions 16 and 31.

In most cases, removing a store instruction i_s generates a chain of "loose instructions" $i_1, i_2, ..., i_{p-1}, i_p$ where i_s is data dependent only to i_1, i_1 is data dependent only to i_2 ..., i_p is data dependent only on i_{p-1}. Since i_1 is the only data dependence of i_s, removing i_s causes i_1 to become independent from all the other instructions in the trace. Therefore, since i_1 is no longer part of the cone-of-the influence, we can safely remove it from the trace. In the same way, $i_2...i_{p-1}, i_p$ are removed in a chain-reaction fashion once their only dependence is removed. The above procedure is implemented by the function *removeLooseInst* of Algorithm 2. The inputs of *removeLooseInst* are the store instructions c_{sel} removed in the previous iteration of *reduce*, the DPDG *dpdg* and the stripped trace $trace^s$. The procedure works in two phases executed for every instruction in c_{sel} (line 23). First, it finds the nodes *visited* corresponding to loose instructions in *dpdg* using function *findLooseNodes* (line 24–26). Second, the found instructions are removed from $trace^s$ (line 27). Function *findLooseNodes* performs the same task of *backwardDFS*, except that it returns when a node with more than one dependence is found (line 32). By removing instructions 16 and 31 in the running example, we generate the loose instructions 14, 15 and 29, 30, respectively. These instructions are removed automatically through the *removeLooseInst* function. Overall, step three of the methodology removes instructions 14, 15, 16, 29, 30, 31 whose corresponding nodes are highlighted in blue in Fig. 3.

5   Bug Explanation with Temporal Assertions

In this section, we describe how to extend the methodology in Sect. 4 to perform bug explanation where the unexpected behaviour is identified through a failing temporal assertion. First, we describe how to handle the advancement of time (Sect. 5.1). After that, we report how to extract an execution trace that makes a temporal assertion fail (Sect. 5.2). Finally, we show how to modify the extracted trace in order to apply the techniques explained in the second and third steps of the methodology (Sect 5.3).

5.1   Time Flow

Temporal assertions are an invaluable tool to verify synchronous RTL designs where the advancement of time is usually defined through a clock signal. Each time a clock signal reaches a positive (or negative) edge, time advances by 1 unit inside the assertion. However, in the specific domain of application of this work, there is no signal that is responsible for articulating the advancement of time. To solve this issue, in this work time advances by one time unit each whenever a new input is provided to the design. The values of the variables inside an assertion at time t_i (corresponding to the i-th input) are equal to the values of the corresponding variables inside the design before executing the instructions necessary to read $input_{i+1}$. In the running example, the value of variable a is equal to 0 at time t_0, before reading the first input. a becomes equal to 5 after receiving the first input $\langle input_1, 0 \rangle$ at time t_1. Note that inside the assertion, the first evaluation unit is t_1 (first sample of the variables) and not t_0.

If the executions reads multiple consecutively inputs, they are all considered part of the same time unit. For example, if the execution is currently at time t_j and the simulation must execute the following instructions

```
1        in1 = getNextInput1();
2        in2 = getNextInput2();
3        in3 = getNextInput3();
```

then, time is equal to t_{j+1} after executing the third statement. This is necessary to allow the evaluation of multiple inputs on a single time unit.

In this work, we consider only safety assertions following the template $always(antecedent \rightarrow consequence)$ (see Definition 7) where both the antecedent and the consequent can be any LTL temporal formula.

5.2   Trace Extraction

Evaluating temporal assertions while performing symbolic simulation presents several additional issues, we describe the main challenges below.

– The assertion is no longer part of the source code of the design; therefore, it must be handled by the simulator outside the simulation.

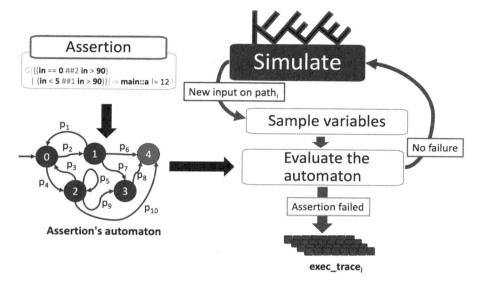

Fig. 4. Trace extraction with temporal assertion

- The variables used inside an assertion might not be always available during simulation; this happens because the existence in memory of a variable depends on the scope in which it is declared.
- The symbolic simulation explores several computational paths; therefore, the simulator must keep track of the state of the temporal assertion for every path.

To solve the above issues, we have developed the procedure described in Fig. 4.

Before starting the simulation, the LTL assertion is translated to a checker in the form of a deterministic finite-state automaton. The automaton always contains a root node as the initial state of the checker and a rejecting node where the assertion fails. The state of a checker is completely identified with an unsigned integer. Each edge is labelled with a propositional formula. Given a checker ch in state s_i and a proposition p_k on the outer edge connecting s_i with s_j; if p_k is true for the current sample, then s_j is the next state of the checker. A sample is a set of couples $S_i = \{(var_1, val_1)_i, ..., (var_n, val_n)_i\}$ where each element $(var_j, val_j)_i$ corresponds to value val_j at time i of variable var_j; $var_1, ..., var_n$ are the variables contained in the LTL assertion. To determine value val_j, the simulator must know the scope in which to find the corresponding variable var_j; therefore, the user has to add such information in the assertion by appending the scope to the variable. In the assertion of Fig. 4, variable a is used as $main :: a$ since it is declared in the main function; likewise, variable in is used without any additional information to specify that it is declared in the global scope. If the simulator tries to make a sample of variable var_k that does not exist in memory at time i, then the sample will contain a val_k equal to 0.

Algorithm 3. Automaton's evaluation

```
 1: function evalAutomaton(aut, samp)
 2:     for all outEdge in aut.currState.outEdges do
 3:         if outEdge.prop.evaluate(samp) then
 4:             aut.state = edge.toState
 5:             if outEdge.toState.type == Rejecting then
 6:                 return false
 7:             end if
 8:             break
 9:         end if
10:     end for
11:     return true
12: end function
```

Function *evalAutomaton* of Algorithm 3 formalises how to perform an evaluation for an automaton *aut* and a sample *samp*. The function searches for an outer edge *outEdge* labelled with a proposition that is true for sample *samp* (line 2–3). After that, the state of the automaton is updated (line 4). If the next state is rejecting (line 5), then the function returns false to notify that the assertion failed (line 6). If the next state is not rejecting, then the function returns true as the assertion did not fail on the current time unit (line 11).

Once the checker and all the utilities to evaluate it on a trace are prepared, we perform symbolic simulation to identify a computational path on which the assertion fails. To do that, we have extended the KLEE framework [27]. In particular, each time a new input must be read in the execution (new symbolic value), the simulator creates a sample of the variables and evaluates the checker on the current time unit. Note that each computational path (called Execution-State in KLEE) contains a unique instance of the checker stored as an unsigned integer (we only need to keep track of its current state). If the evaluation of $checker_i$ on $path_i$ returns false, then the assertion failed and a faulty execution trace $exec\_trace_i$ is found; otherwise, the simulation continues. As in Sect. 4.1, if the user provided the inputs necessary to make the assertion fail, then only one path is explored by the symbolic simulation.

5.3 Trace Decoration

In this section, we describe how to modify an extracted execution trace to include the information of the failure of a temporal assertion. The result of this procedure is a set of decorated execution traces on which to apply steps 2 and 3 of the methodology described in Sect. 4. To simplify the exposition, we will refer to the example in Fig. 5. The example involves the same implementation reported in listing 1.1 that generates the same execution trace reported in Table 1 on which assertion a_1 fails.

The methodology is based on the assumption that the failure of a temporal assertion can be described as a sequence of propositions $\langle p_1, ..., p_n \rangle$ that are true

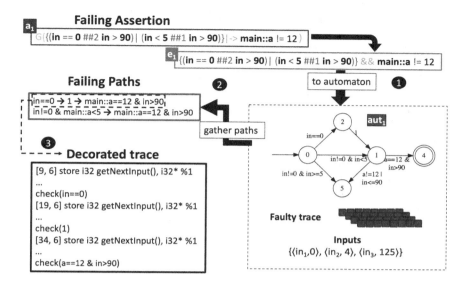

Fig. 5. Trace decoration of the running example

on a sequence of time units $\langle 1, ..., n \rangle$, where p_i is true at time i. For example, assertion a_1 of Fig. 5 fails if the sequence of propositions $\langle in! = 0 \;\&\; a < 5,\; a == 12 \;\&\; in > 90 \rangle$ is true on two consecutive time units. This sequence of propositions corresponds to an accepting path of the automaton generated from the expression $ant \;\&\; !con$, where ant and con is the antecedent and the consequent of the original assertion. The simulator deduces that the assertion fails on the execution trace by checking that all the propositions in the sequence are true on the corresponding time units.

The whole procedure consists of three main steps. First, the original assertion $G(antecedent \rightarrow consequent)$ is converted to the expression $antecedent \;\&\; !consequent$ and translated to an automaton. Note that this automaton contains both accepting and rejecting states. Figure 5 contains the conversion of assertion a_1 to expression e_1 and its translation to automaton aut_1.

In the second step, the procedure retrieves the paths of the automaton justifying the failure of the assertion on the execution trace. This process is formalised in function $retrievePaths$ of Algorithm 4. The idea of the algorithm is to evaluate the edges of the automaton using the samples of the execution trace to build the sequences of propositions that make the assertion fail. The inputs of function $retrievePaths$ are the automaton aut and the list of samples $samps$. Variables $paths$ contains the list of retrieved paths, and $currPath$ is a utility variable used to build the paths (line 2–3). The algorithm starts by evaluating the edges of the accepting state of the automaton (where the assertion fails) with the last sample of the execution trace (lines 4–6). In the running example, the algorithm starts from state 4 of aut_1 with the sample obtained after the

---

Algorithm 4. Function to retrieve the paths triggering the failure

---

1: **function** $retrievePaths(aut, samps)$
2:    $paths = \emptyset$
3:    $currPath = \emptyset$
4:    **for all** $inEdge$ in $aut.accState.inEdges$ **do**
5:        $visitAut(inEdge, aut, samps, paths, currPath, samps.size() - 1)$
6:    **end for**
7:    **return** $paths$
8: **end function**
9:
10: **function** $visitAut(currEdge, aut, samps, paths, currPath, si)$
11:    **if** $currEdge.prop.evaluate(samps[si])$ **then**
12:        $currPath.push\_front(currEdge.prop)$
13:        $si--$
14:        **if** $currEdge.fromState == aut.rootNode$ **then**
15:            $paths.push\_back(currPath)$
16:        **else if** $si >= 0$ **then**
17:            **for all** $inEdge$ in $currEdge.fromNode.inEdges$ **do**
18:                $visitAut(inEdge, aut, samps, paths, currPath, si)$
19:            **end for**
20:        **end if**
21:        $si++$
22:        $currPath.pop\_front()$
23:    **end if**
24: **end function**

---

third input $\langle in3, 125 \rangle$}. For each edge $aut.accState.inEdge$, the algorithm calls function $visitAut$. Among the inputs of $visitAut$ we have the edge $currEdge$ with which the function is trying to build a path and the index si to keep track of which sample must be used to evaluate the proposition on $currEdge$. At line 5, $visitAut$ he is called with si equal to $sample.size() - 1$ to specify that the path is built from the last sample (last time unit). Function $visitAut$ recursively visits the inner edges of each state of aut in a DFS fashion (line 10–24). Each time the function manages to build a path that connects the root state with the accepting state of aut (line 14), a new path is found and stored in $paths$ (line 15). Figure 5 reports the two failing paths retrieved from assertion a_1 in the running example.

In the final step of the procedure, each sequence of propositions is used to generate a decorated execution trace. Formally, a sequence of propositions $\langle p_1, ..., p_n \rangle$ is used to decorate an execution trace with a sequence of checkpoints $\langle c_1, ..., c_n \rangle$ where c_i is a function that returns true if p_i is true at time i, false otherwise. If all checkpoints return true, then the assertion must fail on the execution trace. Figure 5 reports the execution trace decorated with one of the failing paths.

Once a decorated execution trace is generated, we can easily apply the techniques described in the second and third steps of the methodology by considering the differences highlighted below.

- The DPDG must consider the fundamental addresses of all the propositions in the checkpoints
- To determine if an assertion fails on a decorated execution trace, the simulator must verify that all the checkpoints return true.

6   Experimental Results

The proposed methodology has been implemented in an automatic tool extending the KLEE symbolic engine. Its effectiveness and efficency has been evaluated on four well-known C benchmarks compiled to LLVM:

- *xtea* implements the Extended Tiny Encryption Algorithm;
- *matrix mult* is a matrix multiplication algorithm;
- *graph DFS* is a depth first search algorithm;
- *Newton-Raphson* is the famous root finding algorithm.

The experimental results have been carried out on a 2.9 GHz Intel Core i7 processor equipped with 16 GB of RAM and running Ubuntu 20.04 LTS.

Table 2 reports the results in terms of execution time and reduction quality referred to an execution trace exposing a bug for each design. In particular, Table 2 compares the results of our tool with a *baseline* obtained by applying the best achievable reduction, that is, by manually inspecting the trace and removing the unnecessary instructions; indeed, this procedure can be performed only on short traces. The second column (*Original length*) reports the length of the original execution trace that makes the assertion fail, before applying any reduction. The third column (*Our approach*) reports the final length of the trace after applying our approach. The fourth column (*Manual Inspection*) reports the baseline. The fifth column reports the reduction quality as a ratio between "Manual inspection" and "Our approach". Here we can observe that our tool produces results very close to the baseline (reduction quality close to 1) for all the reported tests. The last column reports the execution time of our tool.

Table 3, instead, shows the scalability of our approach. It reports, for the *Netwon-Raphson* benchmark, the reduction percentage and the execution time at the increasing of the length of the target execution trace. These results show that our tool is capable, in a few seconds, of providing a reduction of over 60% of the original trace, even for traces hundreds of instructions long.

Table 2. Analysis of the reduction quality

Name	Original length	Reduced length		Reduction quality	Reduction time
		Our approach	Manual inspection		
xtea	190	155	155	1	1830 ms
Matrix mult	150	127	122	0.96	2631 ms
Newton-Raphson	213	76	76	1	2056 ms
Graph DFS	236	207	205	0.99	4623 ms

Table 3. Analysis of the approach's scalability

Original length	Reduced length	Reduction time	Reduction
482	154	3 s	68.05%
1379	389	36 s	71.79%
10283	2888	437 s	71.91%

7   Conclusions

In this paper, we presented a new methodology and a related tool to automatically remove irrelevant instructions from execution traces identifying unexpected behaviours in system-level designs. Starting from an unexpected behaviour formalised through an assertion, the tool generates a reduced execution trace that triggers such behaviour, thus highlighting the essential instructions related to it. To achieve that, we perform a preliminary reduction involving a DPDG and dynamic program slicing; then, the remaining instructions are further reduced through an instruction clusterization procedure. One of the main aspects of our methodology is that we verify by simulation if the remaining trace is still capable of triggering the unexpected behaviour; therefore, the output trace corresponds to an executable program.

After that, the methodology was modified to support temporal behaviours. This last extension opens a whole new world of possibilities, allowing the application of old and new program slicing techniques to systems implementing functional behaviours described by means of LTL formulas.

Experimental results show the effectiveness and scalability of the approach.

References

1. Lattner, C., Adve, V.: LLVM: a compilation framework for lifelong program analysis & transformation. In: Proceeding of CGO (2004)
2. Bragaglio, M., Donatelli, N., Germiniani, S., Pravadelli, G.: System-level bug explanation through program slicing and instruction clusterization. In: 2021 IFIP/IEEE 29th International Conference on Very Large Scale Integration (VLSI-SoC), pp. 1–6 (2021)

3. Weiser, M.: Program slicing. In: IEEE Transactions on Software Engineering, vol. SE-10, no. 4, pp. 352–357 (1984)
4. Ottenstein, K. J., Ottenstein, L.M.: The program dependence graph in a software development environment. In: Proceedings of the First ACM SIGSOFT/SIGPLAN Software Engineering Symposium on Practical Software Development Environments, ser. SDE 1. New York, NY, USA. Association for Computing Machinery, pp. 177–184 (1984). https://doi.org/10.1145/800020.808263
5. Ferrante, J., Ottenstein, K.J., Warren, J.D.: The program dependence graph and its use in optimization. ACM Trans. Program. Lang. Syst. **9**(3), 319–349 (1987)
6. Bergeretti, J.-F., Carré, B.A.: Information-flow and data-flow analysis of while-programs. ACM Trans. Program. Lang. Syst. **7**(1), 37–61 (1985). https://doi.org/10.1145/2363.2366
7. Kuck, D.J., Kuhn, R.H., Padua, D.A., Leasure, B., Wolfe, M.: Dependence graphs and compiler optimizations. In: Proceedings of the 8th ACM SIGPLAN-SIGACT Symposium on Principles of Programming Languages, ser. POPL 1981, New York, NY, USA. Association for Computing Machinery, pp. 207–218 (1981). https://doi.org/10.1145/567532.567555
8. Reps, T., Bricker, T.: Illustrating interference in interfering versions of programs. In: Proceedings of the 2nd International Workshop on Software Configuration Management, ser. SCM 1989, New York, NY, USA. Association for Computing Machinery, pp. 46–55 (1989). https://doi.org/10.1145/72910.73347
9. Korel, B., Laski, J.: Dynamic slicing of computer programs. J. Syst. Softw. **13**(3), 187–195 (1990)
10. Chen, T., Cheung, Y.: Dynamic program dicing. In: Proceeding of IEEE CSM, pp. 378–385 (1993)
11. Renieres, M., Reiss, S.: Fault localization with nearest neighbor queries. In: Proceeding of IEEE ASE, pp. 30–39 (2003)
12. Wong, W.E., Qi, Y.: Effective program debugging based on execution slices and inter-block data dependency. J. Syst. Softw. **79**(7), 891–903 (2006)
13. Germiniani, S., Danese, A., Pravadelli, G.: Automatic generation of assertions for detection of firmware vulnerabilities through alignment of symbolic sequences. In: IEEE Transactions on Emerging Topics in Computing (2020)
14. Duanzhi, C.: A collection of program slicing. In: Proceeding of ICCASM (2010)
15. Field, J., Ramalingam, G., Tip, F.: Parametric program slicing. In: Proceedings of the 22nd ACM SIGPLAN-SIGACT Symposium on Principles of Programming Languages, ser. POPL 1995, New York, NY, USA. Association for Computing Machinery, pp. 379–392 (1995). https://doi.org/10.1145/199448.199534
16. Field, J., Tip, F.: Dynamic dependence in term rewriting systems and its application to program slicing. In: Hermenegildo, M., Penjam, J. (eds.) PLILP 1994. LNCS, vol. 844, pp. 415–431. Springer, Heidelberg (1994). https://doi.org/10.1007/3-540-58402-1_29
17. J. Q. Ning, J.Q., Engberts, A., Kozaczynski, W.: Automated support for legacy code understanding. Commun. ACM, **37**(5), 50–57 (1994). https://doi.org/10.1145/175290.175295
18. Venkatesh, G.A.: The semantic approach to program slicing. In: Proceedings of the ACM SIGPLAN 1991 Conference on Programming Language Design and Implementation, ser. PLDI 1991, New York, NY, USA. Association for Computing Machinery, pp. 107–119 (1991). https://doi.org/10.1145/113445.113455
19. Kramkar, M., Fritzson, P., Shahmehri, N.: Interprocedural dynamic slicing applied to interprocedural data flow testing. In: Conference on Software Maintenance, vol. 1993, pp. 386–395 (1993)

20. Choi, J.-D., Miller, B.P., Netzer, R.H.B.: Techniques for debugging parallel programs with flowback analysis. ACM Trans. Program. Lang. Syst. **13**(4), 491–530 (1991). https://doi.org/10.1145/115372.115324
21. Liu, C., Fei, L., Yan, X., Han, J., Midkiff, S.: Statistical debugging: a hypothesis testing-based approach. IEEE Trans. Softw. Eng. **32**(10), 831–848 (2006)
22. Liblit, B., Naik, M., Zheng, A. X., Aiken, A., Jordan, M.I.: Scalable statistical bug isolation. In: Proceeding of ACM SIGPLAN PLDI, pp. 15–26 (2005)
23. Wen, W.: Software fault localization based on program slicing spectrum. In: Proceeding of IEEE ICSE, pp. 1511–1514 (2012)
24. Wang, T., Roychoudhury, A.: Hierarchical dynamic slicing. In: Proceedings of the 2007 International Symposium on Software Testing and Analysis, ser. ISSTA 2007, New York, NY, USA. Association for Computing Machinery, pp. 228–238 (2007). https://doi.org/10.1145/1273463.1273494
25. https://llvm.org/docs/LangRef.html
26. Standard for property specification language (PSL). In: IEC 62531:2012(E) (IEEE Std 1850–2010), pp. 1–184 (2012)
27. Cadar, C., Dunbar, D., Engler, D.: Klee: unassisted and automatic generation of high-coverage tests for complex systems programs. In: Proceeding of USENIX OSDI (2008)
28. Harrold, M.J., Malloy, B., Rothermel, G.: Efficient construction of program dependence graphs. In: Proceeding of ACM ISSTA, pp. 160–170 (1993)

A DfT Strategy for Detecting Emerging Faults in RRAMs

Thiago Santos Copetti(✉), Tobias Gemmeke(✉),
and Leticia Maria Bolzani Poehls(✉)

Chair of Integrated Digital Systems and Circuit Design - IDS,
RWTH Aachen University, Aachen, Germany
{copetti,gemmeke,poehls}@ids.rwth-aachen.de
https://www.ids.rwth-aachen.de/

Abstract. Limitations on Complementary Metal Oxide Semiconductor (CMOS) technology scaling combined with the increasing demand for emerging applications requiring high computing and storage capabilities pose significant challenges to device technologies and computer architectures. From the point of view of device technology, memristive devices have become the most promising candidate to complement and/or replace CMOS technology. The key advantages are the memristive device's CMOS manufacturing process compatibility, zero standby power consumption, high scalability and density, as well as the memristive device's capability to implement high-density memories as well as new computing paradigms. Despite all these advantages, these novel devices are also susceptible to manufacturing deviations that may cause faulty behaviors not observed in CMOS technology, significantly increasing the test complexity. In such context, this paper presents a Design-for-Testability (DfT) strategy able to detect traditional as well as unique faults in Resistive Random Access Memories (RRAMs). In more detail, an on-chip sensor able to perform electrical measurements, while performing a predefined operating sequence, was implemented using an X-Fab technology library. The obtained results demonstrate the proposed strategy's capability to detect unique faults in RRAM cells. Finally, the paper provides a discussion about introduced overheads and implementation granularity.

Keywords: RRAMs · DfT strategy · Traditional faults · Unique faults

1 Introduction

Over the last fifty years, Moore's and Dennard's laws dictated the CMOS technology miniaturization rate [1,2]. Limitations on the continued transistor scaling and the increasing demand for emerging applications, requiring high-performance systems with strict constraints, pose significant challenges to device technologies and computer architectures. Device technology faces the following three walls, preventing further transistor scaling [3,4]: (a) the reliability wall - associated with a failure rate increase and lifetime reduction; (b) the leakage wall - meaning that the static power consumption becomes even more important than the dynamic power consumption when considering the overall power

© IFIP International Federation for Information Processing 2022
Published by Springer Nature Switzerland AG 2022
V. Grimblatt et al. (Eds.): VLSI-SoC 2021, IFIP AICT 661, pp. 93–111, 2022.
https://doi.org/10.1007/978-3-031-16818-5_5

consumption, and (c) the cost wall - showing that the cost per transistor via pure geometric scaling is plateauing, with no tendency to get cheaper. From the computer architecture point of view, the following walls can be identified: (a) the memory wall - due to the limited memory bandwidth that impacts performance and energy consumption of data-intensive applications as well as the growing gap between memory and processor speeds; (b) the power wall - as the practical power limit for cooling is reached and consequently, there is no possibility to further increase the CPU clock frequency; and (c) the Instruction Level Parallelism (ILP) wall - related to the always increasing complexity of keeping all cores running in parallel. These aspects limit the use of CMOS technology and von Neumann architectures as solutions for emerging applications' implementation and increase the necessity for novel devices and architectures. Memristive devices represent one of the most promising candidates to complement and/or replace CMOS technology mainly due to their CMOS manufacturing process compatibility, zero standby power consumption, as well as high scalability and density [4]. However, the fabrication of memristive devices is prone to manufacture deviations, including process variation and manufacturing defects, that can result in faults [5]. A fault is defined as any deviation from the memristor's expected behavior due to process variations, manufacturing defects, or design-induced anomalies [5]. The fault size is related to the deviation's magnitude and can be categorized into three different classes. A deviation higher than the tolerance limit is classified as catastrophic. However, if the deviation only degrades the performance, it is categorized as parametric. Finally, if the deviation's magnitude is insignificant, the fault is called benign. Thus, the use of these novel devices depends on being able to guarantee their proper behavior after manufacturing. Memristive devices are usually integrated during the CMOS Back-End-Of-Line (BEOF) manufacturing process. In this context, it becomes mandatory to properly test the fabricated devices after manufacturing, which requires accurate fault models derived from realistic manufacturing defects. In [6], the authors provide a review of the memristive device manufacturing process as well as a discussion related to the possible defects that may affect these novel devices, identifying the relation between manufacturing failure mechanisms and faulty behaviors. Literature shows that Resistive Random Access Memory (RRAM) cells can be affected not only by traditional faults, but also by unique faults [6–9], demanding the development of new manufacturing test procedures able to properly detect these faults [10,11]. In the last few years, some strategies were proposed in order to test memristor-based circuits. A fault model and two Design-for-Testability (DfT) schemes for RRAMs are presented in [7]. The DfT schemes exploit the access time duration and supply voltage level of RRAM cells to facilitate the detection of unique faults. Moreover, the traditional March Tests that explore the execution of predefined read and write operations applied at each RRAM cell are extremely time-consuming and are also not able to guarantee the detection of all unique faults. In [12] the authors presented a scheme based on "sneak-path sensing" able to test multiple elements of Phase Change Memories (PCM) at the same time (1R RRAM cells). The detection is based on a comparison between the output current related to a specific group of cells and the ideal current. The groups are accessed based on the execution of March elements. The main drawback of this scheme is related to the fact that it only works for RRAMs that have sneak-paths as well as the fact that the amount of cells that can be tested in parallel is limited.

In such context, this paper proposes a DfT strategy based on the introduction of an on-chip sensor able to perform electrical measurements, while performing a predefined operating sequence to detect both traditional and unique faults in RRAMs. Note that this paper extends the work described in [13]. In more detail, this paper presents an optimized version of the on-chip sensor proposed in [13], making the DfT strategy able to detect all unique faults that can affect RRAM cells. The validation of the proposed strategy was performed using a 1T1R RRAM cell implemented using a 350 nm X-Fab technology library and a memristive model described in [14]. A defect injection scheme based on the introduction of resistors on the 1T1R RRAM cell was adopted. The obtained results demonstrated that the proposed approach is able to detect traditional and unique faults. Finally, the paper also provides a more complete analysis and discussion about introduced overheads and possible implementation granularity when considering a crossbar memory array.

2   Background

This Section presents concepts related to memristive devices as well as existing fault models associated to these novel devices.

2.1   Memristive Devices

In 1971, Leon Chua postulated the fourth basic circuit element named memristive device, or memristor, while trying to establish a missing constitutive relationship between electrical charge and magnetic flux [15]. A memristive device is a passive element that can be described by the time integral of the current (charge q) through the time integral of the voltage (flux ϕ) across its two terminals [15]. The memristive device has at least two distinct states, the High Resistance State (HRS) and the Low Resistance State (LRS), and can switch from HRS (LRS) to LRS (HRS) by applying a voltage VSET (VRESET) with an absolute value larger than its threshold voltage (Vth). The essential fingerprint of memristive devices is the pinched current-voltage (I-V) hysteresis loop, illustrated in Fig. 1(a). Note that when the memristive device is floating, or when the voltage v(t) across the device is zero, the current i(t) is also zero [16]. An RRAM data storage element is a three-layer device consisting of a dielectric sandwiched between two metal electrodes. In more detail, the memory cell is based on Metal/Insulator/Metal (MIM) structure [17]. The "M" in MIM denotes any reasonably good electron conductor, often asymmetric for the two sides with respect to the materials' work function and oxygen affinity, while "I" stands for insulator, often an ion or mixed conducting oxide or higher chalcogenide. Figure 1(b)

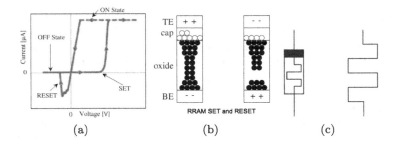

Fig. 1. (a) I-V characteristics of a bipolar resistive switching device [16], (b) Conductive filament in bipolar RRAM, and (c) Symbols used for representing memristive devices [18].

depicts the RRAM device including the Bottom Electrode (BE), the Top Electrode (TE) and the internal structure (metallic oxide and capping layer). When VSET is applied, the oxygen ions are attracted to the capping layer (cap) and leave behind a conductive chain of vacancies that is called a Conductive Filament (CF). However, when VRESET is applied, some of the oxygen ions move back into the oxide and rupture the CF. Figure 1(c) shows two optional symbols used for representing memristive devices, where the black square of the left symbol represents the device's terminal for positive voltage switching [18].

Memristive devices can be initially classified into two types: (a) ionic thin film and molecular memristors, and (b) magnetic and spin-based memristor [19]. When used as memory devices, ionic thin film and molecular memristors are called resistive memories, more precisely RRAMs, being classified as a non-volatile memory [19,20]. Note that RRAMs can be further classified as unipolar or bipolar, filamentary or area dependent switching-based, and finally according to their switching mechanism as Valence Change Mechanism (VCM), Electrochemical Mechanism (ECM) and, Thermochemical Mechanism (TCM) [17]. When considering filamentary switching, the CF is formed through the electroforming process, which is a soft breakdown phenomenon that creates a locally degraded region with a high defect concentration [20]. Note that the CF is made out of metallic impurities or oxygen vacancies, which are responsible for charge transport. Thus, filamentary, memristive VCM cells can be manufactured using different materials, such as TaOx, HfOx, and TiOx. The memristor can be manufactured on a silicon-based substrate or on a processed integrated circuit with planarized contact pads. In general terms, the memristor's fabrication includes the same basic processes, such as lithography, deposition, and etching [3,21]. It is important to highlight that after manufacturing, especially the oxide-based filamentary-type devices, usually have a very high electrical resistance and a large voltage is required for the very first SET operation, also known as the forming process [16]. This process, a controlled soft breakdown, drastically reduces the device resistance allowing the resistance switching behavior in the subsequent cycles.

2.2   Defect Injection Schemes and Fault Models

The manufacturing process of memristive devices aims to create devices composed of three main parts, the BE, the Transition Metal Oxide (TMO) and finally, the TE [6]. The fabrication of memristive devices includes the same basic processes as CMOS circuits, including lithography, deposition and etching [6]. Thus, like any other device, memristors are prone to defects potentially generated during the manufacturing process due to deviations and failure mechanisms. These defects need to be properly modeled in order to guarantee an accurate identification of possible faulty behaviors of RRAM cells. Functional faults always impact the memory's functionality and can be also referred to as strong faults [22]. Contrarily, parametric faults cause parametric deviations and can be also referred to as weak faults [22]. Faults can also be further classified according to their detection conditions. In more detail, faults whose detection is guaranteed using only read and write operations, March elements, are classified as functional Easy-to-Detect (ETD) faults. They have deterministic behavior, and therefore will always lead to a logic faulty behavior that can be detected by writing into or reading from the memory cell. However, faults whose detection is not guaranteed using only read and write operations are classified as Hard-to-Detect (HTD) faults [23].

Defect Injection Scheme: According to literature, manufacturing defects can be injected based on the following two different models: (a) Resistive Defect (RD) model or (b) Defect Oriented (DO) model [11]. On one hand, the simulation of memristive device's faults can be done by adopting defect injection schemes based on the introduction of resistors, known as RD model. In such models, the resistance values correspond to the strength of the defects [16]. On the other hand, the simulation of a memristive device's faulty behavior can be done by altering the electrical properties of the device itself, known as DO model. It is important to highlight that all traditional and unique faults considered in this paper are modeled using the RD model.

Conventional Fault Model: The conventional fault model of RRAMs is composed of faults that are also observed in CMOS-based memories, such as:

- Stuck-at-Fault (SAF): the cell has its logic value stuck-at in one state, LRS or HRS [24];
- Transition Fault (TF) or Slow Write Fault (SWF): the cell fails to undergo a RESET or SET operation in the allowed time [11]. Note that the fault may occur only in one transition direction, from '1' to '0' or from '0' to '1';
- Read Disturb Fault (RDF): the cell returns a correct logic value when a read operation is performed, while the data that is stored by the cell is flipped by the read operation [11];
- Incorrect Read Fault (IRF): the cell returns an incorrect logic value when a read operation is performed, while the data stored by the cell is correct and not affected by the read operation [11];

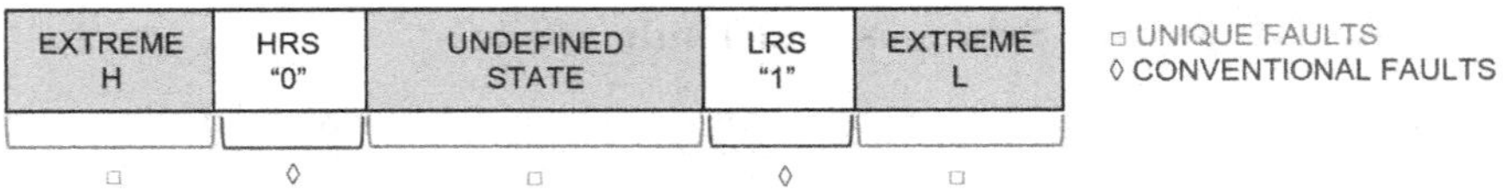

Fig. 2. Unique fault model: resistance intervals of faulty-free and faulty memristive devices.

- State Coupling Fault (CFst): the state of an a-cell (aggressor) impacts the data of a v-cell (victim) [25];
- Write Disturbance Fault (WDF): a write operation in a-cell changes the data in the v-cell. This fault can appear after a cycle of operations (dynamic WDF - dWDF) [26].

Unique Fault Model. As previously mentioned, there are some exclusive faulty behaviors for RRAMs, including the following emerging faults:

- Undefined Write Fault (UWF): after a writing operation the cell is brought into an undefined state 'U' between '0' and '1', HRS and LRS [11];
- Deep State Fault (DeepF): the resistance in the cell is beyond the boundaries for each state of the cell [27];
- Unknown Read Fault (URF): the read operation results in unknown data, which means a random logic value at the output, independent from the reading conditions [11,12]. A URF can occur when LRS and HRS are close to each other or when a state 'U' is stored in the cell. Note that the state 'U' needs to be detected because it indicates misbehavior in the memristor.

Figure 2 depicts the faulty resistance intervals of memristive devices, where the regions highlighted in blue represent emerging faults associated to the unique fault model.

3   The Proposed DfT Strategy

This Section describes the proposed DfT strategy including details related to its specification as well as implementation.

3.1   Specification

The DfT strategy proposed in this paper is based on the introduction of an on-chip sensor that performs electrical measurements of the RRAM cell while executing a predefined operating sequence, including READ, SET, and RESET operations. Figure 3 depicts the general idea of how the on-chip sensor is connected to the 1T1R RRAM cell. Forward, will be proposed a DfT strategy that could be adopted on a column basis introducing just one on-chip sensor per column. From the functional point of view, the on-chip sensor was designed to operate during the execution of READ operations only, reading the voltage between the memristor (1R) and the memristor node (MEM), and comparing this signal with an input reference voltage (V_REF). Note that two control signals are used in order to activate the target resistor, which generates the correct internal reference voltage, the Voltage associated with High Resistance Reference (VHRR) or the Voltage associated to Low Resistance Reference (VLRR). A Sensor Enable (SE) signal is used in order to enable the on-chip sensor during the execution of the predefined operating sequence only, minimizing the power consumption linked with the DfT strategy's introduction. Finally, the Sensor Output (SO) indicates the result related to the comparison between the voltage at the MEM node and the internal reference voltage. Figure 4 depicts the block diagram of the proposed on-chip sensor including the 1T1R RRAM cell. Note that was included extra hardware in order to detect DeepFs. The on-chip sensor consists of a two-stage sense amplifier [28], which compares two voltage outputs, and a set of reference resistors, named Extreme High Resistance Reference (EHRR), High Resistance Reference (HRR), Low Resistance Reference (LRR), and Extreme Low Resistance Reference (ELRR). The first resistor generates the Extreme High Reference Voltage (V_REF_EH) and the second resistor the High Reference Voltage (V_REF_H), the third, the Low Reference Voltage (V_REF_L), and finally the fourth, the Extreme Low Reference Voltage (V_REF_HL). More precisely, the sense amplifier compares the voltage of the memristor (1R) on the memristor node (MEM) with the voltage related to the set of reference resistors on the reference node (REF). Moreover, four nMOS access transistors, VEHRR, VHRR, VLRR, and VHLRR, are used to provide a reference voltage to the REF node. This reference voltage at the REF node is obtained based on the current that flows through the set of reference resistors when applying a voltage reference at VREF.

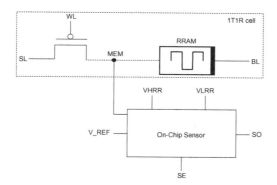

Fig. 3. DfT strategy: proposed on-chip sensor.

3.2   Implementation

The on-chip sensor proposed in this paper was implemented using a 350 nm X-FAB technology library. The selection of this particular CMOS technology node is justified by the fact that some specific size constraints for a tape-out have been posed by the group at Research Center Jülich (FZJ), Germany, that is going to manufacture the memristive devices (BEOL). Figure 5 shows the layout of the proposed on-chip sensor. Note that the presented layout does not include the set of reference resistors (EHRR, HRR, ELRR and LRR).

The fault detection capability of the proposed methodology is guaranteed based on monitoring and comparing the voltage value of the MEM node with four distinct references (EHRR, HRR, ELRR and LRR). Note that the proposed DfT strategy was especially designed to detect the unique faults, but the on-chip sensor is also able to detect traditional faults, such as SAFs. It is important to mention that a high voltage in the MEM node is observed when a high current flows through the memristor, indicating that the memristor is in LRS or storing the value '1' (V_{READ_1}). Similarly, a low voltage in the MEM node is measured when a low current flows through the memristor, indicating that the memristor is in HRS or storing the value '0' (V_{READ_0}). Thus, the on-chip sensor compares the voltages associated to LRS and HRS with the respective reference voltages, LRR, and HRR. Note that LRR assumes a value slightly lower than LRS and HRR a value slightly higher than HRS. Figure 6 depicts the adopted voltage levels for enabling the detection of unique faults (UWF and DeepF). The voltage associated with reading a '1' (V_{READ_1}) is the highest voltage to be observed in the MEM node, 1.30 V, followed by the LRR with a value of 1.16 V, the value of HRR with 1.09 V, and finally, the voltage associated to reading a '0' (V_{READ_0}) with 0.95 V. In order to guarantee the detection of DeepFs an extra comparison

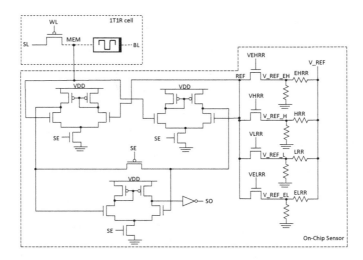

Fig. 4. Electrical schematic view of the proposed on-chip sensor.

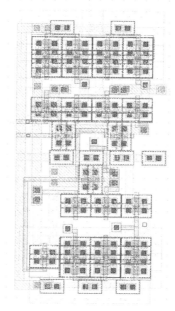

Fig. 5. Layout of the designed on-chip sensor.

needs to be made. In this case, the extreme LRR (ELRR) was set to 1.32 V and the extreme HRR (EHRR) to 0.87 V.

Thus, when the on-chip sensor is enabled, the voltage associated to the memristor's resistance state is compared with its respective reference voltage. The results of such comparison are presented as a pulse in the SO signal, that can be stored by a latch. Figure 7 presents implemented comparison logic. In more detail, Fig. 7 summarizes the expected values of SO when considering one traditional fault (SAF) and two unique faults (UWF and DeepF). Thus, when performing a read operation in which a '1' is expected as output, but the voltage value in the MEM node is smaller than HRR, SO is going to be '0', hence indicating that the RRAM cell presents a SAF-0. However, if the voltage at the MEM node is higher than HRR but lower than LRR, the RRAM cell assumed an undefined state 'U', indicating the occurrence of an UWF. A SAF-1 occurs when the current that flows through the memristor is higher than LRR. The DeepF Low (High) is detected when the current that flows through the memristor is higher (smaller) than ELRR (EHRR). An SO equal to '1' indicates a DeepF Low and an SO equal to '0' a DeepF High. Finally, a fault-free behavior is detected if the voltage in the MEM node is higher than LRR (SO is set to '1') or lower than HRR (SO is set to '0').

It is important to point out that the detection of UWFs requires the execution of two consecutive READ operations, since the on-chip sensor has to perform two comparisons, one considering the value of HRR and another the value of

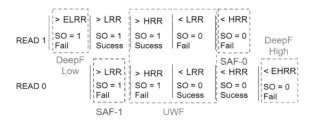

MEM (V)
REF (V)

1.32 V ---------------------------- ELRR
1.30 V ————————————— READ 1
1.16 V ---------------------------- LRR
1.09 V ---------------------------- HRR
0.95 V ————————————— READ 0
0.87 V ---------------------------- EHRR

Fig. 6. Adopted voltage levels MEM and REF nodes: READ1/LRS, LRR, READ0/HRS, HRR, ELRR, and EHRR.

	> ELRR	> LRR	> HRR	< LRR	< HRR	
READ 1	SO = 1 Fail	SO = 1 Sucess	SO = 1 Sucess	SO = 0 Fail	SO = 0 Fail	DeepF High
	DeepF Low	> LRR	> HRR	< LRR	SAF-0 < HRR	< EHRR
READ 0		SO = 1 Fail	SO = 1 Fail	SO = 0 Sucess	SO = 0 Sucess	SO = 0 Fail
	SAF-1		UWF			

Fig. 7. The output of the on-chip sensor according to the performed comparisons.

LRR. However, the detection of SAFs and DeepFs can be assured performing one READ operation only. Note that the fact that the proposed on-chip sensor can detect faults from both fault models, conventional and unique, renders the solution more attractive.

4   Case Study and Experimental Setup

This Section presents the adopted case study and the defined experimental setup used for validating the detection capability of the proposed DFT strategy.

4.1   Case Study

In order to validate the proposed DfT strategy, a case study composed of a single 1T1R RRAM cell was implemented using the 350 nm X-Fab technology and the memristor model defined in [14]. Figure 8(a) depicts the 1T1R RRAM cell and Fig. 8(b) the adopted defect injection scheme, which is based on the injection of two resistors. In this scheme, one of the resistors is in series and the other is injected in parallel with the memristor. The resistor in series (Rs) is used for reducing the current that flows through the memristor, increasing the LRS, and consequently the voltage on the MEM node. On the contrary, the resistor in parallel (Rp) is used to increase the memristor's current flow, decreasing the HRS, and the voltage on the MEM node. Note that the MEM node is connected to the on-chip sensor's input and the following three signals are used to control the memristor: Bit Line (BL), Word Line (WL) and Source Line (SL).

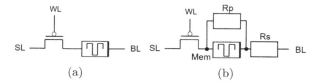

Fig. 8. (a) Case Study 1T1R, (b) Fault injection scheme used for the Memristor.

4.2   Simulation Results Related to Detection Capability

To demonstrate the detection capability of the proposed DfT strategy a set of electrical simulations using SPECTRE from Cadence was performed. As previously mentioned, the adopted case study is composed of a 1T1R RRAM cell, and the on-chip sensor was connected to the MEM node between the memristor and the transistor, see Fig. 4.

In order to validate the DfT scheme, a simulation considering a defect-free RRAM cell was performed. Figure 9 presents the behavior of the on-chip sensor when the RRAM cell is fault-free, which means that no defect was injected. Figure 9(a) presents the sensor output when performing a read operation where the expected value is '1' (LRS) and (b) when the memristor stores the value '0' (HRS). The first line of the graphs presents the voltage values applied on the memristor (BL) as well as on the sensor (VREF). The second line shows the voltages used as VHRR and VLRR. The third line of the graphs shows the voltage value associated with the resistance state stored in the RRAM cell. The last two lines of the graphs depict the SE signal and the output of the sensor (SO), respectively. Thus, the graphs depicted in Fig. 9(a) show that, when SE is enabled and a read operation with an expected value of '1' is executed (Read 1), the SO is high, reflecting a fault-free RRAM cell. However, when performing a read operation expecting a '0', a fault free situation will be indicated by a low SO. Note that when reading a '1', the reference voltage adopted is the LRR and when reading '0', HRR's value is used as reference.

The next graphs, Figs. 10, 11, 12 and 13 depict the on-chip sensor's behavior when injecting defects (Rs and Rp) able to cause the following faults: SAF-0, SAF-1, UWF, DeepF High as well as DeepF Low. Although the on-chip sensor was not specifically developed for detecting traditional faults affecting RRAMs, since the main goal of the proposed DfT was to guarantee the detection of unique faults, the proposed approach is also able to detect traditional faults, such as SAFs. The detection of SAF-0 occurs when the current that flows through the memristor is lower than the expected one, see Fig. 10(a). In that case, the on-chip sensor compares the voltage value at the MEM node with HRR and sets the SO signal to low. Note that in order to model a SAF-0, Rs was set to 70 kΩ. Figure 10(b) depicts the results associated with the injection of a defect that was modeled by setting Rp equal to 1 kΩ. The graph in 10(b) shows the detection of a SAF-1, since the expected output of the performed read operation was '0'. Note that the detection of SAF-1 is indicated by setting SO to high.

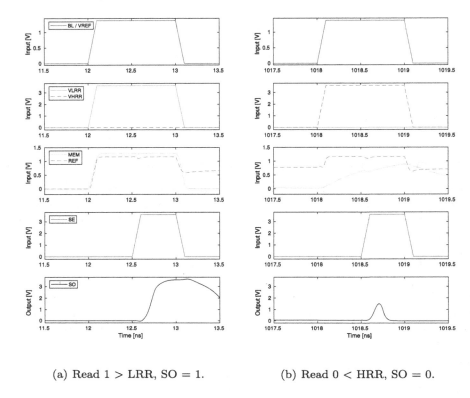

(a) Read 1 > LRR, SO = 1.   (b) Read 0 < HRR, SO = 0.

Fig. 9. Validation of the on-chip sensor considering fault free RRAM cell.

Figure 11 and 12 demonstrate the proposed on-chip sensor's detection capability with respect to UWFs. As previously mentioned, the detection of these faults requires the execution of two consecutive read operations, since two comparisons are required (one with HRR and another with LRR). Two different simulations were performed, one injecting a defect using an Rs set to 15 kΩ (a read operation of '1') and another using an Rp with 30 kΩ (a read operation of '0'). Observing the graphs in Fig. 11 it is possible to see that the on-chip sensor was able to detect the UWF when *Read*1 is performed since SO was set to low when comparing the value of MEM node to LRR and set to high when compared to HRR. The detection of the UWF when performing a read operation with an expected output of '0' is depicted in Fig. 12. In that case, SO is set to low when compared to LRR and to high when compared to HRR. Note again that the detection of UWFs is only possible by executing two comparisons. When considering a read operation expecting a '1', the faulty behavior is detected when the voltage at the MEM node is both smaller than LRR and bigger than HRR.

Figure 13 shows the on-chip sensor's detection capability with respect to DeepFs. Note that the detection of these unique faults requires one read operation only, and the signals in the second line now show the voltages VEHRR and

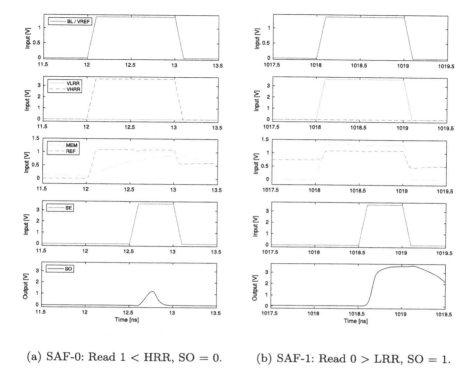

(a) SAF-0: Read 1 < HRR, SO = 0.   (b) SAF-1: Read 0 > LRR, SO = 1.

Fig. 10. On-chip sensor detection capability: SAFs.

VELRR. The DeepF Low was modeled injecting an Rp of 500 Ω and the Deep High an Rs of 1 MΩ. Observing the graphs depicted in Fig. 13 it is possible to see that a read operation expecting a '1' is performed in order to detect a DeepF Low. The SO is set to '1' when the voltage at the MEM node is bigger than ELRR. However, a DeepF High is detected when the voltage at the MEM node is smaller than EHRR. The detection of a Deep High is indicated by a SO equal to '0'.

Finally, it is important to mention that the DfT strategy is also able to provide the detection of the other faults associated wtih the RRAM conventional fault model, such as TF and RDF. The simulation results related to these traditional faults were omitted because the main goal of this Section is to demonstrate the detection capability of the proposed approach with respect to unique faults only since their detection represents the most important challenge when dealing with RRAMs.

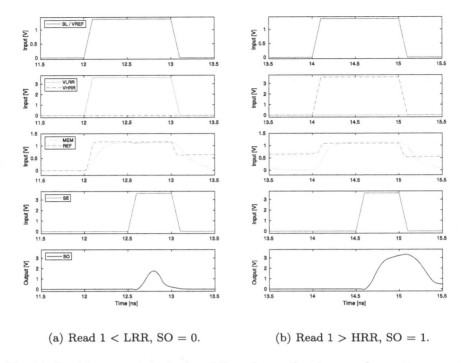

(a) Read 1 < LRR, SO = 0.   (b) Read 1 > HRR, SO = 1.

Fig. 11. On-chip sensor detection capability when performing a read operation expecting '1': UWF.

4.3 Discussion About Introduced Overheads and Implementation Granularity

The proposed DfT approach introduces an area overhead that is not observed when using software-based manufacturing test procedures, such as March Tests. However, March Tests can not guarantee the detection of all unique faults in RRAMs. It is important to highlight that memory faults can be classified as strong or weak faults [10]. Strong faults are functional faults that can always be sensitized by applying a sequence of write and read operations. In contrast, weak faults cause parametric faults and can not be detected with any sequence of write and read operations, since they do not cause functional errors. These faults, when not detected after manufacturing, may become a reliability issue during their lifetime. Thus, as previously mentioned, depending on the effort needed to detect faults caused by manufacturing defects, these faults can be further categorized into ETD and HTD faults. Note that strong faults consist of ETD and HTD faults, while weak faults are all HTD. To resume, the proposed DfT approach is able to provide the detection of HTD faults, which justifies the introduced area overhead. The area of the proposed on-chip sensor is around 278 μm^2, assuming the technology node adopted in this work (350 nm X-Fab technology). Note that this value does not include the transistors related to the reference voltages. In

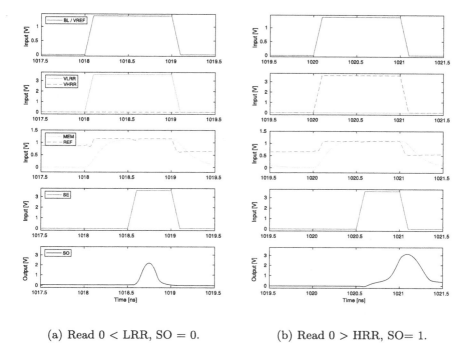

(a) Read 0 < LRR, SO = 0.   (b) Read 0 > HRR, SO= 1.

Fig. 12. On-chip sensor detection capability when performing a read operation expecting '0': UWF.

order to understand the area impact related to the introduction of the proposed DfT strategy, it is important to mention that the area associated to a 1T1R RRAM cell is around 40 μm^2 for the transistor and the memristor can have an area of around 50 μm^2, when fabricated based on the Microcrosbar technology, or 0.1 μm^2 if using the Nano-crossbar technology. This area overhead could be considered relevant with respect to a 1T1R RRAM cell. However, the overhead becomes irrelevant when considering a complete RRAM composed including the 1T1R cell array as well as all peripheral circuitry. Figure 14 depicts one possible implementation of the proposed DfT strategy, where one on-chip sensor is connected to each column of the RRAM block. In more detail, the on-chip sensor could be connected to the Source Line (SL) of the block. During a read operation, the on-chip sensor compares the current of the 1T1R RRAM cell column with the two reference voltages, the V_REF_H and the V_REF_L. Thus, based on this comparison, the on-chip sensor identifies the resistive state associated with the current that flows through the 1T1R RRAM cell column. A possible limitation of this implementation granularity is associated to the on-chip sensor resolution, since depending on the CMOS technology node, the on-chip sensor could be susceptible to process variation, impacting its ability to properly indicate a faulty behavior. Note that in order to assume this granularity, the on-chip sen-

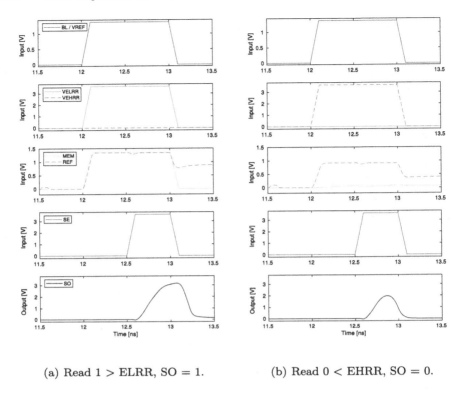

(a) Read 1 > ELRR, SO = 1.   (b) Read 0 < EHRR, SO = 0.

Fig. 13. On-chip sensor detection capability to detect DeepFs

sor needs to measure the current consumption, instead of the voltage. Another important point to be considered is related to the power overhead. The on-chip sensor has a power consumption of around 2.4 mW, while the 1T1R RRAM cell consumes approximately 1.76 mW during the SET operation and 2.2 μW during the RESET operation. Note that in order to reduce the power overhead introduced by the proposed approach, the on-chip sensor is only enabled when used, which means during the execution of read operations included in the predefined operating sequence only. Finally, it is important to highlight that the DfT strategy significantly reduces the time required for performing the manufacturing test with respect to March Tests, since the operating sequence applied in combination with the electrical measurements is significantly smaller.

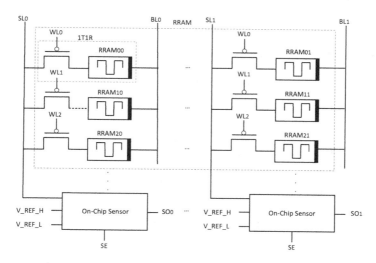

Fig. 14. Electrical schematic view of the proposed on-chip sensor in the block.

5 Final Remarks

The use of RRAMs to replace classic CMOS-based memories represents an interesting alternative in order to guarantee the storage of high data volumes as well as implement emerging applications. However, aspects regarding their quality after manufacturing are still a challenge, since functional test algorithms cannot guarantee the detection of unique faults, which are classified as HTD faults. This paper presents a DfT strategy able to detect traditional and unique faults caused by manufacturing deviations in RRAMs. The proposed strategy consists of introducing an on-chip sensor able to compare the voltage associated with HRS and LRS with a set of predefined reference voltages while executing a predefined operating sequence. This set is composed of at least two resistors, representing the reference voltage associated with HRS and LRS. The results obtained through electrical simulations demonstrate the fault detection capability of the proposed DfT strategy. When compared to state-of-the-art solutions, the DfT strategy has the advantage of detecting not only traditional faults but also all unique faults that can affect RRAMs. The introduced area overhead can be minimized and become tolerable when assuming an implementation granularity considering one on-chip sensor per each RRAM column. Finally, the power consumption of the proposed on-chip sensor does not represent a significant overhead when considering the power associated with a 1T1R RRAM cell executing SET and RESET operations.

Acknowledgment. This work was supported by the Federal Ministry of Education and Research (BMBF, Germany) within the NEUROTEC I & II projects 16ES1134 and 16ME0399.

References

1. Moore, G.E.: Cramming more components onto integrated circuits with unit cost. Electronics 38(8), 114 (1965). https://newsroom.intel.com/wp-content/uploads/sites/11/2018/05/moores-law-electronics.pdf
2. Dennard, R., Gaensslen, F., Yu, W.-N., Rideout, L., Bassous, E., Le Blanc, A.: Design of ion-implanted small MOSFET. S dimensions with very. IEEE J. Solid State Circ. 9(5), 257–268 (1974)
3. Hamdioui, S., et al.: Memristor for computing: myth or reality? In: Proceedings of the 2017 Design, Automation and Test in Europe, DATE 2017. Institute of Electrical and Electronics Engineers Inc., pp. 722–731 (2017)
4. Mazumder, P., Kang, S.M., Waser, R.: Memristors: devices, models, and applications. Proc. IEEE 100(6), 1911–1919 (2012)
5. Chaudhuri, A., Chakrabarty, K.: Analysis of process variations, defects, and design-induced coupling in memristors. In: 2018 IEEE International Test Conference (ITC), pp. 1–10 (2018)
6. Poehls, L.M.B., et al.: Review of manufacturing process defects and their effects on memristive devices. J. Electron. Test. 37(4), 427–437 (2021). https://doi.org/10.1007/s10836-021-05968-8
7. Hamdioui, S., Taouil, M., Haron, N.Z.: Testing open defects in memristor-based memories. IEEE Trans. Comput. 64(1), 247–259 (2015)
8. Haron, N.Z., Hamdioui, S.: DFT schemes for resistive open defects in RRAMs. In: 2012 Design, Automation & Test in Europe Conference & Exhibition (DATE), pp. 799–804. IEEE (2012)
9. Hamdioui, S., Taouil, M., Haron, N.Z.: Testing open defects in memristor-based memories. IEEE Trans. Comput. 64(1), 247–259 (2013)
10. Fieback, M., et al.: Device-aware test: a new test approach towards DPPB level. In: Proceedings - International Test Conference, vol. 2019-Novem (2019)
11. Fieback, M., Taouil, M., Hamdioui, S.: Testing resistive memories: where are we and what is missing? In: 2018 IEEE International Test Conference (ITC), pp. 1–9 (2018)
12. Kannan, S., Rajendran, J., Karri, R., Sinanoglu, O.: Sneak-path testing of crossbar-based nonvolatile random access memories. IEEE Trans. Nanotechnol. 12(3), 413–426 (2013)
13. Copetti, T.S., Gemmeke, T., Poehls, L.B.: Validating a DFT strategy's detection capability regarding emerging faults in RRAMs. In: 2021 IFIP/IEEE 29th International Conference on Very Large Scale Integration (VLSI-SoC), pp. 1–6 (2021)
14. Jart vcm v1b. http://www.emrl.de/JART.html. Accessed 11 Apr 2021
15. Chua, L.: Memristor - the missing current element. IEEE Trans. Circ. Theory CT−18(5), 507–519 (1971)
16. Vatajelu, E.I., Prinetto, P., Taouil, M., Hamdioui, S.: Challenges and solutions in emerging memory testing. IEEE Trans. Emerg. Top. Comput. 7(3), 493–506 (2017)
17. Waser, R.: Electrochemical and thermochemical memories. In: Technical Digest - International Electron Devices Meeting, IEDM (2008)
18. Yu, J., Du Nguyen, H.A., Xie, L., Taouil, M., Hamdioui, S.: Memristive devices for computation-in-memory. In: 2018 Design, Automation & Test in Europe Conference & Exhibition (DATE), pp. 1646–1651. IEEE (2018)
19. Ielmini, D., Milo, V.: Physics-based modeling approaches of resistive switching devices for memory and in-memory computing applications. J. Comput. Electron. 16(4), 1121–1143 (2017). https://doi.org/10.1007/s10825-017-1101-9

20. Waser, R., Dittmann, R., Staikov, C., Szot, K.: Redox-based resistive switching memories nanoionic mechanisms, prospects, and challenges. Adv. Mater. **21**(25–26), 2632–2663 (2009)
21. Hardtdegen, A., La Torre, C., Cuppers, F., Menzel, S., Waser, R., Hoffmann-Eifert, S.: Improved switching stability and the effect of an internal series resistor in HfO2/TiOx Bilayer ReRAM cells. IEEE Trans. Electron Devices **65**(8), 3229–3236 (2018)
22. Medeiros, G.C., et al.: Hard-to-detect fault analysis in finfet srams. IEEE Trans. Very Large Scale Integr. (VLSI) Syst. **29**(6), 1271–1284 (2021)
23. Arvindam, S., Kumar, V., Nageshwara Rao, V., Singh, V.: Automatic test pattern generation on multiprocessors: a summary of results. In: Ramani, S., Chandrasekar, R., Anjaneyulu, K.S.R. (eds.) KBCS 1989. LNCS, vol. 444, pp. 39–51. Springer, Heidelberg (1990). https://doi.org/10.1007/BFb0018367
24. Haron, N. Z., Hamdioui, S.: On defect oriented testing for hybrid CMOS/memristor memory. In: 2011 Asian Test Symposium, pp. 353–358. IEEE (2011)
25. Chen, C.-Y., et al.: Rram defect modeling and failure analysis based on march test and a novel squeeze-search scheme. IEEE Trans. Comput. **64**(1), 180–190 (2014)
26. Chen, Y.X., Li, J.F.: Fault modeling and testing of 1T1R memristor memories. In: 2015 IEEE 33rd VLSI Test Symposium (VTS), pp. 1–6. IEEE (2015)
27. Kannan, S., Rajendran, J., Karri, R., Sinanoglu, O.: Sneak-path testing of memristor-based memories. In: 2013 26th International Conference on VLSI Design and 2013 12th International Conference on Embedded Systems, pp. 386–391. IEEE (2013)
28. Rabaey, J.M., Chandrakasan, A.P., Nikolić, B.: Digital integrated circuits: a design perspective, vol. 7. Pearson education Upper Saddle River, NJ (2003)

FMEA on Critical Systems: A Cross-Layer Approach Based on High-Level Models

Julie Roux[1,2], Katell Morin-Allory[2], Vincent Beroulle[1], Lilian Bossuet[3], Frederic Cezilly[4], Frederic Berthoz[4], Gilles Genevrier[4], Francois Cerisier[5], and Regis Leveugle[2(✉)]

[1] Univ. Grenoble Alpes, CNRS, Grenoble INP Institute of Engineering Univ. Grenoble Alpes, LCIS, 26000 Valence, France
[2] Univ. Grenoble Alpes, CNRS, Grenoble INP Institute of Engineering Univ. Grenoble Alpes, TIMA, 38000 Grenoble, France
`regis.leveugle@univ-grenoble-alpes.fr`
[3] Laboratoire Hubert Curien, Université de Lyon, 42000 Saint Etienne, France
[4] THALES, 26000 Valence, France
[5] AEDVICES, 38430 Moirans, France

Abstract. Designing embedded systems for critical applications requires meeting strict safety constraints according to official standards. In current practice, safety analysis (e.g., Failure Mode and Effects Analysis) is often only relying on human experience and therefore lacks detailed data. Performing more detailed analyses on complex systems is a major challenge to avoid pessimistic assumptions and consequently to avoid over-design of the system, i.e., adding too many protections with respect to the system specifications and risk. Many fault injection techniques have been previously proposed to better evaluate the robustness of circuit designs described at various abstraction levels. However, very few take into account the global system constraints. Also, fault injection experiments become very time-consuming for complex designs. At the highest levels of abstraction (e.g., Transaction level), simulations are faster but suffer of the lack of realism of high-level models. Our contribution is to propose both an increase in safety analysis precision and a fault injection flow improving the analysis duration. The flow is based on an iterative process, taking into account the global system specifications and allowing improvements of high-level models to achieve both precision and efficiency. Improvements are based on metrics, and results are shown on a real airborne system.

Keywords: Safety · Embedded system · FMEA · Fault simulation · Cross-layer

1 Introduction

When developing embedded systems for critical applications, Original Equipment Manufacturers (OEMs) must perform Failure Mode and Effects Analysis (FMEA) to demonstrate the robustness of each component. Standards guide the development of these critical systems. Standards such as ARP5580 [1] for airborne systems and DO254 [2] for

© IFIP International Federation for Information Processing 2022
Published by Springer Nature Switzerland AG 2022
V. Grimblatt et al. (Eds.): VLSI-SoC 2021, IFIP AICT 661, pp. 113–133, 2022.
https://doi.org/10.1007/978-3-031-16818-5_6

electronic embedded systems in aircraft recommend that robustness analysis starts early in the design flow.

FMEA aims et analyzing the failure effects of a component on the system and consists in 3 steps:

- Definition of possible failures and their probability of occurrence,
- Determination of the failure effects on the functional block,
- Determination of the global effect on the whole system and computation of the probability of occurrence of unacceptable events.

Designers must perform detailed FMEA considering:

- Single Event Upsets (SEUs), i.e., single bit-flips,
- Multiple Bit Upsets (MBUs), i.e., multiple bit-flips in the same logic word,
- Multiple Cell Upsets (MCUs), i.e., multiple bit-flips in the several logic words.

This FMEA, called SEU FMEA (even if it also relates to MBUs and MCUs) is often based solely on engineer experience. Some solutions to assist FMEA have been proposed [3, 4] but these tools do not allow early estimations of the robustness of complex systems.

Evaluating the robustness of a circuit can be based on different fault models, at different levels from functional to gate or transistor level. Low levels (transistor or gate level), or even Register Transfer level (RTL) can be used, but are very time-consuming to perform the robustness evaluation of complex systems. Furthermore, some errors observed using RTL fault simulations have no real effect on the overall system because these errors are filtered out or detected by the system. Thus, the interactions of the circuit with other parts of the system must be taken into account. High-level modeling at the Transaction level (Transaction Level Modeling or TLM) allows the quick simulation of complex systems. Such high-level simulations with adequate fault modeling accelerate fault simulations and make possible to account for the whole system. Nevertheless, high-level modeling requires details to be removed (such as a clock or internal signals), which causes some realism issues.

Previous works [5, 6] have studied these issues. For example, results in [6] show that some of the faults injected at RT-Level have no high-level equivalent and conversely, some high-level faults have no RTL equivalent. Cross-layer methods aim to take advantage of fault injections in both RTL and TLM (or e.g., Matlab models) to take into account the whole system [7–11]

However, as far as we know, no previous study proposed a way to build relevant high-level models of the system and of the faults. Safe-Air approach presented in [11] is a cross-layer fault simulation approach allowing speeding up SEU FMEA on circuits used in critical applications. This approach is composed of three steps: (1) system high-level fault simulations, (2) block-level RTL fault simulations, and (3) evaluation of the high-level models. It allows the high-level model realism validation but this validation happens late in the process. In particular, no improvement of the high-level models related to the obtained results was proposed in [11].

As proposed in [12], an iterative process can lead to both perform an early robustness analysis and to improve the realism of the high-level models using the robustness analysis results. The method makes use of "quick and dirty" iterations to speed up the validation of the high-level models. Each round allows improving the high-level models that are simulated with a small number of randomly injected faults. The first rounds are performed on approximate models with a small number of randomly injected faults (dirty), in order to get a quick simulation. Then, the quality of the high-level fault simulation is evaluated through several metrics. The main novelty of this approach relies on these "quick and dirty" rounds with randomly injected faults and on the definition of several metrics.

Our main contributions, in particular with respect to [12], is to present a more detailed discussion with respect to the state-of-the-art, and to show a more detailed analysis of the results with a comparison between the results obtained and data from the initial case study.

This paper is organized as follows. More details on the state-of-the art are presented in Sect. 2. The Safe-Air methodology is briefly reminded in Sect. 3. The proposed iterative flow based on the "quick and dirty" evaluations is presented in 4. Section 5 presents and discusses results applied to a case study. Section 6 concludes the paper.

2 State-of-the-Art and Discussion

2.1 Fault Injections

For more than twenty years, an efficient technique to evaluate the robustness of electronic circuits is fault injection. The results are used to complete FMEAs performed by human specialists, specially to quantify the risks. There are mainly three categories of fault injection techniques: simulation, emulation and physical injection.

When using simulation, faults derived from a given model (e.g., SEUs) are voluntarily introduced in some elements at different execution times. The main advantage of simulation is the possibility to use system models designed with different abstraction levels, from TLM (Transaction Level Modeling) down to transistor-level or even physical device descriptions. Of course, the fault models have to be adapted to each level. Simulations at the highest levels are less precise but when coming to lower levels the simulation times are much higher and quickly become intractable, even when using statistical fault injections [13]. The lowest levels are therefore used to characterize small cells and the results are used to make the highest fault models more realistic.

Even simulations at RT-Level can lead to very long simulation times, thus requiring the use of emulation (or hardware prototyping). In that case, the system is implemented on a hardware platform where faults are injected using logic modifications during the application execution. The advantage is to speed-up the execution for each injected fault, compared to simulation, but at the expense of a non-negligible time to prepare the hardware set-up. Also, such emulations cannot be performed for all description levels of the system; in general, they are limited to RT-Level descriptions.

The third type of method that can be used is physical injection. There are mainly two techniques used to mimic the effects of environmental disturbances: laser [14, 15], or particle accelerators (e.g., [16]). Experiments in natural conditions (so-called life-time experiments) are also possible, in space or on the earth e.g., on mountains or underground, depending on the type of particle that has to be considered. Such experiments are in all cases very costly, especially when particles are used, and a lot of effort is required to prepare them. Furthermore, they need of course to have the final circuit available and any required improvement of the robustness implies a long and expensive process. Such experiments should therefore be restricted to the final product characterization and cannot be considered in early development phases.

Combining laser-based experiments, statistical fault injections and beam experiments was also proved worthwhile in [17]. However, once again, the final circuit must be available to complete the evaluation process.

As mentioned in the introduction, standards for critical embedded systems require an early evaluation of the robustness. Also, reducing costs and time to market imply having a quick identification of weak points in the system. We will therefore focus in the sequel on approaches based on behavioral simulation, aiming at reducing the time required to perform the fault injections while achieving an efficient early analysis of the system-level robustness.

Within this context, many authors have made proposals. We will cite the main approaches related to our proposal.

2.2 Simulated Fault Injections

Injection of faults during a simulation can use two types of approaches: with or without modifying the system description. Most works target RTL descriptions, but similar approaches can be used with TLM descriptions or at lower levels.

Avoiding modifications of the model requires the use of simulator commands to modify signals or variables at a given time. It is therefore not intrusive but depends on the simulator used. To avoid this dependency, it is possible to add control signals to the model, that command internal injection logic. This logic can be added to internal interconnections between blocks or gates in order to force the value of a signal; this is called saboteur insertion. Some types of errors cannot be injected using saboteurs and the behavioral model of the block must then be modified; this is called mutant generation. The pioneer work in [18] proposed both simulator commands and saboteurs. An example of mutant generation can be found in [19]. Of course, modifying the model of the system can become very complex and may also lead to functional errors. We will therefore avoid model modifications in our methodology.

As previously mentioned simulations even at RT-Level are very expensive when the system complexity increases. Furthermore, some errors observed at the circuit level have no real effect on the global system due to intrinsic tolerance properties on some parameters, to detection/tolerance logic or to masking effects during the error propagation. Thus, the global interactions within the system and the system specifications have to be taken into account to avoid a too pessimistic safety evaluation [7, 20].

In order to speed-up the evaluation, TLM models can be used. However, in that case many system characteristics are not yet defined (e.g., communication protocols or timing). Consequently, results are less accurate. This paper will show how it is possible to achieve both accelerated simulations and accuracy.

2.3 Limitations of High-Level Fault Models

Since most of the registers in the system are not yet defined, injecting faults in a TLM description is generally done using specific high-level fault models rather than for example SEU/MBU/MCU. Of course, saboteurs can be used but since the description is quite far from the following RTL model the results obtained are in general not very useful.

High-level modeling removes for example clocks or detailed data types, so some RTL faults have no high-level equivalent as shown in the case study presented in [21], based on a TLM SoC model written in SystemC.

Other works have studied this problem of fault model realism at high-level.

In [22], gate-level fault injections are used to define a realistic high-level fault library. The library is obtained from the circuit without safety mechanisms and used to perform high-level simulations after adding such mechanisms. Such an approach has several limitations. First the RTL description (and even the gate-level description) must be available, thus the high-level fault models are obtained very late in the design process. Then, gate-level simulations are very slow. Finally, the system specifications are not taken into account.

In [5], RTL and TLM faults are compared using a formal approach. More precisely, the TLM faults equivalent to an RTL fault are extracted. The study shows again that some RTL faults have no high-level representation, but also that a single RTL fault can have several equivalences at high-level.

In conclusion, there is no TLM fault model allowing a complete and realistic safety evaluation with this level of description.

2.4 Cross-Layer Approaches

Since a complete evaluation is not possible on high-level models only, many authors considered Cross-layer approaches. This can be used for example to co-simulate an RTL description and the gate-level description of some circuit blocks, but we will focus here on earlier evaluations.

The CLERECO project [8] aimed at performing cross-layer reliability evaluations in order to accelerate the analysis. However, it was focused on microprocessors and software.

Simulations are also performed at several levels in [9], to guide architecture and RTL hardware designers of a critical embedded system. The approach allows early decision making and avoids time-consuming design iterations. However, the problem mentioned in the previous section is not addressed and no verification is made about the realism of the results obtained at high-level. Also, the global system specifications are not taken into account to decide what errors are actually critical.

In [23], faults are injected at both high-level and RT-Level in a processor. The high-level description is used to simulate longer scenarios but there is no comparison between the results obtained at the two levels.

These examples show that there is usually no proof of relevance of the results obtained at high-level with respect to the results obtained at lower levels, and the scope is sometimes limited to a part of the system, in particular microprocessors.

2.5 Safety Analysis Tools

Tools have also been proposed to assist engineers when doing FMEA, in particular:

The AltaRica project [24] aimed at safety analyses in airborne systems. Systems are described at very high level with states and transitions, and critical scenarios are identified with a formal approach. This level of description is useful for the global system validation, but no link is made with hardware implementations.

A tool was proposed in [3], to help extracting quantitative information useful for FMEA. Here some specific parts of an RTL description are chosen and exhaustive fault injections are performed. The RTL description must therefore be available, and the complete system and its specifications are not taken into account.

3 Methodology Based on Cross-Layer Fault Simulation

As shown in the previous section, there are currently strong limitations to available approaches. The goal of the work presented hereafter is to reduce some of them. First, fault injections in high-level TLM models allow early robustness evaluations, but are not completely realistic. The other advantage of simulations at that level is to be able to take into account the whole system and its global specifications (no matter if it is completely implemented as a circuit or designed with several circuits, and even other types of components). It is however necessary, when a lower description level is made available, to check the accuracy of the results obtained at high-level. This can be done using a cross-layer approach, with RTL simulations made at the block level and keeping the TLM model for the whole system, thus noticeably reducing the simulation times compared to a full RTL simulation while being able to take into account the global system specifications. None of the approaches and tools presented in the state of the art has such characteristics. Our methodology allows extracting critical ranges at high-level, then verifying the relevance of the obtained statistics, and also refining the high-level fault models.

The cross-layer fault simulation methodology has been detailed in [25]. We give here an overview of it to keep the paper self-contained. In the sequel of the paper, we will insist more on the extensions of the approach that were presented in [12] and on the comparison with a classical FMEA for one case study.

Our methodology can be divided into three steps illustrated in Fig. 1.

Step 1: We perform a fault injection on a high-level system model at each interface signal of each block: a function corrupts the original value of signals by a fixed amplitude. We analyze the results according to the system specification. The signal corruptions that propagate to outputs and are not detected by any specific mechanism are analyzed to extract critical parameter ranges on the interface signals. Critical parameter ranges are converted into assertions to observe the behavior of these signals: if the assertion is not verified, the value of the signal is not in the range that can be tolerated and leads to a critical behavior of the whole system. This step allows detecting critical blocks.

Step 2: We statistically inject faults [13] in each RTL block leading to critical behaviors at the system level. Statistical fault injections are based on computing the number of faults required to achieve robustness evaluation with a predefined accuracy. The number

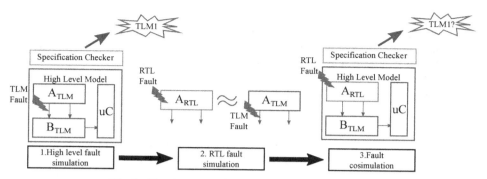

Fig. 1. The three steps in our cross-layer methodology.

of faults depends on three parameters: the number of possible faults (i.e., number of targets multiplied by the number of execution cycles), the margin of error, and the level of confidence (the probability that the exact value is in the margin of error). The usually chosen level of confidence is at least 90%. This method highly reduces the number of faults to inject while the confidence level remains high and the error margin can be reduced to a small percentage. Injected faults are simulated along with the assertions. The values of the assertions allow sorting faults into two categories: critical faults (if assertions are violated) and silent faults (if assertions are satisfied).

Step 3: It verifies the relevance of the high-level models used in step 1. Each RTL block is co-simulated within the high-level system model, and we inject the same faults on it as in step 2. Since the simulation is on the whole system but with a component modeled at lower level with more precise faults to inject, this step requires much more simulation time. Faults are sorted according to the observed behavior of the system. For each block, we obtain a confusion matrix (see Table 1). The "Predicted" column in this matrix corresponds to the results from steps 1 and 2. The "Co-simulation" line corresponds to the results of step 3 and is considered as the reference behavior.

Table 1. Confusion matrix.

Predicted \ Co-simulation	Critical	Silent
Critical	True Critical (TC)	False Critical (FC)
Silent	False Silent (FS)	True Silent (TS)

From this confusion matrix, we extract three metrics: the precision, the true silent rate, and the accuracy.

The precision is the proportion of true critical behaviors:

$$\text{Precision} = TC / (TC + FC) \tag{1}$$

A low precision indicates that too many faults are critical in step 2. The assertions are too restrictive, and critical parameter ranges are too large. Since critical parameter ranges are computed according to the fault amplitude, the low precision may be due to the high-level fault model used in step 1 that is not accurate enough: the amplitude of the fault should be modified.

The True Silent Rate (TSR) is the proportion of true silent behaviors:

$$TSR = TS / (TS + FS) \tag{2}$$

A low TSR means that assertions have not been able to detect correctly the critical faults. Since the critical behaviors are detected during the co-simulation, but not in the RTL simulation, it may mean that no assertion was generated to detect it. If the assertion is not created, it means that the critical behavior was not generated in step 1. This critical behavior is present at the RT-Level but not in the high-level model; it may be due to a bad high-level system modeling.

The accuracy defines the proportion of true results among injected faults:

$$Accuracy = (TC + TS) / (TC + TS + FC + FS) \tag{3}$$

This metric is a kind of trade-off between TSR and precision. It allows us to know the weight of each of the two other metrics. If the accuracy is high, but one of the two others is low, it indicates that the number of faults (either critical or silent) not correctly sorted in step 2 is small according to the whole number of faults. It may not be useful to modify the fault model (low precision) or the high-level model (low TSR).

4   Quick and Dirty Flow

The "quick and dirty" flow aims at highly speeding up the validation of high-level models and the overall evaluation of the system robustness. It is based on successive "quick and dirty" evaluations of the cross-layer fault simulation. It allows obtaining early evaluations of:

- the blocks leading to critical behaviors (step 1),
- the approximate probability of critical SEU (step 2),
- the realism of the high-level system model (step 3),
- the realism of the high-level fault model (step 3).

The flow is illustrated in Fig. 2. According to the design, we empirically define a threshold on metrics that indicates confidence in the high-level models. This threshold constrains the accuracy; we recommend at least 90%. Below, the quality of the high-level system model may not be sufficient. The next rounds depend on the value of the threshold:

- If the threshold is achieved, we perform a final statistical fault injection (arrow from the metric computations to step 2) with a very high confidence level and a low margin of errors to get an accurate evaluation of the probability of critical events. This last round may be very long but it is performed only once.

- If the threshold is not reached, the designer manually improves the high-level models. If the precision is low, he/she modifies the fault model. If the TSR is low, he/she analyzes the location of false silent faults to understand the origin of the model inaccuracy and to correct the system model. Then, a new round is performed (arrow from the metric computations to high-level models).

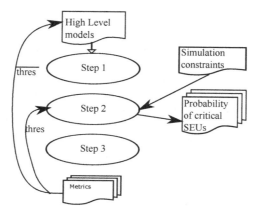

Fig. 2. Quick and dirty flow.

For each round, we define a maximum simulation time. This maximum time impacts the number of faults that can be injected in each block and therefore the couple (confidence level, margin of errors) that can be chosen. We evaluate the RTL simulation time of all blocks (simulation time of each block multiplied by the number of injected faults) for three confidence levels usually used in statistical fault injections (90%, 95%, and 99.8%) and several values of the margin of error. We then select a couple (confidence level, margin of error) that is below the maximum simulation time but still presents a correct robustness evaluation accuracy. During the first rounds, as the high-level model realism is not known, it is useless to obtain a very accurate robustness evaluation. Unaccurate (or dirty) evaluations allow us to quickly validate or improve high-level models. The simulation time per round can be progressively increased with the progress of the model quality.

5   Analysis Results on a Case Study

In this section, we apply the quick and dirty flow on a system converting the frequency of the oscillations of a sensor into a digital value. This design is used in aeronautic. For confidentiality reasons and without loss of generality, all names have been concealed, and all values normalized. The fault model used during the simulations is the SEU fault model (single bit-flips).

5.1   Case Study: System Description

We study an embedded system SYS_X that measures a physical value X, which is sent to the main airplane ECU (Electronic Control Unit). From other collected information, the ECU deduces the flight information. The system inputs the oscillations of a sensor which depend on the physical value X and converts the oscillation frequency into a digital value. Since SensorX is sensitive to temperature, a second sensor SensorT is used to capture the temperature, also generating oscillations. The architecture of the whole system is presented in Fig. 3. It contains a FPGA, a microcontroller, and a memory. Dividers and counters are used to obtain the digital values and are implemented in the FPGA. The microcontroller periodically reads the number of cycles counted during the measurement window of 100 ms (an interrupt occurs when new values are written in the output registers of CounterX and CounterT). The value of X is then computed based on a sensor table (series of points containing the values X corresponding to a given couple of periods of SensorT and SensorX) characterizing each type of sensorX. An interpolation method is used by the microcontroller to calculate an accurate value of X. The microcontroller then transmits the calculated value and some maintenance information (error detection mechanism outputs) to the FPGA in charge of the communication. The communication block then formats the frame in order to transmit the data to the ECU.

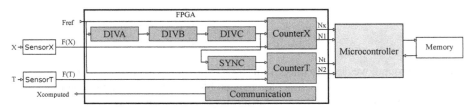

Fig. 3. Architecture of the system used for the case study.

Table 2. System specifications.

Property	Specification
Data flow rate	100 ms ± 3.3 ms
Time to alarm	300 ms ± 3.3 ms
Accuracy	±0.8 U (confidential unit)
Transmission period	<100 ms
Computation period	<100 ms
Transport delay	300 ms ± 3.3 ms

The system specifications are summarized in Table 2. "Data Flow Rate" is the time between two value transmissions. The "Time to Alarm" property corresponds to the minimum error duration before notifying the error during data measurement. The "Transmission Period" is the time spent by the communication block to transmit the data.

"Computation Period" is the maximum time spent by the microcontroller to compute the final value and to transmit it to the communication block when an interrupt occurs. "Transport Delay" is the time between the beginning of a measure window and the data transmission by the communication block to the ECU. Several error detection mechanisms are also implemented in the system: counters overflow, detectors of periods out of the sensor table, detection of X value out of the possible range, etc. These system specifications are taken into account in our approach to classify an error as critical or not. As an example, the exact computation time of the controller is not critical; what is critical is to be under the maximum time allowed by the system. Also, a detected error is managed by the ECU or other redundant elements in the airplane and is therefore not critical.

5.2   Case Study: Initial FMEA

The usual FMEA process, managed mainly thanks to experienced engineers, is illustrated in Fig. 4. The global analysis involves several steps.

The first step is performed considering the architecture description (equivalent to our use of a high-level model, but in current practice it is most often a written description). At that step, a functional FMEA is performed in compliance with the ARP5580 standard (since it is an airborne system). This step early identifies the level of criticality of the different parts in the system. It only takes into account a subset of potential faults and all those are not necessarily realistic.

The second step goes into more details with respect to the implementation. It evaluates the probability of critical errors if a perturbation occurs in one block, especially in one block identified as critical during the first step. One part of this second step is focused on permanent failure of the block (or component) and is very global because this type of event is less frequent than the others, especially with the regular maintenance processes. The second part is focused on transient disturbances and in particular atmospheric particle effects for airborne systems. These events have a much higher probability than permanent failures. This is the SEU FMEA mentioned in introduction.

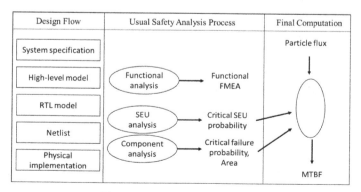

Fig. 4. Classical FMEA process.

Knowing the conditions in which the system will be used (e.g., flight altitude), a particle flux can be characterized and used to evaluate the flux per block (or component) with respect to the area of each block and to the sensitivity of the component in which it is implemented (depending on the technology). Taking into account the probability of critical errors if a SEU (or MBU/MCU) occurs in this block, it is possible to compute the probability of critical failures and, summing this over all the blocks, it is possible to derive the Mean Time Between Failures (MTBF) for the system.

Since the analysis is empirically managed by humans, any doubt about a potential SEU effect leads to the decision that it is critical in order to be conservative and the repartition between the types of failure modes is very rough. The result is often a pessimistic calculation of the MTBF, leading potentially to over-protect the system with consequences on cost and time-to-market. In addition, the analysis is only performed at the level of macro-components and with few failure modes, as illustrated in Table 3. This indicates the most critical components and the main failure modes but cannot give precisions on the criticality of each individual function in the architecture. In this case, the probability of faults per hour due to the particle flux is higher for the FPGA than for the microcontroller and the probability of each major failure mode is just estimated at 50%.

Table 3. Initial SEU FMEA for the case study.

Block	Particle flux per component (per hour)	Failure mode	Ratio
Microcontroller	0.03E−07	Erroneous X value	50%
		Reset	50%
FPGA	0.15E−07	Erroneous X value	50%
		No transmission	50%

For this system, taking into account before the actual implementation that about 25% of the logic resources should be used in the FPGA, and that all SEUs in these resources lead to a critical event, the critical error probability was evaluated around 1E-7 faults per flight hour for the functions in the FPGA.

5.3 Quick and Dirty Flow: First Round

We have modeled the whole system in SystemC at the transaction level approximately timed according to the architecture given in Fig. 3. Each block is implemented by a process. The interface signals between blocks are implemented with sc_fifo communication channels. When a new input is available on a communication channel, the process is notified. The input oscillations are directly modeled by the value of their frequency, i.e. an integer value.

Simulations allow identifying the level of disturbances that may be tolerated on the interface signals. This is illustrated in Table 4 for CounterX. Some signal corruptions can be tolerated thanks to the system specifications, but some others lead to characteristics out of range due to either amplitude or injection time. We can see for example that disturbances have no effect at 150 ms, but have a strong effect if at 100 ms or 200 ms, especially if the value is modified in the range -2% to $+10\%$ because in that case they are not detected by the available mechanisms. This leads to assertions, such as for this case:

Assert always window - > $(Nx < Nx\_gold * 0.98)$ or $(Nx > Nx\_gold * 1.1)$.
or $(Nx = Nx\_gold)$ report « ERR_ASSERTION»;

Table 4. Analysis at high-level of disturbances effects on CounterX (C in red means unacceptable, D in orange means detected, in green it is either silent or tolerable for the system).

	0 ms	50 ms	100 ms	150 ms	200ms
-50%	-	-	D	-	D
-40%	-	-	D	-	D
-30%	-	-	D	-	D
-20%	-	-	D	-	D
-10%	-	-	D	-	D
-5%	-	-	D	-	D
-4%	-	-	D	-	D
-3%	-	-	D	-	D
-2%	-	-	C	-	C
-1%	-	-	C	-	C
0%					
1%	-	-	C	-	C
2%	-	-	C	-	C
3%	-	-	C	-	C
4%	-	-	C	-	C
5%	-	-	C	-	C
10%	-	-	C	-	C
20%	-	-	D	-	D
30%	-	-	D	-	D
40%	-	-	D	-	D
50%	-	-	D	-	D

The first step of the cross-layer fault simulation leads to generate 8 assertions that are used in Step 2 to sort the behaviors. Those assertions monitor the signals on the communication interfaces. In blocks DIVA, DIVB, and SYNC, no fault leads to a critical behavior, so no assertion is generated for these blocks. Only blocks DIVC, CounterX, and CounterY lead to critical behaviors with respect to the system specifications.

To follow the quick and dirty flow, we chose a confidence level (c) greater than 90%, a margin of error (e) less than 10%, and a simulation time less than 3 h. In the third column of Table 5, we have the simulation time of each RTL block that allows us to compute the simulation time for a given number of injected faults. Figure 5 represents this simulation time according to the margin of error for different confidence levels. Three couples (c,e) are compliant with our constraints: either (90%, 4%), (95%, 5%) or (99.8%, 9%). Since a typical value for the confidence level is 95%, we choose the couple (95%, 5%). In Table 5 all the values are computed according to this couple. Columns 4 and 5 give the number of injected faults, then the corresponding simulation time. Columns 6 and 7 give the number of critical faults and the number of silent faults.

Table 5. RTL fault injection during the first round of the quick and dirty evaluation, for $c = 95\%$ and $e = 5\%$.

Block	Number of possible faults	RTL simulation time per fault (s)	Number of faults to inject	Simulation time (min)	Number of critical faults	Number of silent faults
DIVA	2,500	1.1	333	6.1	0	333 (100%)
DIVB	1,500	1.1	305	5.6	0	305 (100%)
DIVC	18,750	1.1	376	6.9	37 (10.0%)	334 (90.0%)
SYNC	2,500	1.1	333	6.1	0	333 (100%)
CounterX	30E6	2	384	12.8	182 (47.5%)	202 (52.5%)
CounterT	150E6	21	384	134.4	157 (40.9%)	227 (59.1%)

The fault simulations of all RTL blocks may take 171 min. Since DIVA, DIVB, and SYNC were not considered critical at Step 1, all the faults are silent (there is no assertion) and the number of critical errors will be null. For this second step, it was therefore not useful to simulate them. For the other blocks, results show that some are more vulnerable than the others: in CounterX and CounterT, quite half of the faults lead to a critical error.

For the three blocks considered as critical at Step 1 and for which assertions have been generated, Table 6 illustrates the interest of taking the system-level specifications into account. In a classical fault injection process, all "tolerable faults" would be considered as critical, significantly reducing the MTBF and increasing the fault tolerance requirements.

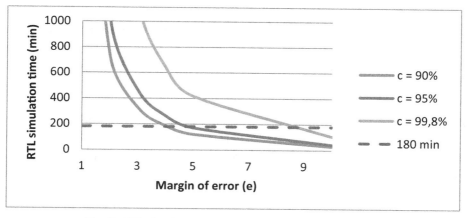

Fig. 5. RTL simulation time according to the margin of error.

Table 6. Classification of injected faults at RTL taking into account assertions with respect to system-level specifications ("tolerable faults"), for c = 95% and e = 5%.

Block	Number of critical faults	Number of tolerable faults	Number of silent faults
DIVC	37 (10%)	79 (21.0%)	260 (69.0%)
CounterX	182 (47.5%)	165 (42.9%)	37 (9.6%)
CounterT	157 (40.9%)	35 (9.1%)	192 (50%)

The co-simulation (Step 3) takes 278 min. The same faults as in Step 2 are injected, and in this step randomly chosen bit flips are also injected in DIVA, DIVB, and SYNC. We extract for each block the precision, the accuracy, and the True Silent Rate. The first column of Table 7 gives the name of the blocks. Simulation times for each block are displayed in the second column (co-simulation time). In the three last columns, the different metrics are reported, indicating the quality of the high-level models. Let us recall that we fix a threshold for the accuracy at 90%. The precision for blocks DIVA, DIVB, and SYNC is not applicable since they were classified as not critical at step 1. For these blocks, few fault injections led to errors and all of those were tolerated with respect to the system specifications. Block DIVC presents a good accuracy, a perfect TSR, but a very low precision (many critical faults identified in Step 2 turn out to be not critical in Step 3). Since the accuracy threshold is achieved, the low precision rate is not relevant. We do not need to change the high-level fault model.

The accuracy of block CounterX is below the threshold. The two other metrics are relevant. The TSR is very low: quite half the critical errors in Step 3 have not been correctly identified at Step 1. We must refine the high-level model to be closer to reality. We will not dwell on CounterT that is a different instantiation of CounterX.

Table 7. Results of the quick and dirty analysis at Step 3, 1st round.

Block	Co-simulation time (min)	Accuracy	Precision	True silent rate
DIVA	61	100%	N.A	100%
DIVB	45.75	100%	N.A	100%
DIVC	9.4	92%	2.8%	100%
SYNC	6.1	100%	N.A	100%
CounterX	96	71.6%	96.5%	55%
CounterT	70.4	78.1%	92.4%	69.8%

5.4 Quick and Dirty Flow: Next Rounds

CounterX (see Fig. 6) is a block that counts the number of impulsions on signals Fref and F(X) between two impulsions of signal F(D).

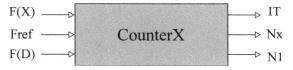

Fig. 6. CounterX RTL model.

Without loss of generality, we will focus only on signal F(X). Signal IT indicates that a fresh value on Nx is available and it interrupts the microcontroller. The behavior of CounterX is illustrated in Fig. 7. Between the two impulsions of F(D), there are 3 impulsions of F(X). On the last impulsion of F(D), signal Nx takes value 3, and signal IT is enabled.

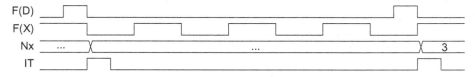

Fig. 7. CounterX behavior.

In the high-level system model, signals F(X) and F(D) were integers and not impulsions. Output Nx was the result of the division of F(X) by F(D). Since Nx is modeled with sc_fifo communication channels that notify the microcontroller when new data is available, signal IT is not modeled.

To improve the quality of the high-level CounterX model, we accurately analyzed the injection results of Step 3. Figure 8 shows the distribution of false silent faults per register. We see that less than 10 registers are sensitive to false silent faults. All these registers are used to compute signal IT.

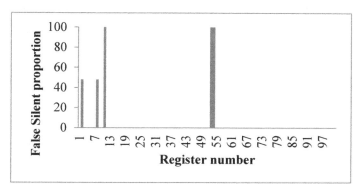

Fig. 8. False silent fault distribution per register.

At the system level, the faults we injected modified the amplitude of the values of Nx but did not modify the instant when they were available. Figure 9 illustrates this behavior: processes CounterX and uC are intrinsically synchronized through the sc_fifo communication channel. At the RT-Level, injected faults modify signal IT so no fresh data may be sent to the microcontroller. It is illustrated in Fig. 10: at T0, signal IT is correct and the microcontroller reads a value Nx1, but at time T1, signal IT is corrupted, CounterX has not finished its computation, and the microcontroller reads value Nx1 again.

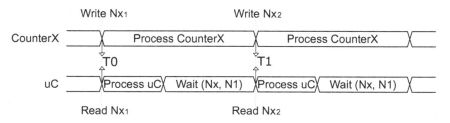

Fig. 9. CounterX TLM model synchronization with the microcontroller.

To avoid this problem, we changed the high-level model: an interruption signal was explicitly described. The second round of the quick and dirty method is then performed. At the end of this round, we get the metrics displayed in Table 8. We observe that in step 2, more faults are critical (column 2), both in CounterX and in CounterT. It means that

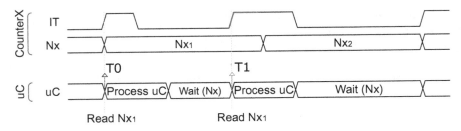

Fig. 10. CounterX RTL model with fault injection propagating on IT signal.

these blocks are more critical than initially assumed. TSR and accuracy are considerably improved. The threshold on the accuracy is reached, we are confident on the high-level model, and we can stop the quick and dirty rounds.

Table 8. Results of the quick and dirty analysis at Step 3, 2nd round, for $c = 95\%$ and $e = 5\%$.

Block	Critical (step 2)	Accuracy	Precision	True silent rate
CounterX	73.4%	94.4%	93.7%	95.4%
CounterT	56.5%	95.4%	95.3%	95.3%

Table 9. Results of the quick and dirty analysis at 3rd round for $c = 99.8\%$ and $e = 2\%$.

Block	Critical (1st round)	Critical (3rd round)	Silent (1st round)	Silent (3rd round)
DIVA	0%	0%	100%	100%
DIVB	0%	0%	100%	100%
DIVC	10.2%	10.2%	89.8%	89.8%
SYNC	0%	0%	100%	100%
CounterX	47.5%	73.4%	52.5%	26.6%
CounterT	40.7%	70.2%	59.3%	29.8%

The final step is to improve the accuracy of the robustness evaluation in Step 2. We increase the confidence level and decrease the margin of error. With a confidence level of 99.8% and a margin of error of 1%, we inject 23,855 faults in CounterX for a simulation time of 14 h. The percentage of critical faults is 73.8% (very close to the percentage obtained after the second round). More complete results are shown in Table 9, with a global simulation time of 41 h.

5.5   Comparison Between the Proposed Flow and the Initial FMEA

The comparison with the initial FMEA stands on two aspects: the functional analysis and the SEU analysis.

For the functional analysis, the simulations of high-level models allows getting a quick and automatic first insight about critical blocks or components in the architecture, more precise that what can be done by an expert from paper specifications. In addition, it is possible to get data about the criticality range of some blocks and timings as illustrated in Table 4.

For the SEU analysis, several strong points can be mentioned. First, with the "quick and dirty" flow, it is possible to keep simulation times acceptable and at the same time to refine the high-level models. Second, results can be obtained not only on components (e.g., FPGA) but also on the different blocks implemented inside the component, as illustrated in Table 10. This is much more precise than the type of analysis illustrated in Table 3 and can help a designer in focusing protection techniques on the most critical parts e.g., in that case, the counters. Also, comparing the figures in Table 10 and the initial estimation for the FPGA component (with the same flux of neutrons but with a conservative assumption that each SEU is a critical fault) the evaluated probability of critical errors is clearly reduced (4.62E−8 vs. 1E−7), leading to a better MTBF and potentially to a reduced need of additional design.

Table 10. Results after the last round assuming a particle flux of $\alpha = 7.2E-11$ neutrons/bit/h.

Block	Critical (3rd round)	Criticality per block (f/h)
DIVA	0%	0
DIVB	0%	0
DIVC	10.2%	1.59E−9
SYNC	0%	0
CounterX	73.4%	2.28E−8
CounterT	70.2%	2.18E−8
Total		4.62E−8

6   Conclusion

This contribution presents an iterative flow to quickly and accurately evaluate both circuit robustness with a cross-layer methodology and improving the realism of high-level models. This approach complies with aeronautics standards that recommend performing robustness analysis at different modeling levels and early in the design flow, from functional level models when possible. The method is based on iterative statistical fault injections that allow during first rounds quick fault simulations with an adapted level of confidence and improvement of the high-level models. When the high-level models are accurate enough, RTL fault simulations of each block with a high number of faults are performed. These RTL fault simulations determine if the faults are critical using the critical parameter ranges given by system high-level fault simulations. The proposed flow allows evaluating quickly and accurately the robustness of each block. It also allows identifying the most critical SEUs and then proposing fair cost countermeasures. This method has been applied to a critical airborne embedded system and demonstrated that, after improvement of high-level models, some RTL blocks were more critical than others. In comparison with the human FMEA analysis available as reference, much more details are available on the different blocks used in the application. The global MTBF is better and so should reduce the need for over-design, while the additional information allows focusing the required protections on the most critical blocks.

At that time, the approach has been applied to only one "real-life" case study. Results are promising, but in future works, we will apply this approach to other test cases. Also, metrics and thresholds used to measure the realism of the high-level models will have to be assessed further.

Acknowledgment. This work is part of the Safe-Air project, from the "Pack ambition recherche" program, funded by "La Region Auvergne-Rhone-Alpes".

References

1. Recommended failure modes and effects analysis FMEA practices for non-automobile aplications ARP5580, Standard (2012). www.sae.org/standards/content/arp5580/
2. Fulton, R., Vandermolen, R.: Airborne Electronic Hardware Design Assurance: A Practitioner's Guide to RTCA/DO-254. CRC Press, Boca Raton (2014). ISBN: 1482206056
3. Mariani, R., Boschi, G., Colucci, F.: Using an innovative SoC-level FMEA methodology to design in compliance with IEC61508. In: 2007 Design, Automation and Test in Europe Conference Exhibition Proceedings, pp. 1–6 (2007)
4. Bernard, R., Aubert, J.-J. , Bieber, P., Merlini, C., Metge, S.: Experiments in model based safety analysis: flight controls. In: 1st IFAC Workshop on Dependable Control of Discrete Systems Proceedings (2007)
5. Herdt, V., Le, H.M., Grosse, D., Drechsler, R.: On the application of formal fault localization to automated RTL-to-TLM fault correspondence analysis for fast and accurate vp-based error effect simulation - a case study. In: 2016 Forum on Specification and Design Languages (FDL) Proceedings, pp. 1–8 (2016)
6. Miele, A.: A methodology for the design and the analysis of reliable embedded systems. Ph. D. Dissertation, Politecnico di Milano (2010)
7. Leveugle, R., Cimonnet, D., Ammari, A.: System level dependability analysis with RT-level fault injection accuracy. In: 19th IEEE International Symposium on Defect and Fault Tolerance in VLSI Systems Proceedings, Cannes, France, pp. 451–458 (2004)
8. Vallero, A., et al.: Cross-layer reliability evaluation, moving from the hardware architecture to the system level: a CLERECO EU project overview. Microprocess. Microsyst. **39**(8), 1204–1214 (2015)
9. Perez, J., Azkarate-Askasua, M., Perez, A.: Codesign and simulated fault injection of safety-critical embedded systems using SystemC. In: 2010 European Dependable Computing Conference Proceedings, pp. 221–229 (2010)

10. Mueller-Gritschneder, D., Maier, P.R., Greim, M., Schlichtmann, U.: System C-based multi-level error injection for the evaluation of fault-tolerant systems. In: 2014 International Symposium on Integrated Circuits (ISIC) Proceedings, pp. 460–463 (2014)
11. Roux, J., et al.: High level fault injection method for evaluating critical system parameter ranges. In: 27th IEEE International Conference on Electronics Circuits and Systems (ICECS) Proceedings, pp. 1–4 (2020)
12. Roux, J., et al.: Cross-layer approach to assess FMEA on critical systems and evaluate high-level model realism. In: 29th IFIP/IEEE International Conference on Very Large Scale Integration (VLSI-SoC) Proceedings, Singapore (2021)
13. Leveugle, R., Calvez, A., Maistri, P., Vanhauwaert, P.: Statistical fault injection: quantified error and confidence. In: 2009 Design, Automation Test in Europe Conference Exhibition Proceedings, pp. 502–506 (2009)
14. Habing, D.H.: The use of lasers to simulate radiationinduced transients in semiconductor devices and circuits. IEEE Trans. Nucl. Sci. **12**(5), 91–100 (1965)
15. Pouget, V., Lewis, D., Lapuyade, H., Briand, P.F.R., Sarger, L., Calvet, M.-C.: Validation of radiation hardened designs by pulsed laser testing and spice analysis. Microelectron. Reliab. **39**, 931–935 (1999)
16. Constantinescu, C.: Neutron SER characterization of microprocessors. In: 2005 International Conference on Dependable Systems and Networks (DSN) Proceedings, pp. 754–759 (2005)
17. Guibbaud, N., Miller, F., Molière, F., Bougerol, A.: New combined approach for the evaluation of the soft-errors of complex ICs. IEEE Trans. Nucl. Sci. **60**(4), 2704–2711 (2013)
18. Jenn, E., Arlat, J., Rimen, M., Ohlsson, J., Karlsson, J.: Fault injection into VHDL models: the MEFISTO tool. In: Randell, B., Laprie, JC., Kopetz, H., Littlewood, B. (eds) Predictably Dependable Computing Systems, pp. 66–75. Springer, Cham (1994). https://doi.org/10.1007/978-3-642-79789-7_19
19. Leveugle, R., Hadjiat, K.: Optimized generation of VHDL mutants for injection of transition errors. In: 13th Symposium on Integrated Circuits and Systems Design (SBCCI2000) Proceedings, pp. 243–248 (2000)
20. Champon, R., Beroulle, V., Papadimitriou, A., Hely, D., Genevrier, G., Cezilly, F.: Comparison of RTL fault models for the robustness evaluation of aerospace FPGA devices. In: IEEE 22nd International Symposium on On-Line Testing and Robust System Design (IOLTS) Proceedings, pp. 23–24 (2016)
21. Miele, A.: A methodology for the design and the analysis of reliable embedded systems. Ph.D. Thesis, Politecnico di Milano (2010)
22. Tabacaru, B., Chaari, M., Ecker, W., Kruse, T., Novello, C.: Fault-effect analysis on system-level hardware modeling using virtual prototypes. In: 2016 Forum on Specification and Design Languages (FDL) Proceedings, pp. 1–7 (2016)
23. Mueller-Gritschneder, D., Maier, P.R., Greim, M., Schlichtmann, U.: System C-based multi-level error injection for the evaluation of fault-tolerant systems. In: 2014 International Symposium on Integrated Circuits (ISIC) Proceedings, pp. 460–463 (2014)
24. Bernard, R., Aubert, J.-J., Bieber, P., Merlini, C., Metge, S.: Experiments in model based safety analysis: flight controls. IFAC Proc. Vol. **40**(6), 43–48 (2007)
25. Roux, J., et al.: High-level fault injection to assess FMEA on critical systems. Microelectron. Reliab. **122**, 114–135 (2021)

Design and Mitigation Techniques of Radiation Induced SEEs on Open-Source Embedded Static RAMs

Sarah Azimi, Corrado De Sio, Andrea Portaluri, and Luca Sterpone[✉]

Dipartimento di Automatica e Informatica, Politecnico di Torino, Torino, Italy
{sarah.azimi,corrado.desio,andrea.portaluri,
luca.sterpone}@polito.it

Abstract. Static RAM modules are widely adopted in high performance systems. Single Event Effects (SEEs) resilient memories are required in many embedded systems applied in automotive and aerospace applications to increase their overall resiliency against SEEs. The current SEE resilient SRAM modules are obtained by applying radiation-hardened by design solutions which leads to elevated area overhead and difficulty to tune the resiliency capability with respect to the particle's radiation profile. To overcome these limitations, we propose a methodology for the analysis and mitigation of embedded SRAMs generated by the OpenRAM memory compiler. A technology-oriented radiation analysis tool is presented to support the interaction of the charged radiation particles with the SRAM layout and depict the sensitive transistors of the SRAM memory. A selective duplication of the sensitive transistors has been applied to the 6T-SRAM cell designed at the layout level. The designed cell is included in the OpenRAM compiler and used to generate a mitigated 8 Kb SRAM-bank, a DMA interface is also added to the bank in order to evaluate the interface capabilities. We evaluated the SEEs sensitivity by comparative simulation-based radiation analysis observing a reduction more than 6 times with respect to the original 6T-SRAM cell for the SEE sensitivity at high energy heavy ions particles, with negligible degradation of operations margins and power consumption and area overhead of less than $\sim 4\%$. The performance of the developed OpenRAM module has been also evaluated considering its application on a neural network behavioral model that demonstrate the feasibility of the proposed solution on large scale memory block circuitry.

Keywords: Radiation effects · Single event effects · SRAM memory · Transistor layout

1 Introduction

Embedded Static Random Access Memories are widely applied in various kinds of commercial applications, and they are today an integrated module of aerospace and automotive microprocessor systems [1]. RAMs are crucial components in System-on-chips (SoCs) and due to their wide application, SRAM modules are characterized by

V. Grimblatt et al. (Eds.): VLSI-SoC 2021, IFIP AICT 661, pp. 135–153, 2022.
https://doi.org/10.1007/978-3-031-16818-5_7

several memory configuration requirements and constraints especially when they are adopted in harsh environments [2]. SRAMs are vulnerable to two main effects, on one side they are really sensitive to wear-out mechanisms such as aging, where the Bias Temperature Instability (BTI) has been discovered as the main reliability concern. On the other side, SRAM cells are extremely sensitive to radiation-induced errors such as Single Event Effects (SEEs) caused by charged particles passing through the semiconductor device and generating electron-hole pairs along the particle track. The collected charge (Q_{coll}) of electron-hole pairs may change the memory cell state in the case it is greater than the critical charge (Q_{crit}) [3]. The radiation sensitivity of embedded SRAM is more emphasized considering that the area used by SRAM memory is dominating the physical layout of CPUs or GPUs [3]. Hence, SRAM layout is typically characterized by minimum device geometry that tends to reduce the Q_{crit} and conversely increase the sensitivity to radiation-induced errors. In order to manufacture robust SRAM modules and to increase the immunity to SEE, design and mitigation strategies for SRAM apply radiation-hardened-by-design (RHBD) that are generally adopting special epitaxial or eventually SOI substrate to limit ionizing radiation particle track length and including high-density capacitors and resistors to avoid circuit response to the collected charge [4]. Since the elevated cost of RHBD, typically error detection and correction (EDAC) approaches are applied to SRAM modules such as caches and shared memory [5]. However, the inclusion of extra combinational logic, such as the one used for Error Correction Mechanism, may also increase the occurrences of Single Event Transients (SETs) since these errors are not easily protected by EDAC.

Considering the growing role of embedded SRAM in system performances, several memory compiler tools have been recently developed [6]. The need for these tools was supported by the fact that most academic ICs design approaches are limited by the effective availability of memories. Nowadays, with the advent of an open-source customizable compiler, researchers are able to design their own memory module with the proper regular structure and configuration. This represents an undoubted advantage in hardware design since the basic building blocks are provided by foundries in technology process design kits (PDKs) and they are essential for hardware and device realization [7]. Thanks to the availability of open-source PDKs for RAMs, several researchers recently started to investigate the applicability of reliability analysis and mitigation of open-source hardware designs [8].

In this work, we propose an analysis and mitigation framework targeting the Single Event Effects (SEE) radiation-induced phenomena on Open-RAM physical design, extending the methodology introduced [8]. The OpenRAM project is an open-source memory compiler freely available under BSC license [6]. The compiler may be used for the design of new architectures in order to evaluate power, performances and area overhead on the other side, OpenRAM is usable to prototype and evaluate technological modification [9] We selected Cyclone, the cyclotron of the University Catholic the Louvain (UCL) heavy ions high-penetration cocktail as a reference for the radiation characterization. We perform a complete radiation sensitivity evaluation of the RAM block core cells in order to individuate the SEE cross-section and potential weak points of each memory component. Secondly, we apply selective mitigation solutions to the 6T cell of the SRAM by hardening the most sensitive transistor. Finally, we evaluated the performances and fault tolerance capability considering the OpenRAM bank connected to a DMA module and stimulated in different data transfer conditions. Furthermore, an extended performance evaluation of the developed solution has been integrating the developed OpenRAM memory bank into the simulation model of a Neural Network with DSP-oriented neuron architecture.

The hardening insertion has been automatized by the development of a tool to manipulate the physical layout of each cell and to insert a resized duplicated transistor into the 6T cell physical layout structure capable to increase the critical charge of the 6T cell structure.

This work has two main scientific contributions. The former is characterized by the first heavy ions radiation sensitivity evaluation of open-source embedded RAMs showing promising results and a large margin of improvements. The second is the realization of a tool to manipulate physical layout on large scale and to introduce mitigation strategies, the tool may be also ported to commercial technology nodes using library technology files. In order to evaluate the developed methodology, we designed two memory blocks using the physical implementations at 45 nm technology with the OpenRAM compiler adopting the FreePDK45 design kit and we performed comparative simulation-based radiation analysis. Experimental results demonstrate that the mitigated Open-RAM memory is approximately 35% more robust than the original Open-RAM design with a marginal degradation of the circuit performance and an area overhead of less than 4%.

This paper is organized as follows. Section 2 presents previous works related to analysis and mitigation methods for SEE effects on SRAM modules. Section 3 gives an overview on the OpenRAM analysis method, while the mitigation approach is described in Sect. 4. The experimental results are reported in Sect. 5. Finally, Sect. 6 drafts some conclusions and future works.

2   Related Works

Several previous works have already analyzed the impact of radiation particles on SRAM cells. With the progressive technology scaling, the number of errors within SRAM module drastically increases. This effect can be explained by both the SRAM cell junction reduction and by the reduced space between cells and lower values of critical charge [9, 10].

Radiation tests and 3-D simulations already demonstrated that the bipolar parasitic physical mechanism of the MOS transistors is activated by radiation particle strikes and is the cause of memory upsets [11]. In the last decade, real-time radiation test explored the sensitivity of 45 nm SRAM modules and identify the soft error projection with respect to the type of radiation particles and energies. The obtained results demonstrated the importance of the device manufacturing and the thick interconnect metallization and dielectric layers with respect to the effective sensitivity to charged particles [12].

On the other hand, two main categories of mitigation techniques targeting the corrections of single and multiple cell upsets were proposed. The first category relies on the insertion of Error Correction Code (ECC) mechanisms at the architectural level, while effective for Single Event Upsets (SEUs) these approaches are not able to cope with many Multiple Event Upsets (MEUs), usually happening in the same word and not necessarily in adjacent cells [6]. Besides, traditional error detection and correction approaches introduce critical timing on memory access making these solutions difficulty applicable in cache memories [13].

The second category is based on radiation-hardened-by-design (RHBD) techniques that allows to apply radiation mitigation circuit solutions to the manufacturing process of commercial foundries in order to minimize the impact of radiation particles [14]. The focus of RBHD techniques have been on Single Event Upsets (SEUs) affecting the 6T-SRAM cell. The developed mitigation solutions were based on resizing of the sensitive transistors [15] or adding extra transistors to reduce the proximity of the radiation strike and distribute the charge collection. The insertion of extra transistors to the original 6T-RAM cell has been also provided in the 8T-SRAM [16] where two transistors are added to eliminate the charge sharing effect between the bit lines or in the differential-ended 10T-SRAM [17] for increasing the speed of the bit line signal or even as 12T-SRAM to reduce the noise disturbance of the bit cell interleaving structure. The performance of the memory block is strictly dependent on the Central Processing Unit (CPU) or Direct Memory Access (DMA) modules.

In particular, the DMA module allows to speed up the data transfer versus and from the memory. In System-on-a-Chip (SoC), DMA module is implemented through the allocation of a controller physically close to the memory layout in order to provide a high-bandwidth infrastructure. In order to provide error tolerant data transfer mechanisms, radiation tolerant heterogeneous multi DMA core systems have been developed to support Single Event Upsets (SEUs) tolerant high-rate connections between the multi-core module and the memory elements [18].

In order to evaluate the performance of the developed OpenRAM memory block with respect to the typical DMA data transfer, we evaluated the Scatter-Gather (SG) algorithm, which consist on the data transfer initialization on blocks of 32-bit words through Buffer Descriptors (BD). A set of DMA configurations have been evaluated considering different direction of the data transfer, parametric data length and different test of read and write addresses (random and full burst transfer mode). We also evaluated single data request from the DMA with data transfer request of a low number of data packets in order to evaluate the performance limits of the OpenRAM block versus the DMA data transfer routines.

In this work, we investigate specifically the sensitivity and mitigation of recoverable SEEs phenomena affecting a SRAM memory bank. Typically, this type of SEE effect happens in ground and avionics applications or, for aerospace applications at Low Earth Orbit (LEO), where the eventuality of ultra-high energy radiation particle is nullified by the Earth magnetic field. Thanks to the layout-oriented radiation analysis we implement a RHBD mitigation solution at the layout level increasing the robustness of the original 6T-SRAM cell by adding two parametrizable transistors that can be tunable with respect to the radiation particle energy required.

3   Radiation Analysis of VLSI Technology

In order to achieve an accurate radiation sensitivity of the SRAM module, we developed the radiation particle simulation environment illustrated in Fig. 1. The simulation flow is based on the 3D radiation particle propagation tool presented in [20] and available as open-source code. We extracted the physical layout description of the OpenRAM basic cell library, and we inserted the layer material, thickness, and depth to the Graphic Data Systems (GDS) description.

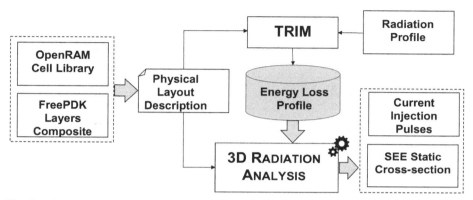

Fig. 1. The developed 3D simulation for the radiation particle analysis on the OpenRAM cell library layout geometry.

The physical description and the particle radiation profile generated by the Transport of Ions in Matter (TRIM) tool are used to calculate the energy distribution released by the ions traversing the layer section of the cell. The last step of the analysis consists on the analysis of the physical layout description and the energy loss of the radiation particle used to calculate the transient sensitivity of the logic cells in terms of SEE cross-section and the correspondent current injection pulses generated within the cell geometry.

3.1 The FreePDK 45 nm Technology Node

The OpenRAM memory module is generated by the open-source compiler using the open-source variation-aware physical design kit FreePDK [19] based on Scalable CMOS design rules. The cell library includes variation-aware tools compatible with commercial design tools based on a theoretical 45 nm technology where each cell is described by a proper structure including rectangular vias, metallizations and interconnects as well as silicon active regions. We integrated the FreePDK library information building a 3D model of the cell library adding thickness and layer material adopting the modeling provided by the 45 nm high performance bulk logic platform technology lithography [21]. The generated model consists of 13 layers from the Active region, the Well and implant sections up to three aluminum metallizations connected by copper vias. The data of the generated model are represented in Table 1 while a structural view of a 6T-SRAM cell of the OpenRAM module is illustrated in Fig. 2.

The size of each layer and the position of each volumetric region of the FreePDK library has been modeled considering the thickness and the implant position in order to achieve a compliant three-dimensional model.

Table 1. 45 nm FreePDK layers, thickness, and composite materials.

Layer name	Layer [#]	Thickness [nm]	Layer material
Active	1	520	SiO_2
N-Well	2	100	n-Si
P-Well	3	110	p-Si
N-implant	4	100	n-Si
P-implant	5	110	p-Si
S-Block	6	85	SiN
Poly-Silicon	9	85	Poly-Si
Contact	10	150	Si_3N_4
M1	11	130	Al
Via1	12	120	Cu
M2	13	140	Al
Via2	14	120	Cu
M3	15	140	Al

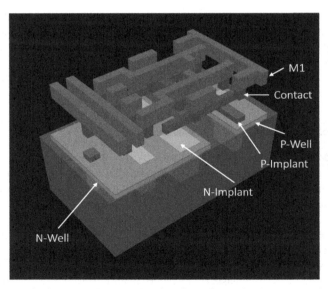

Fig. 2. The 45 nm 6T-SRAM cell 3D model view from the Active layer up to the metallization M1.

3.2 SEE Radiation Analysis

The radiation analysis is performed considering four heavy ions energy profile related to the UCL facility [22]. Table 2 reports the energies, ion range and Linear Energy Transfer (LET) used. The analysis starts by extracting the geometry and size data of layer volumes, material composition as well as the radiation profile for the considered particles. The TRIM application calculates the energy loss level of the particle for each layer of the cell. Figure 3 represents the amount of released energy in each layer of the cell considering the *Aluminium* and *Xenon* heavy ion particles at the energies defined in Table 2. Interestingly, *vias* are the volumes with the highest value of energy loss, while the metalizations, contacts and in implants and well have a low energy loss.

Table 2. Radiation particle characteristics

Ion	DUT energy [MeV]	Range [μmSi]	LET [MeV/mg/cm^2]
$^{13}C^{4+}$	131	269.3	1.3
$^{27}Al^{18+}$	250	131.2	5.7
$^{58}Ni^{18+}$	582	100.5	20.4
$^{124}Xe^{35+}$	995	73	62.5

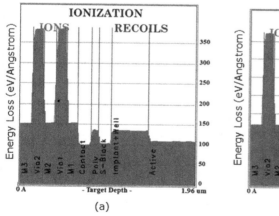
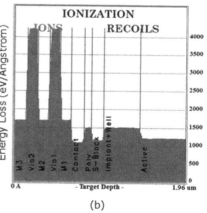

(a)   (b)

Fig. 3. Release energy profile for the different layers of the 45 nm cell for the Aluminum (a) and the Xenon (b) energy levels.

The developed tool elaborates the physical description of the cell, generating the 3D mesh structure of the layout of the logic cell. Based on the size, shape, and material of metallization and volumes of the cell with respect to the radiation profile of the mission represented in Table 2, the developed radiation analysis tool simulates the effects of highly charged particles traversing the silicon junction of the device and calculate the generated eV transmitted to the Silicon matter by the particles and provide the current profile for each particle strike.

3.3 OpenRAM Radiation Sensitivity and SoC Interface

The System-on-Chip (SoC) under evaluation consists on an OpenRAM module and a DMA core. They are connected through two buses: a control bus with read, write and enable signals, and a data-bus of 32 bit wise. The overall scheme is illustrated in Fig. 4, where it is also possible to distinguish the eight blocks of the OpenRAM architecture. The hierarchical blocks of the memory bank are based on six main logic cells: Data Flip-Flop (DFF), Master and Slave Flip-Flip (MS-Flop), Write Drivers, Three states buffer, Sense Amplifier and the 6 Transistors RAM cell. The hierarchical decoder and the control logic gates are outside of the memory bank; however they are mainly based on DFFs and combinational logic cells which radiation sensitivity can be determined with traditional analysis method [23]. We analyzed the memory bank cells with 10,000 heavy ions particle using the 3D simulation approach and we computed the SEE cross-section for each cell. The results are illustrated in Fig. 5.

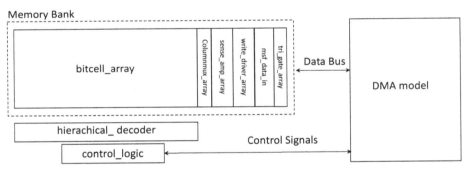

Fig. 4. The overall OpenRAM hierarchical blocks. The hierarchical decoder and control logic modules are outside from the memory bank. The DMA model directly configure the control logic and performs the data transfer through the data bus.

The SEE cross-section may vary from $5.44 \cdot 10^{-14}$ up to $5.46 \cdot 10^{-13}$. The DFFs and the MS-Flops are the most sensitive cells while the 6T-RAM cell is interestingly the cell with the lower cross-section curve. However, considering the number of cells per block, the memory bank cross-section is fully determined by the sensitivity of the 6T-SRAM cell. For example, considering a memory bank of 8 Kb, the cross-section is equivalent to $1.43 \cdot 10^{-9}$ totally due by the 6T-SRAM radiation sensitivity.

We performed a Monte Carlo analysis in order to depict the vulnerability regions of the 6T-SRAM cells and individuating the parasitic thyristor resistance spectrum distribution on the cell layout considering a static and unpowered condition of the cell. In Fig. 6, it is possible to observe that the SRAM has various sensitive area, most of them correlated to the layout position of the 6 transistors. Besides, we calculated the distribution of the current pulses observing that 96.62% of the radiation particle injected over the 40,000 injections performed by the selected ions are generating current pulse below 0.5 μA with a maximal peak of 17.4 μA.

4 8T-SRAM Mitigation Strategies

Traditional 8T-SRAM schemes are based on the insertion of 2 additional transistors to the 6T scheme depending on the target application of the memory. In case of mitigation solutions for soft-errors, extra transistors are generally added to introduce redundancy to the bit-lines or to the NMOS and PMOS used to implement the SRAM storage. The main purpose of our approach is to insert two redundant transistors in parallel to the original PMOS transistors, in order to distribute the radiation particle charge injected by those particles directly crossing MP5 and MP6 and to increase the overall Q_{crit} margins for the transient effects introduced by particles crossing other regions of the cell.

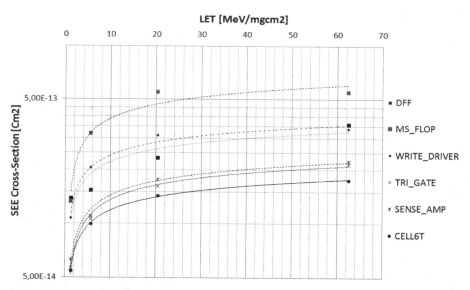

Fig. 5. The Single Event Effects (SEEs) cross-section sensitivity for the OpenRAM memory bank individual cell components.

We adopted a different approach to insert the redundant transistors to the original scheme. Thanks to the availability of the OpenRAM layout, instead to start the mitigation insertion from the electrical scheme, we considered at first the 6T-SRAM original layout available regions that can be modified without introducing area overhead to the cell. We identify on the top of the MP6 and MP5 transistors enough physical space to introduce to redundant transistors without affecting the SRAM cell size.

We introduced the following layers for each transistor: an active layer with $h = 0.02$ μm and $w = 0.19$ μm; a P-implant layer with $h = 0.02$ μm and $w = 0.18$ μm centered with respect to the active layer; the poly-silicon section vertical to the active

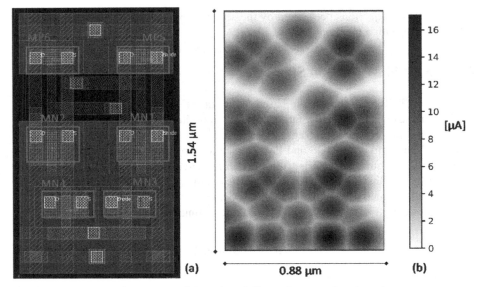

(a)   1.54 μm   0.88 μm   [μA]   (b)

Fig. 6. The 6T-SRAM layout (a) and the vulnerability region reporting the μA current spectrum for the Xenon energy analysis on the overall area (b).

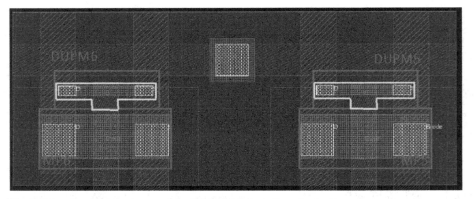

Fig. 7. The view of the top area of the SRAM cell including the duplicated transistor T structure, highlighted in yellow. (Color figure online)

layer has been extended of 0.05 μm in order to be effective with respect to the active layer; two contact regions of $h = 0.02$ μm and $w = 0.035$ μm, finally, we extended the metallization M1 of 0.06 μm in order to connect properly the VDD source and the drain and source junctions.

The result of this modification is a *T-structure* added on the top of the original transistor as illustrated in Fig. 7. The layout insertions have been validated by a commercial layout editor tool configured with the FreePDK45 library design rules check. Finally,

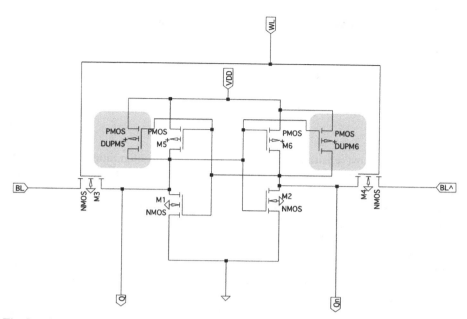

Fig. 8. The electrical scheme obtained from the layout technology extraction of the mitigated 8T-SRAM cell with the highlights on the added transistors replica.

we performed the technology extraction and conversion to an H-spice model, reported in Fig. 8, using the same layout editor tool.

5 Experimental Results

We designed two 8 Kb memory modules with 1 memory bank, 256 words and 32-bits configuring the OpenRAM compiler with the original 6T-SRAM and with the developed 8T-SRAM adopting the T-structure redundant transistors. We performed two experiments evaluating the static behavior of the memory bank. The former consists on a fault injection campaign for evaluating the mitigation capability of the developed 8T-SRAM cell, the latter consists on the comparative analysis of area, leakage current and SRAM performance characteristics.

5.1 SEE Radiation Analysis

The fault injection simulation setup consists on modeling the SEE at the circuit level by inserting transient current sources at the impact nodes. The fault injection has been executed in two different campaigns. The former campaign measures the maximal current pulse threshold tolerated before to create the upset for each individual transistor. The latter campaign measures the dynamic sensitivity of the cell by injecting the current pulse extracted from the current pulse profile generated by the radiation analysis tool applied to the cell.

Table 3. SRAM cell SEE threshold current

SRAM configuration	SEE threshold current pulse [μA]	
	$Q = 1\ Q_n = 0$	$Q = 0\ Q_n = 1$
6T-Original	0.93	0.46
8T-Proposed	3.83	2.12

In general, the most sensitive part of the SRAM inverter configuration is the drain of the n-mos transistor which is in the off stage; however, we performed the fault injection in all the transistors, and we extracted the SRAM cell threshold current for creating a bit-flip within the cell. The obtained results are reported in Table 3, as it possible to notice the proposed mitigated cell increases the maximal current threshold of around 4 times at the static condition $Q = 1$ and $Q_n = 0$ and more than 4.6 times for the condition $Q = 0$ and $Q_n = 1$.

A plot of the injection of the maximal current pulse for the configuration $Q = 1$ and $Q_n = 0$ is illustrated in Fig. 9. The injections are performed at the static storage condition of the SRAM cell and for a duration of 2 ns which is 18% longer than the maximal current pulse width measured by the 3D radiation simulation. In details, the current pulse effect has a duration of around 800 ps when the Q and Q_n are simultaneously at low voltage. As consequence, the two values are upset for 2.05 ns. Once the current pulse expires, the original SRAM values are restored in less than 420 ps.

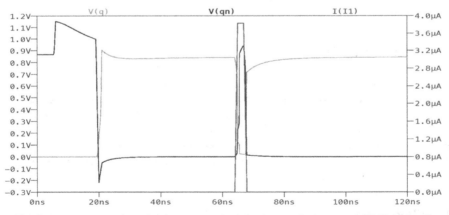

Fig. 9. An example of maximal current pulse injection on the proposed 8T-SRAM cell.

We evaluated the overall robustness of the mitigated OpenRAM memory bank considering the radiation particle spectra described within the radiation analysis section and we performed 40,000 particle injection comparing the achieved SEE cross-section. The results, illustrated in Fig. 10, show that the developed 8TSRAM is robust more than 6 times with respect to the original cell at higher energy. Please note, that the proposed

8TSRAM is drastically more robust for low energy particles, since it is resilient more than one order of magnitude at energies below 10 meV/mgcm².

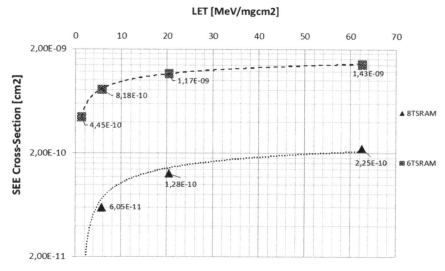

Fig. 10. The OpenRAM 8 Kb memory bank SEE cross-section comparison.

5.2 DMA Performance Analysis

The main goal of the benchmark analysis is to mimic the hardware computing operations of Direct Memory Access (DMA) data transfer considering a single core. As benchmark DMA we selected a data transfer module capable to perform the Scatter-Gather algorithm on memory blocks of 32-bit. We hypothesized to configure the DMA with a single channel mode managing data transfer individually per data transfer direction. We settled two data transfer directions: *Memory Mapped-to-Stream* (MM2S) mainly based on reading operation from the block RAM and *Stream-to-Memory Mapped* (S2MM) which is performing continuous writing on the block RAM. The directions are addressed by different buffer descriptor allocated in a dedicated memory within the DMA module. Please note that the interrupt signals typically coming from the DMAs and connected to the CPU have been properly monitored by the simulation model in order to measure the performance of the memory block. A software routine running on the DMA is settled in order to initialize and stimulate the memory and collect the reports on the simulation environment. The achieved data are reported in Table 4, where we reported the minimal clock period that allows to perform an error immune data transfer.

5.3 Comparative Analysis

The power dissipation, area and delay are marginally affected by the insertion of the two redundant transistors. The size of the SRAM cell is not changed by the insertion

Table 4. OpenRAM memory block DMA performances

32-bit words [#]	Original 6TSRAM [ns]		Proposed 8TSRAM [ns]	
	MM2S	S2MM	MM2S	S2MM
1	2.18	2.19	2.94	3.02
8	17.41	17.49	23.55	23.55
64	139.31	141.45	148.41	159.41
256	556.05	562.08	645.66	682.32

of the T-structure transistors since we included them in the original 6T-SRAM layout. However, in case of further optimization, our insertion will limit the reduction of the SRAM cell area for less than 3%.

Table 5. SRAM cells characteristics comparison

Characteristic	Original 6TSRAM	Proposed 8TSRAM
$V_{DD}(V)$	1.5	1.5
Leakage current (μA)	0.81	0.88
SNM	41.53	43.20
RSNM	27.40	38.42
WSNM	129.62	141.75

Considering the power consumption and the functional characteristics, we compared the original and mitigated cells in order to compare the Static Noise Margin (SNM), the Read Static Noise Margin (RSNM) and the Write Static Noise Margin (WSNM). As expected, the results reported in Table 5 indicates that the proposed 8T-SRAM cell is slightly degrading the leakage current while maintaining almost equivalent the SNM.

We compared the reading and writing delays characteristics of a single SRAM cell. The delay is degraded due to the additional parasitic resistive capacitive load effects that increases the average response time from 68 ps up to 92 ps. Finally, we also compared the standby power for the traditional 6TSRAM cell with the developed 8TSRAM observing a negligible increasing of power consumption from 6.30 μW to 6.83 μW.

6   OpenRAM Module Within Neural-Network Structure

The typical NN structure illustrated in Fig. 11, where floating point data are used for weights, inputs and outputs. In order to implement a complete CNN, a number of parallel neurons can be instantiated in parallel. All the data flow traversing the structure from the synapse inputs up to the post rectified linear output are represented by 16 bits. Considering that the data are generally representing values in a range from 0 to 1 and that

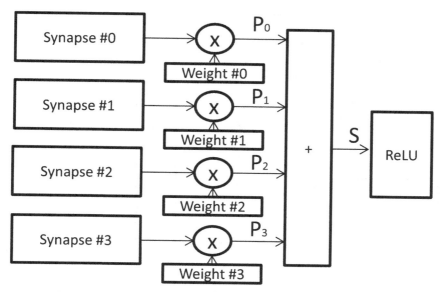

Fig. 11. The neuron structure: the basic element of CNN architecture.

weights are signed values with a limited range of precision; the product will mandatory requires higher resolution for the multiplication and extra range for the accumulation to avoid overflow conditions of any arithmetic process. For the sake of this work, we implemented a full neural network model consisting in a behavioral description of fully parallel neurons in order to evaluate the impact of OpenRAM mitigated module on a large scale circuit.

A feasible solution to insert the developed OpenRAM module in its original unmitigated version and with the developed 8TSRAM cell is to adopt a Digital Signal Processing (DSP) architecture for each neuron. The scheme of the developed implementation is illustrated in Fig. 12.

The structure of the hardware synthesizable neuron consists of an input stream of 256 16 bits data words simultaneously read by all the neuron in the same layer. The layer of parallel neurons is reducing the limitations on the input bandwidth thanks to the essential data caching. The data inputs are multiplied with the weights; typically, each weight value is used several times by the neurons depending on the position related to the data set. The OpenRAM module is inserted in order to store the neuron weight. The architecture used is the classical convolutional network [24] with reduced size, suitable to evaluate mapping and implementation tools.

We tested the network with an input data stream consists of a 224 by 224 image crop with 3 colors map convolved with 96 filters at the first layer, each one with a size of 7 by 7and adopting a stride of 2 on both x and y. The feature map is then passed through a rectifier linear function, max pooled with a 3 × 3 matrix with stride 2 and finally normalized across feature maps and generating 55 × 55 elements feature map. The intermediate layers 2 to 5 repeat the same operation, while the final two layers are fully connected and are elaborating the features from the top convolutional layer in a

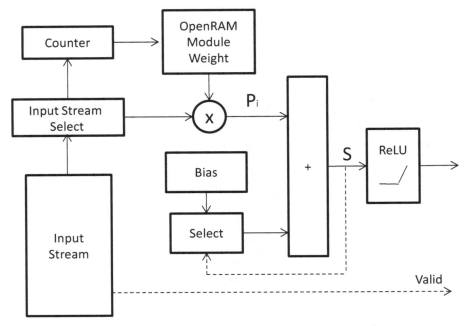

Fig. 12. The hardware neural network structure implementation.

vector of 9,216 dimensions. Finally, the last layer is a soft-max function with i-way, with i being the number of classifications.

The developed design flow has been applied on the NN implemented and simulated using the ModelSIM simulator instrumented with the OpenRAM structural netlist. The NN has been implemented in five different implementation:

- *Original*: implemented with timing performance optimization considering a customized memory block obtained by synthesis
- *+Open*: implemented with the original 8 Kb OpenRAM module used for the storage of the neural node weights.
- *+OpenOptiRead*: implemented with the original 8 Kb OpenRAM module used for the storage of the neural node weights, optimized for the reading operations
- *+OpenMit*: implemented with the developed mitigated 8 Kb OpenRAM module used for the storage of the neural node weights.
- *FullOpen:* implemented with the developed mitigated 8 Kb OpenRAM module used for the storage of the neural node weights and for the storage of the input and data output of the NN.

The obtained results are presented in Table 6 where we show the computational time to elaborate a classification of 10 images. The performance results show the overall computational time considering a simulation frequency of 100 MHz, however, we estimated that that maximal working frequency of 220 MHz can be reached without incurring in errors within the OpenRAM blocks.

The result shows that the insertion of the OpenRAM memory block provides an improvement of performances versus the original implementation of the Neural Network with a customized memory block. We believe that this optimization is due to the faster decoding circuitry of the OpenRAM block versus the customized ones. On the other hand, it is possible to notice a comparable trend on the NN with the mitigated OpenRAM, as expected we observed a marginal degradation of the computational time. However, we believe that this degradation is mainly due to the smaller size of the developed OpenRAM block with respect to the requested size which may reach up to 33 Kb for the largest Neural Network layer.

Table 6. Neural network performances considering the OpenRAM integration

Characteristic	Overall computational time [ms]
Original	12.4
+Open	11.8
+OpenOptiRead	11.4
+OpenMit	12.1
FullOpen	14.9

7 Conclusions and Future Works

In this paper, we propose a methodology for the analysis and the mitigation of SRAM circuit generated by the open-source OpenRAM memory compiler. The main novelty of the proposed methodology is the capability to details the interaction of the radiation particle with the SRAM memory layout, to depict the sensitive transistors and to selectively mitigate the radiation effects by layout-oriented modifications. We applied the workflow methodology to the design and mitigation of the 6TSRAM cell. Thanks to the availability of the layout description provided by the OpenRAM project, we developed a new mitigation strategy to increase the current thresholds and reduce the voltage transients. An experimental analysis performed on an 8 Kb memory module generated by the OpenRAM compiler demonstrates that the developed 8TSRAM-based memory module is 6 times more resilient than the original memory block at high energy particle. The resiliency is improved up to one order of magnitude at lower energies, as specifically target for ground and low earth orbit applications. We compared the functional characteristics with the original cell, and we observed a minimal deviation in leakage current and an evident improvement versus reading and writing noise margins. The performance analysis of the developed cell has been also experimentally evaluated considering a DMA System-on-a-Chip and a Neural Network simulation. Thanks to these two analyses it has been possible to evaluate the proposed solution considering an high performance architecture and large scale memory block usage. As future works, we plan to extend the mitigation features to other memory components and to evaluate the robustness versus destructive Single Event Latch-up (SEL) effects and to evaluate the application of error detection and correction schemes.

References

1. Sierawski, B.D., et al.: Muon-induced single event upsets in deep-submicron technology. IEEE Trans. Nucl. Sci. **57**(6), 3273–3278 (2010)
2. Karnik, T., Hazucha, P.: Characterization of soft errors caused by single event upsets in CMOS processes. IEEE Trans. Depend. Secure Comput. **1**(2), 128–143 (2004)
3. Azimi, S., Du, B., Sterpone, L.: On the prediction of radiation-induced SETs in flash-based FPGAs. Microelectron. Reliab. **64**, 230–234 (2016)
4. Dodd, P.E., Massengill, L.W.: Basic mechanisms and modeling of single-event upset in digital microelectronics. IEEE Trans. Nucl. Sci. **50**(3), 583–602 (2003)
5. Lacoe, R., et al.: Application of hardness-by-design methodology to radiation-tolerant ASIC technologies. IEEE Trans. Nuc. Sci. **47**(6), 2334–2341 (2000)
6. Yao, X., Clark, L.T., Patterson, D.W., Holbert, K.E.:Single event transient mitigation in cache memory using transient error checking circuits. In: IEEE Custom Integrated Circuits Conference 2010, San Jose, CA, USA, pp. 1–4 (2010)
7. Guthaus, M.R., Stine, J.E., Ataei, S., Chen, B., Wu, B., Sarwar, M.: OpenRAM: an open-source memory compiler. In: 2016 IEEE/ACM International Conference on Computer-Aided Design (ICCAD), Austin, TX, USA, pp. 1–6 (2016)
8. Azimi, S., Sio, C.D., Sterpone, L.: On the evaluation of SEEs on open-source embedded static RAMs. In: 2021 IFIP/IEEE 29th International Conference on Very Large Scale Integration (VLSI-SoC), pp. 1–6 (2021)
9. Azimi, S., Sterpone, L.: Digital design techniques for dependable high performance computing. In: IEEE International Test Conference (ITC), pp. 1–10 (2020)
10. Yoshimoto, S., et al.:A 40-nm 0.5-V 20.1-μW/MHz 8T SRAM with low-energy disturb mitigation scheme. In: 2011 Symposium on VLSI Circuits - Digest of Technical Papers, Kyoto, Japan, pp. 72–73 (2011)
11. Baumann, R.C., Smith, E.B.: Neutron-induced 10B fission as a major source of soft errors in high density SRAM. Microelectron. Reliab. **41**(2), 211–218 (2001)
12. Chiu, Y.-W., et al.: 40nm bit-interleaving 12T subthreshold SRAM with data-aware write-assist. IEEE Trans. Circ. Syst. I **61**, 2578–2688 (2014)
13. Seifert, N., Kirsch, M.: Rea-time soft-error testing results of 45nm high-K metal gate, bulk CMOS SRAMs. IEEE Trans. Nucl. Sci. **59**(6), 2818–2823 (2012)
14. Li, J., Chen, W., Li, R., Wang, G., Yang, S.: Study on transient ionizing radiation effect of 40nm SRAM. In: 3rd International Conference on Radiation Effects of Electronic Devices (ICREED), pp. 1–4 (2019)
15. Mohr, K., Clark, L.: Delay and area efficient first-level cache soft error detection and correction. In: IEEE ICCD Proceedings, pp. 88–92, October 2006
16. Hoang, T., et al.: A radiation hardened 16-Mb SRAM for space applications. In: IEEE Aerospace Conference, pp. 1–6 (2006)
17. Mohammad, B.S., Saleh, H., Ismail, M.: design methodologies for yield enhancement and power efficiency in SRAM-based SoCs. IEEE Trans. Very Large Scale Integr. (VLSI) Syst. **23**(10), 2054–2064 (2015)
18. Solokhina, T., et al.:Radiation tolerant heterogeneous Multicore "system on chip" with built-in multichannel SpaceFibre switch for onboard data management and mass storage device: components, short paper. In: 2016 International SpaceWire Conference (SpaceWire), pp. 1–6 (2016)
19. Chang, L., et al.: An 8T-SRAM for variability tolerance and low-voltage operation in high-performance caches. IEEE J. Solid-State Circ. **43**, 518–529 (2008)
20. Chang, J., et al.: A 32 Kb 10T sub-threshold SRAM array with bit-interleaving and differential read scheme in 90nm CMOS. IEEE J. Solid-State Circ. **44**, 650–658 (2009)

21. Stine, J.E., et al.: FreePDK: an open-source variation-aware design kit. In: IEEE International Conference on Microelectronic Systems Education, pp. 173–174 (2007)
22. Sterpone, L., Luoni, F., Azimi, S., Du, B.: A 3-D simulation-based approach to analyze heavy ions-induced SET on ditigal circuits. IEEE Trans. Nucl. Sci. **67**(9), 2034–2041 (2020)
23. Azimi, S., De Sio, C., Sterponet, L.: A radiation-hardened CMOS full-adder based on layout selective transistor duplication. IEEE Trans. Very Large Scale Integr. (VLSI) Syst. **29**(8), 1596–1600 (2021)
24. Zeiler, M.D., Fergus, R.: Visualizing and understanding convolutional networks. In: Fleet, D., Pajdla, T., Schiele, B., Tuytelaars, T. (eds.) Computer Vision – ECCV 2014. LNCS, vol. 8689, pp. 818–833. Springer, Cham (2014). https://doi.org/10.1007/978-3-319-10590-1_53

Design of a Reconfigurable Optical Computing Architecture Using Phase Change Material

Parya Zolfaghari[✉] and Sébastien Le Beux[✉]

Department of Electrical and Computer Engineering, Concordia University, Montreal, Canada
{p_zolfag,slebeux}@encs.concordia.ca

Abstract. Silicon photonics is an emerging technology allowing to take the advantage of high-speed light propagation to accelerate computing kernels in integrated systems. Micrometer-scale optical devices call for reconfigurable architectures to maximize resources utilization. Typical reconfigurable optical computing architectures involve micro-ring resonators for electro-optic modulation. However, such devices require voltage and thermal tuning to compensate for fabrication process variability and thermal sensitivity. This power-hungry calibration leads to significant static power overhead, thus limiting the scalability of optical architectures. In this chapter, we propose to use non-volatile Phase Change Materials (PCM) elements to route optical signals only through the required resonators, hence saving calibration energy of bypassed resonators. The non-volatility of PCM elements allows maintaining the optical path. We investigate the efficiency of the PCM elements on the Reconfigurable Directed Logic (RDL) architecture. We also evaluate the static power saving induced by the use of couplers instead of microring to redirect WDM signals into a single waveguide. Finally, we show that the couplers can be efficiently used to cascade the architectures, allowing to increase the number of inputs to be processed without opto-electronic conversions. Compared to a ring-based implementation of RDL architecture, results show that the proposed implementation allows reducing the static power by 53% on average.

Keywords: Nanophotonics · Phase Change Material (PCM) · Reconfigurable computing architectures

1   Introduction

Silicon photonics have attracted attention due to the compatibility with CMOS manufacturing process. The technology allows integrating high speed photonic devices to provide high bandwidth low latency chip scale interconnects [1, 2]. As the technology continues to mature, emerging optical computing architectures are developed to accelerate neural networks applications [3] and microwave processing [4]. The design of optical circuits dedicated to matrix multiplications, logic functions [5] and adders [6] are also investigated. Logic circuits relying on integrated optics involve electro-optic devices such as micro-ring resonators. In [7, 8] the rings are organized as an array of

V. Grimblatt et al. (Eds.): VLSI-SoC 2021, IFIP AICT 661, pp. 155–174, 2022.
https://doi.org/10.1007/978-3-031-16818-5_8

optical switches to control light propagation. Such architecture allows to simultaneously controlling switching operation of the rings, which lead to low latency processing. Reconfigurable optical architectures [9, 10] allow to efficiently use, bulky, optical devices for multiple operation, thus allowing to reduce the cost overhead induced by the technology. A feature shared by such architecture is the need to calibrate ring resonators in order to control optical signal transmissions. While high contrast can be achieved, the method requires voltage and thermal tuning to calibrate the rings, which accounts for up to 40% [10] of the static power consumption. Disruptive materials and architectures are thus needed to overcome the low energy efficiency of optical devices calibration. Phase Change Material (PCM) has been widely studied to design non-volatile photonic circuits such as neural networks [11]. Indeed, the non-volatility of PCM based devices allows to maintain the configuration of optical device without consuming energy. Typical configurations involve amorphous (am) and crystalline (cr) states, which can be obtained by heating the device [12]. Among recently demonstrated PCM based devices, a Directional Coupler (DC) reported in [13] leads to 0.16 dB and 0.72 dB attenuation under cr and am states respectively at wavelength 1521.5 nm. Such low attenuation and the associated high optical contrasts allow to envision new optical architectures involving reconfigurable optical paths. In this chapter we propose an optical architecture allowing to bypass unused optical devices. To achieve this, PCM-based directional couplers are placed before and after resonating devices, thus allowing either to transmit optical signals to devices for modulation purpose or to bypass them. The use of the bypass path allows to avoid calibration of the optical devices, thus leading to significant reduction in the static power consumption. We investigate the efficiency of the proposed design on the RDL architecture. We also investigate the cascading of the proposed cell using directional couplers combined with lasers source placed between the cells. The architecture involves the use of coupler which induces loss resulting in laser power overhead.

To evaluate the proposed architectures, we define a loss model allowing to estimate the laser power overhead and the reduced ring calibration power consumption. We also investigate the impact of the architecture reconfiguration frequency on the power saving. Results show coupler based implementation of PCM based RDL leads to 53% of static power reduction compared with baseline while ring based implementation of RDL shows 19% of saving.

The chapter is organized as follows. Section 2 presents an overview of micro ring resonator-based computing architectures and introduces PCM based photonic devices. In Sect. 3, we present the proposed reconfigurable PCM-based architecture. Section 4 describes the power model and Sect. 5 presents results and discusses the cascading of the proposed architecture for multi-input logic. Section 6 concludes the work.

2 Related Work

In this section we present works related to optical computing architectures and the application of PCM in nanophotonic circuits.

2.1 Optical Computing Architectures

Numerous optical accelerators have been designed to execute both arithmetic and logic operation. They involve key optical devices such as micro rings, micro-disks, photonic crystal cavities and waveguides. A common objective is to reduce the critical path delay, which can be obtained by simultaneously applying multiple electro-optic modulation on optical signals propagating along a waveguide. By doing so, an 8-bit ripple carry adder with a 20ps critical path delay has been demonstrated in [14]. The same approach has been used in [15] for the design of an n-bit multiplier. Directed logic (DL) architectures have been proposed to efficiently utilize optical devices by simultaneously executing AND and NAND [16], the outputs being available on through port and drop port of a ring resonator. The approach has then been extended to XOR and XNOR operations [17]. A key issue with the above-mentioned architectures is the limited number of operations that can be executed, which is solved by the Reconfigurable Directed Logic (RDL) [10]. The RDL involves parallel waveguides on which modulators are serially placed, thus allowing to map sum-of-product functions. To do so, the architecture relies on modes (named pass/pass, pass/block, block/pass and block/block) which are configured by calibrating the modulator using thermal tuning. Hence, the main drawback of the architecture is the need to constantly thermally tuning ring resonators, even if no modulation is carried out, which is power consuming. In [22], we solved the problem by using PCM based directional couplers [13]. The directional couplers allow to bypass rings when no modulation is needed, thus avoiding to thermally tuning unused modulators. We investigated the efficiency of PCM based DC on RDL architecture. Results showed an average power saving of 32.8% and architecture is more power efficient for frequencies lower than 158 kHz. In this chapter we investigate the power consumptions of RDL in [10] and our proposed RDL [22] taking into account the power consumed by filter rings. We also extend the architecture to support multi-inputs logic through a cascading of the reconfigurable cells.

2.2 Phase Change Material (PCM)

The use of Phase-Change Material (PCM) in photonic platforms has been widely studied in recent years. Indeed, sub-nanosecond phase transition, femtojoule-scale phase transition energy consumption, 10^{15} switching cycle endurance and years long state retention have provided the ground for the massive deployment of PCM in numerous applications. Crystalline and amorphous states show significant differences in optical properties [12, 18]. Hence, binary applications such as memory set and reset can be achieved using phase transition of PCM, which is obtained by thermal annealing using external heaters, optical pulses or electrical pulses [12]. The use of intermediate phase levels, i.e. not fully crystalline or amorphous, leads to multi-level memories [19] and weighting functions in spiking neural networks [11]. PCM is also commonly used for on-chip optical routing applications due to the high optical contrast they provide. For instance, an optical switch based on GST (germanium-antimony-tellurium) sandwiched between the branches of a directional coupler is reported in [20]. In the design, amorphous and crystalline states of the GST lead to cross and bar transmission of optical signals respectively. The design has been further improved in [13] in order to reach 0.16 dB and 0.72 dB Insertion Loss (IL) for cross and bar transmissions respectively. Low transmission loss and non-volatility are the skey characteristics of the directional coupler we are using to bypass unused modulators in the proposed architectures.

3 Proposed Cell

In this section, we first present an overview of the proposed reconfigurable logic cell. We then detail the cell configurations according to the state of the PCM elements and the detuning of the ring resonator. The implementation of the AND is presented using the proposed cell and finally, we present two implementations of the RDL involving the proposed cell.

3.1 Cell Overview

The proposed cell is composed of two phase change Directional Coupler (DC_1 and DC_2) and one micro ring resonator, as shown in Fig. 1. The state of the PCM in DC is electrically configured using a dedicated control signal. As defined in Sect. 3, cross and bar are obtained for Amorphous (Am) and Crystalline (Cr) states respectively. Depending on the state of DC_1, two signal paths can be configured: i) modulation is obtained for Cr state and ii) bypass is obtained for Am state. In the modulation path, the optical signal propagates through a micro ring resonator, where modulation of the input data is carried out, before reaching DC_2. In the bypass path, the optical signal directly propagates towards DC_2. Depending on the state of DC_2, signals are transmitted either to the output of the cell or to a terminator.

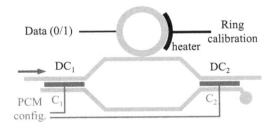

Fig. 1. Proposed cell based on micro ring resonator and phase change directional coupler

The cell is configured according to i) the state of the PCM elements in the DCs and ii) the tuning of the ring. By combining the states of the PCM and ring tuning, the following cell configurations are defined:

- Pass/Pass: Both DC_1 and DC_2 are in the Amorphous state as shown in Fig. 2.a. The input signal propagates through the bypass path and is transmitted to the output. Since the signal does not propagate through modulation path, no thermal calibration of the ring is needed.

- Block/Block: Fig. 2.b represents the block/block mode. Similarly to pass/pass mode, the signal propagates through the bypass path since DC_1 is set to the amorphous state. However, instead of transmitting the signal to the output, DC_2 is configured to the crystalline state, which leads to a transmission of the signal to the terminator. Hence, the optical signal is strongly attenuated on the output.
- Pass/block: The input signal is transmitted to the modulation path, which is achieved with DC_1 is configured in the crystalline state as shown in Fig. 2.c. The signal is first modulated by the input data and is then transmitted to the output (DC in crystalline state). Since a modulation occurs, the ring is thermally calibrated to the signal wavelength (λ_s). Therefore, data input '0' leads to the coupling of the signal, which results in a strong attenuation, while data input '1' detunes the resonance of the ring, which leads to a high transmission of the signal.
- Block/Pass: Similarly, to Pass/block, the signal propagates through the modulation path, as illustrated in Fig. 2.d. However, the ring is tuned to $\lambda_s - \Delta_\lambda$, i.e. the ring is off signal resonance for data input '0'. Data input '1' leads to a red shift of the ring and hence a strong attenuation of the optical signal.

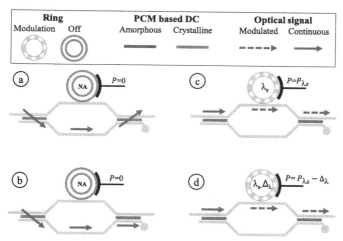

Fig. 2. Non-volatile implementation of a) pass/pass. b) block/block. c) pass/block d) block/pass modes from RDL [10] using PCM-based directional couplers

3.2 Implementation of AND Function

In order to implement the multiplication of two operands, the cell is cascaded as shown in Fig. 3. To reduce the design complexity, DC_2 from the first cell is merged with DC_1 from the second cell. Hence, the configuration of block/block mode is only available in the second cell, which implies to configure the first cell in the pass/pass mode. The design allows to implement functions such as A, B, AB, AB'. Figure 3 illustrates the implementation of AB'. For this purpose first and second cells are configured in pass/block and block/pass modes respectively. This is obtained by configuring DC_1, DC_2 and DC_3 in crystalline state and tuning the first and second cell to λ_0 and $\lambda_0 - \Delta_\lambda$ respectively.

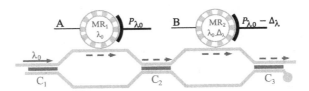

Fig. 3. Implementation of AB'.

3.3 Non-volatile RDL Architecture

In order to implement the function OR, the architecture in Fig. 3 is duplicated on two parallel waveguides. Signals propagating from waveguides are transmitted to multiband photo detector which results in the sum of products.

Proposed PCM based RDL architecture feature the implementation of XOR function, i.e. $AB' + BA'$, with AB' being implemented in the upper waveguide. It is obtained by configuring first and second cell in pass/block and block/pass modes respectively. This is achieved by configuring DC_1, DC_2 and DC_3 in crystalline states and tuning the first and second rings to λ_0 and $\lambda_0 - \Delta_\lambda$ respectively. Therefore, signal at λ_0 is transmitted to the output when rings are off resonance, which requires $A = 1$ and $B = 0$. BA' is implemented on the lower waveguide by configuring first and second cells in block/pass and pass/block modes respectively.

In the following, we present two non-volatile implementations of the RDL architecture as illustrated in Fig. 4.a and Fig. 4.b.

- Ring filter based RDL (Fig. 4.a): The MRR filters on the left-hand side are used to couple signal from lasers to the horizontal waveguides. The modulated signals are transmitted to a photo detector through MRRs located on the right-hand side. The filter MRRs require constant calibration.
- Coupler based RDL (Fig. 4.b): Lasers are placed on each waveguide allowing to turn them off when signal is not used. Therefore block/block mode is not needed which allows to remove the terminator. Signals propagating from two waveguides are merged through coupler.

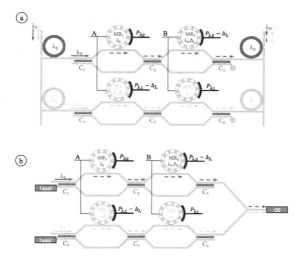

Fig. 4. Configuration of RDLs for XOR, a) Ring filter based RDL, b) coupler based RDL

Table 1 summarizes the configurations of PCMs and the rings according to the logic function for filter ring based RDL architecture. Functions involving a single product induce block/block mode for the lower waveguide which leads to bypassing of signal. XOR and XNOR functions involve modulation on all the rings, which requires to configure all the DCs in the cr state. MR_3 modulates data when functions involving a second product include operand 'A' (e.g. XOR and XNOR). Since all functions can be executed

Table 1. Device state according to the configured function for RDL with PCM and filter rings

Device	Functions						
	A	B	AB	AB'	$A + B$	$A + B'$	$AB + A'B'$
DC_1	cr	am	cr	cr	cr	cr	cr
DC_2	am	am	cr	cr	am	am	cr
DC_3	am	cr	cr	cr	am	am	cr
MR_1	λ_0	off	λ_0	λ_0	λ_0	λ_0	λ_0
MR_2	off	λ_0	λ_0	$\lambda_0 - \Delta_\lambda$	off	off	λ_0
DC_4	am	am	am	am	am	am	cr
DC_5	cr	cr	cr	cr	am	am	cr
DC_6	cr	cr	cr	cr	cr	cr	cr
MR_3	off	off	off	off	off	off	$\lambda_1 - \Delta_\lambda$
MR_4	off	off	off	off	λ_1	$\lambda_1 - \Delta_\lambda$	$\lambda_1 - \Delta_\lambda$

without reconfiguring DC_6, the device could be removed for reduced hardware complexity purpose. However, since keeping DC_6 offers the opportunity to map single produce function on the lower waveguide, we didn't consider this optimization.

Table 2 summarizes the PCM configuration and ring tuning for coupler based RDL. Laser is turned off on lower waveguide for functions involving the use of one waveguide such as A, AB. This allows to avoid the configuration of PCMs which are shown with don't care (i.e. x) in the table.

Table 2. Device state according to the configured function for RDL with PCM and coupler

Device	Functions						
	A	B	AB	AB'	$A + B$	$A + B'$	$AB + A'B'$
DC_1	cr	am	cr	cr	cr	cr	cr
DC_2	am	am	cr	cr	am	am	cr
DC_3	am	cr	cr	cr	am	am	cr
MR_1	λ_0	off	λ_0	λ_0	λ_0	λ_0	λ_0
MR_2	off	λ_0	λ_0	$\lambda_0 - \Delta_\lambda$	off	off	λ_0
DC_4	x	x	x	x	am	am	cr
DC_5	x	x	x	x	am	am	cr
DC_6	x	x	x	x	cr	cr	cr
MR_3	off	off	off	off	off	off	$\lambda_1 - \Delta_\lambda$
MR_4	off	off	off	off	λ_1	$\lambda_1 - \Delta_\lambda$	$\lambda_1 - \Delta_\lambda$

4 Power Model

In this section, we present the proposed power model. It takes into account the power consumption of i) lasers, ii) rings resonators and iii) PCM, as defined by:

$$P\_total = P\_laser + P\_ring + P\_reconfig \tag{1}$$

where P_laser is the laser power needed to reach the targeted optical power. P_ring is power consumption induced by both ring tuning and data modulation. $P\_reconfig$ corresponds to the power consumption required to change the state of the PCMs when the architecture is reconfigured.

4.1 Laser Power

The optical signals propagating through the architecture experience losses induced by micro ring resonator and directional coupler. The worst-case Insertion Loss (IL_{wc}) allows estimating the laser power consumption according to the received power ($P_{received}$) and the laser efficiency (*eff*), as defined by:

$$P_{laser} = (P_{received} + IL_{wc})/eff \qquad (2)$$

We estimate the losses for each device of the architecture as follows:

$$IL_{wc} = IL_{ring} + IL_{DC} + IL_{coupler} \qquad (3)$$

$$IL_{ring} = \sum_{m=1}^{M} IL_{\lambda s} + \sum_{n=1}^{N} IL_{\lambda s - \Delta \lambda} \qquad (4)$$

$$IL_{DC} = \sum_{k=1}^{K} IL_{cr}^{bar} + \sum_{f=1}^{F} IL_{am}^{cross} \qquad (5)$$

where IL_{ring}, IL_{DC} and $IL_{coupler}$ are the ring, DC and coupler losses respectively. M and N are the number of rings tuned to λ_s and $\lambda_s - \Delta_\lambda$ respectively. K is the number of bar transmission for PCM configured in *cr* state and F is the number of cross transmissions for PCM in *am* state. As previously explained, *am* state leads to the cross transmission of most signal power $\left(IL_{am}^{cross}\right)$ while only small fraction of the power is transmitted to bar $\left(IL_{am}^{bar}\right)$ as shown in [13]. The opposite occurs for *cr* state: most of the signal power is bar transmitted while a small fraction of the signal power is cross transmitted $(IL_{cr}^{cross} \ll IL_{cr}^{bar})$ (Fig. 5).

Fig. 5. IL for DC according to the state of PCM and output port, a) am: cross transmission of most signal power, b) cr: bar transmission of most signal power

In our model, we do not consider the crosstalk induced by bar and cross transmission through IL_{cr}^{cross} and IL_{am}^{bar} respectively. However, in block/block mode where signal mostly propagates toward the terminator, we consider IL_{cr}^{cross} for the last DC to obtain the ratio of signal propagation to the output. Table 3 summarizes the ring transmission parameters according to the selected tuning resonance wavelength and the modulated data. Tuning ring to λ_s (resp. $\lambda_s - \Delta_\lambda$) leads to IL_s (resp. $IL_{\lambda s - \lambda} + ER_{\lambda s - \lambda}$) and $IL_{\lambda s} + ER_{\lambda s}$ (resp. $IL_{s-\lambda}$) for logic inputs of '1' and '0' respectively. When the ring is tuned to $\lambda_s + \Delta_\lambda$, the loss is independent from the data.

4.2 Ring Power

The total ring power is defined by i) the calibration power of modulating rings (i.e. rings which are not bypassed using the directional couplers) ii) the calibration power of ring filters and iii) the modulation power P_M, as defined by:

$$P_{ring} = \sum_{i=1}^{I} P_{\lambda s} + \sum_{j=1}^{J} P_{\lambda s - \Delta \lambda} + \sum_{k=1}^{K} P_{\lambda s + \Delta \lambda} + \sum_{l=1}^{I+J} P_M \qquad (6)$$

Table 3. Ring loss according to the tuning and modulated data

Tuning	Data	
	0	1
λ_s	$(IL)_{\lambda_s} + ER_{\lambda_s}$	IL_{λ_s}
$\lambda_s - \Delta_\lambda$	$IL_{\lambda_s - \Delta\lambda}$	$(IL)_{\lambda_s - \Delta\lambda} + (ER)_{\lambda_s - \Delta\lambda}$
$\lambda_s + \Delta_\lambda$	$IL_{\lambda_s + \Delta\lambda}$	

where I, J and K represent the number of rings calibrated at λ_s, $\lambda_s - \Delta_\lambda$ and $\lambda_s + \Delta_\lambda$ respectively.

4.3 Reconfiguration Power

The configuration of a given function involves changing the state of PCMs (cr→am or am→cr). While the static power consumption depends only on the losses induced by the directional couplers, the dynamic power, $P_{reconfig}$, depends on the PCM state conversion energy E_{sc} and the function reconfiguration frequency f. In our model, we first consider the worst-case scenario since i) we assume that all PCM elements change state when a new function is configured and ii) we use the largest of $E_{(cr→am)}$ and $E_{(am→cr)}$ for the state conversion, as defined by:

$$E_{sc} = max(E_{cr→am}, E_{am→cr}) \tag{7}$$

$$P_{reconfig} = f \sum_{i=0}^{\substack{number of \\ PCMs}} E_{sc} \tag{8}$$

We also consider a scenario in which we take into account the actual number of PCMs that change state for each possible reconfiguration.

5   Results

In this section, we evaluate the power consumption of the proposed architectures. We first estimate the laser power overhead needed to compensate for losses induced by PCM elements and coupler. We then estimate the impact of the reconfiguration frequency on the cell power efficiency. Table 4 summarizes the considered parameters for micro ring resonator and DC at 1521.5 nm wavelength. We assume 0.9 mW modulation power (P_M) [10].

Table 4. Cell parameters

Device	Parameter type	Parameter		
MR	Tuning power (mW)	$P_{\lambda s}$	9.9 [10]	
		$P_{\lambda s-\Delta\lambda}$	9.7 [10]	
		$P_{\lambda s+\Delta\lambda}$	12.9 [10]	
	Loss (dB)	$IL_{\lambda s}$	−1.25 [10]	
		$ER_{\lambda s}$	−12.25 [10]	
		$IL_{\lambda s-\Delta\lambda}$	−1.25 [10]	
		$ER_{\lambda s-\Delta\lambda}$	−8.75 [10]	
		$IL_{\lambda s+\Delta\lambda}$	0 [10]	
DC	Phase transition energy (nJ)	E_{sc}	2 [13]	
	Loss (dB)	IL_{cr}^{bar}	−0.16 [13]	
		IL_{cr}^{cross}	−13.7 [13]	
		IL_{am}^{bar}	−22.9 [13]	
		IL_{am}^{cross}	−0.72 [13]	

5.1 Cell Insertion Loss

We evaluate the cell insertion loss for each configuration, as reported in Table 5. Pass/pass leads to the lowest loss since the signal propagating from input to the output cross two DCs in the am states. Assuming $IL_{am}^{cross} = 0.72$ dB, this leads to 1.44 dB total loss. Block/block leads to the 14.42 dB loss, i.e. the highest attenuation, by configuring DC_1 and DC_2 in am and cr states respectively. Pass/block involves using the modulation path, i.e. DC_1 and DC_2 are in cr state and ring is tuned to λ_s. Depending on the modulated data, the ring involves an attenuation of $IL_s = 1.25$ dB (data '1') and $IL_s + ER_s = 13.5$ dB (data '0'). The only difference for block/pass is the ring detuning, which is set to $\lambda_0 - \Delta_\lambda$. This leads to 1.57 dB and 10.32 dB loss for data '0' and '1' respectively, thus resulting in high extinction ratio for both modulation modes. Since comparable insertion losses are obtained for all the modes, data '1' on the cell output will be represented by

Table 5. Cell insertion loss wrt cell configuration

Mode	Device configuration			IL (dB)	
	DC_1	MR	DC_2		
pass/pass	am	NA	am	$2 \times IL_{am}^{cross}$	1.44
block/block	am	NA	cr	$IL_{am}^{cross} + IL_{cr}^{cross}$	14.4
pass/block	cr	λ_s	cr	$2 \times IL_{cr}^{bar} + IL_{\lambda s}$	1.57
block/pass	cr	$\lambda_s - \Delta_\lambda$	cr	$2 \times IL_{cr}^{bar} + IL_{\lambda s-\Delta\lambda}$	1.57

similar power levels. We thus conclude that a same laser power can be used for all the configurations and that no laser power tuning is needed.

5.2 Laser Power

In order to estimate the required laser power, we estimate the worst-case loss at the architecture level for each implementation of the non-volatile RDL architecture. Figure 6 illustrates the loss breakdown for each RDL. The worst-case loss occurs for functions in which signal is propagating through two modulating rings such as AB and XOR, which involves $3IL_{cr}^{bar}$ and $2IL_{\lambda s/\lambda s - \Delta\lambda}$ and results in 2.98 dB. For same functions RDL in [10] leads to 2.5 dB loss.

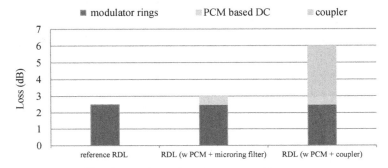

Fig. 6. Loss breakdown for RDL architectures

To compensate the 0.48 dB and 3.48 dB additional loss for RDLs with ring filters and coupler, the injected optical power are set to 2.25 mW and 4.5 mW respectively. Assuming a 25% lasing efficiency [22], this leads to 1 mW and 10 mW laser power overhead respectively. In the following, we discuss how energy saving can be achieved for RDL with PCM and ring filters thanks to i) the use of the bypass path, which allows to avoid tuning unused rings. For coupler based RDL extra saving is achieved thanks to the ii) removal of ring filters which reduces MRR calibration power and iii) turning off laser for functions which involves the use of one waveguide such as A and AB.

5.3 Power Saving Analysis

In the following we investigate the power saving of the two implementations of non-volatile architecture wrt RDL in [10] as reported in Fig. 7. For functions A and B, three rings out of four are bypassed thanks to the PCM based DC. This results in 35% saving for RDL with ring filters. For coupler based RDL in addition to bypassing rings, turning off the laser on the lower horizontal waveguide and saving the calibration power of ring filters lead to 72% power saving. This is achieved despite of 10mW laser power overhead needed to compensate for the loss induced by DCs and coupler. Functions involving two operands (A + B, AB, AB′, A + B′) allow bypassing two rings, thus leading to 22% power saving for RDL with ring filters. For coupler based RDL, functions AB and AB′

lead to 61% power saving, while functions A + B and A + B′ result in 50% power saving. While in all the above mentioned functions two rings are bypassed and calibration power of ring filters are saved, however turning off laser for functions of AB and AB′ leads to extra saving. XOR and XNOR involve the use of all rings. Therefore due to the higher laser power needed to compensate loss induced by PCM, RDL with ring filters leads to slight power increase of (+0.2%). For coupler based RDL calibration power saving of ring filters outperforms the laser power overhead and results in 29% power saving. Therefore while RDL with ring filters leads to 19% average power saving, 53% is obtained for coupler based RDL.

The results demonstrate that using PCM to bypass ring resonators not needed to modulate data lead to significant improvement in the power efficiency. While PCM leads to saving in both implementations of proposed RDLs, keeping laser off for some functions and saving the calibration power of ring filters result in extra saving for coupler based RDL.

While we investigated the use of PCM on the reconfigurable directed logic architecture, we believe that the same approach could be applied to other computing architecture such as OLUT or to reconfigurable nanophotonic interconnects, which we will investigate in our future work.

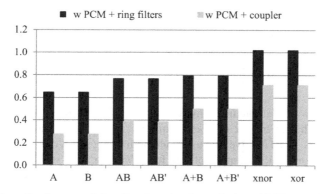

Fig. 7. Normalized power of ring filter based and coupler based RDLs wrt RDL in [10]

5.4 Power Saving Analysis of Coupler Based RDL

In this section we investigate the impact of MRR calibration power and laser efficiency on power saving of coupler based RDL. For this purpose, we consider laser efficiencies of 10% and 25% and we focus the study on functions A + B and XOR, as illustrated in Fig. 8 and Fig. 9. We assume MRR calibration power ranging from 1 mW to 10 mW for pass/block mode, which corresponds to the power consumption needed to detune the rings from the signal wavelength. We also consider MRR calibration power for block/pass and pass/pass modes to be respectively 0.2 mw below and 3 mw above the caliobration power for pass/block mode.

The implementation of A + B with coupler based RDL considering 25% laser efficiency is more power efficient for all considered MRR calibration power, as shown on Fig. 8. However, for 10% laser efficiency, the proposed implementation is power efficient from 6 mW. Implementation of A + B on coupler based RDL involves saving the calibration power of four filter rings and two modulating rings. However, the PCM also involves laser power overhead. Therefore the architecture is more power efficient when laser efficiency is 25% or MRR calibration power is greater than 6 mW.

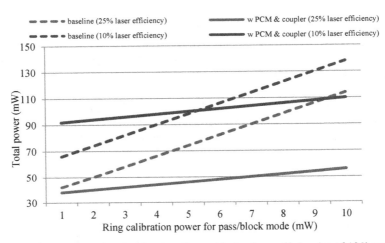

Fig. 8. Total power consumption for A + B considering laser efficiencies of 10% and 25%

Figure 9 shows the implementation of XOR on both RDLs. Coupler based RDL is more power efficient from 2 mW and 9 mW for laser efficiencies of 25% and 10% respectively. Since XOR involves the use of all modulating rings, the coupler based RDL is less efficient for implementation of this function compared with A + B. However considering laser efficiency of 25% makes coupler based RDL a more power efficient candidate for implementation of functions for calibration power ranging from 2 mW to 10 mW.

5.5 Reconfiguration Power

We evaluate the impact of state change of PCM elements according to the architecture reconfiguration frequency. For this purpose, we assume a 2nj [13] energy consumption to change the state of a PCM element. We assume a minimum reconfiguration period of 100 ns since, according to [18], the amorphization and crystallization times are in the range of ps to ns. To obtain reconfiguration power two scenarios are considered. First we assume all PCMs are reset between each reconfiguration which leads to the worst case. In second scenario we take into account the actual number of PCMs that change state between each possible reconfiguration. For this purpose we assume that architecture is initially configured for a function then we consider its reconfiguration

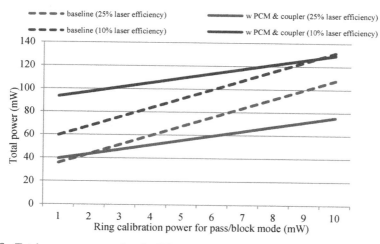

Fig. 9. Total power consumption for XOR considering laser efficiencies of 10% and 25%

Table 6. Number of PCMs state changes for each reconfiguration

		Function after reconfiguration							
		A	B	AB	AB'	A+B	A+B'	xnor	xor
	A	-	2	2	2	1	1	3	3
	B	2	-	2	2	3	3	3	3
Function	AB	2	2	-	0	3	3	1	1
before	AB'	2	2	0	-	3	3	1	1
reconfiguration	A+B	1	2	3	3	-	0	4	4
	A+B'	1	2	3	3	0	-	4	4
	xnor	2	2	1	1	4	4	-	0
	xor	2	2	1	1	4	4	0	-

to all other functions and obtain the number of PCMs that must change state for each reconfiguration as summarized in Table 6.

Figure 10 illustrates an example in which the initial function is A + B. Reconfiguring the architecture for A + B' does not require any PCM state change. Only ring tuning on lower waveguide changes from λ to λ−Δ$_λ$. However implementing XOR requires four of PCMs to be reset and all rings to be tuned. To obtain reconfiguration power we consider the average of all PCM reconfiguration listed in Table 6.

While average power consumption of all functions for RDL in [10] is 107 mW, the power consumption for PCM based RDL with ring filters and with coupler is 87.3 mW and 51 mW respectively. Here we investigate the impact of the reconfiguration frequency on total power consumption. Figure 11 illustrates the power consumption for each reconfiguration scenario for two implementation of PCM based RDLs. Both coupler based

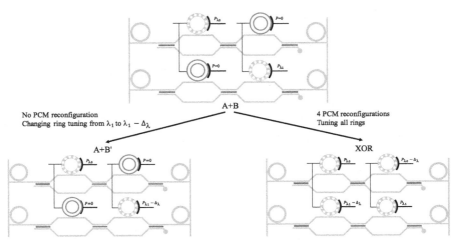

Fig. 10. Reconfiguration of architecture to A + B′ and XOR considering the initial function of A + B

RDL and ring filter based RDLs are most power efficient when no reconfiguration is required. The higher the reconfiguration frequency the higher the power consumption. Ring filter based RDL is power efficient up to 1.7 MHz and 5 MHz for worst case and actual scenarios respectively and coupler based RDL is power efficient up to 4.7 MHz and 14 MHz for corresponding scenarios respectively. This demonstrates that taking into account the current state of PCMs is needed to efficiently reconfigure the architecture. This is especially important when the architecture is extended to process large numbers of inputs, as discussed in the following.

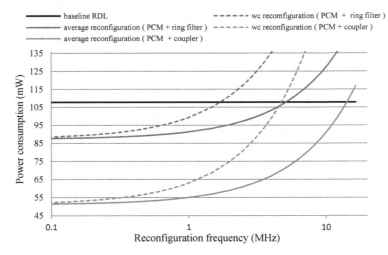

Fig. 11. Power consumption according to reconfiguration frequency for PCM based RDLs

5.6   Toward Large Scale Architectures

In this section, we study the usage of the architecture to enable the processing of multi operand functions. From the coupler based architecture, which is the most energy efficient design, we define architecture illustrated in Fig. 12. It is essentially composed of two cascaded cores which are interconnected using waveguides linking upper and lower branches of DC_3 and DC_9 to DC_4 and DC_{10}. The other two branches are used to sum the output signals and transmit the results to a photodetector. Therefore, different optical connection between the cores are obtained depending on the PCM configurations. In following we show how sum of products for four operands can be achieved using proposed architecture. We also discuss the limits of the architecture and introduce future works.

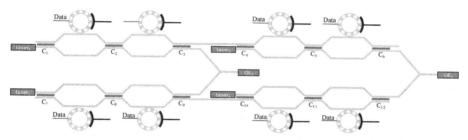

Fig. 12. Architecture for processing multi operand functions

Figure 13 illustrates the implementation of ABCD + EFGH. Both ABCD and EFGH are implemented through configuring all cells in pass/block mode. In order to transmit the signal from first core to the second one, both DC_3 and DC_9 are configured in cr state. This allows to avoid turning on the laser$_3$ and laser$_4$. Signals transmitting from lower and upper waveguides propagate to the OE of second core through configuring DC_6 and DC_{12} in am state. Therefore the sum of products are obtained.

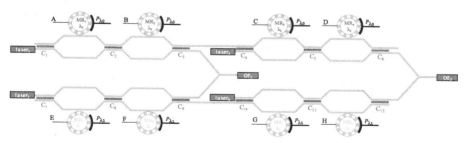

Fig. 13. Implementation of ABCD + EFGH

Although the cascading of computing cores using PCM based directional couplers appear promising, the architectures suffer from several limitations. For instance, the implementation of multi-input XOR cannot be achieved since it requires crossing of data between the cores. While using electro-optical solutions would solve the issue, the use of electronics would also considerably limit the advantages of the such architectures. Hence, topologies involving heterogeneous and specialized cores [17, 23] are probably needed. Another challenge remains the losses induces by PCM material; while we have shown that crossing relatively small number (<10) of PCM based directional couplers doesn't have a significant impact on the required laser power, the power consumption of large circuits involving hundreds or thousands of PCM may be dominated by static power. This will call for synthesis tools enabling the mapping of functions to minimize the crossing of PCMs [24]. Finally, as already previously discussed, PCM suffers from a limited endurance and high reconfiguration time. This will call for synthesis tools able to map the application while taking into account the current PCM state to minimize changes of states.

6   Conclusion

In this chapter, we investigate two implementations of non-volatile PCM based RDL defined as ring filter based RDL and coupler based RDL. Both involve the use of PCM to bypass unused microring resonator. Ring filter based RDL includes MRR to direct WDM signal to horizontal waveguide and to direct the modulated signal to the photodetector where OE conversion occurs. In coupler based RDL lasers are placed on each waveguide allowing to turn it off when signal is not used. The modulated signals of waveguides are merged through coupler. Bypassing MRRs in ring filter based RDL leads to 19% of saving in power consumption compared with baseline. Coupler based RDL results in 53% saving due to the reduced MRR calibration power of ring filters in addition to bypassing of non-modulating rings. We also investigate the impact of the PCM reconfiguration frequency on total power consumption considering two reconfiguration scenarios. Results show that as the reconfiguration frequency is decreased the architectures are more power efficient. Considering current state of PCM leads to reduced number of required PCM reconfiguration which leads to actual assumption of the reconfiguration power. We also investigated the cascading of the architecture to enable multi operand function. The architecture is extended to involve the AND of multi operands without opto-electronic conversion. The drawback however is its limitation in implementing XOR, which requires the electrical connection between cores which we intend to investigate in more details in future.

Acknowledgment. This research was supported by the Fonds de recherche du Québec – Nature et technologies (FRQNT) under grant 2021-NC-286424.

References

1. Atabaki, A.H., Moazeni, S., Pavanello, F., et al.: Integrating photonics with silicon nanoelectronics for the next generation of systems on a chip. Nature **556**, 349–354 (2018)
2. Jalali, B., Paniccia, M., Reed, G.: Silicon photonics. IEEE Microw. Mag. **7**(3), 58–68 (2006)
3. Xu, S., Wang, J., Wang, R., Chen, J., Zou, W.: High-accuracy optical convolution unit architecture for convolutional neural networks by cascaded acousto-optical modulator arrays. Opt. Express **27**, 19778–19787 (2019)
4. Minasian, R.A.: Photonic signal processing of microwave signals. IEEE Trans. Microw. Theory Tech. **54**(2), 832–846 (2006)
5. Zhao, Z., Wang, Z., Ying, Z., Dhar, S., Chen, R.T., Pan, D.Z.: Optical computing on silicon-on-insulator-based photonic integrated circuits. In: IEEE 12th International Conference on ASIC (ASICON), Guiyang, China, pp. 472–475 (2017)
6. Ying, Z., et al.: Silicon microdisk-based full adders for optical computing. Opt. Lett. **43**, 983–986 (2018)
7. Li, Z., Le Beux, S., Monat, C., Letartre, X., O'Connor, I.:Optical look up table. In: Design, Automation and Test in Europe Conference and Exhibition (DATE), Grenoble, France, pp. 873–876 (2013)
8. Tian, Y., et al.: Reconfigurable electro-optic logic circuits using microring resonator-based optical switch array. IEEE Photonics J. **8**(2), 1–8 (2016)
9. Xu, Q., Soref, R.: Reconfigurable optical directed-logic circuits using microresonator-based optical switches. Opt. Express **19**, 5244–5259 (2011)
10. Qiu, C., Gao, W., Soref, R., Robinson, J., Xu, Q.: Reconfigurable electro-optical directed-logic circuit using carrier-depletion micro-ring resonators. Opt. Lett. **39**, 6767–6770 (2014)
11. Chakraborty, I., Saha, G., Sengupta, A., et al.: Toward fast neural computing using all-photonic phase change spiking neurons. Sci. Rep. **8**, 12980 (2018)
12. Abdollahramezani, S., et al.: Tunable nanophotonics enabled by chalcogenide phase-change material. Nanophotonics **9**(5), 1189–1241 (2020)
13. Xu, P., Zheng, J., Doylend, J., Majumdar, A.: Low-Loss and broadband nonvolatile phase-change directional coupler switches. ACS Photonics **6**(2), 553–557 (2019)
14. Ishihara, T., Shinya, A., Inoue, K., Nozaki, K., Notomi, M.:An integrated optical parallel adder as a first step towards light speed data processing. In: International SoC Design Conference (ISOCC), Jeju, Korea, pp. 123–124 (2016)
15. Shiomi, J., Ishihara, T., Onodera, H., Shinya, A., Notomi, M.: An integrated optical parallel multiplier exploiting approximate binary logarithms towards light speed data processing. In: IEEE International Conference on Rebooting Computing (ICRC), McLean, VA, USA, pp. 1–6 (2018)
16. Tian, Y., Zhang, L., Yang, L.: Electro-optic directed AND/NAND logic circuit based on two parallel microring resonators. Opt. Express **20**, 16794–16800 (2012)
17. Zhang, L., et al.: Electro-optic directed logic circuit based on microring resonators for XOR/XNOR operations. Opt. Express **20**, 11605–11614 (2012)
18. Zheng, J., et al.: GST-on-silicon hybrid nanophotonic integrated circuits: a non-volatile quasi-continuously reprogrammable platform. Opt. Mater. Express **8**, 1551–1561 (2018)
19. Ríos, C., Stegmaier, M., Hosseini, P., et al.: Integrated all-photonic non-volatile multi-level memory. Nat. Photonics **9**, 725–732 (2015)
20. Ikuma, Y., Saiki, T., Tsuda, H.: Proposal of a small self-holding 2×2 optical switch using phase-change material. IEICE Electron. Express **5**(12), 442–445 (2008)
21. Sun, C., et al.:DSENT - a tool connecting emerging photonics with electronics for opto-electronic networks-on-chip modelling. In: IEEE/ACM Sixth International Symposium on Networks-on-Chip, Lyngby, Denmark, pp. 201–210 (2012)

22. Zolfaghari, P., Beux, S.L.: A reconfigurable nanophotonic architecture based on phase change material. In: 2021 IFIP/IEEE 29th International Conference on Very Large Scale Integration (VLSI-SoC), pp. 1–6 (2021)
23. Zhang, L., Ji, R., Tian, Y., et al.: Simultaneous implementation of XOR and XNOR operations using a directed logic circuit based on two microring resonators. Opt. Express **19**, 6524–6540 (2011)
24. Zhao, Z., Wang, Z., Ying, Z., et al.: Logic synthesis for energy-efficient photonic integrated circuits. In: 23rd Asia and South Pacific Design Automation Conference (ASP-DAC), pp. 355–360 (2018)

END-TRUE: Emerging Nanotechnology-Based Double-Throughput True Random Number Generator

Shubham Rai[1(✉)], Nishant Gupta[1], Abhiroop Bhattacharjee[1], Ansh Rupani[1], Michael Raitza[1], Jens Trommer[2], Thomas Mikolajick[2], and Akash Kumar[1]

[1] Chair of Processor Design, Technische Universität Dresden, Dresden, Germany
shubham.rai@tu-dresden.de
[2] NaMLab gGmbH, Dresden, Germany

Abstract. True Random Number Generators (TRNGs) are essential primitives in any cryptographic system. They provide the foundation to secure authorization and authentication. This work proposes a generator that exploits the metastability effect of cross-coupled logic gates, as found in SR latches. Based on emerging reconfigurable transistor technology, a random number generator design has been proposed that doubles the throughput, compared to a similar standard CMOS design, by exploiting transistor-level reconfiguration. The proposed design is superior in terms of the number of transistors per block, power consumption and in critical path delay with respect to its CMOS counterpart. Random Number bit sequence are generated by operating the given design at three operating frequencies of 10 MHz, 100 MHz and 200 MHz. Firstly, the Shannon entropy for the generated bit sequence is measured, and then the generated bit sequence are subjected to statistical evaluation using the NIST benchmark suite. The P' values for the NIST benchmarks is above the accepted threshold, which underlines the assumption that the designed circuit produces the random numbers based on the metastability effect.

Keywords: Reconfigurable field effect transistor (RFET) · True Random Number Generator (TRNG) · Metastability · NIST benchmark suite · Von-Neumann extraction

1 Introduction

Hardware security is an area of prime concern in the current era of *Internet of Things* (IoT) owing to the growing security threats and adversarial vulnerabilities to embedded devices [1]. To this end, reliable and secure hardware primitives are required to be interfaced with low-cost and resource-constrained embedded devices for secure communication, identification or authorization and privacy protection. These security primitives can manage digital keys, perform encryption and decryption for digital signatures, strong authentication and various

© IFIP International Federation for Information Processing 2022
Published by Springer Nature Switzerland AG 2022
V. Grimblatt et al. (Eds.): VLSI-SoC 2021, IFIP AICT 661, pp. 175–203, 2022.
https://doi.org/10.1007/978-3-031-16818-5_9

other cryptographic functions [32]. Generating secrets is a cornerstone of cryptographic applications [1,10,18,38], whose randomness, as a measure of unpredictability, is the defining property of a secure secret key.

Random Number Generators. (RNGs) produce uniformly distributed sets of numbers for secret keys. There are two kinds of RNGs: True Random Number Generators (TRNGs) and Deterministic Random Number Generators (DRNGs). Hardware-based TRNGs extract the noise from chaotic physical processes in the form of an unpredictable sequence of bits (e.g., thermal noise, flicker noise, clock-jitter, metastable states, power supply fluctuations) [1,18,40]. On the other hand, DRNGs use one or more inputs known as 'seeds' and are used in generating '*pseudo random numbers.*' These numbers are generated using deterministic algorithms and satisfy every requirement posed by random numbers. However, the only drawback is that these sequences can easily be retraced if the seed is known. Hence, to make DRNGs truly random, the seeds must be generated from some TRNG. A TRNG comprises of three main components: 1) an entropy source, like the one proposed in this work. It is used to generate unpredictable and independent values. 2) A conditioning component, which is usually optional. It is used to reduce the bias in the random outputs. 3) A health test, which checks for the failure of the entropy source [60].

There are various places where a TRNG can be used, including providing security against existing adversarial attacks, such as spoofing and cloning, because of their ability to generate unique secret keys [1]. They are also used as initialization vectors, random masks, challenges and nonces in side-channel attack countermeasures [14]. To guarantee a high level of random output, a compromise in terms of speed, power and area is generally considered [28]. However, TRNGs which are to be installed in embedded devices have certain criterion to fulfil. They need to be area and power efficient and should utilize existing hardware elements such as logic gates for random number generation [8,47,60]. Hence, it is imperative to explore emerging nanotechnology-based solutions.

Recent developments in emerging technologies have opened up new avenues to bring security from the technology side within the hardware system [2,41,48, 67]. Various emerging technologies have been explored in works such as [5,35,40, 65] which cater for random number generations with low power requirements.

Runtime reconfigurable technologies form an interesting class of such emerging devices. Transistors based on these technologies (such as silicon [6,17] or germanium [55,62] nanowires) show electrical symmetry and can be reconfigured between p- and n-type behavior at runtime. Due to their transistor-level reconfiguration, devices made of such nanotechnologies are often termed as *Reconfigurable FETs* (RFETs). RFETs can encapsulate more logic and functionality into a smaller area and are able to achieve reduced power consumption and higher speed during their operation [34,40,44,50,74]. Due to their extended functionality, they have shown great potential for hardware security applications, particularly in the domain of logic locking and layout camouflaging [2,3,5,45,50,50].

In this work, a TRNG design based on RFETs that is referred as *Emerging Nanotechnology - based Double - Throughput True Random Number Gener-*

ator (END-TRUE) is proposed. It introduces a *bistable* device/circuit responsible for generating random numbers. The occurrence of a *metastable* state in any bistable circuit is unavoidable. There are three static equilibrium points in the proposed circuit, two of which are stable (bistable) and known as accurate output states, while the third point is known to be the metastable state. The metastable state, in simple terms, can be defined as a state where the output of the circuit is unpredictable. The output can settle down to either of the two stable states (the bistable states). The proposed TRNG consists of a metastable RFET-based SR latch and a dual-edge triggered *True-Single Phased Clock D-Flip Flop* (TSPC DFF). Conventionally, each random bit generated using metastability-based TRNGs is a result of two cross-coupled elements entering into a metastable state at the rising (or falling) edge of an input clock signal. This implies that each clock period translates to one random bit at the output, thereby making the throughput of the TRNG equal to the input clock frequency. However, in this design, the property of transistor-level reconfigurability allows to have both cross-coupled NAND and NOR operations in a single clock cycle, which are triggered into metastable states at the rising and falling clock edges respectively, thereby generating two random bits per clock cycle. However, when the design is fabricated, it introduces some device variations which influences the outcome of the TRNG. As this mismatch increases, the 50-50 probability of resolving the output to two different stable states gets unbalanced [39].

The proposed TRNG is able to generate random numbers achieving double-throughput over a similar architecture of a TRNG using CMOS technology (which would need additional hardware components for reconfiguration). This work also shows that the END-TRUE is more efficient in terms of area (60% saving in number of transistors), delay (77.3% reduction) and power consumption (94.5% lower leakage power and 70.7% lower dynamic power) over its CMOS counterpart.

The present work is an extension of an earlier work [1]. Compared to the previous work, this work contains a detailed experimental evaluation and discusses PVT robustness in the case of RFETs, which is integral to any TRNG design.

Contributions: Major contributions of this work are as follows:

– Use of a Verilog-A model from a predictive RFETs design kit [13], to propose a *Minority*-based SR latch which allows reconfiguration between a NAND and NOR-based SR latch. This is essential to achieve double throughput and forms the core for the proposed TRNG.
– An improved design for a reconfigurable dual edge-triggered TSPC D-flip flop using RFETs based on TSPC logic. This allows random number generation at both edges of the clock.
– It has been demonstrated the runtime reconfigurability of RFETs can be exploited to design the double-throughput TRNG (END-TRUE) using less hardware than its CMOS counterpart. The proposed design is better in terms of transistor count, power consumption and critical path delay.

– It has been further shown that the raw random bit sequence obtained from the TRNG, upon post-processing using Von-Neumann extraction have sufficient entropy to pass the statistical tests.

Experimental evaluation over NIST benchmark suite [49] at three different frequencies – 10 MHz, 100 MHz and 200 MHz, demonstrate that the proposed END-TRUE returns raw bit sequence with high values of Shannon entropy.

The remainder of the chapter is organised as follows: Sect. 2 presents the fundamentals of RFET device operation and RFET-based circuits. It also describes various kinds of TRNGs with an emphasis on metastability-based TRNGs. Section 3 deals with the circuit design of the reconfigurable dual edge-triggered D-flip flop followed by the proposed design. Section 4 begins with the simulation results using the proposed design and presents a comparison between the END-TRUE and its equivalent CMOS counterpart on the basis of number of transistors, power consumption and critical path delay. It culminates with the results of various statistical tests carried out on the raw bitstreams generated from END-TRUE. Section 5 involves analysis of the test results along with assessment of the impact of post-processing (using Von-Neumann extraction) on the raw bit sequences from the END-TRUE. Some consideration on the impact of process, voltage and temperature (PVT) variations on the TRNG functionality are given. Finally, Sect. 6 presents the conclusions to this chapter.

2   Background

2.1   Reconfigurable FETs

Reconfigurable transistor functionality has been demonstrated on a variety of materials such as 1D silicon [6,17] or germanium nanowires [55,62], carbon nanotubes [72], graphene nanoribbons [15], or by planar 2-D devices based on materials such as $MoTe_2$ [36] or graphene p-n junctions [57]. More recently also the integration into an existing fully depleted silicon on insulator 22nm technology was demonstrated [52]. This chapter focuses on nanowire-based RFETs since it is one of the most actively researched emerging technologies having Verilog-A models [13] as well a first physical synthesis flow [43] available.

Reconfigurable nanowire-based transistors, unlike conventional CMOS based transistors, feature two types of gate terminals, a *Program Gate* (PG) and a *Control Gate* (CG). The PG is used to reconfigure the channel between p-type and n-type by selectively suppressing the injection of one type of charge carrier. Whereas the CG receives a voltage input to the FET and modulates the flow of the other type of carrier [34,44,74]. This is shown in (Fig. 1). Figure 1a shows how an RFET logically encapsulates both PMOS and NMOS together [42]. The electrical symmetry in I-V characteristics for nanowire transistors for both p- and n-type behavior can be seen in Fig. 1d [47]. This electrical symmetry is necessary while realizing complementary circuits.

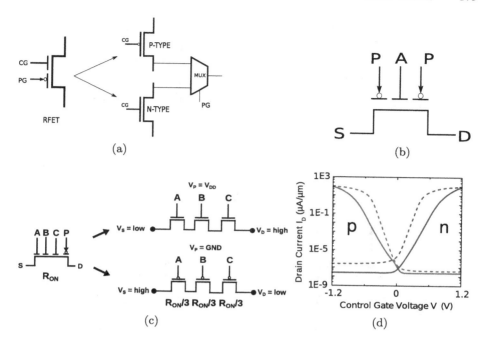

Fig. 1. (a) Transistor level-equivalent model of the RFET showing how it encapsulates both p- and n-type behavior. The runtime-reconfigurability is represented by the MUX.; (b) All-around *Three-Independent Gate FET* (TIGFET) with the control gate (A) and program gates (P) marked [6]; (c) multi-gate RFET with inputs A, B and C, and a program signal P [44]. It shows how the channel resistance is reduced as compared to a series of conventional CMOS transistors; (d) Ambipolar transfer characteristics for SiNW RFET [47]. Bold lines corresponds to the high-V_t operation and dotted lines corresponds to the low-V_t operation.

As shown in Fig. 2, to switch the device into an n-type FET, V_{PG} should be larger than 0, whereas to convert the device into p-type FET, V_{PG} should be below 0. When V_{CG} is equal to 0, then both the FETs are switched off because of the barrier induced by the opposing potential of CG and PG. On the other hand, when V_{CG} is above 0, it allows the conduction of current through tunneling in an n-type FET, and when V_{CG} is below 0, p-type FET switches ON. A small amount of thermionic emission also contributes to the overall I_{DS} current flowing through the RFET. This tunneling and thermionic current is possible because of the strong band bending which takes place at the source contact leading to injection of electrons and holes from the metal to the semiconductor through the thinned barrier respectively.

RFET can also exist is multi-independent gated form. The authors in [17,74] have shown that multi-independent-gate RFETs allow merging of two or more series transistors in CMOS technology into a single RFET as shown in Fig. 1c. RFETs having two or more inputs on a single channel in a wired-AND [54] con-

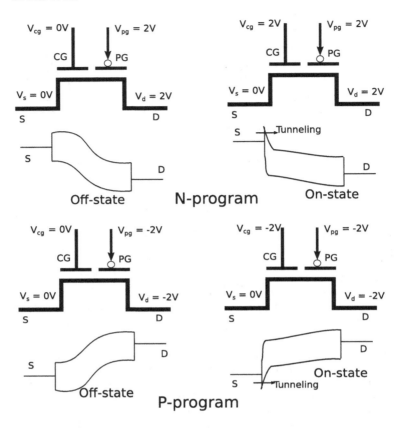

Fig. 2. Working principle of a reconfigurable FET [46]

figuration operates with a virtually lower channel resistance per input (Fig. 1c) thereby dramatically reducing transistor count in digital circuits as well as the parasitics and delays. This is due to the presence of Schottky barrier in the on-state of the RFETs [61]. This helps to design compact digital circuits with added functionalities [44].

2.2 RFET-Based Logic Gates

In this work, an RFET variant with *Three Independent Gates* has been used to design digital circuits. The devices is thus often called TIGFET in literature. A typical layout having a single-input configuration with CG (input A) in the middle of the channel and the program signal (P) is used to alter between p-channel ($P = $ '0') and n-channel ($P = $ '1') behaviour is shown in Fig. 1b. Figure 3a shows an extension of the TIGFETs for two inputs. If one chooses to operate a TIGFET as shown in Fig. 3a, then there are 8 possible configurations in which it could be operated. Out of these possible 8 configurations, only 6 are

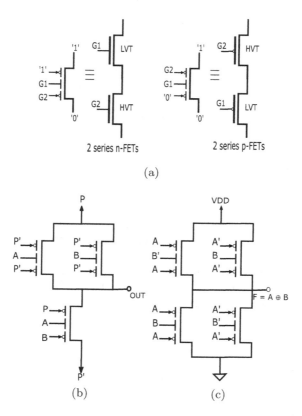

Fig. 3. (a) N-MOS and P-MOS transistor level equivalent models for TIGFETs in dual-threshold voltage configuration; (b) A configurable MIN gate behaving as a NAND gate when P = '1' and NOR gate when P = '0' (c) XOR gate

useful to us. These 6 configurations are (assume, $V_{DS} = V_{DD}$): 1) ON state: When the V_{PGS} (voltage of program gate at the source) = V_{PGD} (voltage of program gate at the drain) = V_{CG} (voltage of control gate present in the middle). When this condition is applied on the RFET, one of the Schottky barriers is very thin, allowing the tunneling of the majority charge carriers. 2) OFF state: This state occurs when $V_{PGD} = V_{PGS}$ and V_{CG} has opposite biasing to the polarity gates. In this state, there is still a small number of charge carriers that can cross the barrier. 3) Low-leakage OFF state: This state occurs when $V_{PGS} = $ S and $V_{PGD} = $ D. This condition creates a thick enough barrier across the channel, which is sufficient enough to prevent the tunneling at both ends. The unused states must be avoided while implementing the RFET in the circuit. This could be done by fixing the $V_{PGS} = 0$ ($V_{PGD} = 1$) for p-RFET (n-RFET) as shown in the Fig. 3a or by using $V_{PGD} = V_{PGS}$ [74].

The authors in [74] have shown that it is a dual-threshold voltage config-uration wherein, input $G1$ has lower threshold voltage (**LVT**) and input $G2$

has higher threshold voltage (**HVT**) (corresponding to lower leakage current). This feature of configuring threshold in RFETs is used later for the TSPC-based DFF as discussed in Sect. 3.3. The dual-threshold feature helps in improving the leakage power of the circuit. Leakage power is a critical issue in the present-day circuits. It comprises around 30% - 50% of the current SoC power consumption. Low V_t devices are used in the paths that are critical, in order to meet the timing constraints while high V_t devices which have low leakage are used in slack paths [74].

Note - In the world of CMOS technology, implementation of multi-V_t devices is a bit difficult task. CMOS devices require an extra technological step which increases the cost of fabrication and affect the regularity of the layout. Another method which can help in decreasing the leakage power in the CMOS technology is by employing adaptive body biasing. But it adds a separate overhead in terms of area consumption by additional circuits and routing resources, thus RFET are supposed to shown an advantage over standard CMOS technology in this regard as well.

Figure 3b presents the configuration of a configurable MIN gate that is shown to behave both as a two-input NAND gate ($P = `1`$) and NOR gate ($P = `0`$) [44]. Switching between NAND and NOR occurs because of the interchange in the functionality between the pull-up and the pull-down part of the circuit. This happens when the value of P is modified. In RFET technology, NAND and NOR gates, thus, can be built with equal performance owing to the electrical symmetry of the underlying devices. This helps in simplifying timing constraints [44]. Similarly, an RFET-based 2-input XOR is shown in Fig. 3c [6].

2.3   Types of TRNGs

True Random Number Generators. (TRNGs) produce unpredictable numbers that originate from some stochastic physical phenomenon [33]. There have been various works on TRNGs in CMOS technology. There are three kinds of TRNG architectures - TRNGs that attribute a logic value to noise (aka. noise-based TRNGs), TRNGs that attribute a time value to noise (aka. jitter-based TRNGs) and metastability-based TRNGs that exploit the random outcome of transient metastable behavior [1].

Noise-Based TRNG. Noise-based TRNGs involve direct amplification of a noise source (e.g., thermal noise), followed by quantization or digitization using a comparator to produce random output [4, 20]. However, noise-based TRNGs are difficult to interface with highly dense digital ASICs owing to the presence of thermal analog sensors and amplifiers [1, 12].

Jitter-Based TRNG. Jitter-based TRNGs amplify the frequency noise, called jitter, of voltage-controlled oscillators (VCOs) [56, 64, 70], free-running oscillators (FROs) [12] and ring oscillators. Ring-oscillator based TRNGs have been shown to have resilience to temperature fluctuations [56, 64]. However, factors that affect oscillator-based TRNGs include high power consumption, aging and frequency injection attacks that can result in loss of entropy [12,30].

Metastability-Based TRNG. Metastability-based TRNGs use metastable circuits [16,19,24,31,59,60,63] to generate random numbers. They use cross-coupled elements (for ex. cross-coupled NAND gates in SR latch or cross-coupled inverters) to amplify random noise and generate random bits. The cross-coupled elements are biased precisely to attain a metastable state, which is eventually resolved to a stable random state. Any kind of unbalance/asymmetry in the circuit would cause the output of the TRNG to be biased [12]. Metastability-based TRNGs are well-suited for interfacing with embedded devices due to their small-scale and low power consumption and they have been shown to be robust against temperature and supply voltage variations [60].

3   Design of the TRNG Using RFETs

The potential of using transistor-level reconfiguration in RFETs to develop compact and power-efficient circuits with less parasitics motivates to employ them for the END-TRUE design. The aim of this work is to double the throughput of generation of random binary sequences by exploiting the feature of runtime reconfigurability in *Minority* (MIN) gates based on RFETs. The present section details about the components of the proposed metastability-based TRNG.

3.1   Metastability in SR Latch

The TRNGs employ the metastable state attained by cross-coupled elements as a source of randomness. Figure 4 shows a NAND gate based SR latch unit which initially rests in a ground state when the input clock (A) has a value of '0', i.e. the outputs (B and C) of the unit are '1'. At the rising clock edge of the input clock, the output of the latch begins to race and temporarily enters into a metastable state. However, due to the random noise, the metastability is resolved and the latch eventually generates a random bit sampled using a positive-edge triggered D-flip flop at the output. Again, at the falling clock edge, the output of the latch resets itself to its ground state and the phenomenon is repeated with each clock cycle. Hence, the throughput of the TRNG is equal to the input clock frequency. The raw bit sequence generated at the output for each clock cycle would only be unbiased or perfectly random if driving capabilities of the two NAND gates are same.

3.2   Minority Gate-Based SR Latch for END-TRUE

In the present work, the metastability-based TRNG is designed using reconfigurable MIN gates (Fig. 3b). Figure 5 shows a single SR latch unit consisting of two cross-coupled MIN gates and two buffers. Two clock signals (*clk_Program*

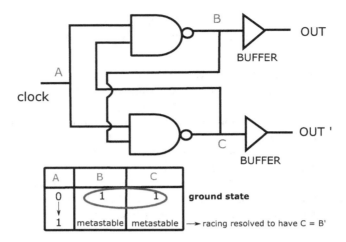

Fig. 4. An SR latch unit for the TRNG in [16] with two cross-coupled NAND gates and two buffers

and clk_IN) with the same time period T are fed into the unit, clk_IN being a time-delayed version of $clk\_Program$, delayed by t_d satisfying the condition $t_d < T/2$. In the first half-period of $clk\_Program$ ($clk_Program = $ '1'), the MIN gates behave as NAND gates and the rising edge of the clk_IN signal occurs (when $clk_IN = $ '0'), the outputs of both the gates are '1' (ground state). Post the transition in clk_IN signal, the outputs begin to race and temporarily enter into metastability. However, owing to the random noise, the output 'OUT' stabilises in order to generate a random bit ('0' or '1'). Similarly, in the second half-period of $clk\_Program$ ($clk_Program = $ '0'), the MIN gates behave as NOR gates and the falling edge of the clk_IN signal occurs. This time in the ground state the outputs of both the gates are '0' and metastability is attained at the '1'→ '0' transition of clk_IN signal, which eventually results in another random bit. Thus, in one complete clock cycle, two random bits are generated implying that the throughput of the SR latch unit is twice the input clock frequency.

3.3 Dual Edge-Triggered TSPC-Based D-Flip Flop

In this section, a compact design of a dual-edge triggered TSPC-based D-flip flop using RFETs (Fig. 6) is proposed that is employed in the TRNG design. At the transistor level, flip flops require the clock signal directly and inverted. This poses challenges to the clock-tree synthesis [58]. However, TSPC-based D-flip flops require only a single clock signal [73]. This, along with the dynamic logic of TSPC-based design, leads to compactness and faster response [22]. Thus, TSPC-based D-flip flop can be used for high speed applications efficiently [58].

The authors in [58] proposed a design of a positive edge-triggered TSPC-based D-flip flop using RFETs that has been shown to have a reduced transistor count and area compared to its CMOS counterpart [73]. Furthermore, since in

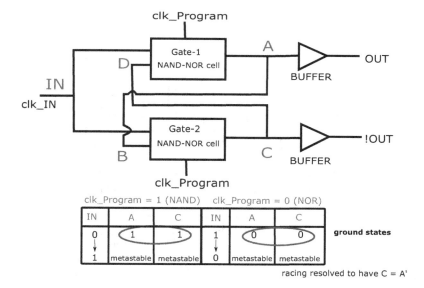

Fig. 5. An SR latch unit for the END-TRUE

the design of the flip flop, each pull-up and pull-down path consists of a single transistor, the parasitics are further reduced, thereby improving the speed of the flip flop [58,74].

This work exploits the runtime reconfigurability feature of RFETs to make the TSPC-based D-flip flop proposed in [58] dual-edge triggered. This can be done by using a program signal (P) instead of the power-rails as shown in Fig. 6. If P = '1', the upper four transistors encircled in red provide the pull-up path while the lower four transistors encircled in blue provide the pull-down path. In this case, the flip flop samples data at the rising edge of the clock and hence, behaves as a positive edge-triggered flip flop. Conversely, if P = '0', the pull-up and pull-down paths get interchanged and the flip flop samples data at the falling clock-edge. This way it behaves as a negative edge-triggered flip flop. Dual-threshold voltage design style as shown in Fig. 3a has been adopted (for three transistors encircled in purple) to make the design compact and reduce leakage power consumption.

Thus, the same circuit of the flip flop can be reconfigured into both positive and negative edge-triggered functionalities based on the program signal during runtime. However, the same TSPC-based design of a D-flip flop in CMOS technology [73] cannot be reconfigured as both positive and negative edge-triggered and it also uses a higher number of transistors (11 transistors) with respect to the proposed design in this work using RFETs (8 transistors). To the best of the author's knowledge, none of the earlier works have explored a TRNG design using device-level reconfigurability offered by reconfigurable emerging nanotechnologies.

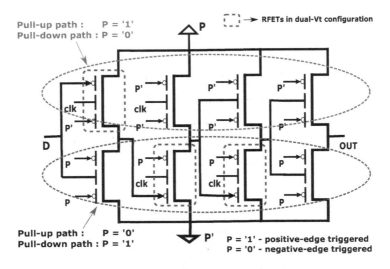

Fig. 6. A configurable dual edge-triggered D-flip flop based on TSPC logic style

3.4 XOR-ing the Outputs

For the purpose of simulation, the outputs of the two SR latch units are XOR-ed and its results are fed into a dual edge-triggered TSPC-based D-flip flop (Fig. 6). Compact implementation of MIN gates (Fig. 3b), XOR gate (Fig. 3c) and the proposed TSPC-based D-flip flop has been carried out using dual-threshold-voltage design style that makes the design area-efficient with improved speed and reduced leakage power consumption [74].

It has been mathematically proven in [7,65] that by XOR-ing outputs from multiple TRNGs (in this case, the SR latch units), the randomness (entropy) of the resultant output sequence can be increased and the TRNG becomes more robust against PVT variations.

Let the ith TRNG produce a probabilistic output signal (bitstream) for which probability of obtaining bit '1' is equal to p_i. In the ideal scenario, the value of p_i should be equal to 0.5 for an unbiased binary sequence (perfectly random). Let the probability deviation from the ideal value be defined as $\alpha_i = |0.5 - p_i|$, $\alpha_i \in [0, 0.5]$. If two such probabilistic output signals are combined by the XOR gate, then the resultant probabilistic signal can be given as -

$$p_{XOR} = p_1(1 - p_2) + p_2(1 - p_1) = 0.5 \pm 2\alpha_1\alpha_2 \tag{1}$$

For n such probabilistic signals, Eq. (1) becomes-

$$p_{XOR} = 0.5 \pm 2^{n-1}\alpha_1\alpha_2...\alpha_n \tag{2}$$

The deviation of the resultant output signal from the ideal value is, therefore, given as-

$$\alpha_{XOR} = 2^{n-1}\alpha_1\alpha_2...\alpha_n \tag{3}$$

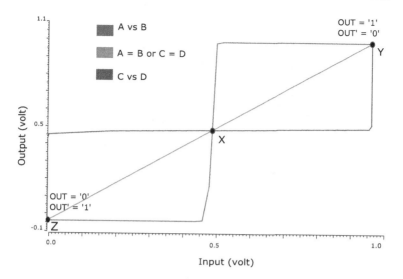

Fig. 7. Butterfly curve in the Voltage-Transfer Characteristic (VTC) for the SR latch unit of the END-TRUE

with $\alpha_{XOR} \in [0, 0.5]$. Smaller the value of α_{XOR}, higher the randomness in the output signal. Furthermore, $\alpha_{XOR} \leq min\{\alpha_1, \alpha_2, ..., \alpha_n\}$. This implies that by XOR-ing the output signals of multiple TRNGs, randomness (entropy) in the resulting signal can be improved.

3.5 Analysis of Randomness

The cross-coupled MIN gates in the SR latch unit (Fig. 5) are analogous to two cross-coupled inverters (such as in an SRAM cell) that are powered-ON when the input clock makes a '0' → '1' transition for $clk\_Program$ = '1' or when it makes a '1' → '0' transition for $clk\_Program$ = '0'. 'B' and 'D' are respectively the inputs to *Gate-2* and *Gate-1* while, 'A' and 'C' are respectively the outputs of *Gate-1* and *Gate-2*. The corresponding butterfly-curve in the *Voltage-Transfer Characteristic* (VTC) for the SR latch unit is shown in Fig. 7. It can be clearly seen that point 'X', which is the point of metastability, lies on the identity line (shown in green). This means that both stable states demarcated by points 'Y' and 'Z' are equally preferred, when the MIN gates in the latch have similar drive capabilities. Eventually, the latch attains either state 'Y' or 'Z' due to noise, thereby producing a random bit at the output (OUT). Thus the SR latch unit in END-TRUE generates a random bit when triggered into a metastable state.

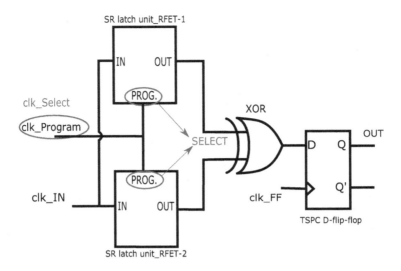

Fig. 8. The simulation model for the END-TRUE consisting of two SR latch units, an XOR gate in DG configuration and the configurable dual edge-triggered D-flip flop **(The signals and nodes in the equivalent CMOS model have been marked in red)** (Color figure online)

Figure 8 shows the complete circuit for the END-TRUE based on RFETs with all the components. In the next sub-section END-TRUE has been compared with an equivalent CMOS-based design.

3.6   Comparison with CMOS-Based Design

Table 1. A comparison between RFET-based SR latch unit and its CMOS equivalent on no. of transistors

RFET SR latch	No. of transistors	CMOS SR latch	No. of transistors
MIN gate	6	NAND gate	8
Buffer	8	NOR gate	8
–	–	Buffer	16
–	–	2 × 1 MUX	14
TOTAL (RFET)	**14**	**TOTAL (CMOS)**	**46**

It has been shown that the transistor-level reconfigurability in RFETs helps to double random bit generation rate per clock cycle in case of the END-TRUE, thereby achieving double-throughput. For the same functionality to be implemented in CMOS technology, the SR latch unit consists of two cross-coupled

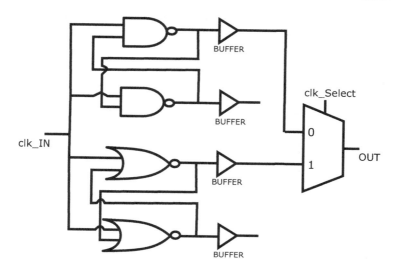

Fig. 9. An SR latch unit for the CMOS equivalent of the END-TRUE

NAND gates, two cross-coupled NOR gates, four buffers and one 2×1 MUX as shown in Fig. 9. In this case clk_Select is fed into the select line of the multiplexer and clk_Select and clk_IN are clock signals having the same time period T, the latter being a t_d time-delayed version of the former satisfying the condition $t_d < T/2$. In one clock cycle of clk_Select, two random bits are generated at the output 'OUT' - one corresponding to the metastability of NAND-based SR latch in one half cycle (clk_Select = '0') and the other corresponding to the metastability of NOR-based SR latch in the other half cycle (clk_Select = '1'). This way a throughput equal to twice the input clock frequency is obtained at the cost of additional hardware and greater number of transistors with respect to the RFET-based implementation.

A tabular comparison of the number of transistors for implementation of the RFET based SR latch unit and its CMOS equivalent is presented in Table 1. It can be observed that there is 69.6% saving in transistor count by using RFET technology.

4   Experiments

4.1   Experimental Setup

The simulation of the END-TRUE has been carried out in Cadence Virtuoso. The Verilog-A model for the RFET in three-independent gate configuration (TIGFET) from [13] was used during the circuit-level simulations. This model has been adapted to incorporate flicker and white noise parameters. Furthermore, according to the current-drive capability of vertically-stacked SiNW technology, it has been assumed that there are four nanowires per stack of

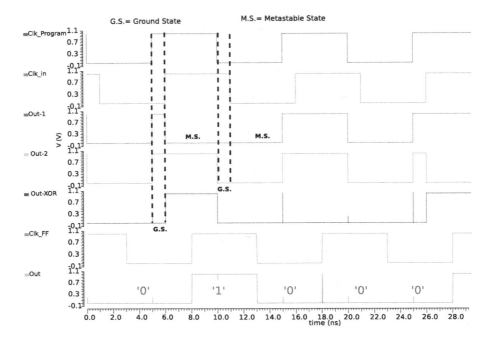

Fig. 10. Transient waveforms on operating the END-TRUE at 100 MHz clock frequency with the ground states and metastable states marked for a clock cycle. Smaller glitches in the *Out* signal appear since the same *clk_Program* is also fed to configure the proposed TSPC D-flip flop as negative or positive edge-triggered. Larger glitches appear during the switching transience of the D-flip flop during data sampling.

TIGFET [13,34,74]. It is to be noted that the main focus in this work is to demonstrate how transistor-level reconfigurability can be used for random number generation at increased throughput and hence [13] has been used for the experimental simulations. Verilog-A models for other ambipolar devices with different performance parameters and model characteristics are orthogonal to this work and can be used as well.

4.2   Simulation and Results

For the circuit shown in Fig. 8, the transient waveforms for the input and output signals are shown in Fig. 10. All the analyses have been done for a supply voltage of 1.0 V. Here, all the clock signals *viz.*, *clk_Program*, *clk_IN* and *clk_FF* operate at a frequency of 100 MHz. Also, *clk_IN* and *clk_FF* are time-delayed versions of *clk_Program*, delayed by 1*ns* and 3*ns* respectively. A transient analysis has been performed using the embedded transient noise feature in *Virtuoso*

Spectre Circuit Simulator and obtain random bits at the 'OUT' node after every 5 ns. The ground states (**G.S.**) and metastable states (**M.S.**) attained by the TRNG in a clock cycle have been marked in Fig. 10. It can be noted that the throughput is equal to 200 Mbps which is twice the input clock frequency of 100 MHz.

In the corresponding CMOS-based implementation (designed for double-throughput) of the END-TRUE, operating at supply voltage of 1.0 V, PTM 16 nm low power based CMOS model has been used for the simulation of the MOSFETs [69]. In this case, *clk_Select* and *clk_IN* signals operate at 100 MHz whereas, the *clk_FF* signal, that samples data entering into the positive-edge triggered D-flip flop, operates at 200 MHz (Fig. 8). Random bits having a throughput of 200 Mbps has been obtained at the 'OUT' node.

The above procedure is repeated for a higher clock frequency of 200 MHz and a lower frequency of 10 MHz in case of the END-TRUE and the output raw bit sequences are recorded.

4.3   Comparison with the Equivalent CMOS-Based TRNG

Table 2 and Table 3 present a comparison between the simulated END-TRUE and its CMOS counterpart (both for double-throughput). It can be seen that there is 60% saving in the number of transistors by employing an RFET based design. Furthermore, Table 3 shows a comparison between one SR latch unit for the END-TRUE and its CMOS counterpart on the basis of power consumption and delay operating at a clock frequency of 100 MHz. A 94.5% reduction in leakage power, 70.7% reduction in dynamic power and 77.3% reduction in critical path delay has been observed in case of the SR latch unit based on RFETs with respect to its CMOS equivalent.

Table 2. Comparison of the number of transistors, to realize END-TRUE and its CMOS equivalent.

No. of transistors	RFET model	CMOS model
SR latch unit	14	46
2-input XOR	4	8
TSPC-based D-flip flop	8	11
TOTAL	**26**	**65**

4.4   Statistical Evaluation of the Generated Bit Sequence

By performing a transient analysis in the *Spectre* simulator, 110,000 bits has been generated as output from the END-TRUE for the clock frequencies of 10 MHz, 100 MHz and 200 MHz respectively. The statistical tests are performed on the random bits generated.

Table 3. Comparison of power consumption and delay of an RFET-based SR latch unit and its CMOS equivalent.

SR latch unit	Leakage power (nW)	Dynamic power (nW)	Delay (ps)
END-TRUE	16.85	79.65	206
CMOS equivalent	308.25	271.5	909

In order to carry out thorough statistical evaluation and owing to the complexity of the simulations due to large number of parameters, high precision and a bulk of simulated and stored data points, two types of analysis are carried out– Firstly, 110 sequences of 1000 bits each are formed from the overall 110,000 bits for each frequency of operation and are subjected to various statistical evaluations. This is required to evaluate the randomness in smaller chunks of the bit patterns. Secondly, statistical analysis is performed by consolidating all the 110 sequences, thereby forming a 110,000-bits long sequence each for the clock frequencies of 10 MHz, 100 MHz and 200 MHz. This is necessary to carry out evaluation for the complete sequence.

For the simulation model as proposed in Sect. 3.2, that is used to extract entropy from the END-TRUE, the output bit sequence can be assumed to be *i.i.d.* (independent and identically distributed). It is because before the occurrence of a metastability event, either at the rising or at the falling clock edge, the output node 'OUT' of the TRNG attains a ground state in which it resets itself before generating another random bit. Hence, the model does not involve correlation between two consecutive bits generated at 'OUT' due to the metastability event.

Shannon Entropy as a Measure for Randomness. Entropy is defined as the average amount of information produced by a stochastic source of data [65]. The amount of randomness in the outcome of an experiment can be measured using a metric called Shannon entropy. For an *i.i.d.* binary sequence that takes values from a finite set $X\{0,1\}$ with a probability distribution function $p : X \rightarrow [0,1]$, the Shannon entropy per bit (H) is given as:

$$H = -\Sigma_{x_i \epsilon X} \ p(x_i) \log_2 p(x_i) \tag{4}$$

For an uniformly distributed (unbiased) sequence of bits for which $p(0) = p(1) = 0.5$, the Shannon entropy per bit is equal to 1.0 which is the maximum value. If the output bit sequence from the TRNG is strongly biased, *i.e.* one bit appears more frequently than the other, then the Shannon entropy deviates significantly from its maximum value, indicating that the given bit sequence is less random and more deterministic.

Figure 11 shows the variation in the Shannon entropy per bit for each 1000 bit-long output sequence when the END-TRUE operates at various clock frequencies. It can be clearly observed that the Shannon entropy for most of the

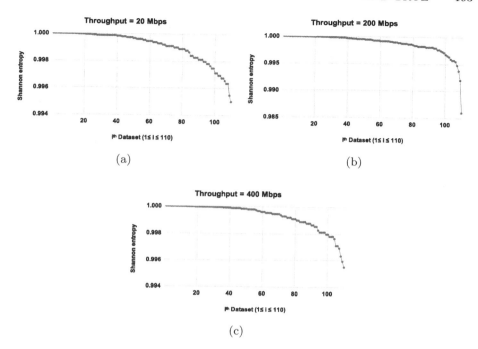

Fig. 11. Plots showing variation in Shannon entropy with the 110 datasets of 1000 bits each for frequencies- (a) 10 MHz, (b) 100 MHz, and (c) 200 MHz

sequences is very close to 1.0, indicating that the raw bit sequences are uniformly distributed. This, however, does not imply deeming the bit sequence as random. It is to be noted that uniform distribution of bits is a necessary but not a sufficient condition to assess randomness and hence evaluation over NIST benchmark suite has been carried out in this work.

NIST benchmark suite (SP800-22 rev. 1a) for statistical evaluation of randomness [49] The *National Institute of Standards and Technology* (NIST) test suite is used to evaluate the randomness of the binary sequences generated at the output of a TRNG. This benchmark suite is commonly used to evaluate both hardware and software-based RNGs and indicates whether the bitstream is likely to come from a uniform i.i.d. [23,49]. The test suite consists of several benchmarks that are run on all the binary sequences and a value, *p-value* corresponding to each sequence per benchmark is generated. An RNG is said to pass a benchmark if the p-value is greater than a particular threshold, which is termed as a 'success' for that specific benchmark. Subsequently, for each benchmark in the suite, two metrics are defined namely, *success rate* and *P'-value*. The success rate for a benchmark is the proportion of the binary sequences passing the benchmark, while the P'-value quantifies the uniformity in the distribution of all the p-values for a benchmark in the suite. The P'-value is a number between 0 and 1. An RNG is said to pass a benchmark if the success rate and the P'-value are greater than a threshold [49]. Only those benchmark are performed from the suite which can be run on the generated number of bits (110,000).[1]

Table 4. Results of the NIST benchmark suite for the END-TRUEusing 110 sequences of 1000 bits each. The threshold for P'-value is 0.0001 and for success rate is 105/110 = 0.954 [23,40]. (**Failed benchmark results have been highlighted in red**)

Benchmark name	10 MHz		100 MHz		200 MHz	
	Success rate	P'-value	Success rate	P'-value	Success rate	P'-value
Monobit Frequency	0.991	0.2238	0.964	0.0052	1.0	0.7757
Block frequency	0.982	0.0004	0.936	3.19E-12	0.918	1.08E-10
Runs	1.0	0.7399	1.0	0.6276	0.973	0.3807
Longest run	1.0	0.5159	1.0	0.5899	1.0	0.1431
DFT	0.991	7.99E-18	0.973	5.04E-14	0.991	2.25E-20
Overlap template matching	0.964	0.0004	0.945	0.0020	0.964	2.02E-07
Non-overlap template matching	0.991	0.0064	1.0	0.3218	1.0	0.6655
Cumulative sum - 1	0.991	0.1359	0.973	0.0002	1.0	0.5526
Cumulative sum - 2	1.0	0.2820	0.945	6.66E-05	1.0	0.5159
Serial - 1	0.991	0.7216	0.954	0.0011	0.973	0.0027
Serial - 2	0.982	0.3654	0.991	0.9230	0.973	0.1506
Approximate entropy	0.991	0.8421	0.964	0.0597	0.982	0.0083
Binary matrix rank	1.0	0.2949	0.991	0.0885	0.982	0.2346

5   Results and Discussion

Table 4 shows the NIST benchmark results (success rates and P'-values) for the 110 raw bit sequences generated from the END-TRUE operating at clock frequencies of 10 MHz, 100 MHz and 200 MHz. Table 5 shows the NIST benchmark results (p-values) and Shannon entropies for the 110,000 bits-long binary sequence each for the clock frequencies of 10 MHz, 100 MHz and 200 MHz.

It can be observed that when the TRNG operates at a lower frequency of 10 MHz, the success-rate for raw output binary sequence passes all the NIST benchmarks as shown in Table 4. At higher values of operating frequency or throughput, only a few benchmarks (in this case, *Block frequency, DFT, Overlap template matching* and *Cumulative sum - 2* benchmarks) fail from the perspective of success rate and/or P'-value. However, the observed success rates for the failed benchmarks are still more than 90% for all the binary sequences tested. Moreover, even without post-processing the raw output bit sequences, it can be observed that the *Monobit Frequency* benchmark is passed for both higher and lower frequencies of operation. It implies that the number of '0's and '1's produced by the TRNG are approximately equal as would be expected for a truly random sequence [49]. It is important to note here that the *Monobit Frequency* benchmark is compulsory to pass as other subsequent benchmarks in the NIST suite depend on it [49].

---

[1] This is because the remaining benchmarks in the suite (*Maurer's Universal statistical, Linear, Radom excursion* tests) require more than 10^7 bits for evaluation and it would amount to an unfeasible time duration to generate the bits using simulation [40] for a TCAD-based verilog-A model for RFETs [13].

Table 5. P-values for the NIST benchmarks with the binary sequences of 110,000 bits from the END-TRUE taken altogether (without post-processing). The threshold for P-value is 0.01 for a benchmark to pass [49]. (**Failed benchmark results have been highlighted in red**)

Benchmark name	10 MHz	100 MHz	200 MHz
Monobit Frequency	0.59	0.21	0.51
Block frequency	0.01	7.32E-05	0.57
Runs	6.15E-08	1.33E-10	6.78E-07
Longest run	0.11	0.68	0.51
DFT	0.72	0.27	0.23
Overlap template matching	0.02	0.46	0.02
Non-overlap template matching	0.42	0.03	0.32
Cumulative sum - 1	0.39	0.25	0.35
Cumulative sum - 2	0.64	0.12	0.67
Serial - 1	6.44E-07	1.23E-17	1.76E-17
Serial - 2	0.08	0.01	0.02
Approximate entropy	9.19E-07	5.69E-17	5.10E-17
Binary matrix rank	0.68	0.35	0.06
Shannon Entropy	**0.9999980685**	**0.9999896832**	**0.9999972186**

Table 6. P-values for the NIST benchmarks after Von-Neumann post-processing of the raw binary sequence of 110,000 bits from the END-TRUE. The threshold for P-value is 0.01 for a benchmark to pass [49]. (**Failed benchmark results have been highlighted in red**)

Test name	10 MHz	100 MHz	200 MHz
Monobit Frequency	0.95	0.46	0.63
Block frequency	0.11	0.75	0.47
Runs	0.87	0.00025	0.04
Longest run	0.39	0.91	0.25
DFT	0.46	0.16	0.26
Overlap template matching	0.25	0.19	0.03
Non-overlap template matching	0.81	0.16	0.998
Cumulative sum - 1	0.44	0.20	0.74
Cumulative sum - 2	0.39	0.72	0.81
Serial - 1	0.59	0.02	0.22
Serial - 2	0.50	0.68	0.28
Approximate entropy	0.60	0.02	0.24
Binary matrix rank	0.31	0.15	0.87
Shannon Entropy	**0.9999999011**	**0.9999854835**	**0.9999937737**

5.1   Post-processing Unit of a TRNG

On fabrication, it is quite plausible that if our proposed metastability-based TRNG generates a raw binary sequence at higher speed (higher throughput), then the sequence has a statistical weakness resulting in a skewed (biased) distribution of '0's and '1's [1,11]. Statistical weaknesses may also arise from PVT variations that hamper the source of entropy among other factors. Thus, typically every metastability-based TRNG has an integration of two units, *viz.* a physical source of entropy (in this case, the SR latch units generating the raw binary sequences) and a post-processing unit that transforms the raw binary sequences with statistical weaknesses into a sequence which is computationally tedious to differentiate from a purely random sequence [11,60].

A very commonly used post-processing technique is the Von-Neumann extraction. This method acts on raw bit streams with statistical weaknesses and outputs a uniformly distributed and uncorrelated bit stream independent from the input raw stream however, at the cost of reduced throughput [37]. In this algorithm, the raw bit stream is grouped into non-overlapping pairs of consecutive bits. For each pair, in case both the bits are equal then the pair is discarded, otherwise, the first bit in the pair is taken to be the output. Thus, this algorithm essentially uses two input bits to produce either zero or one output bit. This algorithm is employed to post-process the raw binary sequences consisting of the entire set of 110,000 bits from the END-TRUE operating at frequencies of 10 MHz, 100 MHz and 200 MHz. Subsequently, all the NIST benchmarks are run on the processed output sequences and the corresponding p-values are recorded in Table 6.

On comparing the data shown in Table 5 and Table 6, a significant improvement in the NIST benchmark results after Von-Neumann processing can be observed, for all the three frequencies of operation. After Von-Neumann processing of the 110,000 bits-long sequence, almost all the NIST benchmarks have been shown to pass.

XOR-ing the Outputs of Multiple SR Latch Units to Increase Entropy: It has been mentioned in Sect. 4 that to have a feasible runtime for simulations, the two outputs of SR latch units has been XOR-ed to generate the output binary sequence of the END-TRUE. However, as discussed in Sect. 2, the outputs of multiple SR latch units can be XOR-ed to further increase the entropy of the output sequence of the END-TRUE and make the device more robust against PVT variations [65]. For the CMOS-based ASIC implementation of the TRNG proposed in [60], it has been shown that XOR-ing the outputs of 256 SR latches can generate a random sequence with sufficient entropy that is able to pass all the benchmarks in the NIST suite without post-processing. This methodology can also be employed for the END-TRUE to obtain a bitstream having sufficient randomness to pass all the benchmarks in the suite. Thus, the optimal number of SR latch units for the END-TRUE that must be XOR-ed to obtain a random sequence with entropy high enough to pass all the statistical tests without post-processing is to be determined when physically implemented in hardware.

5.2   Considerations on PVT Variations

TRNGs should preferably generate high-quality random numbers even in the case of an adverse surrounding environment. Unfortunately, TRNGs based on CMOS and other charge-based technologies are sensitive to the variations of process conditions, supply voltage, and temperature (PVT). An attackers can try to evade the secure device by intentionally providing such PVT variations externally. For example, they can reduce the supply voltage or can put the embedded device in a freezing environment and thus deteriorating the quality of random numbers hence degrading the security of the device [60]. An RFET being CMOS compatible charge-based device is not spared from these variations and hence can compromise the overall functioning of the TRNG if not optimized properly. They may also cause an asymmetry in the electrical characteristics, thus compromising the overall functioning of the reconfigurable circuit. Thus, PVT variations may cause biases in the output of a TRNG. Therefore, to develop secure hardware, one should ideally run simulations corresponding to all the mentioned variations on TRNG and verify the quality of randomness by using NIST benchmarks.

Unfortunately some the limitations posed by the version of the Verilog-A RFET table model used in this work does not allow us to provide quantitative data for our design. To study the effect of voltage variations in the TRNG output, one has to simulate the circuit with the supply voltage variation of V_{DD} $\pm$ 10% and collect up to 110,000 data points, and subsequently perform NIST SP 800-22 tests on those data points. The current version of the model used in this work is too slow and takes considerable resources and time to collect this high amount data points. Further, no temperature dependencies or process variation parameters are integrated into the model. Thus in this work, a qualitative discussion of the PVT impact on our TRNG application based on some results from literature has been done. The conclusions given in this section have to be verified by extensive simulations once better models are available.

Process Variations: The impact of process variation is an important effect that should be considered while designing a robust circuit. They occur because of the manufacturing conditions like temperature, concentration levels, etc. These conditions although extremely well controlled in modern CMOS processes, still have some unavoidable variations, which manifests as slight variations of device parameters. It is an unavoidable variation and bound to exist. The main contributors to the process variations are: Line Edge Roughness (LER) [21,66], Gate Edge Roughness (GER) [75], Work Function Variation (WFV) [25,27], and Random Dopant Fluctuations (RDF) [27]. Threshold voltage and different parasitic capacitance's are two of most the significant parameters which get affected in classical CMOS [51]. Beeing a dopant-free technology, RFETs are expected to show better performance in terms of RDF. Still, to develop a reliable circuit using RFETs, process variation estimation is crucial. It is imperative to calculate reliable process corner information and timing variations [26]. Combining GER, LER, and WFV RFETs have been found to be more vulnerable to process fluctuations overall than CMOS devices [26]. However, this effect can be mainly attributed to the high impact of WFV, which is the main contributor in terms of process variations for RFET technology reasoned in the metallic source and drain electrodes. Thus, to yield a good TRNG, special attention must be given to a highly controlled work function, while mass manufacturing the RFETs [26]. Considering that most silicon nanowire based RFETs are based on sharp $NiSi_2/Si$ junctions with a quasi-epitaxial relation between both materials, it is reasonable to assume that this metric can be achieved [68].

Voltage Variations: Supply voltage variations are also a crucial parameter that is needed to be taken care of. It has been stated that the circuit must at least support a variation of $V_{DD} \pm 10\%$ to be known as a reliable device [51]. In terms of RFET designs, it is mainly crucial, that the symmetric behavior between p- and n-type operation is not lost by the voltage variations. Such an attack scenario was first tested in [9] on various NAND/NOR logic gate design variants. In this work, it was described that increasing V_{DD} lead to no particular differences in the propagation delay values of both configurations. If the nominal operation voltage has been instead decreased the relative difference between individual NAND and NOR rise and fall times increased, but stayed always below 10% difference. A V_{DD} reduction of more than 33% of the initial supply voltage resulted in malefaction of the circuit.

Temperature Variations: The final parameter to be considered for RFET based security solutions are temperature variations. It is well known that in CMOS technology, temperature variation impacts the I-V characteristics of a transistor. It affects the thermal voltage V_T in subthreshold conduction, transistor threshold voltage V_t as well as the μ, due to higher number of scattering events at higher temperatures [51]. Thus, typically the off-state currents of CMOS devices is increased, while the on-state is decreased, leading to lower on/off ratio at higher temperatures. This is different for RFET devices, which rely on the thermionic field-emission based injection of carries over the Schottky junctions at source and drain. With increase in temperature, more carriers are injected, overshadowing the effect of the lower effective channel mobility. As a result, both, on- as well as off-current increase with increasing temperature. It is conceivable, that this behavior makes RFET based circuit solutions more stable with respect to temperature variations than their CMOS based counterpart.

6   Conclusions

In the present work a metastability-based TRNG design has been proposed using emerging reconfigurable nanotechnology. This is referred as *Emerging Nanotechnology -based Double -Throughput True Random Number Generator* (END-TRUE). The transistor-level ambipolarity in RFETs allows us to duplicate cross-coupled SR latches and hence random bits can be sampled at both the edges of the clock. The END-TRUE generates a random bit at each half cycle of the input clock, thereby a throughput of twice the input clock frequency is obtained. This enables the dual edge-triggered D-flip flop operate at the same clock frequency as the input clock signal to the TRNG. Using runtime reconfigurability, the TRNG is shown to use less hardware, be compact in terms of transistor count per block (60% saving in the transistor count), consume less power (94.5% saving in leakage power and 70.7% saving in dynamic power) and has a lower critical path delay (77.3% reduction in delay) with respect to its equivalent CMOS counterpart. Statistical evaluations show that the generated bitstream using our proposed END-TRUE has high values of Shannon entropy as well as successfully passes the NIST benchmark suite (except one) upon post-processing. The technique of post-processing is used regardless to mitigate the effects of process variation [1].

The present work demonstrates a viable circuit implementation for emerging reconfigurable nanotechnology which is a key component in hardware security. Silicon or germanium nanowire-based RFETs follow similar CMOS-like top-down fabrication process [29,53] and come in stacked nanowire geometry [71] and hence are commercially feasible and can complement CMOS technology. While in the present work, a specific application has been demonstrated, it is expected that with better device models, better evaluation can be carried out.

References

1. Bhunia, S., Tehranipoor, M.: Hardware security primitives, chapter 12. In: Hardware Security, pp. 311–345. Morgan Kaufmann (2019). https://doi.org/10.1016/B978-0-12-812477-2.00017-4, http://www.sciencedirect.com/science/article/pii/B9780128124772000174. ISBN 978-0-12-812477-2
2. Bi, Y., et al.: Enhancing hardware security with emerging transistor technologies. In: Proceedings of the 26th Edition on Great Lakes Symposium on VLSI. GLSVLSI'16. pp. 305–310. ACM, Boston, Massachusetts (2016). https://doi.org/10.1145/2902961.2903041, http://doi.acm.org/10.1145/2902961.2903041. ISBN 978-1-4503-4274-2
3. Bi, Y., et al.: Leveraging emerging technology for hardware security - case study on silicon nanowire FETs and graphene SymFETs. In: 2014 IEEE 23rd Asian Test Symposium, pp. 342–347 (2014). https://doi.org/10.1109/ATS.2014.69
4. Bucci, M., et al.: A high-speed oscillator-based truly random number source for cryptographic applications on a smart card IC. IEEE Trans. Comput. 52(4), 403–409 (2003). https://doi.org/10.1109/TC.2003.1190581. ISSN 2326-3814
5. Chen, A., et al.: Using emerging technologies for hardware security beyond PUFs. In: 2016 Design, Automation Test in Europe Conference Exhibition (DATE), pp. 1544–1549 (2016)
6. De Marchi, M., et al.: Polarity control in double-gate, gate-all-around vertically stacked silicon nanowire FETs. In: 2012 International Electron Devices Meeting, pp. 8.4.1–8.4.4 (2012). https://doi.org/10.1109/IEDM.2012.6479004
7. Davies, R.B.: Exclusive OR (XOR) and hardware random number generators (2002)
8. Fujieda, N., Takeda, M., Ichikawa, S.: An analysis of DCM-based true random number generator. In: IEEE Trans. Circuits Syst. II: Express Briefs, 1–1 (2019). https://doi.org/10.1109/TCSII.2019.2926555. ISSN 1558-3791 , 1109–1113 (2019). ISSN 1558-3791
9. Galderisi, G., Mikolajick, T., Trommer, J.: Reconfigurable field effect transistors design solutions for delay-invariant logic gates. IEEE Embed. Syst. Lett. (2022)
10. Gassend, B., et al.: Silicon physical random functions. In: Proceedings of the 9th ACM Conference on Computer and Communications Security. CCS'02, pp. 148–160. Association for Computing Machinery, Washington, DC (2002). https://doi.org/10.1145/586110.586132. ISBN 1581136129

11. Golic, J.D.J.: New methods for digital generation and postprocessing of random data. IEEE Trans. Comput. **55**(10), 1217–1229 (2006). https://doi.org/10.1109/TC.2006.164. ISSN 2326-3814

12. Gong, L., et al.: True random number generators using electrical noise. IEEE Access **7**, 125796–125805 (2019)

13. Gore, G., et al.: A predictive process design kit for three-independent-gate field-effect transistors. In: 2019 IFIP/IEEE 27th International Conference on Very Large Scale Integration (VLSI-SoC), pp. 172–177 (2019). https://doi.org/10.1109/VLSI-SoC.2019.Gore2019

14. Haddad, P., Fischer, V., Bernard, F., Nicolai, J.: A physical approach for stochastic modeling of TERO-based TRNG. In: Güneysu, T., Handschuh, H. (eds.) CHES 2015. LNCS, vol. 9293, pp. 357–372. Springer, Heidelberg (2015). https://doi.org/10.1007/978-3-662-48324-4_18

15. Harada, N., et al.: A polarity-controllable graphene inverter. In: vol. 96(1), p. 012102. American Institute of Physics (2010)

16. Hata, H., Ichikawa, S.: FPGA implementation of metastability-based true random number generator. IEICE Trans. Inf. Syst. **95**(2), 426–436 (2012). https://doi.org/10.1587/transinf.E95.D.426

17. Heinzig, A., et al.: Reconfigurable silicon nanowire transistors. Nano Lett. **12**, 119–24 (2011). https://doi.org/10.1021/nl203094h

18. Holcomb, D.E., Burleson, W.P., Fu, K.: Power-up SRAM state as an identifying fingerprint and source of true random numbers. IEEE Trans. Comput. **58**(9), 1198–1210 (2009). https://doi.org/10.1109/TC.2008.212. ISSN 2326-3814

19. Holleman, J., et al.: A 3 μW CMOS true random number generator with adaptive floating-gate offset cancellation. IEEE J. Solid-State Circuits **43**(5), 1324–1336 (2008). https://doi.org/10.1109/JSSC.2008.920327. ISSN 1558-173X

20. Holman, W.T., Connelly, J.A., Dowlatabadi, A.B.: An integrated analog/digital random noise source. IEEE Trans. Circuits Syst. I: Fundam. Theory Appl. **44**(6), 521–528 (1997). https://doi.org/10.1109/81.586025. ISSN 1558-1268

21. Jiang, X., et al.: Investigations on line-edge roughness (LER) and line-width roughness (LWR) in nanoscale CMOS technology: Part I-modeling and simulation method. IEEE Trans. Electron Dev. **60**(11), 3669–3675 (2013). https://doi.org/10.1109/TED.2013.2283518

22. Yuan, J., Svensson, C.: New single-clock CMOS latches and flipflops with improved speed and power savings. IEEE J. Solid-State Circuits **32**(1), 62–69 (1997). https://doi.org/10.1109/4.553179. ISSN 1558-173X

23. Kim, S.-J., Umeno, K., Hasegawa, A.: Corrections of the NIST statistical test suite for randomness (2004). https://doi.org/10.48550/ARXIV.NLIN/0401040. https://arxiv.org/abs/nlin/0401040

24. Kinniment, D.J., Chester, E.G.: Design of an on-chip random number generator using metastability. In: Proceedings of the 28th European Solid-State Circuits Conference, pp. 595–598 (2002)

25. Ko, K., et al.: Compact model strategy of metal-gate work-function variation for Ultrascaled FinFET and vertical GAA FETs. IEEE Trans. Electron Dev. **66**(3), 1613–1616 (2019). https://doi.org/10.1109/TED.2019.2891677

26. Li, X., et al.: Impact of process fluctuations on reconfigurable silicon nanowire transistor. IEEE Trans. Electron Dev. **68**(2), 885–891 (2021). https://doi.org/10.1109/TED.2020.3045689

27. Li, Y., et al.: Process variation effect, metal-gate work-function fluctuation and random dopant fluctuation of 10-nm gate-all-around silicon nanowire MOSFET

devices. In: 2015 IEEE International Electron Devices Meeting (IEDM), pp. 34.4.1–34.4.4 (2015). https://doi.org/10.1109/IEDM.2015.7409827

28. Liu, N., et al.: A true random number generator using time-dependent dielectric breakdown. In: 2011 Symposium on VLSI Circuits - Digest of Technical Papers, pp. 216–217 (2011)

29. De Marchi, M., et al.: Top-down fabrication of gate-all-around vertically stacked silicon nanowire FETs with controllable polarity. IEEE Trans. Nanotechnol. **13**(6), 1029–1038 (2014). https://doi.org/10.1109/TNANO.2014.2363386. ISSN 1536-125X

30. Markettos, A.T., Moore, S.W.: The frequency injection attack on ring-oscillator-based true random number generators. In: Clavier, C., Gaj, K. (eds.) CHES 2009. LNCS, vol. 5747, pp. 317–331. Springer, Heidelberg (2009). https://doi.org/10.1007/978-3-642-04138-9_23

31. Mathew, S.K., et al.: 2.4 Gbps, 7 mw all-digital PVT-variation tolerant true random number generator for 45 nm CMOS high-performance microprocessors. IEEE J. Solid-State Circuits **47**(11), 2807–2821 (2012). https://doi.org/10.1109/JSSC.2012.2217631. ISSN 1558-173X

32. Mavrovouniotis, S., Ganley, M.: Hardware security modules. In: Markantonakis, K., Mayes, K. (eds.) Secure Smart Embedded Devices, Platforms and Applications, pp. 383–405. Springer, New York (2014). https://doi.org/10.1007/978-1-4614-7915-4_17

33. Menezes, A.J., et al.: Handbook of Applied Cryptography. CRC Press, Boca Raton (1996)

34. Mikolajick, T., et al.: The RFET - a reconfigurable nanowire transistor and its application to novel electronic circuits and systems. Semicond. Sci. Technol. **32** (2016). https://doi.org/10.1088/1361-6641/aa5581

35. Mulaosmanovic, H., Mikolajick, T., Slesazeck, S.: Random number generation based on ferroelectric switching. IEEE Electron Dev. Lett. **39**(1), 135–138 (2018)

36. Nakaharai, S., et al.: Electrostatically reversible polarity of ambipolar- MoTe2 transistors. ACS Nano **9**(6), 5976–5983 (2015). https://doi.org/10.1021/acsnano.5b00736. PMID 25988597

37. von Neumann, J.: Various techniques used in connection with random digits, chapter 13. In: Householder, A.S., Forsythe, G.E., Germond, H.H. (eds.) Monte Carlo Method. National Bureau of Standards Applied Mathematics Series, vol. 12, pp. 36–38. US Government Printing Office, Washington, DC (1951)

38. Pappu, R., et al.: Physical one-way functions. Science **297**(5589), 2026–2030 (2002). https://doi.org/10.1126/science.1074376, https://science.sciencemag.org/content/297/5589/2026.full.pdf

39. Parker, R.J.: Entropy justification for metastability based nondeterministic random bit generator. In: 2017 IEEE 2nd International Verification and Security Workshop (IVSW), pp. 25–30 (2017). https://doi.org/10.1109/IVSW.2017.8031540

40. Perach, B., Kvatinsky, S.: An asynchronous and low-power true random number generator using STT-MTJ. IEEE Trans. Very Large Scale Integr. (VLSI) Syst. **27**(11), 2473–2484 (2019). https://doi.org/10.1109/TVLSI.2019.2927816. ISSN 1557-9999

41. Rahman, F., et al.: Security beyond CMOS: fundamentals, applications, and roadmap. IEEE Trans. Very Large Scale Integr. (VLSI) Syst. **25**(12), 3420–3433 (2017). https://doi.org/10.1109/TVLSI.2017.2742943. ISSN 1063-8210

42. Rai, S., Raitza, M., Kumar, A.: Technology mapping flow for emerging reconfigurable silicon nanowire transistors. In: 2018 Design, Automation Test in Europe

Conference Exhibition (DATE), pp. 767–772 (2018). https://doi.org/10.23919/DATE.2018.8342110

43. Rai, S., et al.: A physical synthesis flow for early technology evaluation of silicon nanowire based reconfigurable FETs. In: 2018 Design, Automation Test in Europe Conference Exhibition (DATE), pp. 605–608 (2018)

44. Rai, S., et al.: Designing efficient circuits based on runtime-reconfigurable field-effect transistors. IEEE Trans. Very Large Scale Integr. (VLSI) Syst. **27**(3), 560–572 (2019). https://doi.org/10.1109/TVLSI.2018.2884646. ISSN 1557-9999

45. Rai, S., et al.: Hardware watermarking using polymorphic inverter designs based on reconfigurable nanotechnologies. In: ISVLSI (2019)

46. Rai, S., et al.: Security promises and vulnerabilities in emerging reconfigurable nanotechnology-based circuits. IEEE Trans. Emerg. Top. Comput. 1 (2020). https://doi.org/10.1109/TETC.2020.3039375

47. Raitza, M., et al.: Raw 2014: random number generators on FPGAs. ACM Trans. Reconfigurable Technol. Syst. **9**(2) (2015). https://doi.org/10.1145/2807699. ISSN 1936-7406

48. Rajendran, J., et al.: Nano meets security: exploring nanoelec-tronic devices for security applications. Proc. IEEE **103**(5), 829–849 (2015). https://doi.org/10.1109/JPROC.2014.2387353

49. Rukhin, A., et al.: NIST Special Publication 800-22: A Statistical Test Suite for the Validation of Random Number Generators and Pseudo Random Number Generators for Cryptographic Applications. NIST Special Publication 800-22 (2010)

50. Rupani, A., Rai, S., Kumar, A.: Exploiting emerging reconfigurable technologies for secure devices. In: Euromicro DSD (2019)

51. Sedra, A.S., Smith, K.C.: Microelectronic Circuits, 5th edn. Oxford University Press, Oxford (2004)

52. Sessi, V., et al.: Back-bias reconfigurable field effect transistor: a flexible add-on functionality for 22 nm FDSOI. In: 2021 Silicon Nanoelectronics Workshop (SNW), pp. 1–2. IEEE (2021)

53. Simon, M., et al.: A wired-and transistor: polarity controllable FET with multiple inputs. In: 2018 76th Device Research Conference (DRC), pp. 1–2 (2018). https://doi.org/10.1109/DRC.2018.8442159

54. Simon, M., et al.: Bringing reconfigurable nanowire FETs to a logic circuits compatible process platform. In: 2016 IEEE Nanotechnology Materials and Devices Conference (NMDC), pp. 1–3 (2016). https://doi.org/10.1109/NMDC.2016.7777085

55. Sistani, M., et al.: Nanometer-scale GE-based adaptable transistors providing programmable negative differential resistance enabling multivalued logic. ACS Nano **15**(11), 18135–18141 (2021)

56. Sunar, B., Martin, W.J., Stinson, D.R.: A provably secure true random number generator with built-in tolerance to active attacks. IEEE Trans. Comput. **56**(1), 109–119 (2007). https://doi.org/10.1109/TC.2007.250627. ISSN 2326-3814

57. Tanachutiwat, S., et al.: Reconfigurable multi-function logic based on graphene p-n junctions. In: Design Automation Conference, pp. 883–888 (2010). https://doi.org/10.1145/1837274.1837496

58. Tang, X., et al.: TSPC flip-flop circuit design with three-independent-gate silicon nanowire FETs. In: 2014 IEEE International Symposium on Circuits and Systems (ISCAS), pp. 1660–1663 (2014). https://doi.org/10.1109/ISCAS.2014.6865471

59. Tokunaga, C., Blaauw, D., Mudge, T.: True random number generator with a metastability-based quality control. In: 2007 IEEE International Solid-State Circuits Conference. Digest of Technical Papers, pp. 404–611 (2007). https://doi.org/10.1109/ISSCC.2007.373465

60. Torii, N., et al.: ASIC implementation of random number generators using SR latches and its evaluation. EURASIP J. Inf. Secur. **2016**(1), 10 (2016)
61. Trommer, J., et al.: Reconfigurable nanowire transistors with multiple independent gates for efficient and programmable combinational circuits. In: 2016 Design, Automation Test in Europe Conference Exhibition (DATE), pp. 169–174 (2016). ISBN 9783981537062
62. Trommer, J., et al.: Enabling energy efficiency and polarity control in germanium nanowire transistors by individually gated nanojunctions. ACS Nano **11**(2), 1704–1711 (2016)
63. Varchola, M., Drutarovsky, M.: New high entropy element for FPGA based true random number generators. In: Mangard, S., Standaert, F.-X. (eds.) CHES 2010. LNCS, vol. 6225, pp. 351–365. Springer, Heidelberg (2010). https://doi.org/10.1007/978-3-642-15031-9_24
64. Vasyltsov, I., Hambardzumyan, E., Kim, Y.-S., Karpinskyy, B.: Fast digital TRNG based on metastable ring oscillator. In: Oswald, E., Rohatgi, P. (eds.) CHES 2008. LNCS, vol. 5154, pp. 164–180. Springer, Heidelberg (2008). https://doi.org/10.1007/978-3-540-85053-3_11
65. Vatajelu, E.I., Di Natale, G.: High-entropy STT-MTJ-based TRNG. IEEE Trans. Very Large Scale Integr. (VLSI) Syst. **27**(2), 491–495 (2019)
66. Wang, R., et al.: Investigations on line-edge roughness (LER) and line-width roughness (LWR) in nanoscale CMOS technology: Part II-experimental results and impacts on device variability. IEEE Trans. Electron Dev. **60**(11), 3676–3682 (2013). https://doi.org/10.1109/TED.2013.2283517
67. Wang, Y., et al.: A novel circuit design of true random number generator using magnetic tunnel junction. In: 2016 IEEE/ACM International Symposium on Nanoscale Architectures (NANOARCH), pp. 123–128 (2016)
68. Weber, W.M., et al.: Silicon to nickel-silicide axial nanowire heterostructures for high performance electronics. Physica Status Solidi (b) **244**(11), 4170–4175 (2007)
69. Zhao, W., Cao, Y.: New generation of predictive technology model for sub-45 nm design exploration. In: 7th International Symposium on Quality Electronic Design (ISQED 2006), vol. 6, p. 590 (2006)
70. Wold, K., Tan, C.H.: Analysis and enhancement of random number generator in FPGA based on oscillator rings. In: 2008 International Conference on Reconfigurable Computing and FPGAs, pp. 385–390 (2008). https://doi.org/10.1109/ReConFig.2008.17
71. Ye, P., Ernst, T., Khare, M.V.: The last silicon transistor: nanosheet devices could be the final evolutionary step for Moore's law. IEEE Spectr. **56**(8), 30–35 (2019)
72. Lin, Y.-M., et al.: High-performance carbon nanotube field-effect transistor with tunable polarities. IEEE Trans. Nanotechnol. **4**(5), 481–489 (2005). https://doi.org/10.1109/TNANO.2005.851427. ISSN 1941-0085
73. Yuan, J., Svensson, C.: High-speed CMOS circuit technique. IEEE J. Solid-State Circuits **24**(1), 62–70 (1989)
74. Zhang, J., et al.: Configurable circuits featuring dual-threshold-voltage design with three-independent-gate silicon nanowire FETs. IEEE Trans. Circuits Syst. I: Regul. Pap. **61**(10), 2851–2861 (2014). https://doi.org/10.1109/TCSI.2014.2333675. ISSN 1558-0806
75. Zhang, Z., et al.: Extraction of process variation parameters in FinFET technology based on compact modeling and characterization. IEEE Trans. Electron Dev. **65**(3), 847–854 (2018). https://doi.org/10.1109/TED.2018.2790083

A First Approach in Using Super-Steep-Subthreshold-Slope Field-Effect Transistors in Ultra-Low Power Analog Design

Matthieu Couriol[✉], Patsy Cadareanu, Edouard Giacomin, and Pierre-Emmanuel Gaillardon

The University of Utah, Salt Lake City, UT 84112, USA
matthieu.couriol@utah.edu

Abstract. The benefits of steep-*Subthreshold Swing* (SS) devices, though plentiful at the device-level, have yet to be fully exploited at the circuit-level. This is evident from a look at the *Three-Independent-Gate Field-Effect Transistor* (TIGFET), a device renowned for its ability for polarity reconfiguration. At the same time, its demonstrated dynamic control of the subthreshold slope beyond the thermal limit has only been studied at the device-level. This latter benefit is referred to as *Super-Steep Subthreshold Slope* (S4) operation and can lead to unprecedented gain, which is ideal for use in an amplifier circuit. In this book chapter, we investigate the impact of S4 operations when designing differential-amplifier circuits while using TIGFET technology. We demonstrate the benefits of our implementation both from a theoretical standpoint and through circuit-level analyses. More specifically, we show that the TIGFET -based amplifier gain is 95.5× better, and that the gain-bandwidth product is improved by 13.8×, compared to an equivalent MOSFET-based design at the 90 nm node. Besides, we show that at equivalent gains, the TIGFET-based amplifier decreases the area and power by 22.8× and 7.2×, respectively, against its MOSFET counterpart. Further investigations prove that TIGFETs could be used in bio-sensing application where noise and power consumption are crucial. We have demonstrated that the use of TIGFETs could improve the thermal noise of low-power, *Low-Noise Amplifiers* (LNA) by 83% and the noise efficiency factor (NEF) by 58%.

Keywords: Low-power analog design · Schottky barrier field-effect transistors · Steep-subthreshold slope · Three-independent-gate field-effect transistors

1 Introduction

The ever-increasing signal and data processing performance demand is driven by the semiconductor industry and its work in scaling down standard technologies

© IFIP International Federation for Information Processing 2022
Published by Springer Nature Switzerland AG 2022
V. Grimblatt et al. (Eds.): VLSI-SoC 2021, IFIP AICT 661, pp. 205–224, 2022.
https://doi.org/10.1007/978-3-031-16818-5_10

such as the *Metal-Oxide-Semiconductor Field-Effect Transistor* (MOSFET) and its Fin-variant [1].

One way to characterize a device's performance is through its *Subthreshold Swing* (SS), which refers to the gate-to-source voltage needed to change the drain current by one order of magnitude [2]. Based on this definition, a small SS value corresponds to a faster switching speed in the digital domain and defines a large intrinsic gain in terms of analog benefits. The minimum subthreshold swing (SS_{min}) in a MOSFET is limited to approximately 60 mV/decade at room temperature (300 K) because the carriers follow the Fermi-Dirac distribution, and their energy is bounded such that only the carriers with enough thermal energy to exceed the source-channel potential barrier will contribute to the ON-current (I_{ON}) of the device [3]. Due to this, MOSFETs are limited in their use for applications requiring fast switching, such as in signal processing applications.

A solution to this MOSFET-limited problem is the use of alternative devices which are not thermal-conduction-limited. These include tunnel FETs [3], Nano-Electro-Mechanical FETs [4], Impact-ionization MOSFETs [2], and Feedback FETs [5]. The alternative device we will consider in this study is not originally intended as a steep-subthreshold-slope device: *Three-Independent-Gate Field-Effect Transistor* (TIGFET) [6]. The TIGFET is best known for its dynamic channel reconfiguration to n- or p-type that gives it a higher expressive capability at the circuit-level than a typical transistor, enabling compact and efficient logic gates [6,7]. This device was also found to be capable of *Super-Steep-Subthreshold-Slope* (S4) operation with an SS_{min} of 3.4 mV/dec and an SS_{avg} of 6.0 mV/dec over 5 decades of current as demonstrated in [8]. This operation is enabled by an effective body biasing, which in turn is enabled by a positive feedback process based on weak impact ionization. By definition, subthreshold swing defines the gate voltage required to change the drain current by an order of magnitude.

The TIGFET and other steep-subthreshold-slope devices are optimal for use in analog circuits, as evidenced by the longstanding use of devices in their subthreshold region, with applications ranging from biological (such as in cochlear implants) [9–11] to microcontrollers [12,13], to improved signal acquisition for ADCs applications [14–16]. Additionally, TIGFET technology can bring benefits in the context of amplifiers. In a regular *Common-Source* (CS) amplifier design, one transistor acts as a Voltage-Controlled CS while the other acts as a resistor, converting the current back to a voltage [16,17]. The value of the subthreshold swing defines the gain of the amplifier in very low current amplifier designs. Overcoming the thermal conduction limits of regular MOSFETs for extremely low current amplifier design applications offers new horizons regarding area reduction, power consumption, and performance improvement. Operation in the subthreshold region results in low power and high gain, resulting in improved performance-to-power consumption efficiency. This is facilitated by the diffusion and tunneling-based carrier movement in the subthreshold limit.

One of the most challenging applications in analog design is biological sensing and implementable electronics. The co-integration of electronics near living tissue requires rigorous constraints on power consumption [28,29] as thermal dissipation from the electronics can cause damage to the cells. Brain implant electronics also suffer from noise and the general expected input referred noise of the analog front-end is within $2\,\mu V_{RMS}$. With the performance increase of S4 devices, TIGFET devices could potentially provide new standards for *Brain-Computer Interface* (BCI). The potential power reduction can greatly increase the number of interfaceable neurons and the noise reduction can benefit the measurement quality.

In this book chapter, we extend our previous work [32] and introduce an amplifier design using TIGFET devices operating in S4 mode and highlight their benefits compared to standard MOSFET transistors. We study the advantages of our implementation both from a theoretical perspective and through circuit-level analyses. In particular, we demonstrate a $95.5\times$ improved gain and a $13.8\times$ higher *Gain-Bandwidth Product* (GBP) for our TIGFET design, compared to an equivalent MOSFET-based design using a 90 nm technology node. Additionally, we show that at equivalent gains, the TIGFET-based amplifier decreases the area and power by $22.8\times$ and $7.2\times$, respectively, against its MOSFET counterpart. We also show how the use of TIGFET devices in biological sensing applications could improve *the Noise Efficiency Figure* (NEF) by 58% and input referred noise by 83% for the input recording amplifiers.

The remainder of this chapter is as follows: Sect. 2 reviews various SS devices and TIGFET technology. Section 3 introduces our proposed TIGFET-based amplifier circuit and provides theoretical gain and bandwidth analyses. Section 4 presents our circuit-level experimental results. Section 5 presents the noise and performance analysis of a typical bio-sensing TIGFET-based amplifier. Finally, Sect. 6 concludes this chapter.

2   Technical Background

In this section, we introduce the necessary background behind sub-60 mV/decade technology, including TIGFET technology and its operations.

2.1   Steep-Subthreshold Devices

Multiple devices have been proposed as candidates to replace MOSFETs with an ability for sub-60 mV/decade SS operation. These include the tunnel FET that has been fabricated with OFF-current down to the $pA/\mu m$ scale and a small *SS* of 52.8 mV/dec [3]. These benefits are mostly neutralized by the low ON-current of approximately $50\,\mu A/\mu m$ exhibited by TFETs fabricated with large band-gap semiconductors such as silicon; the massive loss in current drive makes this device practically unusable for standard designs. Note that the TFET results in an onset strength (ON-OFF current ratio) that is almost the same as that of a conventional MOSFET. Another alternative device capable of steep-substhreshold characteristics is the Nano-Electro-Mechanical FET [4]. This device is limited in operation and device reliability by the mechanical gate with which it realizes its abrupt SS. Besides, impact-ionization MOSFETs are devices that have been shown to achieve less than 5 mV/dec *SS* and high ON-state currents through avalanche breakdown, but constantly being operated using this mechanism leads to reliability issues at the device-level [2]. The Feedback FET has similar benefits to the impact-ionization MOS device, but it is not CMOS-compatible, requires initial programming to set the device states, and suffers from reliability problems [2,3,5].

2.2   The TIGFET as a Standalone Device

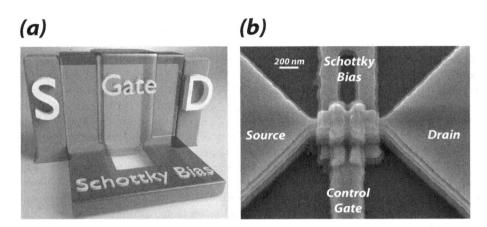

Fig. 1. Schottky-barrier FET: (a) general structure; (b) SEM image of a fabricated fin-based device [8].

Figure 1(a) depicts the general structrue of a Schottky-barrier FET. Such device requires a channel made of a semiconductor material, metallic source and drain contacts, and a minimum of two independent gate electrodes: the *Control Gate* (CG) and a polarity gate at the drain (PG_D) to act as electrostatic doping means at the Schottky barrier interfaces [19,20]. Figure 1(b) depicts a *Scanning Electron Microscopy* (SEM) of a fabricated fin-based Schottky-barrier device [8]. The TIGFET is an enhanced Schottky-barrier FET with a CG and two independent polarity gates: one added at the source (PG_S) and another at the drain (PG_D) [19]. The control gate controls whether the device is ON or OFF. The polarity gate at the drain induces a band-bending opposite to the source band-bending, suppressing the reverse junction leakage. This allows for device reconfigurability between n-type and p-type behaviors after fabrication. Besides, much lower leakage floor values can be reached due to the Schottky-barrier cutoff provided by the individually-gated nanojunctions. The dominant carrier is chosen by the potential on the polarity gate [20]: if the PGs are increased to the supply voltage (V_{DD}), the device will be n-type (electron) carrier-dominated, whereas if the PGs are grounded (0 V), the device will be p-type (hole) carrier-dominated.

Besides its ability for polarity reconfiguration, TIGFETs have demonstrated two additional operation modes: the dynamic control of the threshold voltage [6] and the dynamic control of the subthreshold slope beyond the thermal limit [8].

The latter makes the TIGFET uniquely suited for amplifier applications. This effect, referred to as S4 operation, is enabled by an effective body biasing that is permitted by a positive feedback process based on weak impact ionization.

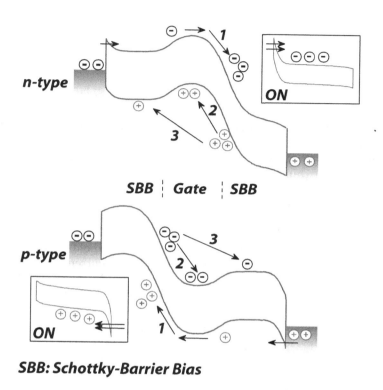

Fig. 2. Energy band diagrams of the TIGFET being operated in steep-subthreshold-slope during the transition from OFF to ON. The inset diagrams show that impact ionization and potential wells vanish when the device is ON [8].

When the device is biased in the subthreshold region, the electrons diffuse from source to drain, and the resulting impact ionization causes the holes to be collected at the potential minimum in the body, thus raising the body potential (V_{BS}) and enhancing the electron supply from the source. This body biasing causes the electron concentration and therefore current in the channel to be much higher than would otherwise be possible in a conventional MOSFET. The increase in I_{DS} and more impact ionization initiates a positive feedback, resulting in an abrupt increase in subthreshold current [2,5]. Figure 2 shows a TIGFET being operated in this steep-subthreshold mode. The benefits reaped are substantial, as seen in the TIGFET device demonstrated in [8]: SS_{min} of 3.4 mV/dec, SS_{avg} of 6.0 mV/dec over 5 decades of current, an onset strength of 10^7, and an OFF-current of 0.06 pA/μm.

3   Proposed TIGFET Differential Amplifier

In this section, we start by introducing the differential amplifier based on MOS-FET and TIGFET devices. We then provide a theoretical comparison of the gain of MOSFET and TIGFET devices. This serves as the backbone for our simulation work.

3.1   The Differential Amplifier

The differential pair is the most widely used structure in analog design [16,17], as it is the input stage of every operational amplifier. The two main reasons for the widespread use of differential amplifiers are that they mitigate interference and do not require bypass or coupling capacitors when biasing the amplifier or coupling amplifier stages together. The performance of the differential pair depends on the matching between the two sides of the circuit. Figure 3(a) shows a basic MOSFET-based differential pair.

V_G and V_{CM} are the biasing voltages; their values set the operating point of our amplifier and define the transconductance of the transistors. I_{tail} defines the DC current going through the transistors and thus also defines the transconductance. I_{tail} is chosen to set the transistor in the subthreshold region so that I_{DS} is at approximately 20 nA while V_G is set by a Widlar current source [16,17].

3.2   The TIGFET-Based Differential Amplifier

As explained in Sect. 2.2, connecting the polarity gates to V_{DD} configures the top TIGFETs as n-types, while connecting the polarity gates to GND configures the bottom devices as p-types. As such, the MOSFET amplifier shown in Fig. 3(a) can be designed with TIGFET devices, as illustrated in Fig. 3(b). V_G, V_{CM}, and I_{tail} are the same biasing sources as in Fig. 3(a) and have the same impact on the amplifier performance. However, since the TIGFET operates at a much higher V_{DS}, the current I_{DS} is lowered to 5 nA to keep the power consumption equal to the standard MOSFET amplifier. While both MOSFET and TIGFET amplifiers employ the same schematic, significant gain improvements are expected by using TIGFET device due to their S4 behavior.

3.3   Theoretical Equations

In this section, we provide theoretical equations for both MOSFET and TIGFET cases. When considering a 90 nm MOSFET technology with a biasing point of 0.6 V for V_{DS} and 20 nA, discussed in Sect. 3.1, the resistance r_0 is defined as [16,17]:

$$r_{0-CMOS} = \frac{V_{DS}}{I_{DS}} = \frac{0.6\,\text{V}}{20\,\text{nA}} = 30\,\text{M}\Omega$$

The 90 nm CMOS device has a slope of 80 mV/dec around this previous biasing point. Using the definition of SS, we calculate the transconductance by

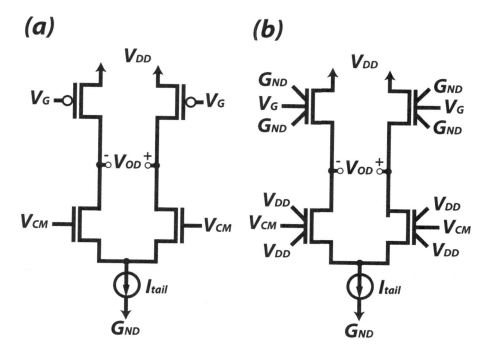

Fig. 3. Transistor-level schematic of a differential pair using: (a) standard MOSFETs; (b) TIGFETs.

picking an order of magnitude of I_{DS} around its operation point of 20 nA. This gives us a transconductance of:

$$g_{m-CMOS} = \frac{\Delta I_D}{\Delta V_{GS}} = \frac{40\,\text{nA} - 4\,\text{nA}}{80\,\text{mV}} = 0.45\,\mu\text{S}$$

Thus, the gain of the differential pair is given by:

$$A_{V-CMOS} = g_{m-CMOS} \cdot R_{0-CMOS}$$

$$\implies A_{V-CMOS} = g_{m-CMOS} \cdot (r_{0-CMOS}//r_{0-CMOS})$$

$$\implies A_{V-CMOS} = 0.45\,\mu\text{S} \cdot 15\,\text{M}\Omega = 6.75\,\text{V/V}$$

Based on the fabricated devices of [6], for the TIGFET operating in S4, the hero device operates at a V_{DS} of 5 V and with an I_{DS} current of 5 nA:

$$r_{0-TIG} = \frac{V_{DS}}{I_{DS}} = \frac{5\,\text{V}}{5\,\text{nA}} = 1000\,\text{M}\Omega$$

The transconductance g_m of the TIGFET is derived using the same approach as for the CMOS; we pick an order of magnitude of current around the biasing point and use the SS definition:

$$g_{m-TIG} = \frac{\Delta I_D}{\Delta V_{GS}} = \frac{10\,\text{nA} - 1\,\text{nA}}{3.4\,\text{mV}} = 2.647\,\mu\text{S}$$

Similarly, the gain A_V of the amplifier is:

$$A_{V-TIG} = g_{m-TIG} \cdot R_{0-TIG}$$

$$\implies A_{V-TIG} = g_{m-TIG} \cdot (r_{0-TIG} // r_{0-TIG})$$

$$\implies A_{V-TIG} = 2.647\,\mu\text{S} \cdot 500\,\text{M}\Omega = 1323\,\text{V/V}$$

The TIGFET exhibits a 196× higher theoretical gain than its MOSFET counterpart, which is particularly appealing for amplifier designs. This improved gain will be verified in the experimental results section.

4   Experimental Results

In this section, we demonstrate the benefits of using an S4-TIGFET device when designing a differential amplifier. First, we describe our experimental methodology, and then we compare this proposed design to a conventional MOSFET implementation using a commercial 90 nm technology.

4.1   Experimental Methodology

To compare the different amplifier designs, we employ a commercial 90 nm technology node for the MOSFET case. For the TIGFET devices, we consider 100 nm gate transistors based on fabricated devices from [8]. We study the performances of differential amplifiers using minimum-sized MOSFET and TIGFET devices through electrical simulations. Besides, both circuits are biased in the subthreshold region with the same power consumption [18]. TIGFETs are modeled using small-signal models of *n-type* and *p-type* transistors, as shown in Fig. 4. DC characteristics such as the transconductance (gm) and intrinsic capacitances are extracted from [8]. Note that the S4 behavior was demonstrated for both *n-type* and *p-type* [8]. As this small-signal model is originally meant to describe MOSFETs, the three TIGFET gate capacitances are assumed to be equivalent as a large single one. The goal of our paper being to showcase a new application for TIGFET technology thanks to their S4 behavior, we believe that this still provides a first good approximation for our study. This model provides accurate performance analysis for small signal AC operations. Large-signal information has not been included for distortion analysis. In a second study, we compare the area and power of both designs while achieving the same gain.

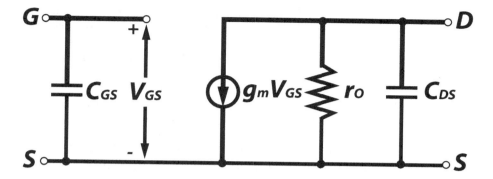

Fig. 4. Small signal model of a TIGFET device.

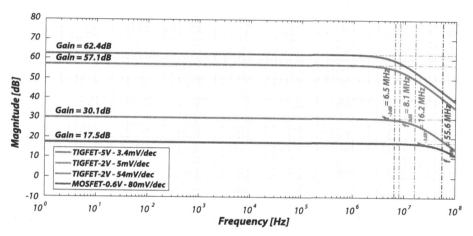

Fig. 5. Frequency responses for differential pairs, considering a 90 nm MOSFET case and different 100 nm TIGFET configurations.

4.2 Frequency and Gain Comparison for Minimum Sized Devices

Figure 5 shows the magnitude responses of differential pairs using conventional MOSFET devices and using TIGFET devices under different configurations. The first TIGFET configuration (*TIGFET-5V-3.4mV/dec*) we studied uses the experimental hero device TIGFET S4 value reported in [19]. This configuration is not easily comparable to the others due to the large V_{DS} biasing voltage of 5 V; this would not be fair as the amplifier would require a V_{DD} of 10 V. However, it results in the best performance due to having an SS_{min} of 3.4 mV/dec. The voltage gain and bandwidth are 62.4 dB, and 6.5 MHz, respectively, as shown in the red plot in Fig. 5. The low bandwidth is a result of the low current used in the design. The second TIGFET configuration (*TIGFET-2V-5mV/dec*) uses the hero TCAD-predicted device characteristics and biases the device with

$V_{DS} = 2$ V and reaches 5 mV/dec of subthreshold slope [8]. As V_{DD} is reduced, the amplifier can be powered with 5 V. As expected, the gain suffered from the 5 mV/dec slope and is only 57.1 dB, though the current can be increased to match the power consumption of the *TIGFET-5V-3.4mV/dec* case while achieving a 8.1 MHz bandwidth. The last TIGFET configuration studied (*TIGFET-2V-54mV/dec*) uses the lower-performance S4 device from [19] with a measured SS of 54 mV/dec. As shown in Fig. 5, the gain is decreased to 30.1 dB. In comparison, the MOSFET (*MOSFET-0.6V-80mV/dec*) suffers in performance due to its thermally-limited SS and only achieves a gain of 17.5 dB. MOSFETs can, however, operate at 1.2 V with higher current and achieve better bandwidth than the TIGFET cases (55.6 MHz). Table 1 summarizes the results of all four cases.

Table 1. Performance results for MOSFET- and TIGFET-based amplifiers.

	Gain (V/V)	Bandwidth (MHz)	GBP (GHz)
MOSFET-0.6V-80mV/dec	7.5	55.6	0.42
TIGFET-5V-3.4mV/dec	1318.3	6.5	8.57
TIGFET-2V-54mV/dec	32.0	16.2	0.52
TIGFET-2V-5mV/dec	716.1	8.1	5.80
Comparison*	**+95.5×**	**−6.9×**	**+13.8×**

*When comparing the *TIGFET-2V-5mV/dec* case against the *MOSFET-0.6V-80mV/dec* case.

The *TIGFET-2V-5mV/dec* results in a 95.5× better gain and a 13.8× higher GBP than the MOSFET case. Besides, even the worst TIGFET case (*TIGFET-2V-54mV/dec*) still achieves a larger gain when biased in the subthreshold than its MOSFET counterpart.

4.3   Area and Power Comparisons

Our second study aims at comparing the area of a TIGFET-based amplifier and a MOSFET-based amplifier of the same performance [16,21]. TIGFET devices are generally larger than MOSFET devices at the same node due to their additional polarity gates. However, to get the same gain from the MOSFET amplifier, a cascoded version of the differential pair shown in Fig. 6 must be used, and requires additional transistors [16,17,22].

This architecture keeps the power consumption low using only 2 branches, similar to the original amplifier in Fig. 3. However, the extra added common-gate transistors are required to increase the gain of the MOSFET-based amplifier to 57 dB to match the TIGFET performance. Both MOSFET- and TIGFET-based amplifiers are shown in Fig. 7(a) and (b), respectively. For a fair comparison, the TIGFET amplifier layout is drawn from fully-custom TIGFETs designed using a commercial 90 nm *Process Design Kit* (PDK) and both designs were verified using the same *Design Rule Check* (DRC) rules. The MOSFET-based amplifier

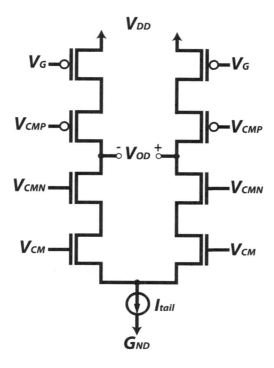

Fig. 6. Schematic of a MOSFET-based cascoded differential pair.

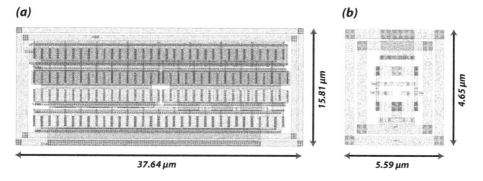

Fig. 7. Layouts of differential amplifiers achieving a same gain of 57 dB: (a) MOSFET-based; (b) TIGFET-based.

has a total area of 595.36 μm^2. In comparison, the TIGFET-based amplifier area is 26.04 μm^2, a 22.8× reduction compared to the MOSFET case, as shown in Table 2.

Table 2. Performance results of MOSFET- and TIGFET-based amplifiers, at the same gain of 57 dB.

	90 nm MOSFET	100 nm TIGFET	TIGFET Benefits
Area (μm^2)	595.36	26.04	$-\mathbf{22.8}\times$
Power (nW)	360	50	$-\mathbf{7.2}\times$

The significant area reduction is due to the TIGFET S4 intrinsic gain being significantly higher compared to a conventional MOSFET gain, as explained in Sect. 2. As a result, the TIGFET devices do not need to employ larger sizes to reach a gain of 57 dB, as in the MOSFET case. Besides, the TIGFET-based amplifier reduces the power consumption by 7.2× compared to the MOSFET implementation. This is because the TIGFET implementation employs smaller devices while achieving the same performance than its MOSFET counterpart.

5   The Benefits of TIGFETs in Biosensing Applications

In this section, we first introduce the concept of bio-sensing and typical design constraints. We then compare a typical CMOS amplifier for bio-sensing applications with its TIGFET-based counterpart and conclude about the potential of TIGFETs for such bio-sensing applications.

5.1   Brain Computer Interfaces Requirements

Neuronal activity can be recorded *in-vivo* through an implanted neural electrode array. The useful information from such electrodes typically consists of two different types of signals, as shown in Fig. 8. The first and most common type is the *Extracellular Neural Action Potential* (ENAP), referred to as spikes and shown in Fig. 8a. Spikes are "short" and biphasic pulses that typically last between 100 μs and 1 ms with peak amplitude of tens of μV to tens of mV. They are the results of firing a neuron in the region near the electrode and the signal of interest is within 500–5,000 Hz. The second type of signal is called a *Local Field Potential* (LFP), shown in Fig. 8b which is a very slow oscillation of <200 Hz up to 5 mV peak amplitude. This signal is the result of many neurons firing in the same large area and affects the "DC" potential of this wide area of tissue. Typically, state-of-the-art bio-sensing ASICs dedicate fewer channels to record LFPs while most of the channels record neuron spikes. LFP recording channels require a 0.1–250 Hz bandwidth and ENAP recording channels require a 300–10,000 Hz bandwidth. Recording high quality signals typically constrains the input referred noise, and commercial state-of-the-art ASICs limit the maximum input referred noise on the analog front-end to <3 μV$_{rms}$, with a 10 kHz bandwidth and a 12bits resolution ADC. In a nutshell, brain machine interfaces are low-frequency monitoring system with rigid requirements on noise.

We have introduced the recording requirements of the BCIs and their expected performance in term of bandwidth and input referred noise. These

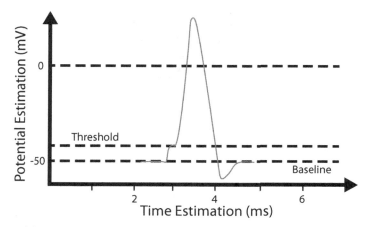

(a) Typical signal from a neuron firing close to an electrode.

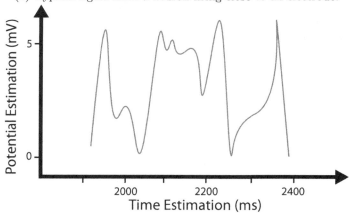

(b) Typical low frequency signal from the field potential induced by the firing of surrounding neurons.

Fig. 8. Typical signals recorded from bio-sensing electronics: a) High-frequency spikes; b)Low-frequency LFP.

BCIs are also subject to very challenging constraints regarding thermal dissipation, and thus power consumption. All BCI devices require either continuous or transient transcutaneous power delivery, and this power dissipates as heat or radiates as electromagnetic radiation. As the implanted device is recording or stimulating, it is dissipating heat into the tissue; the magnitude of this temperature difference is critically important to the safety of the surrounding cells. The recommended specific absorption rate (SAR) for human tissue is 1.6 W/kg for radiation in the 3 kHz to 300 GHz spectrum [28]. The standard limits of a 2 °C temperature increase, of 40 mW/cm^2 heat flux are valid for most tissues in the body and is reasonable targeted thermal power dissipation value for BCI [29].

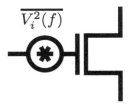

Fig. 9. Simplified noise model for low and moderate operation frequencies of the MOS-FET.

As discussed previously, BCI are low-frequency acquisition systems (<10 kHz) that have strict constraints on power consumption and input referred noise. In order to understand why the TIGFETs could benefit such applications, it is worth mentioning how noise in a MOSFET is determined. For low and moderate frequencies, which is the case for a 10 kHz low-noise amplifier for conditioning the neuron activity, the simplified noise model of the MOSFET shown in Fig. 9 can be used, assuming a large channel device [16] with:

$$\overline{V_i^2(f)} = 4kT(\frac{2}{3})\frac{1}{g_m} + \frac{K}{WLC_{ox}f}$$

The term $4kT(\frac{2}{3})\frac{1}{g_m}$ is the thermal noise of the device and $\frac{K}{WLC_{ox}f}$ is the flicker noise or 1/f noise. The thermal noise is purely dependant on the transconductance g_m of the device while the flicker noise is inversely proportional with the size of the device; this means that a larger device will have a smaller flicker noise, thus we can use the large channel approximation. K is a process dependent factor and widely varies for different devices in the same process. For low frequency applications, the flicker noise tends to be more of a concern and designers tend to increase the size of the input stage as much as is reasonable in order to keep the input referred noise low. However, some BCI [23] have shown that thermal and inband noise actually dominates the total input referred noise to almost 50%. To cover this issue, it is possible to increase the transconductance of the input device, at the expense of increased power consumption since $gm = \frac{I_d}{n \cdot V_t}$ (in sub-threshold), which is not compatible with BCI applications because of the thermal dissipation requirements. Another solution is to use different semiconductors to overcome this device limitation. Section 3.3 shows that the TIGFET transconductance is equal to 2.64 μS compared to the 0.45 μS of the regular CMOS, for the same low biasing current. Thermal noise would be reduced by approximately 5× and would greatly benefit any kind of low-power LNA in a brain-computer interface circuit. This increase in g_m is, generally, very interesting for any kind of low-power, low-noise application [32].

5.2 Typical Analog Front-End for Neuronal Recording

Figure 10 presents an example of the high-level architecture for a typical brain computer interface. The electrodes connected to the neurons are interfaced by

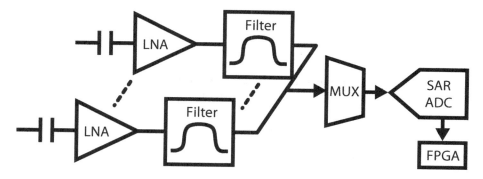

Fig. 10. Typical block diagram of a multi-channel, integrated brain-computer interface.

single channels in parallel through a line capacitor to filter DC signal and allow the spikes to pass through [23, 27, 31]. The low-noise amplifier is the first stage which interfaces the signals and great care must be taken in its design. This first stage must be designed to keep the input referred noise down to $2\,\mu$V. Signals are then filtered to detect either the spikes or the low-frequency LFP. Most BCI [23, 30] then use a multiplexer to digitize an array of channels. The output is processed by a controller and sent to an FPGA or μ-controller through low-power wireless communication. The LNA is the first stage of the acquisition front-end and its noise performance affects the overall acquisition system performance. Since the main trade-off in designing a BCI is between noise and power dissipation, we often use the noise efficiency factor (NEF) [24] or power efficiency factor to estimate the ability of a design to get a certain level of noise for a given power consumption.

NEF is defined as:

$$NEF = V_{ni,rms}\sqrt{\frac{2 \cdot I_{tot}}{\pi U_T 4kT \cdot BW}}$$

where I_{tot} is the current used by the low-noise amplifier, BW is the $-3\,$dB bandwidth of the pass-band filter, and $V_{ni,rms}$ is the input referred noise of the amplifier.

Based on state-of-the-art literature, the current-reuse low-noise amplifier topology is the best-in-class for having the lowest NEF [25].

A typical first-stage current reuse topology [26] is shown in Fig. 11. As this topology is well-known for being very efficient in terms of NEF, we will discuss its noise performance, its power consumption, and its NEF equation. We will also provide some insights on how a TIGFET-based current reuse compares to a standard MOSFET in the next Section. [26] shows that the input referred noise of a single-ended current reuse topology is half the power of a regular single-ended differential pair (when $g_{mn} = g_{mp}$):

$$\overline{V_{in,n}^2} = \frac{8kT}{3(g_{mn} + g_{mp})}$$

The output current noise [26] of the circuit shown in Fig. 11 is defined by:

$$\overline{i^2_{o,noise}} = \frac{16kT}{3} \cdot (g_{mn} + g_{mp})$$

This value is valid for any type of device used in the design. The input referred thermal noise can then be determined by dividing the output current noise by the gain of the first-stage. This leads to:

$$\overline{V^2_{in,therm}} = \frac{\overline{V^2_{out,therm}}}{A_v^2} = \frac{\overline{i^2_{o,noise}} \cdot R_o^2}{(g_{mn} + g_{mp})^2 \cdot R_o^2}$$

$$\overline{V^2_{in,therm}} = \frac{16kT}{3(g_{mn} + g_{mp})}$$

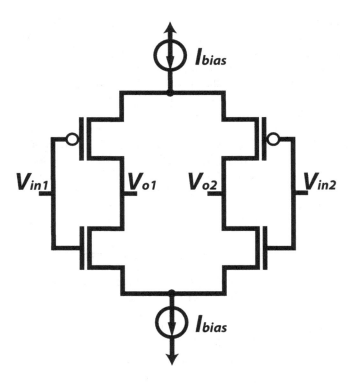

Fig. 11. Typical current-reuse input stage for the LNA.

5.3   Comparison Results

Using the previous equations for the NEF and the input referred thermal noise, and the performance of the TIGFET from Sect. 3.3 and Sect. 4, we can estimate the TIGFET noise level relatively to the MOSFET topology in Fig. 11. The input referred thermal noise of the current reuse stage is a function of the transconductance of the devices and we can derive the thermal noise improvement using the derived transconductance of the device from Sect. 3.3.

$$100 \cdot \frac{\overline{V_{in,therm-TIG}^2} - \overline{V_{in,therm-CMOS}^2}}{\overline{V_{in,therm-CMOS}^2}} = 100 \cdot \frac{g_{m-TIG} - g_{m-CMOS}}{g_{m-CMOS}} = -83\%$$

Considering the TIGFET g_m of $2.64\,\mu S$ and the CMOS g_m of $0.45\,\mu S$ leads to a calculated reduction of 83% in input referred thermal noise which is linearly linked to the improvement in transconductance of the device.

The NEF comparison is more complex because it is both a function of the current consumption and the input referred noise. We can either suppose: 1) two LNAs with the same power consumption but different input referred noise which also leads to a -83% improvement since the NEF linearly depends of noise, or: 2) having two LNAs with the same input noise and compare their power consumption. Since $g_m = \frac{I_d}{n \cdot V_t}$ is a function of I_d, the CMOS LNA's supply current must be $\frac{g_{m-TIG}}{g_{m-CMOS}} = 5.8\times$ bigger for having the same input referred noise. This leads to an increase in NEF of:

$$100 \cdot \frac{NEF_{TIG} - NEF_{CMOS}}{NEF_{CMOS}} = \frac{\sqrt{2 \cdot I_{tot-TIG}} - \sqrt{2 \cdot I_{tot-CMOS}}}{\sqrt{2 \cdot I_{tot-CMOS}}}$$

$$= 100 \cdot \sqrt{\frac{1}{5.8}} - 1 = -58\%$$

This comparison in NEF and input referred noise does not take the flicker noise into account but it is worth discussing flicker noise in more depth. Flicker noise in a MOSFET is defined as:

$$\overline{V_i^2(f)} = \frac{K}{WLC_{ox}f}$$

Flicker noise is inversely proportional to the device size and BCI interfaces use extremely large devices to mitigate the effect of flicker noise. Flicker noise is also decreased by using low currents which is the case in BCI interfaces with thermal limitations. While it may be obvious that, for low-frequencies applications, flicker noise is the dominant source of noise, post-silicon experimental results have often shown that flicker noise is not significant in this application [23,27]. [27] shows that in their design, flicker noise contributes to $0.1\,\mu V_{rms}$ of the total $2.2\,\mu V_{rms}$, a contribution of only 4.5%. For this purpose, this study did not include the effect of flicker noise on BCI.

It is also complex to compare the flicker noise of a CMOS device and a new emerging device because of different K constant terms that depend on how the devices are fabricated. An emerging device is most likely to suffer from a bad K because of the lack of maturity in the device. A TIGFET's *Super-Steep-Subthreshold-Slope* abilities rely on a positive feedback during impact ionization and this effect can influence the noise of the device. It is therefore important to mitigate the noise improvements that TIGFETs ideally show, as it is more likely to be higher that what we derived in this chapter.

6   Conclusion

In this book chapter, we have shown the benefits of S4 devices at a circuit level. While MOSFET devices are limited by their SS of 60 mV/dec, the TIGFET shows SS as low as 3.4 mV/dec. TIGFET-based amplifiers show great performance when biased in their subthreshold region, where they can benefit from their steep slope and high gain. In particular, we showed that a regular differential-pair using TIGFET devices improved the gain by 95.5× and increased the GBP by 13.8×. Besides, we showed that porting the same-performance MOSFET-based amplifier to TIGFET devices reduced the area and power by 22.8× and 7.2×, respectively. This demonstrates that TIGFETs are great devices for high-performance analog applications, where power consumption and cost are crucial. Additionally, this work paves new paths in the extremely low-power and low-noise analog domain for S4-devices in general, and TIGFETs in particular, with an 83% reduction in input referred noise and a 53% expected improvement in NEF.

Acknowledgments. This work was supported by the NSF Career Award #1751064.

References

1. Natarajan, S., et al.: A 14 nm logic technology featuring 2nd-generation FinFET, air-gapped interconnects, self-aligned double patterning and a 0.0588 μm^2 SRAM cell size. In: IEEE IEDM, pp. 3.7.1–3.7.3 (2014)
2. Sze, S.M., Ng, K.K.: Physics of Semiconductor Devices, 3rd edn. (2006)
3. Datta, S., et al.: Tunnel FET technology: a reliability perspective. Microelectron. Reliab. **54**(5), 861–874 (2014)
4. Kam, H., et al.: A new Nano-electromechanical Field Effect Transistor (NEMFET) design for low-power electronics. In: IEEE IEDM, pp. 463–466 (2005)
5. Lu, Z., et al.: Realizing super-steep subthreshold slope with conventional FDSOI CMOS at low-bias voltages. In: IEEE IEDM, pp. 16.6.1–16.6.3 (2010)
6. Zhang, J., et al.: Configurable circuits featuring dual-threshold-voltage design with three-independent-gate silicon nanowire FETs. IEEE TCAS **61**(10), 2851–2861 (2014)
7. Giacomin, E., et al.: Low-power multiplexer designs using three-independent-gate field effect transistors. In: IEEE/ACM NanoArch, Newport, RI, USA, 25–26 July 2017 (2017)
8. Zhang, J., et al.: A Schottky-barrier silicon FinFET with 6.0 mV/dec subthreshold slope over 5 decades of current. In: IEEE IEDM, pp. 13.4.1–13.4.4 (2014)
9. Tsai, T.-H., et al.: Low-power analog integrated circuits for wireless ECG acquisition systems. IEEE Trans. Inf. Technol. Biomed. **16**(5), 907–917 (2012)

10. Harpe, P., et al.: A 3 nW signal-acquisition IC integrating an amplifier with 2.1 NEF and a 1.5 fJ/conv-step ADC. In: ISSCC 2015/Session 21/Innovative Personalized Biomedical Systems/21.2 (2015)

11. Fan, D., et al.: EHDC: an energy harvesting modeling and profiling platform for body sensor networks. IEEE J. Biomed. Health Inform. **22**(1), 33–39 (2018)

12. Chien, T.-K., et al.: Low-power MCU with embedded ReRAM buffers as sensor hub for IoT applications. IEEE J. Emerg. Sel. Top. Circuits Syst. **6**(2), 247–257 (2016)

13. Pullini, A., et al.: Mr. Wolf: an energy-precision scalable parallel ultra low power SoC for IoT edge processing. IEEE J. Solid-State Circuits **54**(7), 1970–1981 (2019)

14. Verma, N., et al.: An ultra low energy 12-bit rate-resolution scalable SAR ADC for wireless sensor nodes. IEEE J. Solid-State Circuits **42**(6), 1196–1205 (2007)

15. Mao, W., et al.: A low power 12-bit 1-kS/s SAR ADC for biomedical signal processing. IEEE Trans. Circuits Syst.-I: Regul. Pap. **66**(2), 477–488 (2019)

16. Carusone, T.C., et al.: Analog Integrated Circuit Design. Wiley, Hoboken (2012)

17. Sansen, W.M.C., et al.: Analog Design Essentials, vol. 859. Springer, New York (2007)

18. Alioto, M.: Understanding DC behavior of subthreshold CMOS logic through closed-form analysis. IEEE Trans. Circuits Syst. I Regul. Pap. **57**(7), 1597–1607 (2010). https://doi.org/10.1109/TCSI.2009.2034233

19. De Marchi, M., et al.: Polarity control in double-gate, gate-all-around vertically stacked silicon nanowire FETs. In: IEEE IEDM, pp. 1–4 (2012)

20. Trommer, J., et al.: Enabling energy efficiency and polarity control in germanium nanowire transistors by individually gated nanojunctions. ACS Nano **11**(2), 1704–1711 (2017)

21. Hastings, A., et al.: The Art of Analog Layout. Prentice-Hall, Englewood Cliffs (2001)

22. Mallya, S., et al.: Design procedures for a fully differential folded-cascode CMOS operational amplifiers. IEEE J. Solid-State Circuits **24**, 1737–1740 (1989)

23. Gao, H., et al.: HermesE: a 96-channel full data rate direct neural interface in 0.13 μm CMOS. IEEE J. Solid-State Circuits **47**(4), 1043–1055 (2012). https://doi.org/10.1109/JSSC.2012.2185338

24. Steyaert, M.S.J., Sansen, W.M.C.: A micropower low-noise monolithic instrumentation amplifier for medical purposes. IEEE J. Solid-State Circuits **22**(6), 1163–1168 (1987). https://doi.org/10.1109/JSSC.1987.1052869

25. Simmich, S., Bahr, A., Rieger, R.: Noise efficient integrated amplifier designs for biomedical applications. Electronics **10**, 1522 (2021). https://doi.org/10.3390/electronics10131522

26. Horestani, F.K., Eshghi, M., Yazdchi, M.: An ultra-low power amplifier for wearable and implantable electronic devices. Microelectron. Eng. **216**, 111054 (2019). ISSN 0167-9317

27. Harrison, R.R., Charles, C.: A low-power low-noise CMOS amplifier for neural recording applications. IEEE J. Solid-State Circuits **38**(6), 958–965 (2003). https://doi.org/10.1109/JSSC.2003.811979

28. IEEE. IEEE Standard C95.1. 1999. Standard for Safety Levels With Respect to Human Exposure to Radio Frequency Electromagnetic Fields, 3 kHz to 300 GHz

29. Wolf, P.D., Reichert, W.M.: Thermal considerations for the design of an implanted cortical brain-machine interface (BMI). In: Indwelling Neural Implants: Strategies for Contending with the In Vivo Environment, pp. 33–38 (2008)

30. Chae, M.S., Yang, Z., Yuce, M.R., Hoang, L., Liu, W.: A 128-channel 6 mW wireless neural recording IC with spike feature extraction and UWB transmitter. IEEE Trans. Neural Syst. Rehabil. Eng. **17**(4), 312–321 (2009). https://doi.org/10.1109/TNSRE.2009.2021607. PMID: 19435684

31. Charvet, G., et al.: A wireless 64-channel ECoG recording Electronic for implantable monitoring and BCI applications: WIMAGINE. In: 2012 Annual International Conference of the IEEE Engineering in Medicine and Biology Society, pp. 783–786 (2012). https://doi.org/10.1109/EMBC.2012.6346048

32. Couriol, M., Cadareanu, P., Giacomin, E., Gaillardon, P.-E.: A novel high-gain amplifier circuit using super-steep-subthreshold-slope field-effect transistors. In: 2021 IFIP/IEEE 29th International Conference on Very Large Scale Integration (VLSI-SoC), pp. 1–6 (2021). https://doi.org/10.1109/VLSI-SoC53125.2021.9606989

A Regulated Sensing Solution Based on a Self-reference Principle for PCM + OTS Memory Array

J. Gasquez[1]([✉]), B. Giraud[2], P. Boivin[1], Y. Moustapha-Rabault[1], V. Della Marca[3], J. P. Walder[3], and J. M. Portal[3]

[1] STMicroelectronics, Crolles, Rousset, France
`julien.gasquez1992@gmail.com`
[2] CEA, LIST, MINATEC Campus, GRENOBLE, France
[3] Aix Marseille Univ, Université de Toulon, CNRS, IM2NP Marseille, France

Abstract. Phase change memory (PCM) device associated with Ovonic Threshold Switch (OTS) selector is a proven solution to fill the gap between DRAM and mass storage. This technology also has the potential to be embedded in a high-end microcontroller. However, programming and reading phases efficiency is directly linked to the selector's leakage current and the sneak-path management. To tackle this challenge, we propose in this paper, a new sense amplifier able to generate an auto-reference taking into account leakage current of unselected cells, including a regulation loop to compensate voltage drop due to reading current sensing. This auto-referenced sense, built on the charge-sharing principle, is designed on a 28 nm FDSOI technology and validated through extensive Monte-Carlo and corner cases simulations. Layout and post-layout simulation results are also provided. From the simulation results, our sense amplifier is demonstrated to be robust for an ultra-large range of sneak-path current and consequently for a large range of memory array size, suitable for embedded memory in high-end microcontroller.

Keywords: PCM · OTS · Non-volatile memory sensing · Sneak-path compensation

1 Introduction

The evolution of edge computing, with AI and data-intensive treatment, exacerbates the requirement in terms of performances and memory capacity on edge devices, such as the high-end Micro Controller Unit (MCU) [1–5]. In this context, high-density memory based on emerging concept could replace current solutions such as 1.5T NOR Flash memory or 1T1R Phase Change Memory (PCM) [6–12]. In this context, to decrease drastically the bit cell footprint, a back-end selector solution could be adopted. Doing so, this new embedded solution could rely on the most mature back-end memory solution namely Phase Change Memory. The PCM which material phase modifications directly affect its resistance (1R) value can be associated with Ovonic Threshold Switch (OTS)

© IFIP International Federation for Information Processing 2022
Published by Springer Nature Switzerland AG 2022
V. Grimblatt et al. (Eds.): VLSI-SoC 2021, IFIP AICT 661, pp. 225–243, 2022.
https://doi.org/10.1007/978-3-031-16818-5_11

selector (1S) [13–18], in order to form an 1S1R bit cell. However, due to process compatibility in an embedded context, OTS may require specific adjustments [19]. Beyond the well-known feature of PCM cells already demonstrated in the literature, i.e. a large resistance ratio of 10^3, a low variability thanks to a bulk phase change (crystalline and amorphous state) compared to the filamentary resistive memory, a mature process, and a large endurance 10^9 [9–12], the performances of memory with OTS as selector is mainly driven by the OTS selectivity. Regarding the OTS selectivity feature, numerous papers have reported very different performances [14, 20, 21], with selectivity ranging from 10^3 to 10^7.

The impact of the selectivity of the OTS at array level is characterized by the level of the leakage current sum due to the unselected cells during the programming and the reading operations. Thus to compensate for the impact of this leakage, defined also as sneak-path current, some circuits design techniques have been already proposed:

- The first technique proposed to limit the sneak-path current impact is based on well-chosen biasing conditions applied on the unselected row and column in the memory array. These techniques are namely *V/2* and *V/3* biasing solutions [22, 23];
- The second technique is based on sneak-path current measurement during a first pre-programming or pre-reading phase in order to adapt the biasing voltage to compensate for the amount of sneak current [24, 25];
- The third technique consists in collecting a mean sneak current coming from a compensation port and add it from a reference [26] during the operation.

As shown, compensation schemes are must-have solutions when dealing with crossbar array, but to the best of our knowledge, sensing circuit solution with auto-compensation of the leaky current and autoregulation of the row and column biasing has never been proposed at circuit level targeting a large range of OTS selectivity. In this context, the main contributions of this paper are as follows:

- we introduce, for the first time, an auto-referenced sense amplifier for PCM associated with OTS, where sensing reference is self-adapted to the leakage level. (Sects. 2 & 3);
- we also introduce a regulation loop to dynamically change the biasing conditions of the lines in the array depending on the sneak-path current but also on the reading current through the selected cell. (Sects. 2 & 3);
- we carry out functional (Sect. 3) and extensive Monte-Carlo simulations taking into account global and local variability, as well as corner cases of process, voltage and temperature (PVT), to demonstrate the robustness of our solution for a large range of OTS selectivity (Sect. 4);
- we evaluate the circuit area on a 28 nm FDSOI technology from STMicroelectronics and propose a layout of the solution together with post-layout simulations in order to assess the robustness of the solution against parasitic elements (Sect. 5).

Compared to our previous publication [27], the area estimation of the solution in an advanced 28 nm FDSOI node is given together with post-layout simulation results. We point out that the area of the proposed solution is dominated by the regulation loop, that is constrained by middle voltage, large load and fast response time.

2 Proposed Sensing Solution Overview

In array consisting of 1S1R bit cell, as presented in the introduction, using a half bias (*V/2*) strategy during a read operation, the cells sharing the same column and the same row as the accessed cell are half biased, inducing sneak-path currents. The consequence is twofold:

- The column sneak-current adds an extra-current to the one crossing the accessed cell with the risk of blurring the cell read current;
- The row sneak-current uses extra-current than the one needed to read the cell with a risk of drop-out of the read voltage *V*.

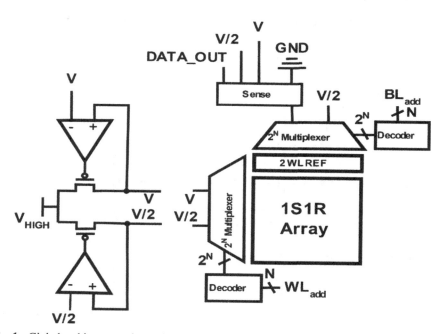

Fig. 1. Global architecture scheme, including LDO to generate V and V/2 voltages regulated from our sense amplifier regulation loop

Both sneak-path currents of course depend on OTS selectivity as well as array size, these two parameters are being linked. Consequently, any sensing solution developed for 1S1R array should be able to:

- Compensate the sneak-path current to solely isolate the contribution of the read current crossing the accessed cell;

- Regulate the applied read voltage V on the selected lines and $V/2$ on the unselected lines to compensate for large read current due to sneak-path and read current above the OTS selector's hold current [24].

Our proposition follows these two requirements. First of all, as illustrated in Fig. 1, knowing the read voltage to be applied on the array, we use a regulator loop inside the sense amplifier solution to compensate the read voltage drop due to the current sensing, which is dependent on the accessed PCM cell state (HRS or LRS) but also of the sneak-path current amplitude. The principle is to add to the read voltage V_{READ} and respectively $V_{READ}/2$, the voltage drop in the sense amplifier in order to have constant voltage, V and respectively $V/2$, applied to the array.

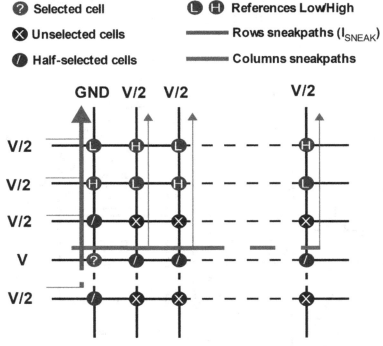

Fig. 2. 1S1R array with 2 references rows, illustrating also row sneak path and column sneak path during bit cell selection.

In a second time, we also introduce two references rows as depicted in Fig. 2. The two reference rows exhibit 1S1R cells with for each column a PCM in HRS and one in LRS. The main idea is to sense, prior to the selected cell of a given column, both references cells sharing the selected column. Doing so, we preserve the sneak-path current context, and we are able to generate a voltage reference that cancels the sneak-path current.

The reference generation is built using the charge sharing principle, in three functional phases. During the first phase, the sense input capacitor is charged using the LRS

1S1R reference cell resulting in a capacitor-voltage given in (1).

$$V_{IN} = \frac{(I_{LRS} + I_{sneak}) * T}{C} \tag{1}$$

With T the charging time, C the sense input capacitor, I_{LRS} the current through the LRS 1S1R cell reference, and I_{sneak} the sneak path current of the selected column.

During the second phase, the input capacitor is further charged using the HRS 1S1R reference cell, resulting in a new capacitor-voltage given by:

$$V_{IN} = \frac{(I_{LRS} + I_{sneak} + I_{HRS} + I_{sneak}) * T}{C} \tag{2}$$

With I_{HRS} the current through the HRS 1S1R cell reference.

In the third phase, a charge sharing process occurs, using a reference capacitor equal to the input capacitor C. Doing so, the reference voltage is given by:

$$V_{REF} = \frac{(\frac{I_{LRS} + I_{HRS}}{2} + I_{sneak}) * T}{C} \tag{3}$$

Thus when reading the selected cell, the input capacitor voltage is determined by:

$$V_{IN} = \frac{(I_{CELL} + I_{sneak}) * T}{C} \tag{4}$$

And knowing that C and T are the same in (3) and (4), it is straightforward to see, that the sneak current is compensated and that I_{CELL} (the selected cell current) is compared solely to $\frac{I_{LRS} + I_{HRS}}{2}$.

It is also important to note that any temperature drift in the 1S1R cell might be compensated by this self-reference generation.

3 Sense Amplifier Circuit Description

3.1 Circuit Description

The full scheme of our new self-referenced sensing solution is illustrated in Fig. 3. It is composed mainly of three blocks:

- The regulation block (Fig. 3a), which is mainly composed of two current mirrors generating the reference voltages V and $V/2$, used as input for the LDOs biasing the array rows and columns, from respectively the inputs V_{READ} and $V_{READ}/2$;
- The capacitor block (Fig. 3b), which exhibits the input capacitor C_{IN} and the reference capacitor C_{REF} both equal to the same value C. They are used for auto-reference generation through charge-sharing;
- The comparator block (Fig. 3c), which is built with a StrongARM comparator [28] followed by an RS latch to produce the sense output DATA_OUT.

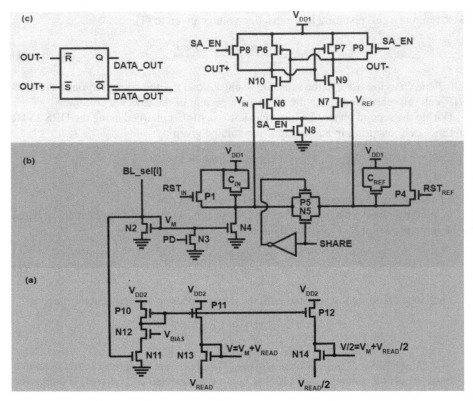

Fig. 3. Schematic of the proposed sense circuit with three main blocks: (a) the regulation block, (b) the capacitor block and (c) the comparator block.

<u>Regulation block</u>: Ideal biasing voltages for a read operation, that should be applied to the selected cell and unselected rows and columns are noted respectively V_{READ} and $V_{READ}/2$ on the Fig. 3.c. However, to ensure a constant read voltage and a constant inhibition, these voltages (V_{READ} and $V_{READ}/2$) have to be regulated depending on the amount of current flowing into the input branch of the sense amplifier during a read operation. Indeed, depending on the selected cell state and the sneak path contribution, the potential V_M is more or less increasing, reducing the applied potential on the selected cell to $V_{READ}-V_M$ and on unselected rows and columns to $V_{READ}/2-V_M$. It is thus mandatory to add the corresponding potential V_M to the ideal biasing voltages V_{READ} and $V_{READ}/2$. In doing so, the LDOs reference voltages (see Fig. 1) are respectively set to $V = V_M + V_{READ}$ and $V/2 = V_M + V_{READ}/2$. Consequently, the resulting potential differences on the selected cell and on the unselected rows and columns, become respectively $V_M + V_{READ}-V_M = V_{READ}$ and $V_M + V_{READ}/2-V_M = V_{READ}/2$. To achieve this task, a copy of the V_M potential is performed through current mirrors composed of transistors P10, P11, and P12. N13, and N14 act as active charges to add respectively V_M to V_{READ} and $V_{READ}/2$. Please note, that N12 safeguards N11 from high swing voltage and needs adequate biasing for quick regulation.

Capacitors block: The principle of current acquisition is based on the voltage discharge of the input capacitor C_{IN} through a current mirror composed of N2 and N4. Thus, prior to any current acquisition, C_{IN} is charged to V_{DD1} through P1 by pooling down signal RST_{IN}. In a similar way, before any reference voltage generation, through sharing activation (signal $SHARE$ = '1'), C_{REF} is charged to V_{DD1} through P4 by pooling down signal RST_{REF}. A pull-down transistor N3 is added to ensure that N4 is cut-off during two current acquisition phases in order to do not disturb the voltage stored on C_{IN}. The sharing between C_{IN} and C_{REF} is ensured by an analog switch (N5, P5) controlled by the signal $SHARE$ (active high).

Comparator block: The comparator block is designed with a StrongARM comparator followed by an RS latch. This block compares the two input voltages V_{CIN} and V_{CREF} to generate the digital output. This comparator works in two distinct phases. In the first phase, all the internal nodes of the structure are pre-charged to V_{DD1} through P8 and P9 when the signal SA_EN is grounded. During a second phase (signal SA_EN = '1'), the pre-charge transistors are inhibited and the foot transistor is activated. Depending on the voltages V_{CIN} and V_{CREF} the StrongARM internal latch capture either a '0' or a '1'. This digital output, available on $OUT+$ and its complement OUT-, is then memorized in the RS latch.

3.2   Functional Validation

The proposed solution has been designed using a 28 nm FDSOI technology from STMicroelectronics, using two different supply voltages: low V_{DD1} equal to 1.0 V and middle voltage V_{DD2} equal to 5.5 V.

Figure 4 illustrates the self-reference generation followed by a read operation on an HRS cell and a read operation on an LRS cell. The self-reference generation takes three phases, whereas any successive read operations take two phases each. Please note, that to ease the representation all addressing changes, row selection, and column multiplexer activation, have been set here to 1 ns as for the sense circuit internal signal change. Of course, addressing timing varies accordingly to the array size and the memory controller feature, when the sense amplifier is embedded in a full memory chip. It is also important to note that; even if the reference generation principle remains similar to the one presented in Sect. 2, we proceed with capacitor discharge and not charge to minimize current copy circuitry.

Self-reference generation: During the 1st phase, the sense amplifier is disconnected from the memory array, accordingly the signal PD is activated and the reset signals (RST_{IN} and RST_{REF}) are activated with a low value to charge both capacitors to V_{DD1}, doing so both capacitor voltages are initialized and $V_{IN} = V_{REF} = V_{DD1}$. Please note that the signal PD is activated, whenever the sense circuit is disconnected from the array. After this 1st phase, the self-reference generation process starts with the selection of first the LRS cell reference and after with the selection of the HRS cell reference, during this complete process, the signal $SHARE$ is activated, thus the discharge occurs simultaneously on both C_{IN} and C_{REF}. With this strategy, the charge sharing between both capacitors is realized during the acquisition. Thus, during the 2nd phase, the sense amplifier is connected to the memory array (PD is disabled) and both capacitors are discharged following (5):

$$V_{IN} = V_{REF} = V_{DD1} - \frac{(I_{LRS} + I_{sneak}) * T}{2.C} \tag{5}$$

It is also important to notice that since the read current I_{LRS} plus the sneak-path current I_{sneak} are absorbed by the structure, the potential V_M rises and has to be added to the regulated voltages V and $V/2$. After the second phase, the sense is first disconnected from the array, the HRS cell reference is addressed, and when the signals are stabilized in the memory array, the sense amplifier is again connected, here also with the $SHARE$ signal activated. During this 3rd phase, here also with regulated loop activated, both capacitors are again discharged, thus the resulting voltages on the capacitors can be expressed following (6):

$$V_{IN} = V_{REF} = V_{DD1} - \frac{(I_{LRS} + I_{HRS} + 2.I_{sneak}) * T}{2.C} \tag{6}$$

This process, similarly to the principle described in Sect. 2, creates a reference voltage image of the mean of the I_{LRS} and I_{HRS} including the sneak path current of the acceded column I_{sneak}. It is interesting to note that the self-reference generation takes three phases, after that, only the input capacitor will have to be charged to V_{DD1} and discharge accordingly to the state of the cell to be read, in two phases. Another advantage of this self-referencing scheme is that after a reference generation and until the leakage current of the MOS (P4, P5, N7, and N5) degrades the voltage reference V_{REF}, numerous reading phases can be performed on the cells of the same column in burst mode, before refreshing the reference voltage.

Read operation: Before any read operation, it is mandatory to disable the $SHARE$ signal and to reset the input capacitor by activating the RST_{IN} signal. Doing so during the *1st phase* of a read operation the voltage V_{IN} is again initialized to V_{DD1}. In the *2nd phase* of the read operation, the sense amplifier is connected to the memory array and the input capacitor is discharged by the read current, accordingly to the state of the addressed cell, while considering the sneak path current I_{sneak}. Depending on the state of the addressed cell, the voltage V_{IN} is above (HRS) or below (LRS) the voltage reference V_{REF}. The comparator is then activated latching the output on the two internal nodes $OUT+$ and OUT-. Please note, that the regulation process is also active during the read operation *2nd phase*.

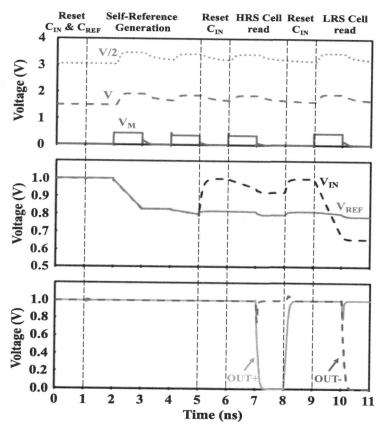

Fig. 4. Simulation of the proposed sense operation, with the self-reference generation (Reset both capacitors & reference generation), followed by the sensing of a cell in a HRS (reset in and read) $V_{IN} > V_{REF}$ and $OUT + = 0$ and respectively of a LRS cell (reset in and read) $V_{IN} < V_{REF}$ and $OUT + = 1.0$ V. Regulated signal are also represented during all phases.

4 Sense Amplifier Validation

4.1 Sense Robustness Versus Variability

The sizing of our new sense amplifier is defined to target, 10 µA of sneak path current, corresponding to the OTS characteristics reported in [29] and considering a 1Mb array. The simulation timings are the ones presented in Fig. 4. First of all, the energy consumption of the sense amplifier has been extracted from simulations in nominal case, per block and per operation (self-reference generation, HRS, and LRS cell read), as shown in Table 1. As expected, since a large current is involved during reference generation and LRS read, these operations are the most consuming. The regulation loop is the main contributor, whereas the consumption of the two other blocks remains below the tens of fJ.

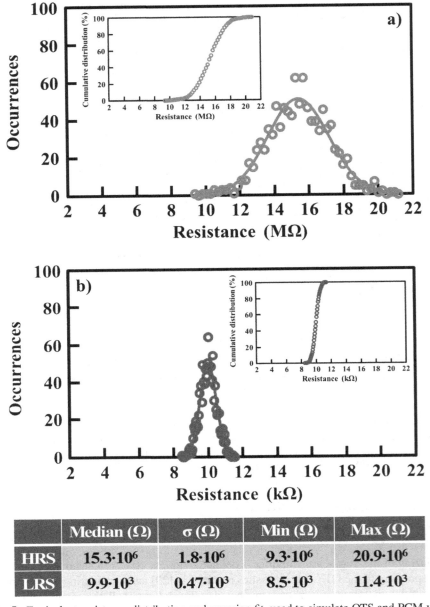

	Median (Ω)	σ (Ω)	Min (Ω)	Max (Ω)
HRS	$15.3 \cdot 10^6$	$1.8 \cdot 10^6$	$9.3 \cdot 10^6$	$20.9 \cdot 10^6$
LRS	$9.9 \cdot 10^3$	$0.47 \cdot 10^3$	$8.5 \cdot 10^3$	$11.4 \cdot 10^3$

Fig. 5. Equivalent resistance distribution and gaussian fit, used to simulate OTS and PCM variability with (a) OTS in off state during the read operation of a PCM in HRS state and, (b) OTS in on state during the read operation of a PCM in LRS state

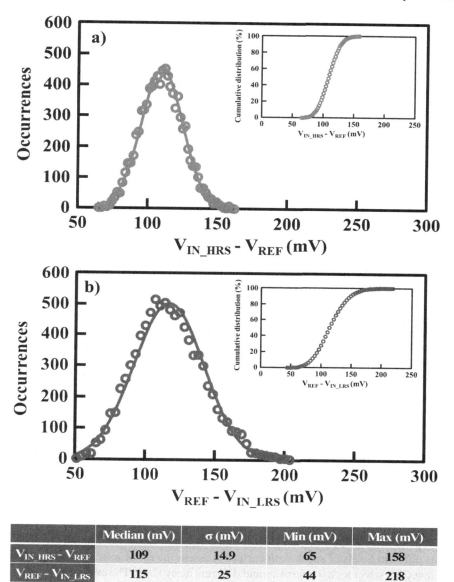

Fig. 6. Margin window distribution including gaussian fit, with (a) V_{IN_HRS} - V_{REF} for a read operation on a PCM HRS and (b) V_{REF} - V_{IN_LRS} for a read operation on a PCM LRS.

	Median (mV)	σ (mV)	Min (mV)	Max (mV)
V_{IN_HRS} - V_{REF}	109	14.9	65	158
V_{REF} - V_{IN_LRS}	115	25	44	218

Then, to analyze the robustness of our sense solution, we first run an extensive set of simulations to take into account Process – Voltage – Temperature variations. Voltage variations are classically set to –10%, nominal, and + 10% of the *VDD1* defining 3 corner cases: 0.9 V, 1 V, and 1.1 V. The operating temperature variations are also defined with 3 corner cases: –55° C, 27° C, and 125° C. So, the validation of our sense solution

Table 1. Sense amplifier energy consumption

Blocks	Operations		
	Ref. Generation	HRS cell read	LRS cell read
Regulation	1.465 *pJ*	384 *fJ*	1.28 *pJ*
Capacitors	16.6 *fJ*	1.05 *fJ*	15.2 *fJ*
Comparator	0.052 *fJ*	0.3 *fJ*	0.68 *fJ*
Total	1.48 *pJ*	385.4 *fJ*	1.3 *pJ*

is performed against this set of 9 corner cases. For the process variations, we consider global as well as the local source of variability at $-3\sigma/+3\sigma$, including mismatch on the typical process corner, considering the implementation of common centroid and inter-digitized layout in order to reduce the mismatch between capacitor and StrongArm comparator. For all simulated voltage and temperature corners, 1000 runs are performed to take into account the process variations. Regarding the OTS and PCM variability [30], we have extracted dispersion reported in [29] for the OTS and in [31] for the PCM respectively. From these extractions and knowing that during a read operation on a PCM in LRS with OTS-on and a PCM in HRS with OTS-off, we have considered a Gaussian distribution whose mean value is 9.93 kΩ and standard deviation is equal to 470 Ω and another Gaussian distribution whose mean value is 15 MΩ and standard deviation is equal to 1.78 MΩ, respectively (Fig. 5).

Figure 6.a reports the margin window ($V_{IN} - V_{REF}$) between the input capacitor voltage V_{IN} and the reference capacitor voltage V_{REF}, considering our 9 Voltage-Temperature corners and with 1000 Monte Carlo runs for each corner, in the case of a read operation on a PCM HRS (noted V_{IN_HRS}). Respectively, Fig. 6b reports the margin window ($V_{REF} - V_{IN}$) in the same conditions, but for a read operation on a PCM LRS (noted V_{IN_LRS}). Both margin windows exhibit a positive value of 65 mV and 44 mV, validating the robustness of our sense solution. This robustness strongly relies on the auto-reference generation, compensating even worst-case variations.

4.2 Sense Robustness Versus OTS Characteristics and Array Size

Keeping the same sizing and timing constraints, the proposed sense solution is evaluated versus different levels of sneak-path current to assess the robustness of the design with different OTS selector characteristics and different array sizes. The evaluated conditions are reported in Table 2 with for each pair of OTS selector characteristic/array size, the corresponding theoretical sneak-path current.

Please note, that sneak-path currents above 1 mA are discarded as non-realistic values in memory chip design-space exploration (noted NA in Table 2). The sneak path current is calculated as follow:

$$I_{sneak} = \sum_{row=0}^{n-1} I_{sneak[i]} \tag{7}$$

with *Isneak[i]* a single cell sneak-current when the OTS is biased at *V/2* and *n* is the number of rows in the array.

Table 2. Sneak Path Current I_{SNEAK}

$I_{sneak[i]}$ (A) at V/2	n×n array size			
	10 kb	1 Mb	100 Mb	3.2 Gb
OTS from [20]: 10 pA	10 nA	100 nA	1μ A	6 μA
OTS from [28]: 1 nA	1 μA	10 μA	100 μA	600 μA
OTS from [21]: 50 nA	50 μA	500 μA	NA	NA

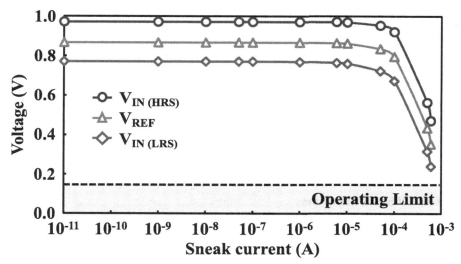

Fig. 7. Input voltage V_{IN} (corresponding to the read of a PCM HRS and respectively a PCM LRS) and voltage reference V_{REF} evolution versus the identified conditions given Table 2 for various OTS selector characteristic and array size.

The simulation results for a typical case are reported in Fig. 7 with the *VIN* voltage for a read operation on a PCM in HRS (noted V_{IN_HRS}), respectively on a PCM in LRS (noted V_{IN_LRS}), and the V_{REF} voltage versus the sneak-path current given Table 2. One can first notice that the auto-reference generation technique is efficient for a broad range of sneak-path current. Actually, for sneak-path current ranging up to 600 μA, the reference voltage level is well balanced in between the LRS voltage level and the HRS voltage level. However, due to the sizing of the capacitor block (Fig. 3.b), when the input current overcomes a given limit (around a few hundreds of μA), one can observe two effects. The first one is a too large potential capacitor-discharge, with possibly V_{IN} and V_{REF} close to the NMOS threshold voltages (noted as operating limit in Fig. 7), with a direct impact on the comparator response time and an over-sensibility to mismatch. The second effect is a nonlinear discharge of the capacitor due to the polarization regime change of the transistor N4, however since the reference is auto-generated, this effect remains partially compensated. Thus depending on selector characteristics as well as array size, careful sizing of the capacitors C_{IN} and C_{REF}. Has to be adopted. Finally, it is worth noting, that using body bias options, the threshold of the MOS at the inputs of the comparator can be trimmed to enhance the sense robustness to large sneak-path current for a given sizing.

	Global & Local variations with Mismatch (1000 Monte Carlos runs)									Process
	0.9 V			1.0 V			1.1 V			Voltage
sneak current	-55 °C	27 °C	125 °C	-55 °C	27 °C	125 °C	-55 °C	27 °C	125 °C	Temperature
1 nA	0	0	0	0	0	0	0	0	0	
1 µA	0	0	0	0	0	0	0	0	0	
10 µA	0	0	0	0	0	0	0	0	0	
100 µA	0	0	0	0	0	0	0	0	0	
200 µA	0	0	0	0	0	0	0	0	0	
400 µA	17	4	1,6	1,2	0,3	0	0	0	0	
600 µA	98	66	71	72	62	15	39	8	1	

Error (%): 100 80 60 40 20 0

Fig. 8. Fail results (shmoo plot) of the PVT simulation of the proposed sensing circuit for various sneak-path currents.

4.3 Overall Sense Robustness

Finally, our sense amplifier is benchmarked on various sneak-path current for the 9 pre-defined corners with Monte Carlo simulations (1000 runs) to include process variations. Figure 8 presents a shmoo plot of the pass/fail sensing results considering the corners cases and the process variation versus different sneak path current values. The first errors occur for a sneak-path current of 400 µA for the most severe voltage corner case. The errors are mainly due to the low voltage corner (0.9 V) since this corner reduces the dynamic across the capacitor, leading to 17% of reading errors. For extreme sneak-path current the solution exhibits errors, whatever the corner, meaning that the C_{IN} and C_{REF} sizing is not sufficient to deal with the extreme amount of sneak-path current. Besides, for this high sneak path, the errors are mainly due to voltage corner (0.9 V) together with low temperature corner. For all other cases representing a large range of sneak-currents including the targeted one (10 µA), due to the auto-reference generation, our new sensing solution has clearly demonstrated its robustness.

5 Sense Amplifier - Layout Evaluation

Figure 9 represents the full layout of the complete solution, including two blocks designed with thin transistors, namely the capacitor block and the comparator block, and a middle voltage block for regulation, designed with thick transistors. The overall area is 28.1 µm by 65.2 µm, whereas if we do not consider the middle voltage regulation block, the area is limited to 7.78 µm by 9.67 µm.

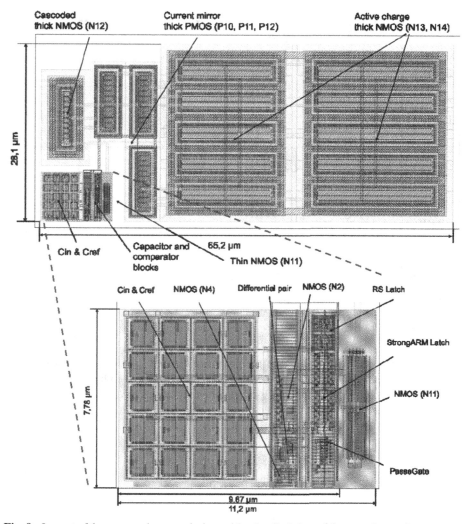

Fig. 9. Layout of the proposed sense solution, with a detailed view of the capacitor and comparator blocks. The regulation block dominates the overall area due to required fast response time and middle voltage devices.

Thus, it appears that the regulation block dominates the area of the solution, with 94.5% of the complete area. The sizing of the regulation block is constrained by middle voltage compatibility, together with important output load and fast response time (ns range). The remaining 5.5% are mainly dominated by CIN and CREF sizing, that account for 4.6% of the total area. The layout of CIN and CREF is realized with a common-centroid approach since both capacitors have to be strictly equivalent [32] to avoid any offset at the input of the comparator.

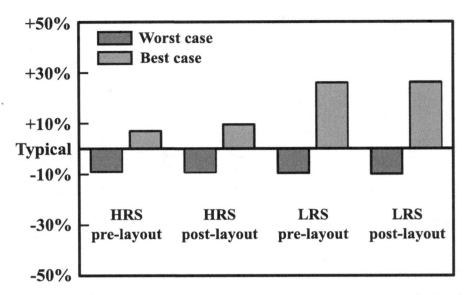

Fig. 10. Post-Layout simulation results for the best and worst corner-cases, normalized to the typical corner-case for ideal scheme (pre-layout) and extracted netlist (post-layout), when reading a LRS cell and a HRS cell

To further assess the robustness of the proposed sensing solution, post-layout simulations are realized. The sizing of the entire circuit is performed to be fully compliant with a leakage current of 10 μA. Thus, post-layout simulations have been performed for such a current, considering three corner-cases as reported Table 3.

Table 3. Post-Layout simulation for a leakage current of 10 μA – corner-cases definition

Corner-cases	Simulation conditions		
	Process	Temperature (°C)	Voltage (V)
Worst	TT	-55	0.9
Typical	TT	27	1.0
Best	TT	125	1.1

The simulation results are given for the three corner-cases, comparing the ideal (pre-layout) and post-layout simulations. The Fig. 10 presents the percentage of variation, normalized versus the typical case, for the worst and best cases, considering ideal and post-layout simulation results. The results are expressed considering the read margin variation in percent (difference between V_{IN} and V_{REF}) for a read operation on a LRS cell and respectively on a HRS cell. As depicted Fig. 10, the percent of read margin reduction is around 9% considering the worst corner-case, whatever the resistance state (HRS or LRS) for ideal and post-layout simulation. For the best corner-case, here also ideal and post-layout simulation results show the same trend with an increase of the read margin versus the typical case, of 7% (ideal) and 9% (post-layout) considering the HRS cell and of 26% for both considering the LRS cell. To summarize, similar results are obtained for ideal and post-layout simulation, assessing the robustness of our layouted sensing solution versus corner cases study.

6 Conclusion

In this work, we propose for the first time a sense amplifier suitable for OTS selector and PCM memory. The main advantage of our sensing solution, is to generate, just when necessary, a self-reference that takes into account the sneak-path current. Thanks to this self-reference generation, the leakage current during the read operation of a 1S1R cell is fully compensated. Moreover, we also introduce a regulation loop to apply a constant reading voltage on the selected cell whatever the sensing current. It is worth to note that this regulation loop is the main contributor (94,5%) of the overall area. Finally, we have demonstrated the exceptional robustness of our approach through extensive corner cases and Monte-Carlo simulations, including post-layout simulations, and thus for a broad range of sneak path current, corresponding to various OTS features and/or memory array size. This new sensing solution opens the way to a robust OTS selector and PCM memory reading operation in high-end microcontroller products.

References

1. Abeysekara, L.L., et al.: Short paper: neuromorphic chip embedded electronic systems to expand artificial intelligence. In: Second International Conference on Artificial Intelligence for Industries (AI4I) (2019)
2. Prutyanov, V., et al.: Developing IoT devices empowered by artificial intelligence: experimental study. In: Global IoT Summit (GIoTS) (2019)
3. Ghibellini, A., et al.: Intelligence at the IoT edge: activity recognition with low-power microcontrollers and convolutional neural networks. In: IEEE 19th Annual Consumer Communications & Networking Conference (CCNC) (2022)
4. Wang, Y., et al.: Home intelligent fire alarm system based on STM32. In: 14th International Conference on Measuring Technology and Mechatronics Automation (ICMTMA) (2022)
5. Nakano, M., et al.: A 40nm embedded SG-MONOS flash macro for high-end MCU achieving 200 MHz random read operation and 7.91 Mb/mm2 density with charge assisted offset cancellation sense amplifier. In: IEEE Asian Solid-State Circuits Conference (A-SSCC) (2021)
6. Lue, H.T., et al.: 3D AND: A 3D stackable flash memory architecture to realize high-density and fast-read 3D NOR flash and storage-class memory. In: IEEE International Electron Devices Meeting (IEDM) (2020)
7. Lue, H.T., et al.: A vertical 2T NOR (V2T) architecture to enable scaling and low-power solutions for nor flash technology. In: IEEE Symposium on VLSI Technology (2020)
8. La Rosa, F., et al.: 40nm embedded select in trench memory (eSTM) technology overview. In: IEEE 11th International Memory Workshop (IMW) (2019)
9. Carissimi, M., et al.: 2-Mb embedded phase change memory with 16-ns read access time and 5-Mb/s write throughput in 90-nm BCD technology for automotive applications. In: IEEE Solid-State Circuits Letters, vol. 2, no. 9 (2019)

10. Navarro, G., et al.: Highly Sb-Rich Ge-Sb-Te engineering in 4Kb phase-change memory for high speed and high material stability under cycling. In: IEEE 11th International Memory Workshop (IMW) (2019)
11. Nolot, E., et al.: Germanium, antimony, tellurium, their binary and ternary alloys and the impact of nitrogen: an X-ray photoelectron study. Appl. Surf. Sci. **536**, 147703 (2021)
12. Disegni, F., et al.: Embedded PCM macro for automotive-grade microcontroller in 28nm FD-SOI. In: Symposium on VLSI Circuits (2019)
13. Laudato, M., et al.: ALD GeAsSeTe ovonic threshold switch for 3D stackable crosspoint memory. In: IEEE International Memory Workshop (IMW) (2020)
14. Verdy, A., et al.; Improved electrical performance thanks to Sb and N doping in Se-Rich GeSe-based OTS selector devices. In: IEEE International Memory Workshop (IMW) (2017)
15. Laguna, C., et al.: Innovative multilayer OTS selectors for performance tuning and improved reliability. In: IEEE International Memory Workshop (IMW) (2020)
16. Chekol, S.A., et al.: Thermally stable Te-based binary OTS device for selector application. In: Non-Volatile Memory Technology Symposium (NVMTS) (2018)
17. Ovshinsky, S.R., Fritzsche, H.: Amorphous semiconductors for switching, memory, and imaging applications. Trans. Electron Devices **20**(2), 91–105 (1973)
18. Gong, N.: Multi level cell (MLC) in 3D crosspoint phase change memory array. Sci. China Inf. Sci. **64**(6), 1–2 (2021). https://doi.org/10.1007/s11432-021-3184-5
19. Chai, Z., et al.: Cycling Induced metastable degradation in GeSe ovonic threshold switching selector. IEEE Electron Device Lett. **42**(10), 1448–1451 (2021)
20. Verdy, A., et al.: Optimized reading window for crossbar arrays thanks to Ge-Se-Sb-N-based OTS selectors. In: IEEE International Electron Devices Meeting (IEDM) (2018)
21. Chien, W.C., et al.: Comprehensive scaling study on 3D Cross-point PCM toward 1Znm node for SCM applications. In: Symposium on VLSI Technology (2019)
22. Li, J., et al.: New write operation scheme for alleviating effect of line resistance on RRAM crossbar array. In: IEEE Advanced Information Management, Communicates, Electronic and Automation Control Conference (IMCEC) (2016)
23. Lei, Y., Liu, M., Song, Z., Chen, H.: 2V/3 bias scheme with enhanced dynamic read performances for 3-D cross point PCM. IEEE Int. Symp. Circ. Syst. (ISCAS) **2020**, 1–5 (2020). https://doi.org/10.1109/ISCAS45731.2020.9181075
24. Levisse, A., et al.: SneakPath compensation circuit for programming and read operations in RRAM-based CrossPoint architectures. In: 15th Non-Volatile Memory Technology Symposium (NVMTS) (2015)
25. Lee, K.W., Park, H.K., Jung, S.-O.: Adaptive sensing voltage modulation technique in crosspoint OTS-PRAM. IEEE Trans. Very Large Scale Integr. (VLSI) Systems, **29**(4), 631–642 (2021). doi: https://doi.org/10.1109/TVLSI.2021.3058150
26. Bae, W., et al.: A variation-tolerant, sneak-current-compensated readout scheme for crosspoint memory based. IEEE Trans. Circ. Syst. II: Express Briefs, **65**(12), 1839-1843 (2018)
27. Gasquez, J., et al.: A self-referenced and regulated sensing solution for PCM with OTS selector. In: 2021 IFIP/IEEE 29th International Conference on Very Large Scale Integration (VLSI-SoC), pp. 1–6 (2021) doi: https://doi.org/10.1109/VLSI-SoC53125.2021.9606969
28. Razavi, B.: The StrongARM Latch [a circuit for all seasons]. IEEE Solid-State Circ. Mag. **7**(2), 12–17 (2015)
29. Lopez, J.M., et al.: Optimization of RRAM and OTS selector for advanced low voltage CMOS compatibility. In: IEEE International Memory Workshop (IMW), Dresden, Germany, pp.1–4 (2020)
30. Moustapha-Rabault, Y., et al.: First 1S1R device based on Gerich GeSbTebased "Wall" phase change memory (PCM) and GeSbSeNbased ovonic threshold switching (OTS) for BEOL Crossbar Arrays. In: 52nd IEEE Semiconductor Interface Specialists Conference (SISC) (2021)

31. Lama, G., et al.: Reliability analysis in GeTe and GeSbTe based phase-change memory 4 kb arrays targeting storage class memory applications". Microelectron. Reliab. **114**, 113823 (2020)
32. Bucher, M., et al.: A scalable advanced RF IC design-oriented MOSFET model. Int. J. RF Microwave Comput. Aided Eng. **18**(4), 314–325 (2008)

An Improved Deterministic Stochastic MAC (SC-MAC) for High Power Efficiency Design

Ming Ming Wong[(✉)], Lu Chen, and Anh Tuan Do

Institute of Microelectronics (IME) A*STAR, Singapore, Singapore
{wong_ming_ming,doat}@ime.a-star.edu.sg

Abstract. Convolutional Neural Network (CNN) is widely acknowledged as an effective machine learning model for various detection and recognition tasks. However, CNN often requires a significant amount of hardware resources and is high in its power consumption. This hinders the widespread deployment of CNN model in embedded systems and wearable devices. Therefore, stochastic computing (SC) which leverages the power-accuracy trade-off, began to gain popularity in various neural network (NN) implementations. This paper presents an improved SC multiply-and-accumulate (MAC) unit that can be utilized as convolution engines in CNN. The proposed SC-MAC is operated using deterministic sequence and the design achieves latency and power reductions through parallelism and split mechanism optimizations. Furthermore, we also introduce decoder-based Stochastic Number Generator (SNG) that is capable of generating uncorrelated and segmented stochastic number (SN) without using random sources. The proposed deterministic and split SC-MAC is synthesized using typical libraries of UMC 40 nm technology for detailed hardware evaluation. The functionality of the presented SC-MAC is also verified in CNN using the MNIST dataset. Overall, our SC-MAC is proven to achieve higher power efficiency (GMACS/mW) and lower in energy consumption (pJ/MAC) as compared to the related works.

Keywords: Stochastic Computing (SC) · Stochastic Number Generator (SNG) · multiply-and-accumulate (MAC) · Shared segmented/split design · Convolution engine

1 Introduction

In recent years, Convolutional Neural Network (CNN) has emerged as one of the most promising artificial neural networks and has been deployed in a wide range of machine learning applications such as image/video classification

This research is supported by Programmatic grant no. A1687b0033 from the Singapore government's Research, Innovation and Enterprise 2020 plan (Advanced Manufacturing and Engineering domain).

© IFIP International Federation for Information Processing 2022
Published by Springer Nature Switzerland AG 2022
V. Grimblatt et al. (Eds.): VLSI-SoC 2021, IFIP AICT 661, pp. 245–266, 2022.
https://doi.org/10.1007/978-3-031-16818-5_12

[4,14], speech recognition [25] and natural language processing [8]. Software-based CNN/DCNN usually requires high-performance computer (with accelerators such as GPUs) to process excessive and intensive computations at a very high processing speed.

The core operation in CNN/DNN computational layer is the convolution function that involves multiplication and accumulation of the receptive field and a set of filters/kernels. Due to the excessive amount of multiply-accumulate (MAC) functions, CNN has rather high implementation cost. With that, MAC unit is also known as system's bottleneck as its design's characteristic fundamentally determines the system's overall area, power and performance [31]. Hence, researchers have placed great emphasis on MAC design optimization techniques, so as to enable neural network (NN) deployment in resource-constrained embedded systems. Instead of exploring new optimization techniques in binary arithmetic computing, this study focuses on the non-conventional computing domain, which is Stochastic Computing (SC) for CNN implementation.

In the recent decade, SC has appeared to be a popular solution for hardware implementation of NN. SC is a form of approximation computing that substitutes complex mathematical operations with simple logic gates. The biggest advantage of employing SC is that the resultant circuitry has significantly smaller hardware footage compared to their binary fixed point counterparts [6,18]. Besides, SC is also proven capable to outperform conventional computing in terms of fault tolerance [23]. It is further reported that DSP and NN in their nature are able to work relatively well using SC, provided its internal computations are able to attain a certain level of accuracy [23,31]. However, the typical approach for binary-to-stochastic domain conversion is rather costly as it requires random number generators (RNGs). Not only that, in order to minimize the conversion error due to the random fluctuations, the required length of the bit-streams is increased exponentially with respect to its binary resolution n. As a result, stochastic bit-stream is larger than 2^{2n} bits [13].

This paper is an extended version of an earlier publication of ours [29], where we provide further descriptions and analysis of our SC-MAC design. To this end, we highlight the following contribution aspects of this work:

- We present a decoder-based stochastic number generator (SNG) that produces deterministic and highly uncorrelated stochastic number (SN). Precision progression of the SNs that are generated from both the positive and negative binary numbers are analyzed. Results proved that our SNG achieves lower representation error and requires smaller resolution bit.
- We address the main challenges in the conventional non-deterministic SC in achieving low latency and high accuracy multiplication. We further demonstrate that SC multiplication using our SNG is free from random fluctuation and accuracy loss due to data correlation.
- We incorporate parallelism and split mechanism in our SC-MAC unit in order to reduce the computational latency. The implementation of both of the optimization techniques is discussed in detail and we further elaborate the integration of approximate parallel counter (APC) in our SC-MAC design.

– Our design's implementation cost and its performance are evaluated using 40 nm process while the computational accuracy is validated in CNN using MNIST dataset.

The rest of the paper is organized as follows. Section 2 briefly introduces the background concepts of stochastic computing (SC) that are used in the rest of the chapter. Section 3 highlights the challenges and the problems in the conventional non-deterministic SNG design. Section 4 describes our new decoder-based SNG design and its analysis results are presented as well. Section 5 elaborates our new SC-MAC solution that is optimized with parallelism and split mechanism. Section 6 summarizes the overall performance analysis and the benchmarks with related works. Finally, the conclusions are drawn in Sect. 7.

2   Theory of Stochastic Computation

Stochastic computing (SC) is a form of non-conventional computation where the computational data is represented as a result of continuous time stochastic process [9]. This section describes the preliminaries of SC that will be used throughout this chapter.

2.1   Architecture of Stochastic Computing (SC)

The general architecture of Stochastic Computing (SC) is illustrated in Fig. 1. The architecture is comprised of stochastic number generator (SNG) that converts (or randomized) binary values into stochastic bit-streams. Meanwhile, the arithmetic functions (i.e. multiplication, addition/subtraction and many more) are implemented as stochastic computational elements (SCE) by using simple logic gates. The final outputs of SCE are converted (or de-randomized) back to the binary representation. This conversion is performed through counting the total number of non-zero bits in the stochastic bit-stream. Further descriptions of the SC components are elaborated in the following subsections.

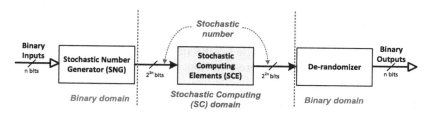

Fig. 1. Stochastic computing architecture that comprises of stochastic number generator (SNG), stochastic computing elements (SCE) and de-randomizer. The SCE is performed in SC domain where its inputs and outputs are represented in stochastic numbers (SN).

2.2 Stochastic Number (SN)

The computational data (i.e. **Stochastic Number (SN)**) is encoded in the form of digitized probability which is defined by the number of non-zero bits in the bit-stream. In other words, the SN value is associated with the ratio of total bit-1s to the total bit number [23]. SN represents computational data in two different formats: *unipolar* and *bipolar* representations [9]. Using unipolar representation, the values are bound within the internal $0 \le s \le 1$, while using bipolar representation, the values are extended to $-1 \le s \le 1$.

With $P(S = 1)$ is the probability of non-zero bits in bit-stream S, both the unipolar (UR) and bipolar (BR) representations are derived using Eq. 1 [9,28]. For example, in Fig. 2, bit-stream S of $2^4 = 16$ bits has 13 bit-1. In unipolar representation, bit-stream S is equivalent to $UR = P(S = 1) = 0.625$. Meanwhile, in bipolar representation, the same bit-stream will be interpreted as $BR = 0.8125$.

$$UR = P(S = 1)$$
$$BR = 2\left(P(S = 1) - \frac{1}{2}\right) \qquad (1)$$

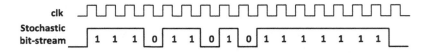

Fig. 2. Stochastic Number (SN) generated in serial, $S = 13/16$ representing 0.625 in unipolar representation and 0.8125 in bipolar representation.

Note that stochastic representation is not defined based on the position of any particular bit in the bit-stream S [28]. Instead, it is based on the probability of total bit-1s at arbitrary position. As SC utilizes non-positional number representation, it is less susceptible towards errors that are caused by bit-flip. Meanwhile, in the conventional 2's complement computation, single bit-flip on the higher-order bit will lead to significant error. As all the bits in the SN bit-stream carry equal significance, single bit-flip in a long bit-stream will only cause a minor deviation in its binary representation.

2.3 Binary-Stochastic Data Conversion

There are two types of converters (refer Fig. 3) that are required in SC architecture, which is the *randomizer* or generally known as the stochastic number generator (SNG), and the *de-randomizer* or simply known as counter.

SNG performs binary to stochastic conversion and it is typically designed using random source and comparator. The conversion is based on the comparison between the binary data and the values from the random source (refer

Fig. 3 (i)). If the binary input is larger than the random value, output bit-1 will be generated, otherwise output bit-0 will be generated. Linear Feedback Shift Register (LFSR) is one of the common choices for (pseudo) random number generator [12]. A k-bit LFSR is able to generate a total of $2^k - 1$ unique k-bit outputs. Therefore, comparing the binary input X (of k-bit) with the LFSR output sequence will generate SN bit-stream of $2^k - 1$ bits. The generated bit-stream contains a total of $X - 1$ bit-1s which the SN of binary input X is represented as $\frac{X}{2^k}$ [12].

On the other hand, converting the SN back to the binary data is simply calculating the total bit-1s in the bit-stream. This can be easily implemented using counter such as shown in Fig. 3 (ii). Following the nature of this stochastic representation, the subsequent SC arithmetic can be implemented using simple logic circuits [2,23] which will be explained next.

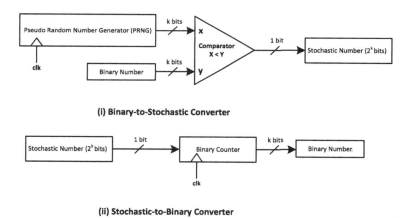

(i) Binary-to-Stochastic Converter

(ii) Stochastic-to-Binary Converter

Fig. 3. Computational data conversion. (i) Randomizer/SNG: From binary data to stochastic representation (ii) De-randomizer/counter: From stochastic representation back to binary data.

2.4   Stochastic Computing Elements (SCE)

Multiplication in SC can be effectively implemented using single logical gate. Assuming the input to the multiplication, X_1 and X_2 are uncorrelated, the derivation of its output Y, is given in Eq. 2. With that, as depicted in Fig. 4, the logical AND gate and logical XNOR gate are used as a SC multiplier in unipolar and bipolar representation respectively.

$$y = P(Y)$$
$$= P(X_1) \cdot P(X_2) + (1 - P(X_1)) \cdot (1 - P(X_2)) \qquad (2)$$

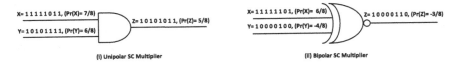

(i) Unipolar SC Multiplier   **(ii) Bipolar SC Multiplier**

Fig. 4. Stochastic Multiplier for (i) unipolar and (ii) bipolar representations.

Addition in SC is performed in a scaled manner such that the output is probability value within the range $[0, 1]$. To be exact, SC addition requires a constant scale, S, such that the sum (Y) of two inputs X_1 and X_2, is defined as Eq. 3.

$$
\begin{aligned}
y &= P(Y) \\
&= P(S)P(X_1) + (1 - P(S))(P(X_2)) \\
&= SX_1 + (1 - S)X_2
\end{aligned}
\tag{3}
$$

Thus, multiplexer with conditional select line S, set as $P(S) = \frac{1}{2}$ can be used to realize the scaled addition of two stochastic bit-streams in digital circuit.

Subtraction in SC is essentially the same as the SC addition but with one of the input is inverted (using logical NOT gate). Both the stochastic scaled adder and scaled subtractor are shown in Fig. 5.

(i) SC Adder   **(ii) SC Subtractor**
(Unipolar Format)   **(Bipolar Format)**

Fig. 5. Stochastic scaled adder/substractor for (i) unipolar and (ii) bipolar representations.

3 Challenges in Conventional (Non-deterministic) Stochastic Computing (SC)

Though SC is a favourable alternative to binary computing, we have identified two main drawbacks in the computation, which also serve as the main motivations of this study. First, the **stochastic number generator (SNG) incurs the major overhead** in the entire SC system. To be exact, conventional SNG that utilizes random sources consumed up to 80% of the overall computational cost [3]. For instance, the LFSR-based SNG that is commonly used for binary-to-stochastic conversion (refer to Sect. 2), has high power dissipation per area as compared to the SC element such as the logical AND or XNOR gates.

Following this, several works either designed compact random source (such as RNG) for SNG [11] or proposed random source sharing between the SNGs in order to reduce the overall hardware area cost [16,20]. However, it is worth a note that the latter approach causes correlation between the input SN bit-streams [20]. This leads to the second challenge in SC circuit design, which the **correlation between the SN bit-streams will degrade the overall computational accuracy**. In other words, correlation in the input data tends to alter the expected outcome of the stochastic logic and this is evident in stochastic multiplication. One of the potential scenarios is to multiply stochastic inputs that are directly inverse of each other and this produces the output Z as zero instead of the product $P_x P_y$.

The technical implication of data correlation in SC context is reported in [1, 22]. The works proved that SC multiplication which involves logical AND/XNOR gates will suffer from accuracy degradation when the inputs are correlated. On the other hand, the study further reported that such output discrepancy does not happen when correlated or uncorrelated input data are used in the multiplexer. Therefore, stochastic scaled addition/subtraction naturally is not affected. This analysis is also summarized using the examples given in Fig. 6.

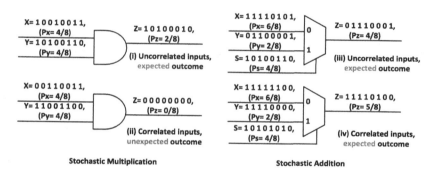

Fig. 6. Analysis of SCE with correlation data. (Left) Stochastic multiplication (i) using uncorrelated inputs and produces accurate/expected result and (ii) using correlated inputs and produces inaccurate/unexpected results. (Right) Stochastic addition with accurate/expected result using (iii) uncorrelated inputs and (iv) correlated inputs.

Based on the discussion above, it is evident that uncorrelated SN generation is essential to obtain high accuracy computation in SC multiplication, as well as SC-MAC. This also implies that random source is not necessarily needed for SNG. Therefore, this study focuses on non-conventional SC approach where the computations are performed on deterministic sequences.

4 New Lightweight and Deterministic SNG Design

In this work, we presented a new SNG that overcomes the drawbacks in the conventional design (refer to Sect. 3). The new SNG is lightweight, and produces deterministic and uncorrelated SN without the need of random sources (PRNG/RNG). Detailed description of our design and its analysis results are elaborated in the following subsections.

4.1   Decoder-Based and Deterministic SNG

The main concept of the proposed SNG is using binary data to produce a primary k-bit pattern which can be repeated p times to generate the deterministic SN bit-stream. An example of the generated SN bit-stream is shown in Fig. 7. Furthermore, both the parameters p and k can be configured in a way that the SN fulfills the required precision and correlation levels in the SC system.

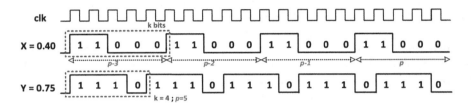

Fig. 7. Deterministic SN examples (i) For X = 0.40, 2/5 is repeated 4 times to generate bit-stream that comprises of 40% bit-1 and 60% bit-0. (ii) For Y = 0.75, 3/4 is repeated 5 times to generate bit-stream that comprises of 75% bit-1 and 25% bit-0.

The core design of this SNG is the k-bit pattern generator, which we implemented using n-to-2^n decoder. With that, the decoder's output is concatenated p times to produce SN bit-stream of $k \times p$ bit length. The design is low in hardware cost and high in efficiency because the SN bit-stream can be generated instantaneously within a clock cycle. The proposed decoder-based SNG and its comparison with the conventional SNG and the existing deterministic SNGs (using source/wave generator) are illustrated in Fig. 8.

In addition to the design complexity, we also analyzed the precision progression of the generated SN in representing the positive and the negative binary numbers. As our deterministic SNG does not utilize random source, the generated SN is free from random fluctuations. Besides, with our SNG, highly accurate SN can be attained with smaller resolution bit. As presented in Fig. 9, conventional SNG (using random source) requires at least 2^{16} bits to accurately represent bipolar real number in the intervals of $[0, 1]$ and $[-1, 0]$. On the other hand, our proposed SNG requires only 2^6 bits to sufficiently represent the same bipolar numbers (refer Fig. 10).

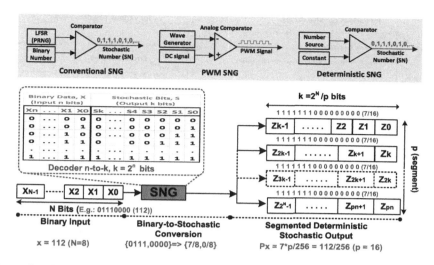

Fig. 8. (Top) SNG designs from prior works. The deterministic SNG design is reported [13] .(Bottom) The proposed decoder-based SNG: SNG conversion for 8-bits input, X, to deterministic SN output of 2^8-bits with ($p = 16$) segments and each segment is ($k = 16$) bit-length. Note that the parameters p and k can be configured according to the application's requirements.

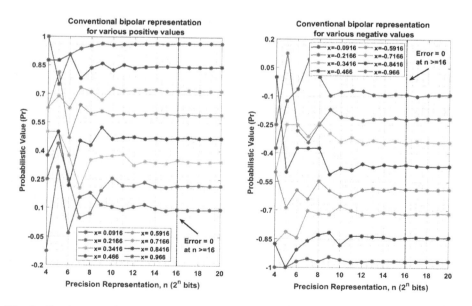

Fig. 9. Stochastic values derived using conventional (non-deterministic) SNG across a range of 2^n precision bits. It is shown that at least 2^{16} bits is required to represent both (i) positive and (ii) negative values in SN without error.

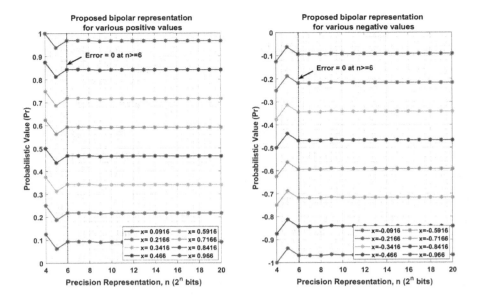

Fig. 10. Stochastic values derived using proposed (deterministic) SNG across a range of 2^n precision bits. It is shown that 2^6 bits is sufficient to represent both (i) positive and (ii) negative values in SN without error.

4.2   Stochastic Multiplication Using Decoder-Based SNG

Since the proposed SNG produces deterministic bit-stream which is comprised of p repetitions of k-bit pattern, we configure these parameters to generate uncorrelated SNs for stochastic multiplications. Given u/x is represented in x-bits with u number of bit-1 and the remaining $x - u$ bits are zeros. Similarly, given v/y is represented in y-bits with v number of bit-1 and the remaining $y - v$ bits are zeros. Assuming both bit-streams are repeated to S-bit length, the stochastic multiplication of $(u/x) \times (v/y)$ can be computed correctly if S is the least common multiple (LCM) number of x and y and that x and y are relatively prime [21].

As an example, the generated SN using the proposed SNG for input X and Y are shown in Fig. 11 and are contrasted with the conventional random SNs. In Fig. 11 (ii), the input $x = 2/5$ is repeated 3 times while the input $y = 2/3$ is repeated 5 times to produce bit-streams of 15-bit (i.e. $LCM(5,3)$). As a result, multiplying (AND) both the bit-streams produces the same result as the conventional stochastic multiplication in Fig. 11 (i). This example demonstrates the generated deterministic SNs are uncorrelated and are feasible for SC multiplication.

We further analyzed the distribution of the output obtained from SC multiplication across a range of different j-bit resolution. In this analysis, SC multiplication is performed using SNs of the same value 0.6 (i.e. 0.6×0.6) that is represented using bit-streams of 2^j length with j varies from 5 to 10 bits. The

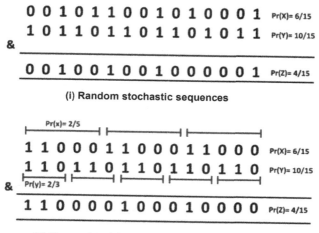

Fig. 11. SC unipolar multiplication (logical AND operation) of two input sequences, X and Y, which are generated in two different probabilistic representations; (i) random stochastic sequence (ii) uncorrelated and segmented stochastic sequence. The example shows that sequences in (ii) that are generated by the proposed SNG can be used to perform multiplication in the same way as the conventional random sequence in (i).

computation is experimented using SNs generated from (i) Conventional SNG, (ii) SNG [16] and (iii) Proposed SNG. The outcome of the SC multiplication using various precision bits is shown in Fig. 12.

In this figure, the accuracy of SC multiplication is reflected in terms of the mean, max and min values where the expected value is $0.6 \times 0.6 = 0.36$. From the observation in Fig. 12 (iii), multiplication using deterministic and uncorrelated SNs produces output that is free from random fluctuation resultant from PRNG/RNG. With that, the output is always consistent and hence, the max and min values are the same as the median value for all the precision bit. Therefore, our SNG in (iii) has outperformed (i) and (ii) in terms of the quality of the generated SN bit-streams. In addition to that, we further extended the experiment to using random inputs to perform SC multiplication. The average errors with respect to the range of precision bits are summarized in Fig. 12 (iv). For $j = 10$ bits, the observed error from the multiplication is less than 3%. This analysis has proven that our proposed SNG ensures both the SC representation accuracy and multiplication accuracy.

4.3 Near Zero Bipolar Representation Analysis

We further evaluate the accuracy of the proposed SNG in converting the near zero binary value to SC bipolar representation. For SC bipolar encoding, it is known that near-zero values tend to generate large random errors and this will affect the accuracy in SC multiplication [15]. In CNN/DNN architecture, the

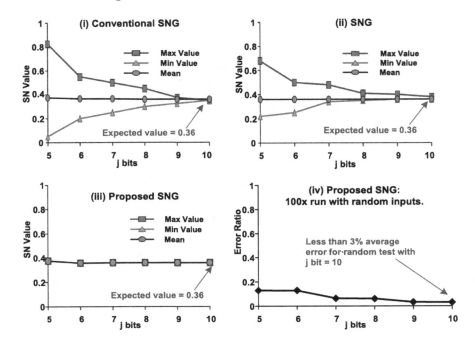

Fig. 12. Accuracy of SC unipolar multiplication (logical AND operation) using inputs 0.6 derived from (i) Conventional SNG (ii) SNG reported in [16] and (iii) Proposed SNG. The expected value is 0.36. (iv) Average error ratio for 100 runs with random inputs.

synaptic weights are often initialized to normally distributed random numbers. At the same time, the weights value are aggregated towards zero (due to L1-, L2-regularization) so as to give penalties to non-zero parameters as a means to prevent over-fitting [10]. Thus, deploying SC for CNN/DNN applications can be challenging where the majority kernel weights are near-zero values. In this case, using deterministic SN which is highly consistent (without random fluctuation) will be a better alternative.

In this analysis, the representation accuracy for zero and near-zero values using deterministic SN (from our SNG) as compared to the conventional random SN is shown in Fig. 13. First, the accuracy obtained from zero values encoding in SC bipolar representation using a range of precision bit is shown in Fig. 13 (i). The result shows that it requires more than 2^{16} bits to achieve error free SC encoding for zero binary value. On the other hand, our deterministic approach only requires 2^4 bits to accurately represent zero value. Next, we analyzed the approximation error obtained for near zero values ($x \in [-0.02, 0.02]$) in SC bipolar representation. Based on the result in Fig. 13 (ii), conventional bipolar representation has significant higher approximation error for near zero values. The error is observed to be higher at the value is closer towards zero.

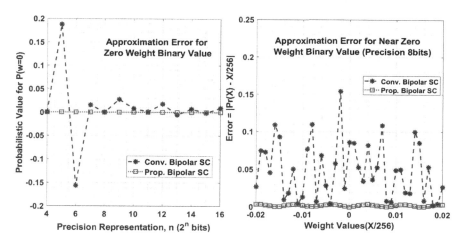

Fig. 13. Error analysis in SC bipolar representation for (i) zero value (ii) near zero values. The analysis results show that the proposed SNG is able to produce SN with lower error.

4.4   Hardware Area and Power Analysis

In this subsection, we present the analysis of the hardware cost (area resource and power consumption) of the proposed SNG. The synthesis result of the existing designs and our SNG are summarized in Table 1. The results show that our SNG has the lowest power consumption and is the most lightweight (area) compared to both the conventional and the other deterministic-based SNGs.

5   New SC-MAC Solution for Convolution Engine

In the previous section, we presented a new SNG design that generates uncorrelated and deterministic SN which (i) is free from random fluctuation errors and (ii) achieves high bipolar representation accuracy. Following this, we propose a new SC-MAC design for convolution engine that computes under deterministic stochastic logic. We further incorporated *parallelism* and *split SC* mechanism in order to achieve energy reduction and power efficiency improvement. Detailed description of the proposed SC-MAC design will be explained in the following subsections.

Table 1. Hardware area and power for various SNG designs for 2 parallel inputs of 8-bits resolution, synthesized using 40 nm process node at nominal voltage.

SNG	Area	Power	Remarks
Work [23]	357.14	366.62	LFSR and comparator
Work [3]	263.90	470.91	Analog-stochastic Converter
Work [30]	211.75	210.17	Error cancellation (ECPCC)
Work [21]	237.04	395.06	PWM (deterministic)
	327.46	NA	Relative prime (deterministic)
Work [13]	436.61	NA	Rotation (deterministic)
	327.46	NA	Clock divider (deterministic)
This work	173.71	4.2	Split SC and decoder (deterministic)

5.1   Parallel and Split SC Computation

Conventional SC often suffers from long computational latency due to SNG that is operated in a serial manner. On the other hand, the decoder-based SNG presented in this work enables the SN bit-stream to be generated instantaneously (refer to Sect. 4). With that, the overall SC performance is no longer constrained by the stochastic input generation rate. Subsequently, speed improvement techniques are feasible to be incorporated in our SC-MAC design effectively.

First, **parallelism** technique can be employed in order to reduce the total execution cycles. Using this approach, bit-parallel processing is incorporated in the SC-MAC operation such that L-bit sequence is partitioned into L/r sequences of r bits. This way, all of the L/r sequences can be processed in parallel as shown in the example in Fig. 14. This figure shows that the 16-bit input is partitioned into four of 4-bit sequences which can be processed simultaneously. Therefore, for our SC-MAC implementation, we have chosen $r = 32$ such that the inputs to the SC-MAC with $L = 256$ can be completed in 8 cycles. In each cycle, the r-XNOR can be processed simultaneously and followed by accumulation, which will be discussed in the next subsection.

Second, **split SC** mechanism can be incorporated to effectively reduce the SN bit-length. We introduced split SC-MAC architecture where the N bits fixed-point binary data is split into k parts prior to the computation. Therefore, the resulting SN is represented as k times of $2^{N/k}$ bit-streams (instead of a single 2^N bit-stream). This results in computation speedup by a factor of k. Similar approach was presented in [7] but the work reviewed that their design incurred higher area and power consumption as compared to the original SC architecture. Furthermore, the design also required additional SNGs to generate parallel bit-streams and this leads to hardware cost overheads.

In this study, we implemented split stochastic processing with $k = 2$ such that the binary inputs are divided into 2 equal segments (refer Fig. 16). In the context of convolution, given two fixed point binary input to the SC-MAC are input feature X, and kernel weights W, these inputs are divided as $X = \{X_H, X_L\}$ and

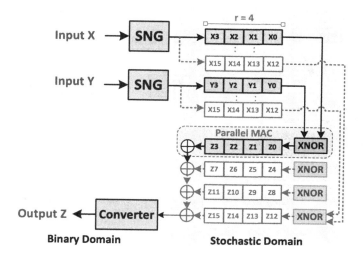

Fig. 14. Bit-parallelism of $r = 4$ for SC-MAC function. This example shows the input sequence of 16-bits that are partitioned into shorter sequences ($r = 4$).

$W = \{W_H, W_L\}$. With that the SNG converts the segments X_H, X_L, W_H, W_L to SN bit-streams prior to MAC operations.

5.2 Optimized Bipolar SC Multiplication and Addition

The overall architecture of our split SC-MAC architecture as the core computation for convolution engine is depicted in Fig. 15. An example is provided in the figure to explain the computation. The bipolar SC multiplication and SC addition for the MAC operation in our design are explained in the following.

SC Multiplication: While the conventional bipolar SC multiplication is described in Sect. 2, the split bipolar SC multiplication used in this work is described in Eq. 4 (also refer to Fig. 16). Note that in Eq. 4, the term $P_r(X_{lo}) \cdot P_r(W_{hi})$ is intentionally excluded from the original dot-product terms (i.e. $P_r(X_{lo}) \cdot P_r(W_{lo})$, $P_r(X_{lo}) \cdot P_r(W_{hi})$, $P_r(X_{hi}) \cdot P_r(W_{lo})$, $P_r(X_{hi}) \cdot P_r(W_{hi})$). For the input feature X, its MSB carries larger significance over its LSB and meanwhile, the kernel weights values are often very small and hence its LSB is more significant compared than its MSB. Therefore, for split SC-MAC, this dot-product term can be omitted in order to reduce the computation complexity.

The split bipolar SC multiplication requires XNOR for dot-product ($\cdot$) and the term $\{P_r(X_{hi}) + P_r(X_{lo})\}$ is simply a bit concatenation. Furthermore, the dot-product is performed using 32 XNORs executed in parallel.

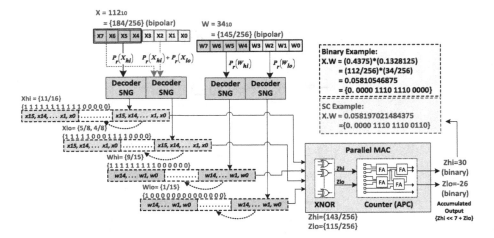

Fig. 15. Architecture of the proposed split SC-MAC. SNG is performed on the LSB and MSB of both the 8-bits input feature (X) and the kernel weight (W). SNGs generate deterministic SN of 256-bits using segments of 16-bits ($\times 15$) and 15-bits ($\times 16$) respectively. The parallel SC-MAC can be referred to Fig. 14 with $r = 32$. The output is converted back via bit-shifting and addition.

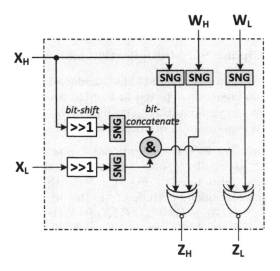

Fig. 16. Split SC and deterministic bipolar multiplication (using XNOR) for input $X = \{X_H, X_L\}$ and $W = \{W_H, W_L\}$. The bipolar multiplication is as derived in Eq. 4.

$$P_r(X) = \{P_r(X_{hi}), P_r(X_{lo})\}$$
$$P_r(W) = \{P_r(W_{hi}), P_r(W_{lo})\}$$

$$
\begin{aligned}
P_r(Z) &= P_r(X) \cdot P_r(W) \\
&= \{P_r(X_{hi}) \cdot P_r(W_{hi}), P_r(W_{lo}) \cdot [P_r(X_{hi}) + P_r(X_{lo})]\}
\end{aligned}
\tag{4}
$$

SC Addition: Stochastic representation values are kept within the probability interval of either $[0, 1]$ or $[-1, 1]$ for unipolar and bipolar format respectively. Therefore, a typical SC addition/subtraction is implemented using multiplexer (with fixed select-and-scale) in order to keep the output value within the interval (see Fig. 17). Given an example where SC-MAC is used as a convolution engine for grayscale images with a filter of $N \times N$ kernel size, there are two potential problems that can be identified. First, there will be an inevitable precision lost as the output can only be scaled up to the closest factor of $\lceil log_2(N \times N) \rceil$. Furthermore, the accuracy will be affected due to the loss of $n - 1$ information [19]. Second, if there are several zero value operands throughout the MAC computation, using a multiplexer with constant selector as the SC scaled-adder will end up over scaling in the accumulated output.

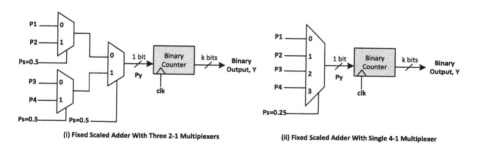

(i) Fixed Scaled Adder With Three 2-1 Multiplexers   (ii) Fixed Scaled Adder With Single 4-1 Multiplexer

Fig. 17. Conventional SC fixed scaled adders for 4-operands.

With that, using a parallel counter (see Fig. 18 (i)) will guarantee accurate accumulation but it is consisted of array of full adders (FA). FA uses binary adder logic circuit and hence it is relatively high in hardware cost [17,19]. Therefore, in this study, we utilize Approximate Parallel Counter (APC) [17] which has reduced number of FA components (see Fig. 18 (ii)). The computation fulfils the same counting function but using less area and power consumption compared to the parallel counter. However, there is a slight trade-off in the accuracy, which is acceptable for approximation computing such as SC. Unlike multiplexers, APC enables us to have the flexibility to scale the accumulated values (i.e. count-and-scale) which the factor can be fine-tuned to suit different applications. Not only that, since the output of the APC is already in binary domain, the stochastic-to-binary conversion/de-randomizer is no longer needed.

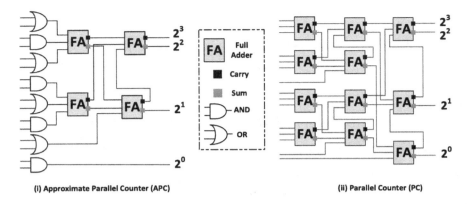

(i) Approximate Parallel Counter (APC)   **(ii) Parallel Counter (PC)**

Fig. 18. Converter/De-randomizer to convert SN bit-stream to binary number using counter [17]. The example shown is to convert 16-bit SN to 4-bit binary using (i) Approximate Parallel Counter (ii) Parallel counter.

6 Experimental Result and Analysis

In this section, we discuss the evaluation result of our proposed SC-MAC unit in terms of its functionality as convolution engine, as well as its performance in hardware implementation. In doing so, our SC-MAC is integrated in CNN and the network's accuracy performance in MNIST classification is analyzed. Therefore, a total of 70, 000 MNIST data samples with each is 28×28 of handwritten digit images in grayscale are used for classification. The CNN topology used in our test case is as the following.

The first hidden layer is a Convolution layer that has 32 filters and all of the filters have 3×3 sliding window with a stride of 1. This is followed by a Max pooling layer with pool size of 2×2. Regularization layer (Dropout) is configured to randomly exclude 25% of the neurons in the layer to avoid over-fitting. This is followed by a Flatten layer that converts 2D convolution matrix data to 1D data, which will then be connected to Fully Connected layer. Dropout layer of 30% is used after that and finally, the output layer has 10 neuron for 10 classes. Using the proposed SC-MAC in the Convolution layer, the accuracy obtained from MNIST classification is 98.2%.

Furthermore, we benchmark our SC-MAC design with the existing works in terms of power efficiency (TOPS/W) and energy per operation (pJ/MAC). For comprehensive hardware analysis, our design is synthesized using typical libraries of UMC 40 nm technology. In Table 2, the works presented in [26] and [27] are the only work besides ours that implemented SC-MAC without using random sources.

The work in [26] presented a new SC multiplication algorithm which is also known as vectorized multiplication (BISC-MVM). In this design, the SNG utilized a finite state machine (FSM) and a multiplexer to generate deterministic SN with bit shuffling pattern. The work is further extended to the implementation in Fully Connected layer and has successfully achieved performance improvement

Table 2. Hardware evaluation and comparison for different SC-CNN/DNN accelerator designs. For benchmarking purposes, the measurement metrics are normalized to 40 nm process node.

Design	Accuracy (%)	Frequency (MHz)	Delay (ns)	Power (mW)	Energy (pJ)	Power Eff. (GMACS/mW)	Energy/MAC (pJ/MAC)	Contribution Descriptions
Work [5] (2017)	97.7	400	650	2.80	1.82×10^6	0.18	3.446	Integral SC, shared LFSR, quasi-synchronous
Work [24] (no.6) (2017)	98.3	200	1,280	3,138	4.0×10^6	0.57	1.744	APC-based inner product, max pooling
Work [24] (no.11) (2017)	96.6	200	1,280	1,360	1.78×10^6	1.32	0.775	APC/MUX-based inner product, average pooling
Work [31] (2017)	99.1	1,667	0.60	3,704	2,222	0.03	33.069	SNG sharing, unipolar SC, SC-based ReLu & Max
Work [15] (2016)	97.6	1,000	5.6	3.20	16.0	11.16	0.085	Shared LFSR, FSM activation, EDT, weight scaling
Work [26] (2017)*	98.5	1,000	1.5	22.28	33.3	7.89	0.126	BISC-MVM, bit shuffling FSM-SNG, CIFAR-10
Work [27] (2019)*	98.2	1,000	1.84	11.74	21.61	11.85	0.084	Extension from [26] to FC layer
This Work*	98.2	1,000	8.0	2.88	23.04	**12.50**[#]	**0.080**	Decoder-SNG, deterministic & split SC-MAC

*SC-MAC implementation without random source (RNG/PRNG)
[#]1 MAC is equivalent to 2 OPs and hence our power eff. is equal to 25TOPS/W

[27]. The study performed quantitative analysis that is inclusive of the end-to-end SC computation only. In addition, the work in [15] proposed LFSR-based SNG and the SNGs are effectively shared in the parallel computation. Despite the fact that the proposed SNG sharing approach does not lead to data correlation, the generated SNs may be susceptible towards random fluctuation error. In addition to that, the reported accuracy is lower compared to our work.

With this study, we have further proven the feasibility of utilizing deterministic sequence for SC. The presented bipolar decoder-based SNG is able to generate deterministic and uncorrelated SN which attains high precision progression with shorter bit-length compared to the conventional SNG. The generated SN bitstream is free from random fluctuations error for both the zero and near-zero bipolar representation. Furthermore, our SNG is the most compact in size and has the lowest power consumption compared to the existing deterministic SNG in digital domain [13,21]. As the SN is generated instantaneously in our design, this enable further latency reduction through parallelism and split mechanism in our SC-MAC design. Overall, our proposed SC-MAC design attained the highest power efficiency (12.5 GMACS/mW or 25TOPS/W) and the lowest energy per MAC operation (80 fJ/MAC) as compared to the prior arts.

7   Conclusion

In summary, we presented a power-efficient deterministic SC-MAC unit, that is suitable to be deployed as a lightweight convolution engine. This SC-MAC utilizes decoder-based SNG that is capable of generating deterministic and uncorrelated SN bit-streams without using random source. Furthermore, the new SNG requires significantly shorter bit-length to accurately encode bipolar SN without random fluctuation. As the SNs are generated instantaneously, the subsequent computation latency can be reduced effectively and this leads to energy savings in the proposed SC-MAC. Our work incorporated parallelism and split mechanism in the presented SC-MAC unit in order to improve the power efficiency of the design without incurring excessive cost. We further demonstrated the proposed SC-MAC as convolution engine in CNN and its functionality is tested in MNIST classification. The experimental results proved that our deterministic SC-MAC surpasses the existing designs in terms of GMACS/W and fJ/MAC metrics.

References

1. Alaghi, A., Hayes, J.P.: Exploiting correlation in stochastic circuit design. In: 2013 IEEE 31st International Conference on Computer Design (ICCD), pp. 39–46 (2013). https://doi.org/10.1109/ICCD.2013.6657023
2. Alaghi, A., Hayes, J.P.: Survey of stochastic computing. ACM Trans. Embed. Comput. Syst. **12**(2), 92:1-92:19 (2013). https://doi.org/10.1145/2465787.2465794
3. Alaghi, A., Li, C., Hayes, J.P.: Stochastic circuits for real-time image-processing applications. In: Proceedings of the 50th Annual Design Automation Conference. DAC 2013, Association for Computing Machinery, New York, NY, USA (2013). https://doi.org/10.1145/2463209.2488901

4. Andrej, K., George, T., Sanketh, S., Thomas, L., Sukthankar, R., Fei-Fei, L.: Large-scale video classification with convolutional neural networks. In: CVPR (2014)

5. Ardakani, A., Leduc-Primeau, F., Onizawa, N., Hanyu, T., Gross, W.J.: VLSI implementation of deep neural network using integral stochastic computing. IEEE Trans. Very Large Scale Integr. (VLSI) Syst. **25**(10), 2688–2699 (2017). https://doi.org/10.1109/TVLSI.2017.2654298

6. Brown, B., Card, H.: Stochastic neural computation. ii. soft competitive learning. IEEE Trans. Comput. **50**(9), 906–920 (2001). https://doi.org/10.1109/12.954506

7. Chippa, V.K., Venkataramani, S., Roy, K., Raghunathan, A.: Storm: a stochastic recognition and mining processor. In: 2014 IEEE/ACM International Symposium on Low Power Electronics and Design (ISLPED), pp. 39–44 (2014)

8. Collobert, R., Weston, J.: A unified architecture for natural language processing: deep neural networks with multitask learning. In: Proceedings of the 25th International Conference on Machine Learning, pp. 160–167. ICML 2008, Association for Computing Machinery, New York, NY, USA (2008). https://doi.org/10.1145/1390156.1390177

9. Gaines, B.R.: Stochastic computing. In: Proceedings of the 18–20 April 1967, Spring Joint Computer Conference, pp. 149–156. AFIPS 1967 (Spring), ACM, New York, NY, USA (1967). https://doi.org/10.1145/1465482.1465505

10. Han, S., Pool, J., Tran, J., Dally, W.J.: Learning both weights and connections for efficient neural networks. CoRR abs/1506.02626 (2015). http://arxiv.org/abs/1506.02626

11. Ichihara, H., Ishii, S., Sunamori, D., Iwagaki, T., Inoue, T.: Compact and accurate stochastic circuits with shared random number sources. In: 2014 IEEE 32nd International Conference on Computer Design (ICCD), pp. 361–366 (2014). https://doi.org/10.1109/ICCD.2014.6974706

12. Ichikawa, K., Yamashita, S.: A multiply accumulator for stochastic numbers without scaling errors. In: 2021 34th International Conference on VLSI Design and 2021 20th International Conference on Embedded Systems (VLSID), pp. 88–93 (2021). https://doi.org/10.1109/VLSID51830.2021.00020

13. Jenson, D., Riedel, M.: A deterministic approach to stochastic computation. In: 2016 IEEE/ACM International Conference on Computer-Aided Design (ICCAD), pp. 1–8 (2016)

14. Karen, S., Andrew, Z.: Very deep convolutional networks for large-scale image recognition (2015)

15. Kim, K., Kim, J., Yu, J., Seo, J., Lee, J., Choi, K.: Dynamic energy-accuracy trade-off using stochastic computing in deep neural networks. In: 2016 53nd ACM/EDAC/IEEE Design Automation Conference (DAC), pp. 1–6 (2016). https://doi.org/10.1145/2897937.2898011

16. Kim, K., Lee, J., Choi, K.: An energy-efficient random number generator for stochastic circuits. In: 2016 21st Asia and South Pacific Design Automation Conference (ASP-DAC), pp. 256–261 (2016). https://doi.org/10.1109/ASPDAC.2016.7428020

17. Kim, K., Lee, J., Choi, K.: Approximate de-randomizer for stochastic circuits. In: 2015 International SoC Design Conference (ISOCC), pp. 123–124 (2015). https://doi.org/10.1109/ISOCC.2015.7401667

18. Li, J., Ren, A., Li, Z., Ding, C., Yuan, B., Qiu, Q., Wang, Y.: Towards acceleration of deep convolutional neural networks using stochastic computing. In: 2017 22nd Asia and South Pacific Design Automation Conference (ASP-DAC), pp. 115–120 (2017). https://doi.org/10.1109/ASPDAC.2017.7858306

19. Li, J., et al.: Normalization and dropout for stochastic computing-based deep convolutional neural networks. Integration **65**, 395–403 (2019). https://doi.org/ 10.1016/j.vlsi.2017.11.002, https://www.sciencedirect.com/science/article/pii/ S0167926017302328

20. Liu, Y., Wang, Y., Lombardi, F., Han, J.: An energy-efficient online-learning stochastic computational deep belief network. IEEE J. Emerg. Sel. Top. Circ. Syst. **8**(3), 454–465 (2018). https://doi.org/10.1109/JETCAS.2018.2852705

21. Najafi, M.H., Jamali-Zavareh, S., Lilja, D.J., Riedel, M.D., Bazargan, K., Harjani, R.: Time-encoded values for highly efficient stochastic circuits. IEEE Trans. Very Large Scale Integr. (VLSI) Syst. **25**(5), 1644–1657 (2017). https://doi.org/10.1109/ TVLSI.2016.2645902

22. Parhi, M., Riedel, M.D., Parhi, K.K.: Effect of bit-level correlation in stochastic computing. In: 2015 IEEE International Conference on Digital Signal Processing (DSP), pp. 463–467 (2015). https://doi.org/10.1109/ICDSP.2015.7251915

23. Qian, W., Li, X., Riedel, M.D., Bazargan, K., Lilja, D.J.: An architecture for fault-tolerant computation with stochastic logic. IEEE Trans. Comput. **60**(1), 93–105 (2011). https://doi.org/10.1109/TC.2010.202

24. Ren, A., et al.: SC-DCNN: highly-scalable deep convolutional neural network using stochastic computing. SIGOPS Oper. Syst. Rev. **51**(2), 405–418 (2017). https:// doi.org/10.1145/3093315.3037746

25. Sainath, T.N., Mohamed, A.R., Kingsbury, B., Ramabhadran, B.: Deep convolutional neural networks for LVCSR. In: 2013 IEEE International Conference on Acoustics, Speech and Signal Processing, pp. 8614–8618 (2013). https://doi.org/ 10.1109/ICASSP.2013.6639347

26. Sim, H., Lee, J.: A new stochastic computing multiplier with application to deep convolutional neural networks. In: 2017 54th ACM/EDAC/IEEE Design Automation Conference (DAC), pp. 1–6 (2017). https://doi.org/10.1145/3061639.3062290

27. Sim, H., Lee, J.: Cost-effective stochastic MAC circuits for deep neural networks. Neural Netw. **117**, 152–162 (2019). https://doi.org/10.1016/j.neunet.2019.04.017, http://www.sciencedirect.com/science/article/pii/S0893608019301236

28. Sousa, L.: Nonconventional computer arithmetic circuits, systems and applications. IEEE Circ. Syst. Mag. **21**(1), 6–40 (2021). https://doi.org/10.1109/MCAS.2020. 3027425

29. Wong, M.M., Chen, L., Do, A.T.: A 25 TOPS/W high power efficiency deterministic and split stochastic MAC (SC-MAC) design. In: 2021 IFIP/IEEE 29th International Conference on Very Large Scale Integration (VLSI-SoC), pp. 1–6 (2021). https://doi.org/10.1109/VLSI-SoC53125.2021.9606972

30. Yang, M., Hayes, J.P., Fan, D., Qian, W.: Design of accurate stochastic number generators with noisy emerging devices for stochastic computing. In: 2017 IEEE/ACM International Conference on Computer-Aided Design (ICCAD), pp. 638–644 (2017). https://doi.org/10.1109/ICCAD.2017.8203837

31. Yu, J., Kim, K., Lee, J., Choi, K.: Accurate and efficient stochastic computing hardware for convolutional neural networks. In: 2017 IEEE International Conference on Computer Design (ICCD), pp. 105–112 (2017). https://doi.org/10.1109/ ICCD.2017.24

Author Index

Printed in the United States
by Baker & Taylor Publisher Services